CW00833252

PROSE POETRY IN THEORY
AND PRACTICE

Prose Poetry in Theory and Practice vigorously engages with the Why? and the How? of prose poetry, a form that is currently enjoying a surge in popularity. With contributions by both practitioners and academics, this volume seeks to explore how its distinctive properties guide both writer and reader, and to address why this form is so well suited to the early twenty-first century. With discussion of both classic and less well-known writers, the essays both illuminate prose poetry's distinctive features and explore how this "outsider" form can offer a unique way of viewing and describing the uncertainties and instabilities which shape our identities and our relationships with our surroundings in the early twenty-first century. Combining insights on the theory and practice of prose poetry, *Prose Poetry in Theory and Practice* offers a timely and valuable contribution to the development of the form, and its appreciation amongst practitioners and scholars alike. Largely approached from a practitioner perspective, this collection provides vivid snapshots of contemporary debates within the prose poetry field while actively contributing to the poetics and craft of the form.

Anne Caldwell is a freelance writer and a lecturer in creative writing for the Open University and has completed a PhD in prose poetry and creative writing at the University of Bolton in 2020. She is a member of the International Poetry Studies Institute (I.P.S.I.) International Prose Poetry Project and the author of four collections of poetry.

Oz Hardwick is a European poet and academic, whose work has been widely published in international journals and anthologies. He has published nine full collections and chapbooks, including *Learning to Have Lost* (2018) which won the 2019 Rubery International Book Award for poetry. Oz is Professor of Creative Writing at Leeds Trinity University.

PROSE POETRY IN THEORY AND PRACTICE

Edited by
Anne Caldwell and Oz Hardwick

Routledge
Taylor & Francis Group

NEW YORK AND LONDON

Cover image: Oz Hardwick

First published 2022
by Routledge
605 Third Avenue, New York, NY 10158

and by Routledge
4 Park Square, Milton Park, Abingdon, Oxon, OX14 4RN

Routledge is an imprint of the Taylor & Francis Group, an informa business

Library of Congress Cataloging-in-Publication Data
A catalog record for this title has been requested

ISBN: 978-1-032-05861-0 (hbk)
ISBN: 978-1-032-05859-7 (pbk)
ISBN: 978-1-003-19953-3 (ebk)

DOI: 10.4324/9781003199533

Typeset in Bembo
by Newgen Publishing UK

CONTENTS

ILLUSTRATIONS

ACKNOWLEDGEMENTS

We would like to thank all the participants at the Prose Poetry UK Symposium in July 2019, at which the seeds of this book were planted, along with Leeds Trinity University for hosting this key event and Arts Council England for their financial support. Special thanks also to members of the Prose Poetry Project at the University of Canberra's International Poetry Studies Institute (IPSI) – and all around the world – for stimulation and sustenance.

NOTES ON CONTRIBUTORS

Cassandra Atherton is a widely anthologised and award-winning prose poet. She was a Harvard Visiting Scholar in English and a Visiting Fellow at Sophia University, Tokyo. She has published 30 critical and creative books and been invited to edit special editions of leading journals. Cassandra is the successful recipient of many national and international grants including a VicArts grant and an Australian Council Grant. Her most recent books of prose poetry are *Pre-Raphaelite* (2018), *Leftovers* (2020), and the co-authored *Fugitive Letters* (2020). She is a commissioning editor of *Westerly* magazine, series editor for Spineless Wonders' Microlit Anthologies, and associate editor at MadHat Press in America. She co-authored *Prose Poetry: An Introduction* (Princeton University Press, 2020) and co-edited the *Anthology of Australian Prose Poetry* (Melbourne University Press, 2020).

Anne Caldwell is a freelance writer and a lecturer in creative writing for the Open University and has completed a PhD in prose poetry and creative writing at the University of Bolton in 2020. She is a member of the International Poetry Studies Institute (I.P.S.I.) International Prose Poetry Project and the author of four collections of poetry. She was co-editor of the *Valley Press Anthology of Prose Poetry* (Valley, 2019) alongside Oz Hardwick. She also jointly co-ordinated the first symposium of Prose Poetry, with Oz Hardwick at Leeds Trinity University, where many of the essays within this book were first presented. She worked for the National Association for Writers in Education for over ten years and is taking up a Royal Literary Fellowship at the University of Huddersfield from September 2021. Her latest prose poetry collection is *Alice and the North* (Valley Press, 2020).

Susie Campbell is currently studying for a practice-based poetry PhD at Oxford Brookes University. Her research project focuses on Gertrude Stein, prose poetry, and spatial form. From 2017 to 2018, she was poet-in-residence for the Oxford Brookes/University of Oxford Mellon-Sawyer Post-War Commemoration series and subsequently a part of a military veterans' poetry workshop team at Oxford Brookes Poetry Centre. Her essays on Stein, prose poetry, and the contemporary lyric have been published in the *Long Poem Magazine* and *Axon* international journal. Her poetry publications include *The Bitters* (Chicago: Dancing Girl Press, 2014), *The Frock Enquiry* (London: Annexe, 2015), *I Return to You* (London: Sampson Low, 2019), and *Tenter* (Cornwall: Guillemot Press, 2020). Her poetry has appeared in many UK and international poetry magazines including *Poetry Review*, *Shearsman*, and *Cordite*, and in anthologies *The Valley Press Anthology of Prose Poetry* (Scarborough: Valley Press, 2019) and *On Commemoration* (Oxford: Peter Lang, 2020).

Oz Hardwick is a European poet and academic, whose work has been widely published in international journals and anthologies. He has published nine full collections and chapbooks, including *Learning to Have Lost* (Canberra: IPSI, 2018) which won the 2019 Rubery International Book Award for poetry, and most recently the prose poetry sequence *Wolf Planet* (Clevedon: Hedgehog, 2020). He has also edited or co-edited several anthologies, including *The Valley Press Anthology of Prose Poetry* (Scarborough: Valley Press, 2019) with Anne Caldwell. Oz has held residencies in the UK, Europe, the US, and Australia and has performed internationally at major festivals and intimate soirees. He has also published widely on Creative Writing, on medieval art and literature, and on medievalism in its varied guises. Oz is Professor of Creative Writing at Leeds Trinity University, where he leads the postgraduate Creative Writing programmes.

Paul Hetherington is a distinguished Australian poet who has published and/or edited 37 books and chapbooks. Among these are the prose poetry collections *Typewriter and Manuscript* (Life Before Man, 2020) and the co-authored *Fugitive Letters* (RWP, 2020). He has won or been shortlisted for more than 30 international and national awards and competitions and undertook an Australia Council for the Arts Literature Board Residency at the BR Whiting Studio in Rome in 2015–2016. He is Professor of Writing in the Faculty of Arts and Design at the University of Canberra, head of the International Poetry Studies Institute (IPSI), and one of the founding editors of the international online journal *Axon: Creative Explorations*. He founded the International Prose Poetry Group in 2014. He co-authored *Prose Poetry: An Introduction* (Princeton University Press, 2020) and co-edited the *Anthology of Australian Prose Poetry* (Melbourne University Press, 2020).

Nicholas Lauridsen is an attorney and scholar conducting research in modern poetry and poetics, reading theory, and cognate practices in verse and music. He holds degrees in literature, writing, and law from the University of California at

Berkeley, the New School, and the University of Virginia. He is a recipient of the Academy of American Poets Prize.

Jane Monson is a poet based in Cambridge, UK. She works as a mentor for disabled students at the University of Cambridge and was Associate Lecturer in Creative Writing at Anglia Ruskin University. She edited the first anthology of contemporary British prose poetry *This Line Is Not for Turning* (Cinnamon Press, 2011), praised by Pascale Petit as "necessary and ground-breaking," and has published two collections of prose poetry with Cinnamon Press, *Speaking Without Tongues* (2010) and *The Shared Surface* (2013). Her PhD, *Crossed Tongues: The Crisis of Speech in the Prose Poetry of Francis Ponge* (Cardiff University, 2008), focused on Modernism and the French prose poem, and she edited *British Prose Poetry: The Poems Without Lines* (Palgrave Macmillan, 2018), the first collection of essays on the British prose poem. Her third prose poetry collection, *The Chalk Butterfly* (Cinnamon Press, 2022), focuses on interconnections between nature, climate change, and mental health.

Divya Nadkarni is a PhD researcher at the Amsterdam School for Cultural Analysis (ASCA), University of Amsterdam. Divya's research focuses on the value and impact of political poetry today, asking the question "what makes a poem political?" Divya obtained their MA in English Literature and Cultural Studies from the University of Mumbai and an MA in Literary Studies from the University of Amsterdam. Divya is the editor of *nether quarterly*, a reputed Mumbai-based literary journal.

Ian Seed is Senior Lecturer in Creative Writing, Department of English, University of Chester, and Programme Leader for the BA in Creative Writing. His collections of prose poetry are: *Threadbare Fables* (LikeThisPress, 2012), *Makers of Empty Dreams* (Shearsman, 2014) (featured on BBC Radio 3), *Identity Papers* (Shearsman, 2016) (featured on BBC Radio 3), *New York Hotel* (Shearsman, 2018) (TLS Book of the Year), *Distances* (Red Ceilings, 2018), and *The Underground Cabaret* (Shearsman, 2020). He also has prose poetry in a number of anthologies, including *This Line Is Not for Turning: An Anthology of British Prose Poetry* (Cinnamon Press, 2011), *The Best British Poetry 2014* (Salt, 2014), *The Forward Book of Poetry 2017* (Faber & Faber, 2016), and *The Valley Press Anthology of Prose Poetry* (Valley Press, 2019). An essay "Nonsense and Wonder: An Exploration of the Prose Poetry of Jeremy Over" was published in Jane Monson (ed.), *British Prose Poetry: The Poems Without Lines* (Palgrave, Macmillan, 2018)

Ruth Stacey received a BA in English Studies from Bath Spa University (2001) and an MA in Literature: Politics and Identity from the University of Worcester (2013). Stacey's current practice-based research considers marginalised historical voices and creates retellings that merge memoir and biography, using Symbolist poetic techniques. Stacey's published collections and pamphlets include *Queen, Jewel, Mistress* (Eyewear, 2015), *How to Wear Grunge* (KF&S Press, 2018), *I, Ursula* (V.Press, 2020), and *Viola, the Virgin Queen* (KF&S Press, 2020). Stacey's collaborative pamphlet of poems *Inheritance* (MM Books, 2017), a duet with Katy Wareham Morris, won Best Collaborative Work in the 2018 Saboteur Awards. Stacey is currently a PhD student at the University of Northumbria where she is writing the imagined memoirs of Pamela Colman Smith, an artist and illustrator most famous for designing the Rider-Waite deck of tarot cards.

Edwin Stockdale has an MA in Creative Writing with Distinction from the University of Birmingham. Red Squirrel Press has published two of his pamphlets: *Aventurine* (September 2014) and *The Glower of the Sun* (January 2019). *The Glower of the Sun* was nominated for the Poetry Book Society Pamphlet Choice, the Michael Marks Award, and the Read Regional Campaign from New Writing North. In 2015, he was one of the runners-up in the Poetry Book Society Student Poetry Competition. He was one of six poets interviewed for the 2016–2017 Arvon/Jerwood Mentoring Award. He has recently submitted his PhD thesis in Creative Writing at Leeds Trinity University. A new pamphlet is due out from Red Squirrel Press in 2022.

Hannah Stone was an academic in the field of Early Christian Theology before completing an MA in Creative Writing at Leeds Trinity University in 2015. Since then she has published *Lodestone* (Stairwell Books, 2016), *Missing Miles* (Indigo Dreams Publishing, 2018), *Swn y Morloi* (Maytree Press, 2019), and several collaborations with other poets, as well as numerous poems in anthologies and print and online journals. She collaborates with composer Matthew Oglesby with whom she wrote the Penthos Requiem for 2018 (www.penthos.uk) and has edited volumes for the Electrifying Women project. She edits *Dream Catcher* literary journal, convenes the poets-composers forum for Leeds Lieder festival, and a monthly discussion with an invited poet for the Leeds Library (Nowt but Verse). Her recent residency as poet-theologian at Leeds Church Institute yielded *Reflections: A Poet-Theologian in Lockdown Leeds* (Maytree Press, 2021). She is poet in residence for the Council of Christians and Jews.

Helen Tookey is Lecturer/Senior Lecturer in Creative Writing at Liverpool John Moores University. She has published two collections of poetry with Carcanet Press, *Missel-Child* (2014; shortlisted for the Seamus Heaney Centre First Collection Poetry Prize, 2015) and *City of Departures* (2019; shortlisted for the Forward Prize for Best Collection, 2019). She is also the author of *Anaïs Nin, Fictionality and Femininity: Playing a Thousand Roles* (Oxford University Press, 2003) and co-editor, with Bryan Biggs, of *Malcolm Lowry: From the Mersey to the World* (Liverpool University Press, 2009) and *Remaking the Voyage: New Essays on Malcolm Lowry and In Ballast to the White Sea* (Liverpool University Press, 2019). She is currently working on a third collection of poetry and on a creative non-fiction book about her engagement with the work of Malcolm Lowry and Elizabeth Bishop.

Jen Webb is Distinguished Professor of Creative Practice at the University of Canberra and Dean of Graduate Research. Recent book publications include *Researching Creative Writing* (Frontinus, 2015), *Art and Human Rights: Contemporary Asian Contexts* (Manchester UP, 2016), and the poetry collection *Moving Targets* (Recent Work Press, 2018). The poetry collection *Flight Mode*, was co-written with Shé Hawke (Recent Work Press, October 2020). She is co-editor of the literary journal *Meniscus* and the scholarly journal *Axon: Creative Explorations* and Chief Investigator on the ARC Discovery project "So what do you do? Graduates in the Creative and Cultural Industries" (DP160101440).

Patrick Wright is a poet and lecturer in English Literature and Creative Writing at the Open University. His first PhD was in English Studies at the University of Manchester, supervised by Terry Eagleton. This was on the concept of the sublime. He is now working on a second doctorate in Creative Writing, at the Open University, which will be a poetry collection and critical commentary on the ekphrasis of modern and contemporary artworks. His first collection of poems, *Full Sight of Her*, is published by Black Spring Press (2020). His poems have appeared in several magazines – most recently *Agenda*, *Wasafiri*, *The Reader*, and *Envoi*. He has twice been included in the *Best New British and Irish Poets* anthology and has been shortlisted for the Bridport Prize.

INTRODUCTION

Anne Caldwell and Oz Hardwick

"The prose has all the high finish, all the glamours, of poetry."[1] So wrote Emile Deschamps in his 1843 review of the posthumously published *Gaspard de la Nuit* (1842) by the French author Aloysius (Louis) Bertrand (1807–1841). Though largely unnoticed at the time, this curious collection of supernaturally-tinged historical *ballades en prose* has become something of a cult classic. Most significantly, it is generally considered, via its profound effect upon Charles Baudelaire, to be the spring to which prose poetry – that seemingly mercurial, even quixotic, genre that defiantly asserts its poetic identity while at the same time adopting a near impenetrable disguise of quotidian prose – can trace its source. Yet, although *Gaspard* presents a recognisable point of origin, most of that which has followed bears all but the scantest similarity. Baudelaire himself, in the dedication of his *Le Spleen de Paris*, acknowledges its debt to his admiration of *Gaspard*, but in a letter of 1861 notes that his own work was shaped by the early realisation that Bertrand's work was "inimitable."[2]

This paradoxical influence of the inimitable is something that is at the heart of prose poetry and may be glimpsed in Deschamps' assessment of Bertrand's singular compositions. For what Baudelaire drew from Bertrand was not that which was on the surface – the notional ekphrasis of an intensely imagined antique Dijon – but the virtuoso, yet simultaneously intangible, "high finish, all the glamours of poetry." Thus, when Baudelaire famously muses on his dream of "the miracle of a poetic prose, musical, without rhythm and without rhyme, supple enough and rugged enough to adapt itself to the lyrical impulses of the soul, the undulations of reverie, the jibes of conscience,"[3] he is responding to these currents which cannot be measured, nor even precisely seen, but which shape the reading – and indeed writing – experience from within. In the wake of such observations, our formal critical vocabulary is less than adequate when confronted with these intriguing

DOI: 10.4324/9781003199533-1

compositions that are neither one thing nor another, yet at the same time more than a grafting of the two. See, for instance, the perfectly serviceable definition of the prose poem offered by *The Princeton Encyclopedia of Poetry and Poetics*: "a composition able to have any or all features of the lyric, except that it is put on the page, though not conceived of, as prose."[4] Few would argue with its applicability across the vast range of works thus defined over nearly two centuries, but fewer still would be able to write one from this description alone.

More picturesquely, Michael O'Neill refers to the prose poem's status as:

> a chimera, even a fabulous unicorn among literary forms; neither anecdotal fish nor symbolic fowl, but a new species; neither parable nor fable, though it may offer some of the fleeting gestures towards insight and story offered by those genres; neither aphorism nor pensée, though there are moments when Pascal, Rousseau, Nietzsche and Wilde seem to anticipate or shadow forth or complement its possibilities.[5]

In this summary account of the historical distrust shown towards prose poetry, O'Neill conflates the factual, the fabulous, the figurative, and the philosophical, thus mirroring what prose poetry does so well; employing (seemingly) lightly-handled juxtapositions to hint at meanings that are always just out of reach or, as he later says of the works which he goes on to discuss, "approaching."[6] An analogous description may be to consider the prose poem as akin to musical improvisation, particularly jazz, where a musician might take a phrase or idea and riff around it to explore just how far the musical phrase can be played with or pushed, never quite resolving the melody that teases both player and listener before further ideas suggest themselves.[7] And just as a musician can tune into a phrase with their whole body, a prose poem can also been seen as a living cell, capable of osmosis, characterised by its permeable frame.

This notion of a liberation from the more familiar "frames" of poetry is inherent in the subtitle of Jane Monson's 2018 anthology of critical essays on British prose poetry. She succinctly characterises the form as "The Poems Without Lines." While this appears the most serviceable definition, we would like here to posit a slight shift in perspective and suggest that they should more properly be considered as single-line poems, each poem a sustained and self-contained metrical unit that intuits rhythm and internal rhyme without recourse to the hard return. And as for their unique character? In his review of Paul Muldoon's *Annals of Chile* (1994), Seamus Heaney evocatively described poetry as "language in orbit" – brilliantly conveying the way in which each word, although set in its fixed path, is at the same time constantly in motion, its relationships with other words subtly different each time it is observed; aligning and spinning away, sometimes illuminating, and sometimes casting shadows. To push this image further, the prose-like appearance on the page of the prose poem may be considered as resembling an orrery, a discrete miniature simulation of planetary motion; yet, when one looks closely, each circling sphere is in fact a galaxy in itself, like that which hangs round the neck of Orion the cat in the *Men in Black* movie.

There is no doubt that the prose poem is enjoying a surge in popularity in the twenty-first century. *The Penguin Book of the Prose Poem: From Baudelaire to Anne Carson* (2018), edited by Jeremy Noel-Tod, sees the form's rich heritage championed at the heart of the literary mainstream, while a proliferation of critical studies in recent years – notable amongst which are Monson's essay collection cited above, Peter Johnson's *A Cast-Iron Aeroplane That Can Actually Fly: Commentaries from 80 Contemporary American Poets on Their Prose Poetry* (2019), Cassandra Atherton and Paul Hetherington's *Prose Poetry: An Introduction* (2020), and Mary Ann Caws and Michel Delville's *The Edinburgh Companion to the Prose Poem* (2021) – along with a significant number of anthologies and single author collections, attests to a growth of interest amongst both writers and readers.

Along with the emergence of digital literature and flash fiction, the playfulness and flexibility of prose poetry singles it out as a form of writing that deserves further scholarly attention. It provides a condensed yet pliable space for creative work to be shared in both traditional media and on digital platforms. On publication of *The Valley Press Anthology of Prose Poetry* (2019) – our edited anthology of contemporary work in the form from around the British Isles – we marked the occasion with what we believe to have been the first British prose poetry symposium at Leeds Trinity University in July 2019. What we had envisaged as a small celebratory gathering of scholars and practitioners exceeded all expectations, with delegates from all around the UK, Europe, the United States, and Australia. The excitement, energy, and enthusiasm which characterised the event persuaded us that our project was far from over and that a collection of short essays combining insights on the theory and practice of prose poetry, from as broad a range of perspectives as possible, would make a timely and valuable contribution to the development of the form. Following on from Monson's collection of critical essays, we are pleased to gather these further critical engagements with prose poetry, which seek to initiate new conversations relating to the form and to raise its profile amongst practitioners and scholars alike.

In our opening essay, Cassandra Atherton and Paul Hetherington survey the contemporary English-language prose poem in its many current guises, as it reproduces and mutates in response to a world of dizzying change and uncertainty. Their exploration of the ways in which the prose poem's "ongoing disguise" as such a small, ostensibly contained, form so often gives way to reveal a restless "metaphorical, analogical, suggestive and consciously intertextual" urge which crosses, questions, and erases categorical boundaries.

Challenging boundaries is a leitmotif which recurs throughout the present volume, both in terms of the form itself and in the ways in which expectations related to generic categorisation may both engage and wrong-foot the reader. Oz Hardwick's essay explores the way in which prose poetry employs poetic techniques in order to set up and subvert expectations of narrative within its neat paragraphs and goes on to suggest why this makes it such a vital literary form for the early twenty-first century. Hannah Stone, in turn, considers the reader's response to – and recognition of – the prose poem as a distinct form, positing that prose poetry's subversion of formal expectations lends itself to a spiral, meditative process rather than a linear narrative locution. These subversions, and the surprise they initiate in the reader – that instance of "quotidian epiphany,"[8] as Michael O'Neill elegantly puts it – is often described as a manifestation of the surreal. Nicholas Lauridsen's essay, however, interrogates such interpretations through the lens of Russell Edson's work, in order to demonstrate how the separation of poetic metaphor from the formal constraints of lineated verse may surprise or disquiet the reader purely through locating figurative language outside of its familiar contexts.

Since the early writings of Bertrand and Baudelaire, prose poetry has been closely associated with the psychology of immediate experience; of a (possibly constructed) self in a state of heightened attention, often to the extent that the familiar becomes strange. Susie Campbell explores the ways in which, historically, prose poems have destabilised discourses surrounding the domestic environment and even the body within that environment. Anne Caldwell approaches experience of environment through a different lens, exploring the territory between poetry and architecture and examining the particular ways in which prose poetry employs intertextuality, compression, and allusion in order to create a deep sense of place. Yet the prose poem, like all literature, also creates its own worlds and, using the work of Gaspar Orozco as a model, Helen Tookey explores the way in which the prose poem can act as a machine for projecting images which, while vividly striking, constantly recede from the reader's grasp.

These engagements with experience and perception are afforded expressive possibilities through the prose poem's distinct inhabitation of liminal spaces, the form itself imbuing language with immediacy charged with transience. Ian Seed discusses ways in which the prose poem is able to estrange the familiar through registering surprising observations and a sense of "outsider" knowledge, arguably remaining an "outsider" art form in spite of its growing popularity. That this flux between notions of "inside" and "outside" remains the case beyond individual writers and their work is demonstrated by Divya Nadkarni, who sees in Indian prose poetry both continuity with tradition and a simultaneous assertion of cultural independence. Jen Webb, too, considers aspects of individuality and interconnectedness, by addressing the adoption of a *renga*-like mode of practice among prose poets which facilitates international collaborative works.

One of the defining features of the prose poem on the page is its conciseness. Most prose poems take the form of a rectangle of text on a white field, and even longer examples generally employ at least a similar aesthetic. In considering this "framing" aspect on the page, Patrick Wright explores its ekphrastic relationship to painting, and the ways in which formless or "catastrophic" subject matter may be contained within – or may challenge – physical and conceptual boundaries.

Edwin Stockdale, too, interrogates conceptual boundaries, considering prose poetry at the nexus between historical record, imaginative fiction, and the figurative characteristics of poetry, in order to engage creatively with the past. While these writers draw upon visual, as well as written sources, Ruth Stacey expands this further, to consider musical and decorative qualities in relation to the prose poem, further establishing it as a site of dynamic exchange with other forms of expression.

The threads laid out through the course of this book are woven together through Jane Monson's concluding chapter, in which examples from international prose poets, as well as criticism around their work, are used to examine how in practice and scrutiny the prose poem increasingly benefits from its position outside predominantly literary parameters, at which boundaries remain only as faint markers, if that. In so doing, Monson opens and encourages an alternative critical discourse around the prose poem, in which comparisons with non-literature-based disciplines may help to move the conversation away from the prose-vs.-poetry debate towards other spaces within the arts and non-fictions.

Less concerned with the *What?* than with the *Why?* and the *How?* of prose poetry, we hope that the volume you are holding will inspire you as a reader and/or writer to join in this conversation about – and indeed with – this protean, sometimes playful, sometimes perplexing, and always provoking form.

Notes

1 Donald Sidney-Fryer, Introduction to *Gaspard de la Nuit: Fantasies in the Manner of Rembrandt and Callot,* by Aloysius Bertrand, trans. Donald Sidney-Fryer (Encino, CA: Black Coat Press, 2004), 54.
2 Quoted in Sidney-Fryer, Introduction to *Gaspard de la Nuit*, 61.
3 Charles Baudelaire, *Paris Spleen*, trans. Louise Varèse (New York: New Directions, 1970), ix–x.
4 Alex Preminger, Frank Warnke, and O. B. Hardison, Jr., *Princeton Encyclopedia of Poetry and Poetics* (Princeton, NJ: Princeton University Press, 1965), 664, quoted in Jane Monson, "Introduction," in *British Prose Poetry: The Poems Without Lines*, ed. Jane Monson (Cham, CH: Palgrave Macmillan, 2018), 7.
5 Michael O'Neill, "The Marvellous Clouds: Reflections on the Prose Poetry of Woolf, Baudelaire and Williams," in *British Prose Poetry*, ed. Jane Monson, 73.
6 O'Neill, "The Marvellous Clouds," 88.
7 Taking this idea further, N. Santilli notes that the prose poem, like jazz, is not a static form, but rather "a succession of styles [which is] always questioning and moving its boundaries." Nikki Santilli, "Prose Poetry and the Spirit of Jazz," in *British Prose Poetry*, ed. Jane Monson, 280.
8 O'Neill, "The Marvellous Clouds," 75.

1

PROTEAN MANIFESTATIONS AND DIVERSE SHAPES

Defining and Understanding Strategies of the Contemporary Prose Poem

Cassandra Atherton and Paul Hetherington

Introduction

Prose poetry is one of literature's most elusive and protean forms. It is a short form that often looks unremarkable when first encountered but ranges widely in its manifestations – and it is evolving and developing so fast that, as scholars of the prose poem, we keep finding innovative expressions of the form, even when we're not looking for them. Many of these innovations appear in the rapidly growing number of anthologies, critical books, and special journal issues that focus on prose poetry – and an example is Lauren Russell's sequence "Requiem for Elementary Language Acquisition," which we discuss below.[1] This remarkable hybrid piece juxtaposes prose poetry paragraphs with lineated moments while exploring the use of free-lines and colons to quiz and defer meaning and resist completion.

In the face of the great variety of prose poems and a conspicuous lack of consensus about what prose poetry is, various scholars and prose poets have suggested that it is best if the form remains mysterious and that we understand prose poetry primarily through reading individual works. For instance, Kevin Brophy writes:

> It is perhaps impossible to discuss the prose poem sensibly. If you move too far towards categorising the different forms it can take, you can end by defeating its defiant formlessness; and if you move down the path of pointing out its poetic strategies you re-align it with that form of poetry it is deliberately discarding.[2]

John Taylor broadly concurs, although he generalises about the prose poem form by acknowledging that it "express[es] a demotic spirit and rarely avoid[s] the anecdotic, in both the etymological and evolved sense of the term."[3]

DOI: 10.4324/9781003199533-2

It is an understandable impulse in a postmodern period to maintain the sometimes-enigmatic frisson associated with the idea of an unquantifiable literary form. Part of the appeal of prose poetry is that it may represent different things to different prose poets and may even manifest in ways that they do not expect. Thus, the form often brings with it a sense of surprise and an associated sense that every prose poem carries the possibility of newness. When we wrote the book *Prose Poetry: An Introduction* (2020), we were aware of these issues. Prose poetry has long been called a subversive form, and even "hypersubversive,"[4] largely because it fails to conform with conventional expectations of either traditional verse or contemporary free verse. It also does not conform to the expectations associated with conventional, discursive prose – whether fiction or narrative nonfiction.

In this context, we wrote that "the main scholarship written about English-language prose poetry to date defines the form as problematic, paradoxical, ambiguous, unresolved, or contradictory."[5] We also quoted the fine prose poet and editor, Peter Johnson's wonderfully tantalising remark, "Just as black humour straddles the fine line between comedy and tragedy, so the prose poem plants one foot in prose, the other in poetry, both heels resting precariously on banana peels"[6] – a comment he made at a time when prose poems were hard to place in journals and magazines and when there was a powerful sense that the prose poem had been "othered" by mainstream literary culture. Given this, is it possible to say what constitutes a prose poem and, in any case, what should one make of its protean tendencies?

In addressing these questions, we will focus on some of the features of prose poetry we have defined in our scholarship on the form: its fragmentary nature and use of metonymy; its use of sentences rather than poetic lines; its prose-poetic cadences; its relationship to the quotidian; its appearance on the page; and its incorporation into hybrid literary forms. We examine these features primarily through the discussion and explication of particular prose poems, taking the position that, overall, prose poetry belongs to the genre of poetry but is written in the mode of prose.[7] Importantly, we begin with the premise that prose poetry is a literary form with identifiable characteristics, however various actual prose poems may be.

Fragmentation and the Prose Poem

Prose poems belong to the tradition of fragmentary literary forms that came into vogue in the Romantic period, most conspicuously in Germany and England. German poets, philosophers, and philosopher-poets, notably Friedrich Hölderlin, Novalis, and Friedrich Schlegel, made a virtue of the unfinished (and in many cases, fairly brief) work, reflecting on the uncontainable nature of existence and what they tended to see as the inherently fragmentary nature of literature. One of the famous statements about such matters is by Novalis (1772–1801):

> Only what is incomplete can be comprehended—can take us further. What is complete is only enjoyed. If we want to comprehend nature we must postulate it as incomplete, to reach an unknown variable in this way. All determination is relative.[8]

Once poetry, and literature more generally, began to be actively conceived of as "incomplete" – and as a gesture towards incomprehensible immensities – so literature began to be understood as insufficient to the task of comprehending the whole.

The development of prose poetry was one outcome of this preoccupation with literary insufficiency. Whether one takes Charles Baudelaire's preface to the first book of modern prose poetry, *Le Spleen de Paris* [*Paris Spleen*] (1869) at face value – and a few critics have questioned Baudelaire's sincerity – his attitude in this preface is reasonably congruent with some of Novalis's key ideas. He writes, "I will not hold [the reader] to the unbroken thread of some superfluous plot … Chop it into many fragments and you will see how each is able to exist apart."[9] This idea of prose poetry being composed of fragments is of profound importance in understanding how ideas of the small and the large, and of what is contained and what is liberated, may intersect in this literary form. As fragments acknowledge their insufficiency, so they simultaneously claim a kind of self-sufficiency, suggesting that their limitations are part of their point. Fragmentation implies that although there is a whole, and although it may be partly knowable, once one steps back from society's grand and encompassing narratives – of the Biblical story, for example, or aspects of European Enlightenment narratives – fragmentation becomes a recognition of knowledge's limitations.

Prose poems as literary fragments thus have the capacity to suggest a clear-sighted understanding of the power of appreciating the brokenness and partiality – in both senses – of human ways of seeing. Prose poems resonate especially powerfully in the liminal space that exists between the limitations of what they say and know, and the larger world and knowledge at which they gesture. Their own gestures are deliberately circumscribed and poetically suggestive *in order* to reach outwards and, in this reaching outwards, they resist closure. Instead, they open a dialogue with larger and not-completely knowable worlds, sometimes unfathomable states of being and the ineffable. By never trying to tell the full story, they acknowledge that no single narrative is able to be all-encompassing.

If prose poems as fragments gesture towards and invoke larger ideas and meanings, they may be understood as inherently metonymic. Certainly, any analysis of their parts indicates that they regularly employ metonymic gestures – where truncated and limited statements stand in for, or gesture at, larger statements and broader ideas beyond their own forms of representation. Furthermore, because prose-poems-as-fragments acknowledge what one may call their broken-offness, many of the most interesting of them resist the full impetus of narrative even when they employ narrative devices. Prose poems try to point to something about their language or their subject that sits outside of the narrative gestures they make (and frequently outside of the work itself), understanding that narrative gestures alone can rarely do the work of connecting the outside "whole" to the prose poem's relatively brief, fragmentary utterance. The prose poem's language needs to employ metaphorical, metonymic, analogical, and ambiguous figures in order to open conduits between its utterance and what is does not, or cannot, explicitly say.

Thus, prose poems exemplify the art of what we will call the suggestive-implicit – saying just enough to indicate that there is more – somewhere – that might be said but cannot currently be stated. However, in its use of prose, the prose poem's flow of sentences and its box shape initially tend to disguise this suggestive-implicitness; indeed, at a first glance, many prose poems appear to be complete and explicit. This means that many prose poems transform powerfully under the reader's gaze as they are revealed to be fragmentary and open.

Speaking the Unspeakable – Mariko Nagai

Mariko Nagai's prose poems in her collection, *Irradiated Cities*, are a good example of these prose-poetic tendencies at work. She creates works that gesture towards an unspeakable reality, are fundamentally metonymic, and which gain much of their power through their carefully circumscribed modes of address. These works are complemented by a series of black and white photographs which Nagai took in Hiroshima, Nagasaki, Tokyo, and Fukushima. Together, both text and image explore the traumatic history of radiation in Japan. And, to a significant extent, the fully justified blocks of prose poetry and photographs mimic one another as both attempt to capture and reiterate fragmentary experiences in the aftermath of atomic catastrophe.

Metonymically, these works stand in for the nuclear sublime's appeal to the beauty and terror of extinction, while simultaneously acknowledging the ultimate failure of any attempt to convey the end of all forms of life. In this way, the accumulation of prose poems and photographs in *Irradiated Cities* is a stark admission that while each is a part of something much larger, perhaps even infinite in its implications, it must be pieced together from fragments to be effective – an acknowledgement that, in such a context, nothing we know or can name or grasp is truly whole. Furthermore, Nagai highlights the power of fragments to stand in for much more than singular moments in a traumatic past. As Nicholas Wong argues, the juxtapositions in the text haunt and beg us "to confront both the cities and ourselves in pieces."[10]

Nagai's striking use of colons between phrases and clauses in *Irradiated Cities* both separates and unites fragments. The colons signal conclusions that never conclude and may even be read as QEDs that prove nothing. However, this repetitive use of the colon constantly expands the reader's sense of these prose poems because, as John Bradley identifies, "everything is connected to everything else."[11] For example, in "The Living Calls to the Dead," Nagai uses the initial aftermath of the atomic bombing to build a picture of abject suffering and catastrophe. Broken parts of sentences are used to convey a sense of the ruptured, postatomic world. Nagai's fragments are simultaneously joined and separated, stacking up on one another like debris and an uncontainable, immeasurable list of suffering:

> : the city simmers from above & from the ground : houses keep collapsing : rivers stink from decaying bodies : survivors hold each other up because everything else has collapsed : schools : concrete buildings : what used to be hospitals : they stagger : in a day : in two days : people start arriving in the city looking for their loved ones : children wander around the streetless streets looking for where their homes used to be : people arrive with water & food, going from one skeletal building to another : calling : always[12]

Similarly, fragments of dialogue rather than complete conversations convey the destruction of families, homes, and communities. This approach demonstrates that what has happened is ultimately unspeakable; that, while some responses in language are possible, communication and understanding are fundamentally splintered:

> calling : *have you seen ... ? : have you seen my husband? he works here : my children went to school here* : floors of buildings covered with the wounded & the dead : nights do not come : the sky never darkens : the white nights alight with fire from the ground : *have you seen ...?* :
> [...]
> searchers walk amidst the dead & the dying & the city that was but no longer, looking for something. anything familiar : a name tag : a rumor of sighting : anything & everything : they walk : they walk all day : they keep scratching messages : it is another hot day in August : it is still a clear day : they do not know that their bodies now carry a bomb inside : a ticking bomb :[13]

This prose poem, like all the others, ends with a colon – addressing what is to come, resisting closure. Bradley says, "the colon is the perfect punctuation mark for the book as it's logical, neutral and inevitable."[14] Indeed, much has been made of the way in which Nagai ends *Irradiated Cities* sequence with two colons, one after the other: "::".[15] Dennis James Sweeney argues that this:

> might be a final generosity, a gesture toward closure in a work that is primarily concerned with the impossibility of that. It might represent the two pillars that stood beneath the dark pedestal before one disappeared. My feeling, however, is that it represents the interminable present, the fact that

the ongoing interrogation Nagai undertakes must finally end in being—not for those who interrogate, but for the victims of irradiation, whose stories are no longer stories but a life.[16]

Nagai's prose poems are fragments that open out to provide more than commentary on the history of radiation in Japan; they lobby for nuclear disarmament and ecological preservation. They do so by engaging with a highly articulate brokenness and fragmentariness of a horror that resists full understanding.

Cadence and Compression – Marc Vincenz

Generally speaking, prose poetry employs the rhythms and cadences of prose rather than using poetic metre or end rhyme, or the more unpredictable rhythms of contemporary free verse. Although the cadences of anglophone prose poetry have not been discussed very often by critics, these are central to the kinds of effects that prose poems achieve – as is the related way in which many prose poems compress their language. Whereas lineated poems make use of the white space that extends beyond every poetic line, there is little white space of any kind in the tight confines of most prose poems – which appear on the page or screen as right justified boxes of enclosed text. Such prose poems typically exploit for their "poetic" effects a range of juxtapositions, repetitions, and alignments – notwithstanding the way many prose poems are printed with different margins in various publications.

Abigail Beckel states:

> A prose poem finds its tension in sentences, its cadence starts and stops with punctuation, with the long sentence and then the short, with repetition, alliteration and internal rhyme built in.[17]

The squeeze of a prose poem's sentences generally encourages a swift pace of reading. Punctuation such as commas and full stops are the only obvious places to slow or pause. And, even in these brief intervals, the reader is never left to balance (or even teeter) on a poem's line endings. Instead, the language of prose poetry unfolds fairly continuously, inviting the reader to pursue the movement of sentences within a familiar block shape composed of the sorts of stacked sentences one might encounter in almost any prose paragraph. However, reading a prose poem soon destabilises conventional readerly expectations – either because of the striking rhythmic strategies many prose poets employ, or as a result of the intensely figurative language of so much prose poetry.

As prose poems become poetic in this way, so their movement tends to be slowed and they may be said to draw out their "own syntax through lyric rather than narrative motion, through sonic and figurative recursion and retard rather than propulsion."[18] Nikki Santilli writes that the "prose poem form oscillates constantly between what it expresses (presses out) from its miniature physical form and the wider worlds to which it gestures, beyond its own edges"[19] – and much of this gesturing to the wider world happens so succinctly, and even gnomically, that prose poems frequently create a powerful tidal surge and return, dragging wider associations towards their particular expressions.

The cadence of such works inflects the movement of the prose. For example, Marc Vincenz's "Switzerland 911" is a galloping ode that continually presses forward but which simultaneously challenges the reader to make sense of numerous references and ironies. Because the prose is dense and recursive in tendency, a never-fully-resolved tension is created, a kind of double movement that is explicitly gestured at in the image of a navel as "a black hole collapsing in on itself." Perhaps Vincenz is asking the reader to understand this work's abundant energy as not so much pressing forward as circling a mysterious centre of meaning:

> All hail the Alps and their glassine ice-stream, the *Stube* with her calvados and *Kaffeecreme*, or the sausages air-dried in glacial attics in every barn across the heartland; oh, and the cheeses, the little holes that harbor untold secrets even from the magic of physics. Outside, watch the Ibex ascend the tallest crags like stairs. One night we are drinking beers and *Kirsch*, playing blackjack with American tourists. *What did they call it? Six-card stud?* And Armin, decked out in his Swiss Army uniform. The epaulette put him at the rank of Colonel, a leader of men and machines in the hearty mountain division. All hail the Alps and their hollowed out interiors […] *Tor! Tor!* are the cheers that echo Thursday nights across the valley. Finally, you light a cigar and the smoke finds its way up the stairs. On your way up you give me a wink and a note. *My room is 911*, it says. I bow out of the last hand, fold on a perfect bobtail straight. For you the idea of time is self-evident. It must be spent before ascending those final steps where birds migrate the Milky Way, or deep into the liquid of mathematics all compasses pointing true north. So up I arise, engineering and economics leading the way, and in 911, your navel becomes the heart of the galaxy, a black hole collapsing in on itself, all those calvados atoms swirling in a haze of Swiss bravado.[20]

The long sentences mirror the mounting triple excitement of the card game, the soccer game, and the impending sexual hook up in the ironically named room 911 – the number for emergency services in the United States and also a reference to the September 11 terrorist attack and the First World's attendant loss of innocence. The sentence, "For you the idea of time is self-evident" is a self-reflexive moment that refers to the form of the prose poem and its use of a cramped TimeSpace,[21] as well as referring to the lead-up to the sexual act.

Vincenz's use of repetitive and reiterative effects creates a sense that language is tightly wound within the box of text – for instance, the phrase "All hail the Alps" along with the moments where people cheer "*Tor! Tor!*" and the narrator moves to room "911" combine to generate a sense of urgency. At the end of the work, the internal rhyming of "bravado" and "calvados" is an example of what Beckel refers to as "mouthfeel":

> Because the prose poet is working with sentences and does not have enjambment to help determine the pace and rhythm of the poem, the poet's focus must return again and again to the level of individual words. The sonic qualities of precise word choice can be used to create density, repetition, and mouthfeel.[22]

Additionally, in a rather subversive Donnean moment, as the narrator finds room 911, with all "compasses pointing true north," the prose poem moves into the realm of the metaphysical. Vincenz refers to the Milky Way galaxy that contains our solar system, playing with the idea that his prose poem, and the intimate relationship it evokes, constitutes a small galaxy all of its own. Yet, even in this moment, the prose poem's box of text opens into the space around it, and the motif of hollowness – in the cheese's "little holes" and the "hollowed-out interiors" – operates in opposition to the work's packed appearance. This not only suggests the potential insubstantiality of edifices both small and large, but a range of hollowed victories. The fragmentary and cramped confines of the prose poem form give these moments a particular, charged effect as the words within the text box seem to burst outwards.

By contrast, one of Vincenz's lineated poems, "Ode to a Northern Seabird," uses enjambment and unrhymed tercets to explore movement in a very different way. The word "triptych" in the first line is a self-reflexive moment drawing attention to the three lines in each stanza and the joining of two tercets in the final stanza to make a sestet. In this poem, the reader perches on the final word of each line before continuing into the space at the right margin and then onto the next line – which becomes a kind of hesitant verbal mimicry of the seabird's progress. Despite the enjambments at the end of each tercet, the space between tercets also creates a momentary pause, as the reader visually registers the gaps in lines and meanings. The poem begins:

> Now the triptych has moved on,
> seasons see no fair weather,
> and grass, grass grows upward.
>
> Somewhere, Hess knows
> the artichoke taunts the dodo
> and a dial telephone
>
> rings out unanswered
> in an abandoned shack
> upon the bleached coast[23]

It ends with this final stanza foregrounding tenacity:

> You know, even in the flurry
> of ice storms, in the slate sky
> of oceans only the bird knows,
> in the crumpled nothings
> of the north wind—
> he *will* still find her.[24]

The white space in this work – and in so many lineated poems, more generally – allows time for the reader to think and breathe as they progress, evaluating individual poetic lines as key units of meaning and following the unwinding of the poem at a pace that suits them. Vincenz's prose poem, on the other hand, refuses the reader this luxury. It is continually under pressure, carrying the reader through the work without significant pause.

The Quotidian and Contemporary – Peter Johnson

In the second half of the twentieth century and the opening decades of the twenty-first century, prose poetry has frequently addressed the quotidian, often locating the weird, the marvellous, or the mysterious in its characterisations of daily life. Such prose poetry – and this is especially true of American examples – typically employs a rather wry, knowing, or matter-of-fact tonality, and the cadence of these works is sometimes deliberately "flat" and prosaic.

Some of the most conspicuous examples occur in works by the highly influential American prose poets Russell Edson and Charles Simic, but many other writers also adopt similar strategies. In the case of Russell Edson, and more recently Peter Johnson, the cultivation of a particular tonality signals that the works they write are to be understood as fundamentally quixotic and strange because their apparent matter-of-factness helps to open up the truly unusual nature of the poetic worlds they present. Such prose poems simultaneously acknowledge and enliven the monotony of so much urban or suburban quotidian experience – employing nuanced, if often disguised (and recurrently colloquial) rhythms and cadences in doing so.

For instance, in "Vaccination, in the Broadest Sense of the Term," Johnson gives us the detritus of his day in a world affected by COVID-19, itemising apparently never-ending and fairly monotonous obligations and responsibilities. His employment of a seemingly autobiographical persona and his repeated use of the first-person pronoun, along with his utilisation of a hyperbolic vernacular – such as in the phrase, "a Biblical plague of ants" – all contribute to the way his prose poem conjures a sense of what one might call the pressing-contemporary. The compression of the prose poem form is particularly suited to such a conjuring.

This prose poem is a miniature frame narrative, with the frame consisting of the moment the persona is vaccinated at a pharmacist. As he receives the needle's jab and reflects on his day, the work becomes an absurd, suburban parable in which the repetition of hyperbolic tropes increasingly normalises the strangeness of the truncated narrative that is unfolding for the reader. Commonplace moments are enmeshed with the extraordinary – when, for example, the persona's headache is described as "the size of Bangladesh" or he lectures about hopefulness to squirrels under a Japanese Zelkova tree – and, as they are, the quotidian is opened up to the persona's wry, ironic, and sometimes frantic wonderment about contemporary urban/suburban existence and its attendant problems and frailties:

> Just as the pharmacist drove the vaccine into my arm, I thought, "So what did you do today, Peter?" I shaved, then looked into the mirror without disappointment, wondering why it took 69 years for that to happen? I had an argument with my wife about a Biblical plague of ants that had overrun her underwear drawer. I killed a huge spider clinging to the inside of the shower curtain, then washed it down the drain. It crawled out so I killed it again. At 10 a.m. I had a headache the size of Bangladesh. […] I went home. The woodpecker had regained consciousness, then flown away. The spider was back, so I killed it again. I went to the library, spoke of the failure of trickle-down economics with the janitor. I left. I gave a lecture about hopefulness to a bunch of squirrels sharing a bagel under a Japanese Zelkova tree. I stopped at the pond and watched the baby geese make their stunning debut. I called my wife, told her to hang in there, that the sequel would be much better. She laughed, then said there was huge spider clinging to a picture of me on her nightstand, its thorax eclipsing my face. "It's so big you can see its eyes," she said. I told her to ignore it, it had earned the right to live.[25]

Prose poems of this kind make use of exaggerated effects to draw attention to the recurrent absurdities attendant on postmodern life. In addition to the examples already mentioned, it is worth noting the manner in which this prose poem tropes on the motif of the spider's death and resurrection. This is surely a reference to the way animal and insect life has increasingly colonised major cities and suburban spaces, and it also functions as a broader indication of the insecurities that increasingly accompany contemporary life – and, specifically, life in a pandemic where people continuously confront mortality.

Johnson's prose poem is not asking the reader to take its narrative at face value but, instead, to understand the aggregation of tightly packed events as symptomatic of the crisis at the heart of society – where time is at a premium and capitalism (with its failing "trickle-down economics") is teetering. As Johnson's sentences exploit a kind of faux matter-of-factness, they move swiftly through the various layers of detail they present, focusing on the evocation of an apparently unresolvable situation. The spider is resurrected so often that it eventually earns "the right to live," even as it has become truly monstrous, and the work finishes by concluding that contemporary humanity survives through strategies that include the acceptance of absurdity and the willingness to ignore or accept various present and disturbing realities.

Shape-shifting – Lauren Russell

Prose poetry has often been identified by its ubiquitous box shape. Most prose poems appear as a fully justified box on the page, and even those that have ragged right margins tend to be broadly shaped as rectangles. Furthermore, all prose poems have sentences that run to, and wrap at, the right margin. This is generally seen as so important to the identification of prose poetry that any poetic work composed of lines that stop before the right margin is usually identified as a lineated or "lyric" poem.[26] However, even as the definition of prose poetry has come into clearer focus in recent years, prose poets continue to push or skew the boundaries of the form. While Ron Silliman identifies what he defines as single sentence paragraphs,[27] Sally Ashton makes a convincing case for the use of the free-line in prose poetry, allowing spaces into the cramped box:

> With free-line form, the construction varies from poet to poet but generally consists of stand-alone sentences running margin to margin and separated by a skipped line. It's as if stanzas comprised of one sentence made up the poem. The skipped line's empty space achieves a momentary stillness, like an exhaled breath, between sentences.[28]

As prose poets increasingly experiment with form and line, hybrid forms are proliferating. While the Japanese *haibun* demonstrates that the idea of combining prose poetry with lineated poetry goes back at least as far as the seventeenth century (in the case of *haibun*, prose paragraphs were joined with a haiku), there are now multifarious combinations of prose poetry paragraphs and poetic lines. Chard deNiord argues:

> The lure of blurred lines in today's poetic climate reflects not only an iconoclastic urge to find new forms beyond the traditional ones—the line beyond the lines in poetry—but a form that also reflects the blend between genders—new hybrid and liminal forms following discontent with the old order. A form that accurately reflects the blur and ambiguity of trans as both verbal and physical reifications of natural but heretofore verboten human expression.[29]

In particular, many women poets have experimented with notions of containment and liberation in hybrid forms that include the prose poem, and in *Prose Poetry: An Introduction*, we argue that "prose poetry's characteristic brevity and condensations begin to expand in many directions … challenging readers to question or overturn their assumptions about gender roles."[30] While prose poetry "may be understood as one of the contemporary literary forms that most clearly expresses feminist ideas and intent,"[31] we would add to this that prose poetry, through its refusal of closure and its recognition of wider worlds and possibilities, is also a form that is well suited to embracing a range of gender identities outside the restrictive gender binary – and this may be especially true of hybrid forms of the prose poem. As Amy Moorman Robbins argues:

> hybridity can be understood as an implicitly political strategy, one that forces encounters between hitherto incompatible literary traditions and that thereby brings to the surface competing ideologies and their implications for lived experience.[32]

Lauren Russell's sequence, "Requiem for Elementary Language Acquisition," is a compelling example of a hybrid prose poetry sequence that foregrounds the play of signification in language while questioning stereotypical or complacent responses to the making of meaning. It begins with an epigraph "La poésie est une pipe" ("Poetry is a pipe"), a gnomic phrase employed by the surrealists Paul Éluard and André Breton in 1929, and also used by the Belgian painter René Magritte.[33] The phrase functions to conjure René Magritte's famous painting, *The Treachery of Images* (1929), which depicts a pipe with the words "Ceci n'est pas une pipe" ("This is not a pipe") written beneath the image. This painting draws attention to the difference between the representation of a thing and the thing itself and was part of a wide-ranging international discussion and debate about the nature of representation among artists, writers, and intellectuals, including many of the Parisian surrealists, in the interwar period. The vigorous, inventive nature of such exchanges is evidenced by Paul Éluard's and André Breton's pointed response to Paul Valéry's 1929 statement that:

> Poetry is a survival.
>
> In an age when language is being simplified, forms are being altered, and the public is insensitive to them—an age of specialization—poetry is a legacy of the past. By which I mean that no one would *invent* poetry today. Or, for that matter, rites of any kind.[34]

Éluard and Breton assert that "A poem must be a debacle of the intellect. It cannot be anything but … In the poet: / the ear laughs, / the mouth swears; / … Poetry is a pipe."[35]

Russell joins this discussion via her prose poetry sequence. Like Magritte's pipe, her hybrid work quizzes and problematises the relationship between language, the world, and the things that words claim to represent. It questions what we think we know and challenges commonplace and conventional understandings of the way we make meaning. Russell's decision to explore these issues via Magritte – and Éluard and Breton – has significant and multi-layered implications. The French surrealists were an important part of the early twentieth-century prose poetry tradition, and neo-surrealist American prose poets have also been highly influential. These prose poets on both sides of the Atlantic Ocean challenged "rational" assumptions about how human experience should be understood, and how literature might respond to surrealist ideas about the importance of the unconscious mind and its dreamlike imagery. Surrealist intertexts are, as it were, re-interpreted in Russell's hybrid prose poetry sequence – which is replete with a neo-surrealist dream of language – as she shifts the surreal into a postmodern and postfeminist context.

For example, the first prose poem is broken by a series of sentences spaced out down the page, creating a sense that the prose poetry box has been ruptured. While lineated poetry can often be identified as deferring meaning and breaking syntax in lines that turn before the right margin, when the prose poem is split open, its transgressed boundaries and internal breaks constitute a visually striking disruption of the way prose is usually expected to proceed:

> Once a person I loved gave me a bestiary, a book of animal portraits with text in three languages. And although we no longer talk, I still love this person or rather the idea of this person, which is not an idea I invented but an idea he gave me.

> In Brussels I am shuffled about in a dream, a dream that is anxious and wary, filled with narrow brick streets that collide in baffling three-part intersections and languages ricocheting off each other to meet somewhere beyond me. The language app instructs me to climb stairs of syntax patiently:

> Je suis une femme.
> Tu es un chat?
> C'est un homme.
> Nous ne parlons pas.

> Is there a language of loneliness?
> Is loneliness beyond language?

> Le chat a les clés.

> From the window of my study, the black tile roof of the building across the street is a waffle dipped in dark chocolate and gabled steeply, dormer windows and sunroof and chimney jutting out at perfect 45-degree angles. I want to put it all in my mouth but can't decide if I should lick or crunch or gulp without savoring.[36]

In this hybrid prose poem, three languages – English, French, and a notional "language of loneliness" – are foregrounded, "ricocheting off each other," and are just beyond the dreamer's comprehension. And, while the narrator is trying to follow the process of learning French on a "language app," questions and statements become shuffled and meanings start to shift: "I'm a woman. / Are you a cat?" is followed by "It's a man. / We do not talk." The dreamer acquires words and phrases that challenge and ironise conventional social constructions of gender as "woman" and "man" become unreliable, even farcical nouns when read in combination with the question "Tu es un chat?" or "Are you a cat?" In this way, Russell challenges "the male/female binary so essential to our culture's notions of identity,"[37] as Lyn Keller says in her reading of outsiderness in Alice Fulton's poetry.

Significantly, Roland Barthes once chose a dog as a metaphor for the "extension of the self,"[38] writing:

> I find dogs, in particular, interesting, fascinating; because they're pure effect: they have no reason, no redans, no unconscious, no mask; in dogs, effect can be seen in its absolute immediacy and mobility.[39]

In her poem, Russell chooses a cat as a kind of interlocuter – both motif and lynchpin in this prose poem sequence, so that later in the sequence a reference to the cat is directly linked to the title of the poem: "Requiem for elementary language acquisition:/ Le chat n'est pas un homme" ("The cat is not a man"). These lines play with received philosophical notions concerning humans and nonhumans, an early example of which is Aristotle's identification of adult humans as animals with the ability to be rational: "children and the other animals share in what is voluntary, but not in rational choice."[40] Furthermore, in an antimetabolic exposition of loneliness and language, Russell shifts from learning rudimentary French to a question about the ephemeral and unanchored nature of much of language and communication in general. She questions whether knowing the word "loneliness" means that one understands it, introducing the idea of transgressing language's boundaries to find out what is "beyond" it.

In this sequence, Russell uses the imagery of learning a language via a simple bestiary – a book of pictures with words underneath. This reference to a bestiary foregrounds the enigmatic statement, "Le chat a les clés" ("The cat has the keys") and the language triad where Russell has connected the idea of loneliness to the notion of "no longer talk[ing]" and ultimately to the deconstruction of love as an "idea." Instead, "love" is exposed as an "invent[ion]" "given" to the dreamer by a man, now more "idea" or patriarchal subliminal message than reality. The final paragraph focuses on the neo-surreal as the "black tile roof" becomes a "waffle dipped in dark chocolate," and the narrator imagines putting everything she sees in her mouth. This enacts an internalisation of language and its displacement by the idea of being able to encompass and consume the thing itself without recourse to words – no matter how large it may be.

Overall, Russell's hybrid prose poetry sequence ruptures, sutures, alternatively widens and minimises, and duplicates the prose poem box as it challenges the idea that words may in any way directly represent the world or the people in it. Anne

Dewey's analysis of Rosmarie Waldrop's prose poetry trilogy, *Curves to the Apple* is starkly relevant:

> the flexible structure of prose poetry enables ... prying of objects from the sex-gender associations and narratives in which they are embedded to reimagine the body and identity.[41]

Such strategies demonstrate the flexibility, durability, and elasticity of the prose poem form and the way words – fragmented, juxtaposed, and joined in unlikely combinations – may test language's limitations, subvert conventional gender identifications, and probe the limits of what anyone may ever hope to say.

Conclusion

Prose poetry, in its various, sometimes hybrid, manifestations is a very versatile literary form. As the examples we have discussed indicate, every prose poem is a fragment that typically invokes or refers to wider domains and larger worlds that are not fully situated within the work itself. In the case of Mariko Nagai's *Irradiated Cities*, the nuclear sublime is addressed fastidiously through the detailing of particular aspects and residues of an unimaginable horror; in Marc Vincenz's work, desire and galactic turbulence are combined in a reflection on the flaws, hollowed spaces, and entropy of an apparently solid world and its cultures; in Peter Johnson's prose poem, the autobiographical and the domestic become a species of a wry yet disturbing suburban fable, questioning how we measure our lives; and in Lauren Russell's prose poetry sequence, an extended meditation on language opens up possibilities and ambiguities – and the prose poem form itself – to reach beyond the realm of confident human speech and restrictive gender binaries.

Prose poetry, irrepressibly, addresses larger issues than its typically miniature form would seem to allow. It is endlessly metaphorical, analogical, suggestive, and consciously intertextual, and it frequently and restlessly makes use of metonymic gestures – recognising that, as a literary form, it so often represents a part (or fragment) that stands in for a whole. Prose poetry employs its box-like form as a kind of ongoing disguise, questioning relationships between the (apparently) small and the (apparently) large, and between what is contained and what may be liberated. Furthermore, hybrid prose poems demonstrate that, even as prose poetry is finally finding real acceptance in the anglophone literary world, the form itself continues to expand, develop, and diversify. It persistently challenges how we understand both poetry and prose, and much more besides, asking that we reconsider our understanding of ourselves and our most apparently solid assumptions and ideas about the world – including the ways we make meaning and the functioning of language.

Notes

1 Lauren Russell, "Requiem for Elementary Language Acquisition," *The Brooklyn Rail* (June 2021), https://brooklynrail.org/2021/06/poetry/Requiem-for-Elementary-Language-Acquisition.

2 Kevin Brophy, "The Prose Poem: A Short History, a Brief Reflection and a Dose of the Real Thing," *TEXT: Journal of Writing and Writing Programs* 6, no. 1 (April 2002): 1–6.

3 John Taylor, "Two Cultures of the Prose Poem," *Michigan Quarterly Review* 44, no. 2 (Spring 2005), http://hdl.handle.net/2027/spo.act2080.0044.223.

4 Margueritte S. Murphy, *A Tradition of Subversion: The Prose Poem in English from Wilde to Ashbery* (Amherst, MA: University of Massachusetts Press, 1992), 198.

5 Paul Hetherington and Cassandra Atherton, *Prose Poetry: An Introduction* (Princeton, NJ: Princeton University Press, 2020), 3.

6 Peter Johnson, Introduction to *The Best of the Prose Poem: An International Journal*, ed. Peter Johnson (Buffalo, NY: White Pine Press, 2000), 11.

7 We argue at length for these ideas in *Prose Poetry: An Introduction* and recommend this publication to anyone who wishes to pursue these matters further.

8 Novalis, *Novalis: Philosophical Writings*, ed. and trans. Margaret Mahony Stoljar (Albany, NY: State University of New York Press, 1997), 65.

9 Charles Baudelaire, *Paris Spleen: Little Poems in Prose*, trans. Keith Waldrop (Middletown, CT: Wesleyan University Press, 2009), 3.

10 Nicholas Wong, testimonial about *Irradiated Cities*, accessed 2 February 2021, www.mariko-nagai.com/irradiated-cities.

11 John Bradley, Review of *Irradiated Cities*, by Mariko Nagai, *Rain Taxi* (Winter 2017–2018), www.raintaxi.com/irradiated-cities/.

12 Mariko Nagai, *Irradiated Cities* (Los Angeles, CA: Les Figues Press, 2017), 10.

13 Nagai, *Irradiated Cities*, 10.

14 Bradley, Review of *Irradiated Cities*.

15 Nagai, *Irradiated Cities*, 129.

16 Dennis James Sweeney, "'there is only one narrative & nothing else': Building the One-Legged Shrine," Review of *Irradiated Cities*, by Mariko Nagai, *Newfound* 9, no. 1, https://newfound.org/archives/volume-9/issue-1/reviews-irradiated-cities/.

17 Abigail Beckel, "Prose Poem Issue Introduction," *Beltway Poetry Quarterly* 14, no. 4 (Fall 2013), www.beltwaypoetry.com/prose-poem-issue-introduction/.

18 Katharine Coles, "The Poem in Time," *Axon: Creative Explorations* 7, no. 2 (December 2017), www.axonjournal.com.au/issue-13/poem-time.

19 Nikki Santilli, "Foreword," in *This Line Is Not for Turning: An Anthology of Contemporary British Prose Poetry*, ed. Jane Monson (Blaenau Ffestiniog, Wales: Cinnamon Press, 2011), 11.

20 Marc Vincenz, "Switzerland 911," *Westerly Magazine* 66, no. 2 (2021), 35.

21 For an extended discussion of the operation of TimeSpace in prose poetry, see Paul Hetherington and Cassandra Atherton, "Prose Poetry and TimeSpace," in *Prose Poetry: An Introduction*, ed. Paul Hetherington and Cassandra Atherton (Princeton, NJ: Princeton University Press, 2020), 128–50.

22 Beckel, "Prose Poem Issue Introduction."

23 Marc Vincenz, *Here Comes the Nightdust* (County Clare, Ireland: Salmon Poetry, 2019), 36.

24 Vincenz, *Here Comes the Nightdust*, 36.

25 Peter Johnson, "Vaccination, in the Broadest Sense of the Term," in *Old Man Still Howling at the Moon: Collected and New Prose Poems* (Cheshire, MA: MadHat Press, forthcoming).

26 For a discussion of the lyric and of the lyric prose poem, see Paul Hetherington and Cassandra Atherton, "Singing the Quotidian: The Lyric Voice and Contemporary American Prose Poetry by Women," *New Writing* (2021), https://doi.org/10.1080/14790726.2021.1876097.

27 Ron Silliman, comments on *Rain Taxi, Silliman's Blog: A Weblog Focused on Contemporary Poetry and Poetics*, June 2003, https://ronsilliman.blogspot.com/2003_06_15_arch ive.html.

28 Brian Clements and Jamey Dunham, "Free-line Poems," in *An Introduction to the Prose Poem*, ed. Brian Clements and Jamey Dunham (Newtown, CT: Firewheel Editions, 2009), 225.

29 Chard deNiord, "Blurred Lines, Some Thoughts on Hybrid, Liminal, and Prose Poetry," *Plume 100* (December 2019), https://plumepoetry.com/blurred-lines-some-thoughts-on-hybrid-liminal-and-prose-poetry/.

30 Hetherington and Atherton, *Prose Poetry: An Introduction*, 223.

31 Hetherington and Atherton, *Prose Poetry: An Introduction*, 223.

32 Amy Moorman Robbins, *American Hybrid Poetics: Gender, Mass Culture, and Form* (New Brunswick, NJ: Rutgers University Press, 2014), 2.

33 René Magritte, "Poetry Is a Pipe: Selected Writings of René Magritte," ed. Kathleen Rooney and Eric Plattner, trans. Jo Levy, *Literary Hub* (29 September 2016), https://lit hub.com/poetry-is-a-pipe-selected-writings-of-rene-magritte/.

34 Paul Valéry, *Collected Works of Paul Valéry, Volume 14: Analects*, trans. Stuart Gilbert. Bollingen Series XLV, 14 (Princeton, NJ: Princeton University Press, 1970), 98.

35 André Breton and Paul Éluard, "Notes on Poetry (excerpt)," in *Manifesto: A Century of Isms*, ed. Mary Ann Caws, (Lincoln, NE: University of Nebraska Press, 2001), 471–72.

36 Russell, "Requiem for Elementary Language Acquisition." This was written on the occasion of Russell's residency at Passa Porta, International House of Literature in Brussels.

37 Lyn Keller, *Thinking Poetry: Readings in Contemporary Women's Exploratory Poetics* (Iowa City, IA: Iowa University Press, 2010), 57.

38 Seema K. Ladsaria and Rajni Singh, "The 'Semiotic Animal' in Roland Barthes: A Reflection on Calculating the Self as 'Difference in Man,'" *Rupkatha Journal on Interdisciplinary Studies in Humanities* 8, no. 3 (August 2016): 28, http://dx.doi.org/10.21659/rupkatha.v8n3.04.

39 Roland Barthes, *The Preparation of the Novel*, trans. Kate Briggs (New York: Columbia University Press, 2011), 62.

40 Aristotle. *Nicomachean Ethics*, ed. and trans. Roger Crisp (Cambridge: Cambridge University Press, 2002), 41.

41 Anne Dewey, "Gender and the 1980s Prose Poem: Rosmarie Waldrop's *Curves to the Apple*," *Revue française d'études américaines* 147, no. 2 (2016): 66.

2

PROSE POETRY AND THE RESISTANCE TO NARRATIVE

Oz Hardwick

"Humans," writes Gillie Bolton, "are narrative-making creatures; creating stories is our way of making sense of things."[1] The Aristotelian beginning-middle-end offers a comfortingly familiar structure in which the most complex and challenging aspects of human experience may be contained; and even in our postmodern age of distrust in grand narratives, it is a structure that is employed successfully in countless popular novels, as well as other forms of writing, from blockbuster cinema to therapeutic practice, to the concise precision of flash fiction. Appropriately, then, this chapter too will have a beginning, a middle, and an end: at its beginning, I shall consider this impulse towards storytelling, in the middle, I shall consider the relationship between prose poetry and short fiction, and I shall close by suggesting why I think this is interesting as the twenty-first century staggers into its third decade.

One of the most readable accounts of the human impulse towards constructing – one might even say imposing – narratives is Jonathan Gottschall's *The Storytelling Animal*, a title borrowed from novelist Graham Swift, which Gottschall underlines with the subtitle: *How Stories Make Us Human*. In adding this subtitle, Gottschall subtly closes a loop. For Swift, "Man … is the storytelling animal. Wherever he goes he wants to leave behind not a chaotic wake, not an empty space, but the comforting marker buoys and trail signs of stories":[2] making stories from the largely random, sometimes traumatic, often confusing, and frequently rather dull, matter of everyday life is something which, according to Swift, we are compelled to do. Gottschall's formulation goes one step further and posits the idea that we do not just construct stories because we are human: rather, those stories in turn shape us into what we consider to be human. Whether it is a culturally shared creation myth, a biometrically targeted "Fake News" story or, on a smaller scale, how

DOI: 10.4324/9781003199533-3

we shape our memories of an evening spent with family or friends, arguably this demonstrates itself to be true over and over again.

Gottschall goes on to discuss the importance of the storytelling mind, referring to it as "a crucial evolutionary adaptation" that "allows us to experience our lives as coherent, orderly, and meaningful. It makes life more than a blooming, buzzing confusion,"[3] while at the same time acting as an emotional and psychological testing ground for life's possibilities: stories are, he explains, "flight simulators of human life,"[4] which make us less likely to lose control or even crash when we meet severe turbulence in the real world. However, as noted above, the traffic is not one-way. The stories we tell shape the people we are, and this includes those stories we tell about our own lives. As Arthur W. Frank notes, "the stories we tell about our lives are not necessarily those lives as they were lived, but these stories become our experience of these lives."[5]

We shall return to broader considerations of this compulsion – or perhaps even need – for stories shortly and turn now to what this means on a day-to-day basis. Whatever the deeper role of ordered narrative, one of the effects of the centrality of story to human experience is that we all know, more or less consciously, when we are being told a story. Stories announce themselves, whether that be with "Once upon a time," "This bloke came up to me," "All the survivors of the war had reached their homes by now," or "They have lost their baby down a sewer": they alert us to a beginning and – however simple or complex – they make us ask "What happened next?" Concomitantly, they make us ask why we have been led into this constructed story-space, a question we expect them to answer by fulfilling certain expectations we have acquired based on the countless stories we have read, heard, and told throughout our lives. However simple or intricate the plot, we expect the familiar tropes of fiction – the exposition, the inciting incident, the rising and falling action, the climax and the denouement – to tip into each other in, to borrow Gottschall's formulation, a "coherent, orderly" fashion like monumental dominos, leaving us with the aesthetic satisfaction of their neatly tumbled, "meaningful" arrangement.

Of the four possible openings cited above, two – "Once upon a time" and "This bloke came up to me" – are generic, one belonging to the fairy tale, the other to the barroom anecdote, each signalling a type of narrative with which the reader or listener is quite probably familiar. The other two, however, are more specific, and the strategies they employ in gaining the reader's attention warrant closer consideration. "All the survivors of the war had reached their homes by now and so put the perils of battle and the sea behind them. Odysseus alone was prevented from returning ... " is taken from E. V. Rieu's prose translation of Homer's *Odyssey*,[6] one of the central epics of the Western literary tradition. We are a mere 30 words in, and already we want to know what the war has been about, where it was from which nearly everyone has returned, who Odysseus is, why he hasn't been able to return home like everyone else, whether or not he will be able to extricate himself from these circumstances and get home like his fellow survivors, what the consequences will be either way, and so on. We're hooked into the story, and we expect that, over the next 200 pages – or 12,000 or so lines in the verse original – with all their adventures, apostrophes, and other rhetorical flourishes, we'll have sufficient action to hold our attention, and that all of our initial questions will be answered to our satisfaction by the time the story reaches its neat conclusion. Indeed, after investing our attention in such a work, we would probably be very disappointed if this was not the case.

I confess that the final decision regarding an opening to use as a comparison with Homer – "They have lost their baby down a sewer" – was made from countless possibilities as I browsed the selected poems of Russell Edson, purely on the basis of its title, "The Epic."[7] After all, what better to compare with one epic than another? Although it adopts a completely different register to Rieu's translation of Homer, Edson's idiosyncratic opening essentially does much the same in terms of narrative, bombarding us with questions which whet our curiosity and hook us into the story-world in search of answers. Given just these eight words, we want to know who "they" are, how they lost their baby down the sewer, how they will attempt to rescue him (we discover that it is a boy in the next-but-one sentence), whether or not assistance will be required and, if so, how others will help or hinder them, whether the baby will be rescued, and the answers to all the other questions posed by this intriguing opening. Although it is considerably shorter than *The Odyssey* – a mere 165 words – we are still likely to be disappointed if we are not provided with the answers and, via that familiar Aristotelian pattern, given a neatly satisfying, "meaningful" resolution by the end. Unless, that is, we are already familiar with Edson's work: because although his works introduce themselves in the manner of stories, and even look like stories on the page with their paragraphed blocks of text between justified margins, they resolutely frustrate narrative expectations.

Edson is one of the foremost prose poets of the twentieth and early twenty-first centuries, and although a unique and distinctive voice, for me his work exemplifies what prose poetry can do so well: that is, to frame uncertainty in a way that satisfies a need beyond narrative closure.[8] John Berger, in his genre-defying collection of missives and micro-essays *And Our Faces, My Heart, Brief as Photos*, observes that "Poems, even when narrative, do not resemble stories":

> All stories are about battles, of one kind or another, which end in victory and defeat. Everything moves towards the end, when the outcomes will be known.
> Poems, regardless of any outcome, cross the battlefields, tending to the wounded, listening to the wild monologues of the triumphant or the fearful.[9]

Berger posits the difference between narrative and poetry as time: while narrative, for all its sequential possibilities, essentially moves from a beginning to an ending, poetry, suggests Berger, "approaches language as if it were a place, an assembly point, where time has no finality, where time itself is encompassed and contained."[10] Edson takes a different approach to explaining the difference. In a 2004 interview with Mark Tursi, Edson expresses the opinion that "language is consciousness, and this is where fiction is made. Poetry springs from the dream mind, the unconscious. Poetry is never comfortable in language because the unconscious doesn't know how to speak."[11] The difference for both writers is not in the language used, nor is it even in the ways in which that language is used – as Berger notes, "poetry uses the same words, and more or less the same syntax as, say, the Annual General Report of a multi-national corporation,"[12] – but in the individual writer's personal relationship to language.

I suggest that one of the defining features of the prose poem – which, for present purposes I will take simply as being "a composition able to have any or all features of the lyric, except that it is put on the page – though not conceived of – as prose,"[13] and leave its countless other contested characteristics aside – is that it exists at a point at which these approaches to language tip into each other. "Language," says Edson, "is an end in itself,"[14] and the prose poem is where that end is attained and explored, not in a fudged borderland where ideas of prose and poetry overlap, but in a distinct area which is just beyond the territory of either story or poem. Time passes here, but not in the way it (almost always) does in story, with an at least underlying acceptance of logical and explicable sequence: rather, as Paul Munden notes, prose poetry has a tendency to be "relentlessly thoughtful about the nature of time."[15] This "*uncertainty*" about time,[16] "the elastic treatment of the 'moment' – sometimes connecting with both distant past and future – can," Munden suggests, "be identified as one of the form's defining, poetic characteristics."[17] With this in mind, it is fruitful to look at Edson's "The Epic" in its entirety:

> They have lost their baby down a sewer. They might run to the sea where the sewer empties. Or they might wait where they have lost him; perhaps he returns out of the future, having found his manhood under the city.
> Surely they risk his having turned to garbage, an orange peel with a bag of chicken guts.
> She is not sure she could love an orange peel with a bag of chicken guts.
> It's okay, honey, because everything happens under the smile of God.
> But why, in heaven's name, is He smiling?
> Because He knows the end.
> But aren't we still getting there?
> Yes; but He's seen it several times.
> Seen what several times?
> This movie, the one where He produced and directed. The one He starred in … You know, the one where He plays all the parts in a cast of billions … The story of a husband and wife losing their baby down a sewer …
> Oh that movie; I cried through the whole thing.[18]

From the opening hook, "The Epic" begins with the suggestion of conventional narrative through laying out possibilities for the direction the story could take. That the child may return, "having found his manhood under the city," appropriately gestures towards the subject matter of the epic which it claims to be: the hero's quest to fulfil his destiny and the journey through the underworld. Allied to this, there are hints of science fiction – that popular late twentieth-century iteration of the epic with all its mythical trappings – through the possibility of the child returning from the future. However, the striking – grotesque, even – metaphor of the baby's possible transformation into "an orange peel with a bag of chicken guts" suddenly undercuts the conventions of storytelling as it not only shifts from the third-person narrator's detached observation to the character's concern but also shifts from the realm of the figurative to become a real concern. The linguistic moment takes over and narrative conventions are abandoned. None of those questions which were raised by the first sentence is answered: we still don't know who "they" are, how they lost their baby, what course of action they will take, or the fate of the baby.

Edson is undoubtedly the most influential prose poet of the last half-century, his work – characterised by Hetherington and Atherton as "neo-surreal fables that often employ elements of magical realism to heighten their absurdity, even as this is expressed in strangely commonplace terms"[19] – profoundly affecting expectations of the form in the United States and beyond. However, it is important to note that even prose poems which explicitly eschew what Campbell McGrath has called the "dreamily surrealist model [which has come] to dominate the American prose poem,"[20] nonetheless share the same characteristics of subverted narrative expression. McGrath's own prose poem "Rifle, Colorado," for example, beneath its evocative place name title, begins by conjuring a still image redolent of countless Western movies: "I doubt they were used to strangers in the Rifle Café, wrapping their sausage in pancakes a little after dawn."[21] The reader is presented with a still early morning, the sound and smell of a homely breakfast being cooked, and the imminent intrusion of a stranger, that near-mythical intruder and initiator of action in the American West. While the title and opening sentence recall the opening of any number of cowboy movies, though, the poem remains purely observational, pregnant with possibilities, yet resisting all narrative impulse to the extent of explicitly refusing to provide backstories for the sketched-in inhabitants of the town. "I doubt" and "I don't know" dominate the poem, and even when the second verse paragraph commences with the affirmative "I know," this certainty does not extend beyond sensory immediacy. If, as Bolton asserts, "creating stories is our way of making sense of things," McGrath's poem implies that all we may be sure of are phenomenological encounters and that the imposition of story structures based on familiar narrative tropes may indeed detract from the "coherent, orderly, meaningful" experience.

Elsewhere in the present volume, Helen Tookey discusses prose poetry's many similarities to cinema.[22] However, if "Rifle, Colorado" suggests the opening of a movie, the "movie" to which the unnamed characters of Edson's "The Epic" refer may gesture to that dominant mode of late twentieth-century popular storytelling, but its emphasis on the enigmatic and grotesque is more Luis Buñuel or David Lynch than John Ford or Sergio Leone. Viewed as a story, "The Epic" is an abject failure, but viewed as a poem, it uses the energy of language and image to produce a satisfying whole. In a 1999 interview with Peter Johnson, Edson refers to this as the "logic of composition," before expounding:

> My pieces, when they work, though full of odd happenings, win the argu-
> ment against disorder through the logic of language and a compositional
> wholeness. So my ideal prose poem is a small, complete work, utterly logical
> within its own madness.[23]

It is a process which he succinctly describes as "looking for the shape of thought more than particulars of the little narrative." This phrase, "the shape of thought," is I believe key to the successful prose poem because thoughts have their own shape before we impose our conscious or unconscious familiar structures upon them. This is not to say that they should be spontaneous and uncrafted: on the contrary, the writer should pay acute attention to both the writing process and the editing process. Thought rarely comes lineated; nor, as I noted at the outset, does it come with a neat beginning–middle–end structure: it has its own structure and its own internal logic, and putting it onto the page, as Patricia Debney observes, is "a pro-cess of *discovery*, rather than a process of *capture*."[24]

While Edson is a distinctive writer, this broad principle of openness to the thought itself before applying the distinct formal disciplines associated with story or poetry is, I believe, what gives prose poetry – whether it is in the sur-realist or documentary mode – its energy and its distinctiveness from, say, flash fiction or anecdote.[25] The effect, from the reader's point of view, is that conven-tion, internalised through a lifetime of reading experience, dictates that the shape on the page is going to be a story, with all its narrative expectations. When this is subverted, it necessitates a rapid adjustment which requires of the reader an openness to possibility that they may not have originally brought to the act of reading. It is something which I consciously play with in my own prose poems; for example, in the chapbook-length sequence *Wolf Planet*, which begins:

> Ahead of schedule, we're entering the realm of science fiction, strapping
> ourselves into reclining chairs, watching screens fill with a planet that looks
> something like the Earth we remember, but less detailed, less hospitable.
> Entering into the spirit of things, we adopt expressions of heroic concen-
> tration and end each sentence with *Over*. Who'd have thought that dystopia
> would be so mundane? Who'd have thought that parallel worlds would be
> stacked so tight that there'd be no room left to breathe? Rivers run black,
> and when we check the likelihood of a breathable atmosphere, the data's

inconclusive, winking digits demanding caution while confirming the lack of alternatives. Scans estimate a population of almost eight billion humans, but the only voice in our retro headsets, sizzling through static that blisters like boiling fat, is the Big Bad Wolf, suggesting last minute adjustments and promising a warm, warm welcome.[26]

An alliance to a specific fictional genre is invoked right from the start, but as an undisguised metaliterary construct, which is immediately complicated through the direct second-person address of the poem and the foregrounding of real-world matters – in this case, urgent ecocritical concerns – which are more usually clothed in metaphor in science fiction. The closing sentence introduces the figure of the Big Bad Wolf, grafting on a recognisable figure from an alternative set of generic tropes and thereby effectively destabilising any expectations which the reader may have formed up to this point. The 26 prose poems which follow frequently hint at generic narrative forms – myth, folk tale, fairy tale, memoir, science fiction, and creative non-fiction – yet privilege the constantly shifting relationships between allusive fragments over the urge for narrative coherence, pursuing Edson's aesthetic of "the logic of language and a compositional wholeness."[27]

If it is in the nature of prose poems to raise expectations of narrative, only to subvert them in favour of their own internal logic, the question arises as to why such a form should gain such notice and popularity in recent years. Why should a mode of writing which traces its roots to the mid-nineteenth century suggest itself as such an apt form for engaging with the first quarter of the twenty-first century? I believe that the answer is suggested by Berger's distinction between story and poetry cited earlier: stories are essentially about battles, while poems criss-cross the battlefield, tending to the needs of the embattled.[28] While Homer may offer us a prescribed narrative frame in which "All the survivors of the war had reached their homes by now and so put the perils of battle and the sea behind them,"[29] in our media-saturated world, the illusory nature of such frames has never been more explicit. So, while we still feel that deep human urge to impose "comforting marker buoys and trail signs of stories,"[30] we are constantly confronted by the deferral of narrative closure. Prose poetry, as Hetherington and Atherton perceptively assert, "tends to emphasize what *has happened* and *will always be happening*,"[31] and, as such, offers the perfect form with which to explore our uneasy responses to a time in which it so often seems as if the more reassuring a narrative is, the further it is from the truth.

From writing an early draft of this chapter for a conference in 2019, to revising it for publication in 2021, news media have presented a series of seductively comforting implied narratives on behalf of world leaders; yet, at time of writing, here in Britain three successive Prime Ministers have signally failed to "get Brexit done" or "take back control." Likewise, on the other side of the Atlantic, Donald Trump's presidency has ended with little evidence of having made America great again by any of his rather indeterminate criteria. Indeed, from early 2020, infections and fatalities relating to the COVID-19 pandemic in both nations suggest quite the opposite of these rabble-rousing boasts. The pandemic itself has given rise to new narratives. In the UK, the comfortingly militaristic narrative of "beating this virus" sadly owed as much to rhetoric as reality, failing to take into account the virus' indifference to the *happy-ever-after* of implicit Aristotelian closure. Though presented as battles, these micro-flash fictions never reach their promised conclusions, leaving us with a profound need for poetry that can, in Berger's terms, "cross the battlefields, tending to the wounded, listening to the wild monologues of the triumphant or the fearful."[32]

Such oversimplified narratives are not merely misleading: they are potentially socially dangerous. For example, Donald Trump's anti-immigration narrative of "taking our country back," so prominent throughout his presidential campaign,[33] became sufficiently internalised by the far right that it was parroted in the Capitol riots on 6 January 2021 which marked the end of his presidency.[34] The event led to five deaths, along with injuries to around 140 police officers and many others.[35] Likewise, the "taking back control" narrative of the Leave EU campaign leading up to the UK referendum on European Union membership in June 2016, whatever its intention, has had the effect of playing to and legitimising racist attitudes, and even actions, beyond any connection with European politics.[36] Though it is impossible – not to mention counter to my argument – to make claims of neat cause and effect, it is notable that the number of racially motivated hate crimes in England and Wales has increased dramatically since 2014, the year in which campaigning became more urgent following the December 2013 vote in the House of Lords to block the Draft EU Referendum Bill. In spite of the United Kingdom Independence Party's (UKIP) use of the phrase "take back control" on their notorious "Breaking Point" anti-immigration billboards in June 2016, the phrase, with all its associations of closed narratives and easy solutions, still appears in discussions of Brexit – and the number of racially motivated crimes continues to rise.[37]

These examples are, of course, extreme cases, and we have seemingly travelled a long way from Homer. However, as Judi Atkins and John Gaffney have noted, political narratives of this kind echo all of the elements of "structure, purpose, grammar and … rhetoric" defined by the Russian Formalists at the birth of modern narratology in the first half of the twentieth century.[38] Our political reality, they conclude, "is underpinned by a deep structure comprising folk tales, pantomime, tragedy and narratives,"[39] all of which are recognised and expected by an audience primed to do so. After all, in the oft-quoted observation of Jonathan Haidt, "the human mind is a story processor, not a logic processor."[40] In view of this, although I do not wish to invoke postmodernism – I share Edson's amused distrust of movements and isms – such cynical appropriations of the insidious appeal of "the comforting marker buoys and trail signs of stories"[41] surely demonstrate the urgent need to resist their siren seductions, for the buoys so frequently turn out to be rocks and the trail rarely leads out of the dark wood. In order to facilitate this resistance, I believe that it is vital to pull the rug from beneath the neat, tissue-thin stories with which we are constantly bombarded. We cannot take back a country that belongs to all. We cannot take back control when we never had control in the first place. Brexit is a process which will initiate other processes *ad infinitum*. Stories may, as Gottschall suggests, make us human, but our humanity may rest on our interrogation of stories. After all, one man's "great" is a million – two million – more – people's grating disenfranchisement.

We find ourselves living in that tired old trope of "interesting times," and it is our responsibility as writers to respond in kind; to embrace the "shape of thought" in all its untamed, subversive, *interesting* energy. And I believe that prose poetry – still enjoying something of an outsider status – is the perfect form with which to do this. In appearing on the page as a short passage of prose, the prose poem's defiant rejection of Aristotelian narrative expectations explicitly questions the validity of narrative itself and, by extension, asks us to reconsider those compact, oft-repeated stories with which we are confronted on a daily basis. As Hetherington and Atherton point out, in many areas of twenty-first century culture, "fixed beliefs and monocultural assumptions have largely passed."[42] Prose poetry does not just passively reflect this broadening of perspectives and possibilities; it actively embraces plurality and diversity.

None of us, to return to Gottschall, will leave behind a dreaded "empty space," though what we will leave behind is less likely to be a well-defined story than it is a collection of disparate items, gathered more by chance than design, which suggest endless readings in their juxtapositions. Viewed in this way, the intriguing box of accumulated treasures and trash is the perfect form in which to capture human experience.[43] Although stories allow us to view our lives as "coherent, orderly, and meaningful," the prose poem reminds us that, although clearly circumscribed at its edges, it is for the most part *in*coherent and *dis*orderly, and that if we are prepared to view it in this way, in both personal and political contexts, these are the constituent elements of life which render our infinitely complex, story-filled, *human* experience "meaningful."

And what of my promised ending? Jamey Dunham compares the prose poem with a coyote: "a survivor, continually skirting the boundaries of convention and exploiting the expectations of anyone foolish enough to get too comfortable."[44] For me, it has a lot in common with the Big Bad Wolf, sometimes giving the impression of affable domestication but "getting twitchy when the light fades and the howling starts."[45] Either way, that unassuming box of text which promises the satisfaction of a brief story is ready to snap like a canine jaw in sheep's clothing, and a person passing in the neighbourhood says, "that dog is wrong … I don't like to see a dog get like that … It's not over yet … "[46] Odysseus eventually returns home but Argos is off sniffing that orange peel with a bag of chicken guts and, whether we like it or not, our big, messy, lolloping lives won't come to heel.

In the words of Richard Brautigan – surely one of the finest prose poets not always recognised as such – "There are more and more endings: the sixth, the 53rd, the 131ˢᵗ, the 9,435ᵗʰ ending, endings going faster and faster until this [chapter] is having 186,000 endings per second."[47] The prose poem is the form that wouldn't have it any other way.

Notes

1 Gillie Bolton, *Write Yourself: Creative Writing and Personal Development* (London: Jessica Kingsley, 2011), 35.

2 Jonathan Gottschall, *The Storytelling Animal: How Stories Make Us Human* (Boston, MA: Mariner Books, 2013), 95.

3 Gottschall, *The Storytelling Animal*, 102.

4 Gottschall, *The Storytelling Animal*, 58.

5 Arthur W. Frank, *The Wounded Storyteller* (Chicago: University of Chicago Press, 1995), 22.

6 Homer, *The Odyssey*, revised edition, trans. E.V. Rieu (London: Penguin, 1991), 3.

7 Russell Edson, "The Epic," in *The Tunnel: Selected Poems* (Oberlin, OH: Oberlin College Press, 1994), 85.

8 Jeremy Noel-Tod, ed., *The Penguin Book of the Prose Poem: From Baudelaire to Anne Carson* (London: Penguin, 2018) is a landmark anthology, which appears to capture something of the *zeitgeist*, judging by co-incident publications such as Jane Monson, ed. *British Prose Poetry: The Poems Without Lines* (Cham, CH: Palgrave Macmillan, 2018); Anne Caldwell and Oz Hardwick, eds., *The Valley Press Anthology of Prose Poetry* (Scarborough, UK: Valley Press, 2019); Paul Hetherington and Cassandra Atherton, eds. *Prose Poetry: An Introduction*, (Princeton, NJ: Princeton University Press, 2020); Mary Ann Caws and Michel Delville, eds., *The Edinburgh Companion to the Prose Poem* (Edinburgh: Edinburgh University Press, 2021); and many other anthologies and single-authored collections in the past couple of years.

9 John Berger, *And Our Faces, My Heart, Brief as Photos* (London: Bloomsbury, 2005), 21.

10 Berger, *And Our Faces*, 22.

11 Russell Edson, "An Interview with Russell Edson," interview by Mark Tursi, *Double Room* 4 (Spring/Summer 2004), www.doubleroomjournal.com/issue_four/Russell_Edson.html.

12 Berger, *And Our Faces*, 22.

13 Alex Preminger, Frank J. Warnke, and O. B. Hardison, Jr., eds. *Princeton Encyclopedia of Poetry and Poetics*. (Princeton, NJ: Princeton University Press, 1965), 664, quoted in Monson, *British Prose Poetry*, 7.

14 Edson, "An Interview."

15 Paul Munden, "Playing with Time: Prose Poetry and the Elastic Moment," *TEXT Special Issue* 46, *Beyond the Line: Contemporary Prose Poetry* (October 2017): 13.

16 Munden, "Playing with Time," 11 (emphasis in original).

17 Munden, "Playing with Time," 1.

18 Edson, "The Epic," in *The Tunnel*, 85.

19 Hetherington and Atherton, *Prose Poetry: An Introduction*, 117.

20 In Peter Johnson, ed., *A Cast-Iron Aeroplane that Can Actually Fly: Commentaries from 80 American Poets on Their Prose Poetry* (Cheshire, MA: MadHat Press, 2019), 155.

21 Campbell McGrath, "Rifle, Colorado," in *Cast-Iron Aeroplane*, ed. Johnson, 154.

22 Helen Tookey, "'Image Machine': Gaspar Orozco's *Book of the Peony* and the Prose Poem Sequence as Perceptual Trick," Chapter 7 of this volume.

23 Russell Edson, "Interview: The Art of the Prose Poem. Russell Edson," interview by Peter Johnson, reprinted in Peter Johnson, ed., *Truths, Falsehoods, and a Wee Bit of Honesty: A Short Primer on the Prose Poem with Selected Letters from Russell Edson* (Cheshire, MA: MadHat Press, 2020), 43.

24 Patricia Debney, "Wrestling with Angels: The Pedagogy of the Prose Poem," in *British Prose Poetry*, ed. Monson, 323.

25 On "the proximity of the prose poem to neighboring speculative prose genres," see Michel Delville, "The Prose Poem, Flash Fiction, Lyrical Essays and Other Micro-Genres," in *Edinburgh Companion*, ed. Caws and Delville, 137–49.

26 Oz Hardwick, *Wolf Planet* (Clevedon, UK: Hedgehog Poetry Press, 2020), 5.

27 Edson, "Interview: The Art of the Prose Poem," 43.

28 Berger, *And Our Faces*, 21.

29 Homer, *The Odyssey*, 3.

30 Gottschall, *The Storytelling Animal*, 95.

31 Hetherington and Atherton, *Prose Poetry: An Introduction*, 26.

32 Berger, *And Our Faces*, 21.

33 "Don't worry, we'll take our country back" was a typical phrase throughout the campaign. See, for example, Elizabeth Chuck, "Donald Trump: 'Don't Worry, We'll Take Our Country Back,'" *NBC News*, 11 July 2015, www.nbcnews.com/politics/2016-election/donald-trump-freedomfest-you-cant-be-great-if-you-dont-n390546.

34 A member of the Proud Boy militia told a BBC Newsnight correspondent that, "We're taking our country back." "Capitol riots timeline: The evidence presented against Trump," *BBC News*, 12 February 2021, www.bbc.co.uk/news/world-us-canada-56004916.

35 During the editing of this book, a news item of 3 August 2021 reported two further deaths by suicide of officers who responded to the riot. The effects of the pernicious soundbite continue to multiply. Jan Wolfe, "Four Officers Who Responded to U.S. Capitol Attack Have Died by Suicide," *Reuters*, 2 August 2021, www.reuters.com/world/us/officer-who-responded-us-capitol-attack-is-third-die-by-suicide-2021-08-02/.

36 See, for example, Satnam Virdee and Brendan McGeever, "Racism, Crisis, Brexit," *Ethnic and Racial Studies* 41 (2018): 1802–19.

37 Grahame Allen, Yago Zayed, and Rebecca Lees, *House of Commons Briefing Paper No. 8537: Hate Crime Statistics* (2020), 7. Figures show that, between 2012 and 2020, all categories of hate crime reported to police in England and Wales increased considerably. On responses to UKIP's "Breaking Point" campaign, see Heather Stewart and Rowena Mason, "Nigel Farage's Anti-migrant Poster Reported to Police," *The Guardian*, 16 June 2016, www.theguardian.com/politics/2016/jun/16/nigel-farage-defends-ukip-breaking-point-poster-queue-of-migrants.

38 Judi Atkins and John Gaffney, "Narrative, Persona and Performance: The Case of Theresa May 2016–2017," *The British Journal of Politics and International Relations* 22, no, 2 (2020): 296.

39 Atkins and Gaffney, "Narrative, Persona and Performance," 306.

40 Jonathan Haidt, *The Righteous Mind: Why Good People are Divided by Politics and Religion* (London: Penguin, 2013), 328.

41 Gottschall, *The Storytelling Animal*, 95.

42 Hetherington and Atherton, *Prose Poetry: An Introduction*, 245–6.

43 The idea of the prose poem as a box has almost become a commonplace. See Hetherington and Atherton, *Prose Poetry: An Introduction*, 83–5.

44 In Johnson, *Cast-Iron Aeroplane*, 64.

45   Hardwick, *Wolf Planet*, 18.

46   Russell Edson, "The Neighborhood Dog," in *The Tunnel*, 139.

47   Richard Brautigan, *A Confederate General from Big Sur* (New York: Grove Press, 1964), 116. I discuss Brautigan as a prose poet in my article, "Shaping Loss: Prose Poetry and the Elegiac Mode," *Axon: Creative Explorations* 9, no. 1 (May 2019), www.axonjournal.com.au/issue-vol-9-no-1-may-2019/shaping-loss.

3

"IN THE EYE OF THE BEHOLDER"

Prose Poetry in Dialogue Between Reader and Poet

Hannah Stone

David Wheatley has succinctly characterised prose poetry as "the slipperiest of genres,"[1] and other contributors to this present volume, particularly Cassandra Atherton and Paul Hetherington, discuss ongoing debates about this slippery genre's definitions, parameters, and dominant qualities. This essay does not seek to add to their insights on these matters. Rather, it will explore aspects of the individual decision to write prose poetry (rather than lineated verse) when addressing particular subjects, and especially when seeking a hybrid form to express ideas. All of these discussions come with the caveats that prose poetry is, as Anne Caldwell and Oz Hardwick note, "an oxymoron; a contested poetic (and of course prosaic) space; a form more defined by what it doesn't have – line breaks – than by what it does."[2] First, it considers the extent to which the definition or identification of the form of something which is written should be determined by the author, or by its reader or auditor. This is set in juxtaposition to a discussion of the relationship between viewer and creator of visual art. Second, it explores the circumstances under which, as a poet, I choose to write prose poetry rather than lineated verse. Finally, with reference to my own work, I suggest that while sharing many of the same elements of prosody as lineated verse, prose poetry's slippery, debatable form employs these elements in surprising and subversive ways.

In Lewis Carroll's *Through the Looking Glass*, there is a discussion about who is in control of meaning, and whether it can be appropriated.

> "When I use a word," Humpty Dumpty said, in rather a scornful tone, "it means just what I choose it to mean – neither more nor less." "The question is," said Alice, "whether you can make words mean so many different things." "The question is," said Humpty Dumpty, "which is to be master – that's all."[3]

DOI: 10.4324/9781003199533-4

Can we apply the same arguments to the form of the prose poem as to "words"? Lineated verse forms, from sonnets to villanelles, via haiku and sestinas, each have established rules that may be used to determine their place with respect to the broad canon of poetry which has gone before, though these forms are not always strictly observed.[4] Whether observed, ignored or bent, such verse forms establish a degree of reader expectation as well as providing a set of guidelines for the poet endeavouring to write one of these forms. The situation with regard to both writer and reader of prose poems presents different opportunities and choices. Elsewhere in this volume, Hetherington and Atherton discuss the hybridity of the prose poem, its fragmentary and subversive forms, and celebrate its fluidity and evolutionary potential, and, above all, its "protean" quality. The formal fluidity and diversity of prose poetry means that I, as a poet, find that the concept and even form of a "prose poem" *can* mean Humpty Dumpty's "so many different things." Furthermore, Carroll, in the passage cited above, raises another issue of interest to me as a practitioner: that of authority and appropriation of a word (and by extension here, a concept or definition). This leads to the question: who decides whether a piece of writing is a prose poem or something else – is it the author of the text, or its reader? When the reader is "unsettled" by a prose poem, to use Divya Nadkarni's phrase,[5] what does this contribute to the text's meaning? Does the reader's potential misinterpretation of a text de-stabilise its genre further, or is the openness to diverse interpretations granted through an inherently unstable form, by being in dialogue with the author, an intrinsic element of the published/performed prose poem?

To begin to explore this question, I will look at one of my own prose poems. This was first shared with other readers as a Facebook post, a medium I sometimes use almost as a journaling tool to record impressions and experiences, especially when travelling. When I wrote this, I was visiting the city of Iasi in northern Romania, where I was the guest of the Russian Orthodox Church for an academic conference; I spoke no Romanian and had few opportunities to explore the city alone. Posting on social media is intrinsically a process which invites not only engagement from a reader, but response; it suggests that (perhaps subconsciously) the person posting expects feedback from readers of such posts. In the case of my own Facebook posts, many of those readers will be fellow poets, and sometimes their comments may shape the subsequent drafts of a poem. A comment on this particular post from a poet friend (GL) reads: "Is that meant to be a poem? Because it reads like one." I will return to this response in due course. Here is the finished poem:

Unspoken

It's minus 8, and dusk is strolling across the plains towards the city. The afternoon hunkers down, expecting minus 15 overnight. As the streets empty, the buildings drop their guard. The fairy tale palace goes back to being a post office; the fine façade at the bottom of the hill stops pretending to be an art gallery and admits to being the main railway station. It is too cold for artifice. A woman stands in front of a display of handwritten notices in a public space. On her head is the ubiquitous dark beanie worn by the people here; it is sprinkled with snow. She is protesting about something and has been doing so for four months now. I do not know what she is so passionate about. We share no language except respectful silence. I look at her posters; she reads my posture. After an appropriate few moments, we turn to face each other and raise hands and shoulders in generous shrugs and smile. By the time I get back to my room, the coffee in its paper cup is tepid, and her feet are beginning to feel numb.[6]

My intention in writing this poem was not to arrive at a conclusion or to finish a "story," but to muse and brood on an experience, an approach that perhaps illustrates one distinction drawn by Carrie Etter between the mechanics of prose and lineated poetry:

> While a lineated poem's development requires some sort of progression as it moves down the page, most reductively a movement from point A to point B, a prose poem develops without "going" anywhere – it simply wants to inhabit or circle A.[7]

In this poem, I "circle round" the idea that as a visitor – with none of the country's language in my vocabulary – I could not correctly "read" what either its buildings (with their labelled functions and unfamiliar logos) or its people might be telling me.[8] The "messages" were not so much unspoken as untranslatable by me; I projected a sense of "artifice" onto the buildings whose functions were not what their appearance led me, a traveller from a different culture, to expect. The intense cold was a backdrop to the scene; I had the impression that it caused the inhabitants and architecture to draw in on themselves, to become closed off and secretive, and at the same time, I was aware that I was the one least used to such cold. It was quite normal to the inhabitants of Iasi. In drafting this poem, I used familiar poetic devices of personification, alliteration, and assonance to colour the poem and used repetition and allusion within the sentence structure to express the to-ing and fro-ing of unspoken communication between the demonstrator and myself ("I look … she read …"). The recurring image is the subzero temperatures which, like the approaching nightfall, constrained and shaped the experience of both the resident and visitor to the city; we shared the experience of the cold evening (and maybe much else), even though we could not talk about it.

A further point in Etter's article pertains to my practice here: she argues that in prose poetry, where there *is* a narrative thread, "that narrative operates to represent or suggest a single idea or feeling; the story or plot is there at the service of the idea."[9] So in my prose poem, the "single idea or feeling" was not that it was cold, the protester was getting cold, and my coffee was getting cold (which could be "the plot" of the piece), but that I could not read the city and could not communicate with its people, in response to which I mythologised the fabric of the city and its people in order to come to a personal understanding of them. The meteorological coldness, then, acts also as a metaphor for my dullness of insight into the material spaces and inhabitants of the city I was visiting.

To return to GL's comment on my initial Facebook post, I "meant" this as a prose poem, not as a piece of prose. Yet, at the same time, I was aware that it could also be read as several other forms of writing and that other interpretations of what I had written were as valid as my own understanding of it. GL may have read the "story," not the "idea." She might also have had expectations of what a poem would look and read like, compared to some other form of written text. Both reader and author contribute to the meaning of the poem, not only in terms of the individual words but regarding the finished form/genre of the text; rather than the reader simply being a passive recipient, their engagement with it contributes to its actual construction. Their response to what they read is as significant as the author's intention. This bears out Wolfgang Iser's assertion regarding the collaborative nature of the reader's engagement with an author's text, when he argues that "the convergence of text and reader brings the literary work into existence."[10] In this understanding of the reception of a text, the reader brings their prior expectations and experiences to bear, and on reading and re-reading the text will come to it with fresh and newly informed eyes. To quote Iser again, "It will always be the process of anticipation and retrospection that leads to the formation of the virtual dimension which in turn transforms the text into an experience for the reader."[11]

If my friend had merely approached my Facebook post in the expectation of it being a status update, that is all they might have seen. Knowing me to have aspirations as a poet, she perhaps "anticipated" a poem (not least because of the common practice of fellow writers of posting poem drafts online) and therefore read back into the text (in retrospect) a poem. The prose-like appearance of the poem caused her to question her reading of it, as she expected a poem to be lineated verse.

To explore further this issue of whether the labour on the part of reader invalidates, confirms, or replaces authorial intention, I shall digress here in order to consider a very different form of poem, with which I engaged as viewer and reader (rather than author) in August 2020.

Claus Bremer's artwork *ein texte passiert* ("a text happens") (1967) is held in the Tate Modern, London. Bremer was an important exponent of concrete poetry in Germany, and my interest in the fluidity of genres was piqued by finding, in an art gallery, a three-dimensional work of art referred to as a poem. The piece takes the form of a screen print featuring a vertical column of letters, which spell out in fragmented sections of text or individual letters the words "ein text passiert" (literally translated as "a text happens"). The display caption reads: "Bremer thought of his poems as 'engaged texts.' Viewers needed to be active in the structuring of the poem by moving their eyes or the printed poem itself in order to read it."[12] In addition to soliciting the viewer's participation in making meaning of the work, Bremer also seems to be playing with the idea of breaking down boundaries between art forms, since he makes a work of art out of words along with other three-dimensional media: the catalogue description reads "Screenprint on canvas, nylon rope, wooden pole and metal pins," which he then refers to as "a poem." The very structure of Bremer's work, however, requires the viewer's/reader's physical action in viewing and reading it; the text "happens" as the eye scans over the letters, as nowhere is the phrase presented in full; it appears only in fragments (a characteristic feature of prose poetry, according to Hetherington and Atherton). The phrase – which also constitutes the title of the piece – is only fully assembled by the viewer casting their gaze over it.

The tension between vertical and horizontal planes teases the viewer into considering what sort of poem this is. In Jane Monson's discussion of verticality and horizontality in reception of lineated and prose poetry, she refers to discussion by writers and architects on the effect of vertical versus horizontal lines in design.[13] In this discussion, she cites the prose poet Gary Young, whose comments are pertinent here, too, when he states that, "The prose poem's democratic itinerary, its horizontal rather than vertical trajectory, engenders a resistance to hierarchy and to inflation."[14] Glossing the prose poem's "democratic itinerary" as relating to the collaboration between the creator of a work of art and its viewer/reader, we find another interpretation of an "engaged text." Bremer's "poem" in its final form physically presents in much more of a vertical than a horizontal manner (its dimensions are 4580 • 900 mm). An earlier 1965 paper version, however, is a square measuring 480 • 480 mm.[15] On balance, given the demands made on the viewer to decode and piece together the fragments of meaning, I would suggest the artwork may be read as a prose poem, because of this "democratic," rather than top-down, relationship between creator and viewer. The "meaning" of the piece, its full realisation as a form, requires the active participation of the viewer/reader to not only connect the fragments, but also to delete the gaps which break up the words. Furthermore, receiving this mixed media artwork as a so-named "poem" engages with Monson's discussion of visual-based practitioners; there are occasions for prose poetry in a variety of media. Prose poetry is not restricted to words on the page. As the viewer and reader of Bremer's artwork, I felt its designation as "poem" was merited not least by the sense that the word "poetry" comes in part from the Greek word "poiesis" meaning "to make," and because words were used to "make" this piece of artwork. In engaging with the work, had I, therefore, helped establish its identity?

This sense that the engagement by a viewer/reader/consumer of an artistic work helps establish its form could be compared to the engagement by my poet friend with the piece of text I placed on Facebook. This could have been received as a poem, a comment on my travels, or simply a status update; maybe it only became a completed form once it had been commented on and labelled by a reader. Bremer identifies his work as a poem, while listing the non-verbal materials that went into its creation, confounding the viewer's "anticipatory" sense of what type of artwork this might be. By contrast, my Facebook post did not announce its intention or define its nature or genre and thus elicited an element of dialogue with its reader. Perhaps the Facebook post contains the "many different things" of which Alice speaks, as well as embodying some of the "protean" nature of prose poetry. In "Unspoken," I had several intentions beyond the ostensible evocation of a place which was both foreign and in some ways familiar. It was also intended to reflect, in a meditative manner, a recurrent returning to a theme: here the intense cold and the phatic communication in the absence of shared verbal language. In evoking a particular moment, I was perhaps capturing one of those Wordsworthian "spots of time," by which in less happy circumstances "our minds/ Are nourished and invisibly repaired."[16] The function of "Unspoken," then, was not primarily narrative in terms of what Etter describes as "most reductively a movement from point A to point B."[17] Rather, my prose poem is shaped and informed by the interpretative possibilities of hybridity.

The hybridity and diversity of form/source in prose poetry is discussed by Rupert Loydell, who cites various genres of writing, including travelogue, journals, and diaries, which prose poetry may draw upon.[18] Each of these types of writing formed part of my Facebook post which became "Unspoken." To return to Alice and Humpty Dumpty, I sometimes "mean" my prose poetry to encompass and draw on a number of different prose genres in a way I tend not to do so much when writing lineated verse. This reflects the insight that "Prose poetry is not merely poetry, minus line breaks. It borrows from forms outside the world of poetry, such as questionnaires, conversations, dream narrative, and art installations."[19]

One aspect of this appropriation of such forms – to which Kathleen McGookey adds "newspapers, recipes, instruction manuals, *The Polar Express*" – is that, by encountering prose on a daily basis, readers less familiar with poetry don't find paragraphs "intimidating."[20] The familiarity fosters a reader's ability to respond to and engage with prose poetry, though at the same time it may set up conflicting expectations of what they are going to read.[21]

This issue of formal hybridity and the reader's response to what is drafted came together in reflection about my as-yet unpublished prose poetry sequence whose working title is *Twenty Nine Volumes*. I often gravitate towards prose poetry rather than lineated verse especially where I want to "circle round" a subject (to return to Etter's phrase), coming at it from different directions, in place of a linear narrative. In discussing the draft of *Twenty Nine Volumes* with a fellow poet, I was challenged to consider what type of text it was, as it presented to him as a mix of genres: was it memoir, autobiography, short pieces of prose, or prose poetry? To assist my reflection on this issue, I revisited Max Porter's *Grief Is the Thing with Feathers*,[22] described in its prefatory blurb by The Observer as "a beguiling literary hybrid,"[23] and by Andrew McMillan as "part memoir, part novel, part experimental sound-poem."[24] Porter's text begins with a quotation from an Emily Dickinson poem, annotated in handwritten capitals in Porter's appropriation of meaning, with the word "CROW" replacing all the nouns in Dickinson's verse. Readers of Porter's book will know that Crow is narrator, protagonist, villain, symbol of grief and recovery, and more besides. The sections are titles as poems might be, and are set out as chunks of prose, with some scoring out, some recorded speech, and various striking devices which cross genre boundaries and which introduce elements of intertextuality: for example, following a section purporting to be conversation and description of the two young brothers (whose mother's putative death and father's bereavement are the foundation to the whole book), a change of font heralds "Comprehension Questions," reminding the reader of the part played by the boys' schooling during this tragic period of their lives.[25]

Returning to my own sequence after reading Porter, it became clear that some of the reasons I had written *Twenty Nine Volumes* in prose poetry were: that it featured intertextuality (I was appropriating both material from a musical dictionary, specific pieces of music, classical myths and fairy stories, as well as family archives and officialdom); that there were multiple intentions (I was writing both a memoir of my own childhood and also about the process of memory; I was writing contemporary reflection); and that in writing about memory and its erosion through dementia the poetry was inevitably going to "circle round" and repeat phrases or parts of phrases, mirroring the way in which a person living with dementia repeats themselves and also utters fragments of phrases, the meanings of which have to be pieced together by the auditor. The decision to write this collection as prose poetry was further informed by the insights of Emily Berry that this form is frequently a "vehicle for reportage and memoir."[26]

The sequence was originally conceived in order to write about my changing relationship with my father as he disappeared down the rabbit hole of dementia. This stage of our lives caused me to reconsider my childhood and to want to write about how memory both captures and distorts personal histories. The initial prompt – and title – was a set of 29 volumes of *Grove's New Musical Encyclopaedia*, which was housed on a shelf in the home I grew up in, specifically in the room which morphed from being my childhood bedroom to being my father's office for a retirement project, a home-based music publishing business. Classical music was a dominant element in my childhood (and remains very significant in my adult life) and was something I shared with my father but not so much my mother. He insisted my siblings and I learn to read music, take music theory exams, and become proficient on various instruments. This ambition displaced opportunities for unstructured play, and socialising was discouraged. In approaching my prose poetry sequence, the arcane and mystifying-to-the-outsider nature of the musical terminology represented for me the communication difficulties inherent in memory loss (and always present in the context of a challenging relationship with a very domineering parent) as well as capturing a dominant feature of my childhood.

When I started writing the sequence, I envisaged making connections between poems using some elements of musical form, such as sonata form and leitmotifs (both of which involve repetitions and recapitulations). Sonata form can be seen as a type of circling round as it consists of a section *a* (the exposition), followed by a section *b* (the development), followed by a return to section *a* (the recapitulation). This application of a form from one type of art (music) to another (poetry) thus recalled the endeavour of Bremer to create a poem out of mixed media. There was also a sense that choosing prose poetry as a form fostered the sense of "rumination" in this sequence, echoing James Harris's description of "the drifting and circular intelligence" he observed in certain prose poems, and "the way they move through thought and into silence, from rumination to description and back again."[27] It was a childhood dominated by officialdom. (My father had been a senior civil servant and drew from that type of bureaucracy and his military service as models for how to run family life.) Consequently, the prose element was prompted by the poems' engagement with the didactic, dogmatic style of discourse which dominated my father's conversations with his children, an aspect of his need to prove and pin down everything. This was better articulated by prose poems, with their straight, fully justified borders, than by the less tidy rambling across the page of my lineated verse. However, while drafting and revising the poems, I did not formally analyse my intentions or method; the editing was intuitive rather than empirical.

After my father's death, I continued to write the sequence, and then poems about my mother began to emerge. These drew not on formal musical elements (which were a complete mystery to her), but on myth, fairy story, and classical allusion, more representative of the reading she shared with me. Because these poems seemed to belong with the poems about my father, and because he was "in charge," I wrote them in the same prose poem form. By then my mother was also living with dementia, and she now sleeps a lot. She daydreams and tells a lot of "tales" as part of her defence mechanism in the face of unreliable memory and altered cognition. My poems about both parents are interconnected: for example, the musical concept of the "Burden," with its meaning of a repeated refrain, is expressed in my collection also through the metaphor of Sisyphus rolling his boulder up the hill, suggestive of the struggles my brothers and I have in getting my mother to take her medications, or to accept the support and help she needs in conducting her life. The recurrent use of allusion and metaphor also articulated a family trait to approach issues indirectly and to avoid clear statements.

As I moved through various drafts of the sequence, I worked with repeated phrases, which seemed to "circle round" each other and also link the components of the sequence in the manner of a catena or chain. They are intended as a series, and "build on one another," and to some extent "flirt with fiction."[28] Sisyphus, Tithonius, and Sleeping Beauty drift in and out of them rather as my nonagenarian mother drifts in and out of sleep and cognition. The memories I allude to are of a childhood in which the rational and proven was valued far in excess of the imagined and uncertain; the prose form of the poems therefore represents that sort of approved "canon" of experience which did not allow for play or fantasy. Contrary to the frequent emphasis on surrealism as innate in prose poems, in this sequence, it was primarily the relationship of prose to official documentation which promoted the choice of prose poetry. As mentioned above, it was through workshopping the poems that I came to realise that something to do with the "function" or purpose of the sequence possibly suggested my choice of form; the poems contain at one and the same time elements of prose texts such as memoir, bureaucracy, nightmarish surreal reflection, lament, and pseudo-scholarship. They juxtapose a child's voice (sometimes drowned out by adult instructions) with voices of adults both real and imaginary. They quote from prose sources. But I am writing them as a poet, and my choice of imagery, punctuation, alliteration, and so on are very consciously part of my poetic method, and the surreal touches, where present, subvert both the reader's expectation of where something written in what looks like prose might be "going" (if anywhere) and the "canon" on which my childhood was based.

My unconscious intentions in writing *Twenty Nine Volumes* as prose poetry brings me to another "reader response," that of a poet friend (PL) who found my decision to write the sequence in prose poetry rather than what he called "verse poetry" to be "perverse." However, he acknowledged that his reception of these poems had offered him the chance to find within the topics I commented on (which included the nature of memory, dementia, and family) "a sense of universality,"[29] which he had not expected to find in prose poetry. Alongside this, he had also found in them the elements of prosody he expected in poetry. And in confounding the expectations of this particular reader, I was perhaps resonating with Loydell's insight:

> Prose poetry is where a person behaves differently from what is considered normal – and realises that they have stepped into someone else's arms, someone who is as much in control of the world as they are. It is a place where language is all compression and angle; tautness. A signpost to a different meaning. It is a key to a house with no doors. To a library full of books you want to read but must use to stoke the fire – for otherwise there is no warmth.[30]

By not choosing the more familiar, expected, vehicle of lineated verse, I had enabled this particular reader to find multiple layers in a medium he had previously dismissed as not really being poetry. Our discussion acknowledged that as a poet I would continue to write across a range of forms, comparable to how a visual artist sometimes produces watercolour paintings and sometimes line drawings. To complete either of these works, she has likely used a sense of line, juxtaposition of shapes, tonal range, a consideration of the placing of various images or designs, an overall shape to her work, and an intention to convey something to her viewer, be it a representative image or something more abstract. But one piece uses colour and tonal range, and the other uses crosshatching and shading to create depth of texture. The works, although employing some common tools and methods, contain a slightly different mix and use them in different ways. Each work contains a sense of form and presents the viewer with something which they are free to interpret as they wish by collaborating with or participating in finding meaning or aesthetic pleasure in the work. Similarly, whether I am writing prose or lineated verse, I write as a poet, using metaphor, assonance, rhyme, rhythms, repetitions, wordplay, punctuation, and so on. The deliberate use of such techniques distinguishes my prose poetry from when I write flash fiction (its "kissing cousin"[31]), a drabble, a blog entry, or any other type of short prose text.

In order to illustrate these points, here is one of the poems from *Twenty Nine Volumes*, with some brief notes of commentary.

Divisi

"an instruction to divide a single section of instruments into multiple subsections."[32]

We siblings share the care of a widowed parent, who lives alone in the family home. We chaperone her to hospital appointments, order the paperwork, drop the right pills into morning/lunchtime/evening slots in boxes labelled M T W T F S S. A ready meal is split *in partes tres*; one third to catch her elusive appetite, two thirds for whoever is serving it. We eat at our own zones of dining table; at the far end, Dad's place has a table mat in front of a chair piled with unopened mail. We are divided by our history which covers her like a rosy throw, but ties us down with darker threads. When the time comes, we will share out her jewellery between the grand-daughters, as mementos, and unite half of Dad's ashes with his much loved wife's bones. We are kept in place by a wall of expectation. No-one holds the ladder steady but sometimes I climb up and look over, to see what's waiting on the other side.

The musical term which forms the title sets the theme for the poem: as family members, we are at one and the same time a whole entity, but also divided by aspects of our history, our place within the family, and the micro-geography of the family home (such as who sat where at the dining table). Within the sequence of poems, there are repeated threads which feature here: the medication boxes (also subdivided into sections labelled for the days of the week and the time of day); the Latin tag meaning "in three parts," referring to a poem about learning classical languages as a child; the ashes which recur in several of the poems; the confinement expressed by the "wall of expectation" and my attempt to escape over it.

Reflecting on my own composition of prose poetry through the lens of both practitioner and scholarly insights into the genre puts me almost in the position of my readers; although inevitably, as both author and critic of my poetry, my comments cannot be fully objective. In so doing, however, I have endeavoured to present some rationale based on my own work for what may give occasion to write prose poetry; to explore aspects of the reader's reception of poetry (both as author and reader); and to demonstrate that whilst not conforming to the rigid structures of particular verse forms, the prose poem is very much an exercise in poetic craft.

In conclusion, my practice shows that prose poetry can employ and become different forms, and work in collaboration with those who receive it to challenge their expectations of what a poem is and what it may do. To return to Carroll: "That's a great deal to make one word mean," Alice said in a thoughtful tone. "When I make a word do a lot of work like that," said Humpty Dumpty, "I always pay it extra."[33]

As poet, as viewer, my own payment can only be through working to improve my craft and giving attention to responses to it. Particularly in the case of the protean prose poem, that "democratic itinerary" depends on the active collaboration of others.

Notes

1 David Wheatley, "By Soft Return," Review of *The Penguin Book of the Prose Poem: From Baudelaire to Anne Carson*, ed. Jeremy Noel-Tod, *The Poetry Review* 109, no. 1 (Spring 2019): 96.

2 Anne Caldwell and Oz Hardwick, "Introduction," in *The Valley Press Anthology of Prose Poetry*, ed. Anne Caldwell and Oz Hardwick. (Scarborough: Valley Press, 2019), 9.

3 Lewis Carroll, "Through the Looking Glass," in *The Complete Illustrated Works of Lewis Carroll*, ed. Edward Giuliano (London: Chancellor Press, 1982), 184.

4 See, for example, Don Paterson's thought-provoking "Introduction" to his edited anthology, *101 Sonnets from Shakespeare to Heaney* (London: Faber & Faber, 1999), ix–xxiv.

5 Divya Nadkarni, "'A form of howling. A form of chanting. A form of looking out for each other': Poetics and Politics of the Contemporary Indian-English Prose Poem," Chapter 9 of this volume.

6 Hannah Stone, "Unspoken," in *Mystery*, ed. Rosi Gemmell, Jasmin Williams, and Oz Hardwick (Beaworthy, UK: Wordspace/Indigo Dreams Publishing, 2019), 34.

7 Carrie Etter, "The Prose Poem," in *The Portable Poetry Workshop*, ed. Nigel McLoughlin (London: Palgrave, 2017), 72.

8 Etter, "The Prose Poem," 72.

9 Etter, "The Prose Poem," 73.

10 Wolfgang Iser, "The Reading Process: A Phenomenological Approach," *New Literary History* 3, no. 2 (1972): 279.

11 Iser, "Reading Process," 286.

12 Object label, *ein texte passiert*, Tate Modern, London.

13 Jane Monson, "One Foot; Many Places: The Prose Poem's Art of Standing Still While Travelling," Chapter 14 of this volume.

14 Gary Young, "The Unbroken Line," in *The Rose Metal Press Field Guide to Prose Poetry: Contemporary Poets in Discussion and Practice*, ed. Gary L. McDowell and F. Daniel Rzicznek (Brookline, MA: Rose Metal Press, 2010), 113.

15 Claus Bremer, "a text happens," screen print on canvas, nylon rope, wooden pole, metal pins, 1965, Tate Modern, London.

16 William Wordsworth, "The Prelude," Book XII, ll. 208–215, in *Poetical Works* (London: Oxford University Press, 1904), 577.

17 Etter, "The Prose Poem," 72.

18 Rupert Loydell, "The Untaught Module," *TEXT Special Issue 46, Beyond the Line: Contemporary Prose Poetry* (October 2017), 1.

19 Gary L. McDowell and F. Daniel Rzicznek, "Introduction," in *Rose Metal Press Field Guide*, ed. McDowell and Rzicznek, xxvii.

20 Kathleen McGookey, "Why I Write Prose Poems," in *Rose Metal Press Field Guide*, ed. McDowell and Rzicznek, 50.

21 On the appearance of form confounding reader expectations, see Oz Hardwick, "Prose Poetry and the Resistance to Narrative," Chapter 2 in this volume.

22 Max Porter, *Grief Is the Thing with Feathers* (London: Faber & Faber, 2015).

23 Ben East, "Grief Is the Thing with Feathers Review – A Fable of Magic and Mourning," *The Guardian*, 11 September 2016, www.theguardian.com/books/2016/sep/11/grief-is-the-thing-with-feathers-max-porter-paperback-of-the-week.

24 Andrew McMillan, recommendation of *Grief Is the Thing with Feathers*, *The Guardian*, 28 November 2015, www.theguardian.com/books/ng-interactive/2015/nov/28/best-books-of-2015-part-one.

25 Porter, *Grief Is the Thing with Feathers*, 44.

26 Emily Berry, editorial, *Poetry Review* 109, no. 1 (Spring 2019): 5.

27 James Harris, "'Goodtime Jesus' and Other Sort-of Prose Poems," in *Rose Metal Press Field Guide*, ed. McDowell and Rzicznek, 11.

28 Brigitte Byrd, "I Cannot Escape the Prose Poem," in *Rose Metal Press Field Guide*, ed. McDowell and Rzicznek, 34.

29 PL, personal communication to author.

30 Loydell, "The Untaught Module," 2.

31 Denise Duhamel, "Happy (or How It Took Me Twenty Years to Almost 'Get' the Prose Poem)," in *Rose Metal Press Field Guide*, ed. McDowell and Rzicznek, 28.

32 All otherwise unattributed quotations in the poem sequence are from *The New Grove Encyclopaedia of Music and Musicians* (London: McMillan, 1979).

33 Carroll, *Through the Looking Glass*, 184.

4

NOBODY'S STORYBOOK

Reading Russell Edson for the Wrong Reasons

Nicholas Lauridsen

Mis-Thanking Russell Edson

A man had just married an automobile. My father by some strange conjunction had mice for sons. A woman had given birth to an old man. A scientist has a test tube full of sheep. I had charge of an insane asylum, as I was insane.[1] Little prepares you for the poetry of Russell Edson; or rather, little could prepare you, especially for those of us who have resisted marrying our automobiles. Heralded as the "godfather of the prose poem in America," Edson devoted his writing career nearly exclusively to the prose poem form, a kind of literary curio notorious for defying classification and stymying theorists.[2] Yet this form has persisted, and in some sense now flourishes in the hands of contemporary writers and across various languages. In America, abiding interest in the form is owed in large part to Edson's five decades of work, which is at once provocative, familiar but transgressive, and certainly unforgettable.

As with fairy tales, nursery rhymes, and fables, reading Edson's work requires a suspension of disbelief – and, with Edson, a steely literary nerve. As readers dropped into the wild and frankly uninhabitable heterocosms of Edson's prose poem worlds, which, minute but capacious, are themselves like infinite space bounded in nutshells, we land hard. We find ourselves out of range of all the familiar signals and signposts of everyday life; we are immediately caught and set adrift in the unpredictable energies of what feels like a science experiment gone wrong, lost amid the stampede of jumping moons and cow-slaying rabbits and toy wives. The figurative and aesthetic trappings that so endear verse to us become reckless and unruly under Edson's ministrations, and seem to have a runaway life of their own, and in a poetry that consistently declines to form any rapport with the reader. The lyric speaker, a tenuous presence if even appearing at all, constantly threatens to turn into a pumpkin when the poem strikes midnight. And metaphor, in particular, does

DOI: 10.4324/9781003199533-5

not do its usual conjunctive work to elucidate or dazzle or pleasantly disorient, but mangles what it fuses, almost physically hurts in its execution.

And yet these are precisely the unwieldly energies and oddities that attract us to Edson's poetry. Despite his assertion in one poem that "in the end there was only an arrangement of words; and still, no matter," his work retools the presumptions of composition such that having a matter no longer matters.[3] If it is nonsense, it is a well-crafted and exquisite nonsense. For all their preposterousness and probably deliberate silliness, his linguistic experiments make something happen. The use of the surreal within Edson's work is what is most familiar and engaging to us, but it is also perhaps what is least innovative. His genius, rather, is to draw us into an unfamiliar, more primordial stage of the metaphorical process, perhaps in order to pre-empt or override some of our natural inoculation as experienced readers to metaphor's inherent, dizzying oddness. His success then, in a twist on Russian formalism, is in defamiliarising ourselves as readers of poetry.

Critics typically describe Edson's work using language that, even in praise, sounds nearly like detraction and is almost equally viable as psychological diagnoses. For Marjorie Perloff, his poems are "'absurdist' proto-Cubist fables" and "parabolic fantasies"[4]; for Sarah Manguso, "nightmares and dream-visions"[5]; for Robert Hass, the American prose poem tradition of which Edson remains the prime exemplar is "a kind of wacky surreal work,"[6] although Edson himself rejected the Surrealist appellation, calling his early work instead "fables."[7] What Michel Delville hits on in terming "the poetics of fabulation" in Edson's work therefore comes closer to the mark.[8] In her poem "Counting Russell Edson," Lee Upton poeticises two broad reader responses to Edson's poems, the tragic and comic:

> But no, she should not thank Mr. Edson. For he reminds her that terrible things will happen and are happening and those things cannot be explained or predicted. Terrible awful cruelties are committed. People split into parts and walk around stuck all over with jelly. Love dies on a piano's lip. A walnut putters around in a garage and disappoints its parents.

> But no, she should thank Mr. Edson because he makes her want to laugh sometimes. But it is strange laughter. Like the laughter attempted by a mouse suffocating in a holiday cheese ball. Like the laughter of a forlorn bale of hay.[9]

Her poem, aping Edson's style and figures in both homage and reproach, then restates the question of his artistic value: what do we have to thank Russell Edson for?

We can begin to answer this question by looking a little more deeply at several aspects of his work, some broached but not thoroughly investigated by critics: literalisation of metaphor, deployment of violence and humour, and canny exploitation of the prose poem form. His use of metaphor and his treatment of the poetic subject in particular prompt questions about what it means to be poetic and to poeticise in a literary form that in general raises more questions than it answers, but also allows us to experience what poetry more broadly is doing in a raw and unconstrained encounter with even the most familiar of tropes and devices.

Turning Forward: How Narrative Animates the Metaphoric Process

Even before one hazards semantics in Edson's poems, we can acknowledge that most of his poems clearly are narrative, in the sense that a type of story is told in a sequence of events or observations. Routinely in his writing, a narrative world of adequate plausibility and familiar principles (a man lives in a house) is quickly jotted in, which then often skews briskly into the surreal or absurd (a man lives in a house and then tells it to *giddyup*). But we can still track the poems as stories, even if they are repeatedly nonsensical, as we do with nursery rhymes or fairy tales. And as is arguably the case with nursery rhymes and fairy tales, what we might be tempted to parse as semantic content – ideological thrust, cultural *mores* and taboos, coded moral didactics – is usually secondary in interest to the mechanisms by which the story coalesces into an organ of thought and imagining that enthrals its reader.

In attempting (and admittedly failing) to define prose poetry, Robert Hass traces its etymology to the Latin *provertere*, which means "to turn forward" – "Prose turns forward. Verse turns."[10] This forward movement is probably best exemplified in narrative prose, where the reader travels through time, usually sequentially or within an overall implicit sequence, as events occur within the story world. With Edson, such stories and events include chronicling a dog's progress as it climbs up the side of a house or a blow-by-blow recounting of a woman fighting a tree (she loses). Consider for instance, "The Fall":

> There was a man who found two leaves and came indoors holding them out saying to his parents that he was a tree.

> To which they said then go into the yard and do not grow in the living-room as your roots may ruin the carpet.

> He said I was fooling I am not a tree and he dropped his leaves.

> But his parents said look it is fall.[11]

Before engaging its various propositions, we can experience the poem as a simple and perhaps intimately commonplace story. Yet compositionally Edson was less interested in narrative fulfilment than attaining a type of unlikely aesthetic and intellectual coherence. In his words, his work is

> looking for the shape of the thought more than the particulars of the little
> narrative … My pieces, when they work, though full of odd happenings,
> win the argument against disorder through the logic of language and a com-
> positional wholeness. So my ideal prose poem is a small, complete work,
> utterly logical within its own madness.[12]

Part of the effect of this "compositional wholeness" that is "utterly logical within
its own madness" in Edson's approach is that it causes several stages of the metaphor to exist at once. If a metaphor is processual – i.e. metaphorisation – then
here: the man is like a tree, he makes himself into an art object, he denies being a
tree, he's perceived as a tree by his parents, he's perhaps perceived as a tree by the
reader – so he literally is a tree, he figuratively is a tree, he is neither. The poem
doesn't decide for us, and instead plays with the energies of metaphorisation rather
than its semantic or aesthetic ends. His simple declaration that he is a tree becomes
increasingly problematic, since all of these conditions come to exist at once. The
state of the man, then, is essentially impossible to visualise, caught in the midst of
metaphorisation. But that is really the point – we are being carefully shown what
we cannot ordinarily or logically witness. The declarative, sometimes flat anecdotal
tone misleads us into a bracing illogic, saying repeatedly, "This statement is false."

The movement of narrative for Edson then is movement towards a cognitive
or intellectual (or aesthetic) end, even if the primary colour of his compositional
technique is "madness." Of course, as the story moves forward, as readers we move
along with the events, which are both logical in that they tell a story and illogical
in that the story makes no sense. But in parallel to this is the development of
figuration, metaphor, and poetic devices that flower along the narrative lattice
in tandem. The forward movement of prose impels the constitutive tropes and
figures of poetry within the prose poem with velocities and in directions that we
do not encounter in verse. The implicit connectivity of narrative is used here in
prose in a way that it is not usually used in verse, where "time stops," in Edson's
reckoning.[13] Edson posits that verse differs from prose in how we experience time
in them: time "flows through prose, and around poetry."[14] For him, the tendency
of prose is "bringing things into existence, only to have them disappear down into
the end of the plot," whereas verse operates within "a sense of the permanent,
of time held."[15] Thus, the momentum of narrative drives the collision and union
of the discrete particles of vehicle and tenor in a way unique to the prose poem
form. And frankly, we do not experience metaphor the same way in prose as we
do in verse. Here, metaphor comes in a rush typically absent in the more measured
pace of lineated verse, becoming a discursive object rather than an object of figuration organised within or across discrete lines. Beyond the typical dichotomy
of narrative time and discursive time, devices such as figuration and musicality
and image need some breathing room to warm up or unfold in order to occur as
their genesis takes hold; require temporal space in which to realise the phenomena
of themselves, their own sort of poetic time. Though not the exclusive province

of poetry, these devices typically exert their powers through delicate and careful articulation: the allegory's subtextual payload must be attached and aimed, the analogy must be mapped precisely onto its scaffolding, and vehicle and tenor must be separated by the narrow interstice of at least one heartbeat to forestall interference or sheer insensibility. If poetic epiphany is often realised via the custodianship of some instance of verse formalism – as Emily Dickinson reckons, "As Lightning to the Children eased" since "The Truth must dazzle gradually / Or every man be blind –" – instead Edson luxuriates in the force of the lightning itself.[16]

In this manner, the prose happening of metaphor therefore diverges from its verse cognate. Consider an arbitrary lineation of a portion of Edson's "Through Dream and Suppertime":

> The head is death
> with hair upon it. Also
> it is the vehicle upon which
> it is itself to ride
> through dream and suppertime.
> …
> Soon, too soon, the soft
> mouth of the worm is eating
> the idea of itself …

Compare this with:

> The head is death with hair upon it. Also it is the vehicle upon which it is itself to ride through dream and suppertime. . . .
>
> Soon, too soon, the soft mouth of the worm is eating the idea of itself … [17]

Edson harnesses the narrative momentum of prose to fill the poem's field with the rampant associative powers of metaphor and leaves little breathing room. Prose's often banal serviceability, its matter-of-factness, here becomes what startles us. This also has the effect of altering the structure of metaphor as we experience it in the prose poem. Rather than observing the propriety in verse of often segregating vehicle and tenor over the pause of a line break, Edson allows them to clash, jams them up against one another, and bangs them together until the sparks fly, in the process inventing his own impropriety of figuration. The primordial din of this clashing seems irresistible to him throughout his poetry.

In contrast, verse lineation tends to inscribe traditional metaphor in one of two ways: thrusting vehicle and tenor together in close proximity within the same line (a favourite technique of Louise Glück's, for instance) or sifting them apart into discrete lines via enjambment (this is also especially popular with managing the deployment of simile, reaching all the way back to Greek epic). Verse seems uniquely poised to prepare us (or *dis*-prepare us) for its metaphoric disjunctions. The line lifts the machinery of metaphor off the surface of the page. Vehicle and tenor, together in one line or separated into two lines, can be isolated according to the poet's inclinations as specimens of language pinned and suspended like the lepidopterist's butterfly. The force of the paradox of their relationship, existing as intellectually discrete but aesthetically conjoined entities, can be distributed between lines to mitigate its power, or contained under the hermetic seal of a single line. Consider Glück's distributive technique in the opening of "The Archipelago":

> The tenth year we came upon immense sunlight, a relief
> of islands locked in the water. These became our course.[18]

The break after *relief* permits the conjunction of "relief / of islands" to occur more plausibly because, ironically, of the disjunctive effect of the break, which mitigates the force of the union. Yet, in withholding vehicle from tenor even momentarily, the poem generates suspense within a micro-drama of figuration, thereby heightening its effect. The break also allows the subtle overtones and undertones of the metaphorical pairings to intone. The idiomatic "immense relief" rises out of the first line free of the distraction of ensuing metaphor, cuing in the reader to the poem's tone and the condition of the beleaguered sailors; and the multiple denotations of *relief* may come into play before it becomes locked to the figure of the islands. Similarly, in "The Wild Iris":

> At the end of my suffering
> there was a door.[19]

Abiding by the first line, suffering is an act or an event occurring over time; with the metaphorising property of the second line, suffering must become a physical space as well, as there is now a door at the end of it. This careful exploitation of the power of verse to manage metaphor and other devices has no direct analogue in prose, and, without confounding prose expectations, is likely untransposable.

"The Only World That Showed Up": The Prose Poem as Word Problem[20]

What may first strike the reader about Edson's poems is that, notwithstanding their broad formal departure from verse, they make no attempt to resemble traditional lyric poems in approach or tone.[21] They present as less poetic than coolly propositional; while lyric luxuriates in experience and subjectivity, Edson's prose poems are speculative, abstract, ludicrous, and defy penetration. Their setup shares the qualities of both the joke and the philosophical exercise in how they posit their subject matter hypothetically, e.g. "Imagine the man's head is a vehicle … ,"

"Imagine some policemen who are chickens … "[22] In some cases, it can be questionable to view them as poems at all rather than a kind of problematic literary shorthand for a genre-less imaginative process.

But there is also the "problem" of prose poems in the other sense, as puzzles to solve, often with a game-like instantiation of their own terms and objects and rules and, sometimes, the suggestion of a solution – although the draw of the prose poem seems to abide within the substance of those very terms, objects, and rules, a resolution notwithstanding. In Edson's practice, these poems can present themselves more like philosophical, legal, or mathematical hypotheticals rather than what we might consider specimens of literature. And if prose poems often are or tend to be word problem-like or puzzle-like, they are puzzles that new generations of writers seem keen on solving by simply writing more of them. For instance, Matthea Harvey's sequence of "mermaid" poems is a canny example of the form luxuriating in its own undecided or liminal state, where the awkwardness of youth and the impositions of femininity appear as metaphorical problems of transformation and identity rendered in a literary form that, like the figure of the composite mermaid, is neither quite verse nor prose.

Robert Hass' more sober re-working of the prose poem form in *Human Wishes* diverges from the Surrealist norms prose poetry had accrued in the United States, yet at times shares Edson's propositional philosophy-play. If Edson's work suggests the fallacy of the declarative, Hass' prose poems restore some of the dignity of the real to the form. Hass' versions are recognised as a deliberate pivot away from the surreal in the form and are good examples of prose poetry *not* foregrounding metaphorisation in the manner of Edson and Harvey. But what Hass retains of Edson's approach is a return to the normativity of prose that belies the energies of poetic shapes of thought, if sometimes tightly constrained in manner. In such a rendering as his poem "A Story About the Body," the geometric demands of verse would certainly be "distractions," both formally and tonally. Like Edson's, Hass' disarming prose poems eschew the formal occasion of verse, drawing their vitality in being a kind of unnoticed form. Edson would likely endorse Hass' use of the form by telling a narrative with images, by refraining from foregrounding language the way verse almost inevitably does. This prose normativity, one of its affordances, is that it *allows* the sentence, the very way that verse typically does not. By eschewing lineation and enjambment, the sentence may reassert its hierarchy and re-establish its current, even if the image-making and the shape of the thought remain poetic.

Peculiar to Edson's word problems, however, is a kind of unrestrained and absurdist violence in many of his poems, which Lee Upton rightly flags as problematic, though she cannily perceives their heuristic function in exposing "the saturation of the private with ideologies that promote violence and render it inevitable."[23] The incorporation of violence is undeniable and commonplace, whether it is "tides of blood" in a home, dismemberment, the animal world locking horns with the human one ("A rabbit had killed a man in a wood one day."[24]), or merely contentious arguments that presage future violence.

> A large woman has killed her parakeet with an ax; went suddenly berserk; blood all over the house, splashed all over the neighborhood, on the roads leading out of town. It is said that parakeet blood was found in several neighboring towns; that it was even splashed several states away![25]

The horror enlivened through the quasi-cinematic sensationalism and deft camera movement of the telling erodes quite quickly into frank disbelief (just how much blood does a parakeet have?) and perhaps a subtle if mischievous literary nod to the bloodiness of *Macbeth* ("Yet who would have thought the old man to have had so much blood in him?").[26] The violence is full-bodied, sometimes off-putting or even gory, but transpiring within a grossly mismatched tonal world.

Here, too, the conception of prose poems as a type of word problem or philosophical exercise may prove helpful towards understanding not only the presence of this violence but our decided remoteness to it as readers, or even perhaps uneasy indifference. Over the run of Edson's work, we feel encouraged to take the strife and combat and purported tragedy, however nonsensical, in stride with everything else that occurs. We as readers are not invited to feel outrage or grief in response; we no more mourn the loss of the fictional figures in his poems than we might mourn the hypothetical victims of the classic trolley problem of moral philosophy. With the heavily abstracted characters subjected to the misfortunes of an imagined world's brutal whimsy, the depicted savagery does not strike true, and, despite its prevalence, it registers as a kind of cartoon violence, heavy in spectacle but light in gravitas. Like the violence of fairy tale, myth, and parable, for better or worse, it gives permission to itself within a didactic or aesthetic, rather than representational, enterprise.

But the violence is not merely another vector of the absurd. Rather, it is arguable that what we are witnessing as readers is a formal violence more so than a substantive one. Without clear boundaries and with rules simply being invented along the way, the worlds that "show up" in Edson's poems are deliberately disjoined from ours and are meant to shock or provoke or amuse in their transgressions upon what we accept as the real. Part of this is perhaps the messiness of Ovidian transformation that is omitted from myth; part of it is likely a philosophical demonstration by Edson that many properties of a system, when taken to absurd extremes, precipitate a novel form of violence. The untidiness of prose, its lack of organising perimeters and rejection of the authority of form, is what permits this violence; much of the violent spectacle we witness would be unthinkable, or at least unconvincing, in verse.

Moreover, the violence is deployed as a formal agency in the poems. It is less a result or a consequence of actions but rather an elemental energy within the narrative, moving us from plot point to plot point and scene to scene. Here, Edson's approach simultaneously questions and exploits the anonymising and sanitising creature that is the philosophical hypothetical. All the secretive energies of metaphor-making – its collisions, its non sequiturs, and its unlikely and sometimes unholy unions – are made visible to the reader. Even the rabbit slaying the man is a kind of joining, as with the woman and her parakeet – each a destructive joining, to be sure, but enacted through the permissive workings of metaphor. In this way, the absurdity of metaphor generates the absurdity of the narrative, and the "category mistakes" of metaphor, its breaking of deeply rooted cognitive taboos, is realised in the peculiar dramas within the discrete worlds of Edson's poems.

Foregrounding Metaphor

More broadly, Edson's use of the prose poem works to bring metaphor into the foreground to the extent that our experience of the poem's story (if there is one) is primarily mediated through metaphor and only secondarily through its narrative events. We come for the promise of a story but stay for the poetic pyrotechnics. This foregrounding has potent effects and is the primary generator of what has been perceived as Surrealist phenomena in his poems. This results in part in our sense of dislocation and defamiliarisation with ourselves as readers: two steps into a poem and we cannot tell what is real and what is figurative. In part, this is due to the literalisation of metaphors, of endowing them with materiality in the poem, and, as in "The Fall," this literalisation becomes not only the mechanism but the subject of the poem, the man's parents literalising his fancy that he has turned into a tree.

But, more importantly, what is really foregrounded is not metaphor as a device itself, but as a process. We are not so much bombarded with a slew of strange metaphors but are instead swallowed up into the poem's naked act of metaphorising. And as is readily seen in Edson's poems, this is a continuous act. While the events of the poem occur in the background, the foreground of the poem is completely saturated with a kinetic metaphorising process that we can't look away from. In "The Toy-Maker," for instance, Edson pushes a (central) metaphor's proposition past its breaking point, perhaps showing its inherent fallacy as propositional:

> A toy-maker made a toy wife and a toy child. He made a toy house and some toy years.
>
> He made a getting-old toy, and he made a dying toy.
>
> The toy-maker made a toy heaven and a toy god.
>
> But, best of all, he liked making toy shit.[27]

Rather than a coherent system of figuration or signification, what emerges instead – or at least in parallel – is a brightly drawn contour of the metaphorising process. We may certainly be captivated by the obvious strangeness of the trespass of adult concerns into the innocent world of children's play, and we are left to decide whether the toy-maker refuses to make-believe or whether he simply and illogically chooses to make-believe what for us is sobering reality. What is the function of a toy but to operate as a talisman of the imagination? And if so, as Edson seems to propose in one of his typical paradoxical inversions, what happens with the real when it is subjected to the imagination? Or, conversely, aren't years and lives and the bric-a-brac of our brief mortal lives merely toys themselves, existential trifles? (And to what extent is the poem-curio itself simply a toy for imagining?) But equally as intriguing is how both narrative progression and our investment as readers in the poem are less gratified by the suspense of what the toy-maker will *do* next − what toy will the toy-maker make next? − than in where the metaphorising process might take us − what toy metaphor will the poet/speaker come up with next? It is the wild figuration of the toy metaphor that emerges as the true drama here, and it steals the show. In the end, we don't care for whom he's making his toy heaven and his toy god; we really only care to see where Edson will take this toy metaphor next, as it seems to have transgressed into forbidden realms of figuration already − religion, mortality, and potty humour. And as a result, the metaphors in Edson's work are not constrained by the practice of lineation, which is frequently used to regulate the structure of metaphor, but instead occur throughout the overarching structure of the narrative.

And yet as pleasurable as it may be to wade into the surreal or illogical (or simply "mad"), the use of metaphor in Edson's prose poems is not irrational. The energy and momentum of prose and narrative allows Edson to, for example, take the metaphor's inherent proposition, its uneasy and improbable fusion of disparate elements, to its logical conclusion − that is, illogic. Or rather, metaphor in his prose poems is no longer propositional but material; its brazen hypothesis is anchored into the poem's linguistic flesh or embodiment as "story facts"; his metaphors have touch and taste and mass, and often sentience. The effects of these are several, not the least of which is to displace lyric agency almost entirely. A centralised human utterance becomes less compelling when the animal kingdom and inanimate objects suddenly burst into intelligible voices.

Furthermore, in Edson's use, the prose poem form serves to heighten the effect of metaphor along a separate axis from verse. With metaphor foregrounded or "exploded" within the prose poem to the point of saturation, it grates against the more conventional and humble expectations of prose − that is, its familiarity. We are conditioned in everyday life to approach prose perhaps less commonly as a form of literature than of efficient but artless communication, from the newspaper to the high school essay to the "grey literature" of receipts, invoices, office memoranda. As Sarah Manguso opines, in prose, we expect "sequential, logical sense" and rely upon a "linear accumulation of meaning." The result, she discovers, is that Edson's poetry frustrates this expectation by virtue of "[alerting] the reader that semantic jumps are possible and that nonsense can proceed logically."[28]

In "The Love Affair," the poem flows logically but for the actual object of the speaker's love:

> One day a man fell in love with himself, and was unable to think of anything else but himself.
> Of course he was flattered, no one had ever shown him that much interest …
>
> He wanted to know all about himself, his hobbies, his likings in music and sports.
> He was jealous he had not known himself as a child. He wanted to know what kind of a boy he had been …
>
> When asked if he thought it would lead to marriage, he said that that was his fondest wish, that he longed to have babies with himself … [29]

Pushing the metaphor past its breaking point and allowing it to pervade the poem until its absurdity is revealed – and relished – keeps the reader engaged with the poem until the final line, even if overall it doesn't make sense on its surface. We may be tempted (or conditioned) to view prose as a form of mutually supported, reciprocal inference. Sentences lean on each other like the stones in a Roman arch, and suspend it airborne. It sits with a paved certainty; it calmly bears the constant traffic of our perusal. Verse seems delicate in contrast; skittish and slippery before the reader; it bears its metaphorical load differently from prose. Yet here, Edson's prose seems to test the limits to which the absurd and the aesthetic may coexist, in an aberrant prose that is at once meticulously consistent within itself and flagrantly inconsistent with everything else.

Prose enjoys a presumption of continuity; this is conditioned perhaps by the overwhelming prose experience we have in life (we live lives of prose, in essence) with grey literature, the first books we read and are read, and perhaps more insidiously, how we are taught to write and reason as schoolchildren and up into higher education and beyond. Furthermore, we are taught that prose is reducible, susceptible to summary and outline by the attentive reader; this may also condition the manner in which we write it. Verse, on the other hand, often exploits its own discontinuity. Even in the epic poem, in which the verbal action is inevitably, though not invariably, narrative, integrity lies with the line. Especially in pre-modern, pre-Gutenberg literary culture, this is also a mnemonic integrity. The discontinuity of verse, then, is most apt for managing the inherent discontinuity of metaphor; but, lacking the impetus of prose, verse perhaps is less suited to exploring the breaking points of central metaphor and for wilfully intermixing vehicle and tenor in their representation.

In Edson's treatment, the prose poem overall then is written in the condition of metaphor. It becomes a medium in which metaphor is *internalised*; it is no longer a surface phenomenon but persists everywhere, in its atmosphere and climate, in the very formative conditions of the work itself. This reflects Edson's instinct towards anticlosure, leaving us in the midst of the metaphorical lurch, so to speak, the interstellar trip between vehicle and tenor, between idea and figuration, through uncharted cognitive space. Edson sucks us into the netherworlds of his prose poems and then hastily abandons us there. In Edson's prose poems, the metaphor, in a sense, has already occurred, or is on the verge of occurring. It is his unique poetic gesture, however, to strand us as readers within the crisis of union that is metaphor.

"Coordinated in Endless Coincidence": Destabilising the Poetic Subject

If foregrounding and literalising metaphor upon the surface of the prose poem are the short-term effects of Edson's practice, then an overall destabilising of the poetic subject is one of the long-term effects. This is consistent throughout his poetry; the prose in which he casts his subjects constantly distorts or occludes them. Like the narrative, the subject is relegated to the background of the prose poem. The value of metaphor takes hold, and it is not in the union of its unlikely paired vehicle and tenor but in the violent energy created by the disjunction. The chemical imbalance of metaphor constantly attempts to correct itself, to stabilise itself; but Edson is constantly jostling the scales, constantly destabilising his poetic subject so that it is spurred into motions and behaviours that we have never seen before. Sets of tensions arise in Edson's poems – defamiliarisation versus familiarisation, figurative versus literal. While his narrative animates and legitimises the literalisation of metaphor's figuration process, it also leaves the reader unsure what is real or what ought to be taken seriously.

And yet surely Edson's aesthetic of uncertainty and instability is what draws us to his poetry. Exposed to the deep inner workings of rampant metaphorising, we are less likely to find closure in this type of figuration and more likely to take pleasure in its open-endedness, in the poems as gestures and provocations rather than insular and finite objects. While the muted language of prose is perhaps realised in language's temporal transitoriness, the inherent decay of the word when one reads and that verse seeks to preserve, Edson's fashioning of the prose poem into an organ for raw metaphor and unrestricted figuration shores up the prose poem as a viable and potent literary form for expression and experimentation beyond the affordances of verse. Situated at the collision of the centripetal tendencies of verse and the centrifugal tendencies of prose, ultimately the instability of the poetic subject is its own aesthetic, and while not uniquely Edson's, he uses it to great effect and extent.

In reading Edson's work, we might find it at once approachable and forbidding, narratively taut yet logically irresolute, as we are dizzied by the relentless parade of animate furniture, gentlemen floating in meadows, paper-doll factories, pet apes, and subterranean cows. Yet this discomfort is not merely an aesthetic aim of Edson's but a clue into his larger philosophy of writing. For Edson, "[p]oetry is never comfortable in language because the unconscious doesn't know how to speak."[30] In his reckoning, his poems are not settled language but are "always looking for a language" – and perhaps this best explains his open metaphorisation and unstable poetic subjects, where the poems have been set in words to which the shape of his thought cannot wholly commit. His interest in storytelling and discovery distracts us from the fact that these are poems, and instead lures us into the stellar workings of the primordial creative process as we read and watch the poem find its language, coasting along on the raw shapes of his thoughts. And as much as it compels us as readers, Edson's raw approach to the form equally continues to inspire modern practitioners of prose poetry. Writers of prose poems instantly may find in Edson a witting accomplice in unorthodox verbal experiments, as well as an unruly guide into the magic of metaphor-making, cultural taboos, and fairy tale logic, and, perhaps most importantly, the intensely and paradoxically generative power of not taking the form too seriously.

Notes

1 The intrepid first sentences of "The Automobile," "The Pattern," "In All the Days of My Childhood," "Counting Sheep," and "Fire Is Not a Nice Guest," respectively, in Russell Edson, *The Tunnel: Selected Poems* (Oberlin, OH: Oberlin College Press, 1994).

2 Ray Olson, review of *The Tormented Mirror*, by Russell Edson, *Booklist*, April 2001, www.booklistonline.com/The-Tormented-Mirror-/pid=416619.

3 Russell Edson, "The Matter," in *The Tunnel*, 204.

4 Marjorie Perloff, "Book Review: Michel Delville's *The American Prose Poem: Poetic Form and the Boundaries of Genre*," *The Prose Poem: An International Journal* 8 (1999): 134–38.

5 Sarah Manguso, "Why the Reader of Good Prose Poems Is Never Sad," *The Believer*, 11 (March 2004), https://believermag.com/why-the-reader-of-good-prose-poems-is-never-sad/.

6 Robert Hass, *A Little Book on Form: An Exploration into the Formal Imagination of Poetry* (New York: HarperCollins, 2017), 385.

7 Russell Edson, "The Prose Poem in America," *Parnassus* 5, no. 1 (1976): 321–25.

8 Michel Delville, *The American Prose Poem: Poetic Form and the Boundaries of Genre* (Gainesville, FL: University Press of Florida, 1998).

9 Lee Upton, "Counting Russell Edson," *Field* 93 (Fall 2015): 22.

10 Hass, *A Little Book on Form*, 385.

11 Russell Edson, "The Fall," in *The Tunnel*, 60.

12 Russell Edson, "Interview: The Art of the Prose Poem. Russell Edson." *Truths, Falsehoods, and a Wee Bit of Honesty: A Short Primer on the Prose Poem with Selected Letters from Russell Edson*, ed. Peter Johnson (Cheshire, MA: MadHat Press, 2020), 43.

13 Edson, "The Prose Poem in America," 322.

14 Ibid.

15 Ibid.

16 Emily Dickinson, "Tell All the Truth But Tell It Slant –" *The Poems of Emily Dickinson: Reading Edition*, ed. Ralph W. Franklin (Cambridge, MA: Harvard University Press, 1988), J 1129, Fr 1263.

17 Russell Edson, "Through Dream and Suppertime," in *The Tunnel*, 117.

18 Louise Glück, "The Archipelago," *Poetry* (May 1971): 65.

19 Louise Glück, "The Wild Iris," in *The Wild Iris* (Hopewell, NJ: Ecco, 1992), 1.

20 "This is the best of all possible worlds only because it is the only one that showed up, said father." Russell Edson, "Of the Snake and the Horse," in *The Tunnel*, 19.

21 At this point, essentialist questions may arise about prose poetry as a form or genre, but scholars and writers alike do not share any sort of consensus on what the prose poem is; more often, the literary community is forced to define it in the negative – not lineated, no rhyme scheme or meter, etc. More rewarding, perhaps, is to approach it in the terms of Caroline Levine's self-determining *affordances* – what the form may generate, what it facilitates or makes possible, or, in her words, "the kinds of uses or actions that are latent in them – their capabilities" that may be carried "across contexts." See Caroline Levine, *Forms: Whole, Rhythm, Hierarchy, Network* (Princeton, NJ: Princeton University Press, 2015); Caroline Levine, "Forms: Literary and Social," *Dibur Literary Journal* 2 (Spring 2016): 75–9. The prose poem is proof positive of this type of approach to form and, more broadly, questions of genre, when it is tough to pin down a form or genre's exclusive qualities.

22 Adapted from the first sentences of Edson's "Through Dream and Suppertime" and "The Smell of Hay and Stars," respectively, in Russell Edson, *The Tunnel*, 116–17.

23 Lee Upton, "Structural Politics: The Prose Poetry of Russell Edson," *South Atlantic Review* 58, no. 4 (November 1993): 102.

24 Russell Edson, "How a Cow Comes to Live with Long Eared Ones," in *The Tunnel*, 17.

25 Russell Edson, "The Howling," in *The Tunnel*, 141.

26 Lady Macbeth in Act V, Scene i.

27 Russell Edson, "The Toy-Maker," in *The Tunnel*, 129.

28 Manguso, "Why the Reader of Good Prose Poems is Never Sad."

29 Russell Edson, "The Love Affair," in *The Tunnel*.

30 Russell Edson, "An Interview with Russell Edson." by Mark Tursi. *Double Room* 4 (Spring/Summer 2004), www.doubleroomjournal.com/issue_four/ Russell_Edson. html.

5

"BORDERS ON EDGES, WHERE SKIN STOPS, OR BEGINS"[1]

The Prose Poem's Relationship with the Discourses of Fashion and Food, with Particular Reference to Charles Baudelaire, Gertrude Stein, and Harryette Mullen

Susie Campbell

The involvement of fashion and food in the construction of identity, gender, and race has drawn the attention of poets such as Gertrude Stein and Harryette Mullen who are interested in subverting or remaking these discourses. In this chapter, I explore how both poets draw on the particular potential of prose poetry for this subversive work, demonstrating how they develop Baudelaire's tonal complexity to exploit the form's capacity for plurality and open-endedness. In particular, I consider how both Stein and Mullen exploit a tendency in prose poetry to keep multiple frames of reference in play and suggest how this might nuance a reading of Baudelaire. Multiple strategies are available to the prose poet, I suggest, due to the form's involvement with both prose and poetry whose different structures and conventions combine in prose poetry's potential for new forms of linguistic organisation.

From the outset, the prose poem as pioneered by Baudelaire has engaged not only with the streets and crowds of an urban landscape but also with an urban interior, sometimes manifesting as a preoccupation with the discourses of the domestic: food, furnishings, and fashion. Throughout *Paris Spleen*, Baudelaire's 1869 (posthumously published) collection of short prose poems, food, and its associated domestic sphere is presented as ambivalent, both interrupting the poet's creative flow yet also grounding it. In one of the poems, "Soup and Clouds," the speaker experiences the interruption of a meal as a rude and unwelcome awakening. The dreaming poet is dragged out of his creative musings by "a violent fist landed in my back" as his girlfriend announces dinner is served: "Get on with your bloody soup, cloud merchant."[2] However, in the context of other *Paris Spleen*

DOI: 10.4324/9781003199533-6

poems, such as "The Artist's Confiteor," which address the "malaise" of the poet and dramatise how poetic virility may be sapped by too much daydreaming, the speaker's resentment at this interruption becomes ironic: it is only the intrusion of the quotidian that energises the dreamer; the lowly "soup" of everyday life is the essential, if bitter, Viagra for his flagging poetic soul. Some critics have seen in this play of irony an optimistic resolution made possible by what they describe as the "elasticity" of the prose poem form. Martin Sorrell, translator of *Paris Spleen*, for example, claims:

> the prose poem … allows more readily than verse, rapid and random changes of mood, contrasts, incongruities. With fewer formal directives, it offers the flexibility to place side by side such antagonists as lyricism and analysis, the glib and the intense, irony and sincerity, beauty and ugliness.[3]

But there may be something more complex going on. The contemporary prose poem's relationship with the domestic is complicated, frequently mimicking, unpicking, or recycling the discourses of fashion, beauty, and cooking, suggesting that a closer examination might be needed. In particular, this study looks at the possibility that the prose poetry form itself offers particular opportunities for subverting and remaking these discourses, and this is why poets such as Gertrude Stein and Harryette Mullen have chosen it for their engagement with the complex implications of the domestic.

The tropes of food and fashion have held a particular interest for a number of contemporary poets interested in writing about gender and identity. Food and clothing are, for example, key motifs in Lyn Hejinian's *My Life*, Claudia Rankine's *Don't Let Me Be Lonely*, Sophie Robertson's *a,* and Alison Benis White's *Small Porcelain Head*. All of these poets have deployed prose poetry as the form in which they explore the domestic and its relationship with gender, race, and identity. The work of Gertrude Stein and Harryette Mullen is the particular focus of this study because of the centrality of these tropes in their work. In her poetry collection *Tender Buttons* (1914), Stein explores the role of the domestic world in generating language, as well as the role of language in generating what she describes as "the rhythm of the visible world."[4] Mullen is explicit about her indebtedness to Stein in her reimagining of *Tender Buttons* in her 1990s volumes *Trimmings* and *S*PeRM**k*t*. "I was writing poems that talked back to Gertrude Stein's *Tender Buttons*," she says in the "Preface" to *Recyclopedia*, the volume in which *Trimmings* and *S*PeRM**k*t* are collected with *Muse & Drudge*.[5]

Another reason for choosing Stein and Mullen to be the focus of this study is because of their interest not just in clothes and clothing, but in the art of clothing – that is, fashion. Whilst there is not space here to engage deeply with fashion theory, even a cursory engagement with it suggests its implication in constructions of gender and identity. It might come as a surprise to consider Stein as a fashion connoisseur, but it was one of the many art forms in which she was interested. She was friends with the fashion designer Pierre Balmain, visited his atelier, and wrote an article about him for an issue of *Vogue*. Along with Baudelaire, Mallarmé, and Benjamin, Stein is described, in a *Poetry Foundation* article on poetry and fashion, as "one of the great observers of modernist fashion."[6] Mullen, also discussed in this same article, is explicit about her interest in the language of advertising, marketing, and mass consumption particularly around fashion (and, indeed, food). However, her epigraph to *Trimmings* warns us not to over-simplify this interest. In the voice of Sappho, she chides, "don't ask me what to wear."[7] Stein and Mullen's interest is anything but simple. This study seeks to show that they explore the language and discourse of food and fashion from multiple perspectives in order to activate complex and ironic layers of meaning. They contextualise and make polysemous these domestic discourses and their associated constructions of race and gender; to paraphrase Mikhail Bakhtin, they activate a subversive dialogism within these discourses.[8]

One critic who has paid close attention to Stein's interest in the domestic is Margueritte Murphy. Murphy provides a helpful analysis of how Stein uses pun, free association, and non-sequitur to destabilise what she calls the "authoritative discourses of the conventional woman's world," discourses that, whilst largely written by women for women, derive from the ideological constructions of the patriarchal, bourgeois family and the female role within it. Murphy suggests that Stein was deliberately both using and subverting the register that characterised contemporary "domestic guides to living: cookbooks, housekeeping guides, books of etiquette, guides to entertaining, maxims of interior design, fashion advice."[9]

Titles of her poems, such as "A Long Dress" or "A Red Hat" or "A Blue Coat," might lead us to expect some kind of fashion writing; however, Stein both fulfils and subverts any such expectation. Her poem "A Long Dress" depicts the garment from some surprising perspectives and raises questions not usually asked by fashion writers. "What is the current that makes machinery, that makes it crackle, what is the current that presents a long line and a necessary waist. What is this current?" asks the poem, and continues: "Where is the serene length, it is there and a dark place is not a dark place, only a white and red are black, only a yellow and green are blue, a pink is scarlet, a bow is every colour. A line distinguishes it. A line just distinguishes it."[10]

The gaze through which we are shown this dress is not a typical "fashion gaze." In the light of John Berger's discussion of the objectifying power of the look and Laura Mulvey's subsequent coinage of the phrase "male gaze,"[11] we have come to expect the gaze associated with fashion to treat the garment as object, and by extension, to objectify its wearer. The gaze in this poem is not just interested in the dress as a finished object but is also interested in its manufacture. And complicating matters further, it is not clear whether the viewing point of this gaze is from inside or outside, both simultaneously, or whether what is described here is, in fact, visible at all. The dress appears to be moving, either with the residue of its construction or through some kind of static energy or draught, but who is perceiving this? The viewer, the wearer, or the dress itself? Whose line is the "line which distinguishes it"? or rather, whose line of sight? In the third paragraph, any separation between the dress, its viewer, and the language starts to collapse so that it becomes unclear whether the properties of the garment reside in the garment, in the perception of the viewer, or only in the language of the poem. The processes that produced the dress seem to be visible within the poem and yet are absent from it, and so we are left with a materiality that has been rendered elusive and ambiguous. The bow that starts off as a ribbon attached to the dress dissolves into the realm of language as the pun on "rainbow" plays out ("a bow is every colour"). Colours seem to hover somewhere between the perceptual apparatus of the viewer and the material garment: "only a white and red are black, only a yellow and green are blue, a pink is scarlet." In the end, the poem forces us to question the materiality of all these properties, and their relationship with the varying and multiple perspectives of the reader/viewer, making any single point of view uncertain or inconclusive: "a dark place is not a dark place." Even the grammar of the poem is inconclusive with punctuation left indeterminate. Apparent questions might be statements or qualifications; statements are qualified and questioned. Far from describing the dress in this poem as an inert object, Stein renders it as a dynamic participant in a flux of perceptions and processes.

Her use of the language of food, meals, and recipes is equally decentred and unstable. You would not want to sit down for breakfast with Stein. Although her poem "Breakfast" starts on an apparently positive note ("A shining breakfast, a breakfast shining"), it quickly mutates into a Mad Hatter's tea party. Alarmingly, we learn, "A sudden slice changes the whole plate, it does so suddenly," and instead of the shining breakfast, we find "There is no salmon, there are no tea-cups," and all we are left with are "the same kind of mushes as are used by stomachers by the eating hopes that makes eggs delicious." Worse, even these "mushes" are then replaced by images of domestic fracture ("A hurt mended stick, a hurt mended cup") and even potential crisis ("in most violent likely"). However, the poem reassures us none of these worrying arrangements need to be permanent. "Do this temporarily," the poem advises; nothing need be "stationary."[12] In both poems, "A Long Dress" and "Breakfast," Stein ultimately celebrates movement and change.

Despite Deborah Mix's claim that Stein's "poetry of domesticity" can be "silencing,"[13] Harryette Mullen claims the opposite is true for her. Embracing the idea of "recycling," she says in an interview, "I found that on a lot of levels I could use what Stein was doing ... in terms of using a prose-poetry form ... also in her use of subject-matter, where she is dealing with objects, rooms and food, the domestic space that is a woman's space."[14] In *Recyclopedia,* Mullen argues that Stein's *Tender Buttons* should be read as a "meditation on the interior lives of women and the material culture of domesticity," claiming that Stein's verbal objects "illuminate, animate and eroticise the domestic space to which women have been traditionally confined."[15] Mullen draws on the language of advertising and media, and combines it with Stein's techniques of pun and multiple points of view to play with the discourse of fashion in *Trimmings,* and of food in *S*PeRM**k*t.* But, whilst responding to Stein, Mullen has her own concerns as an African American poet. Deborah Mix is valuable here, emphasising how "Stein's critique of white femininity, while a kind of finishing place for Stein, became a starting place for Mullen's own deconstruction of patriarchal formations,"[16] deconstruction which is concerned with race as well as gender. Mullen's interest in intersectionality – that is, how aspects of social, racial, and political identity combine within privilege and inequality – is illustrated in her poem "Tender," one of the poems in *Trimmings* which explicitly responds to Stein's poems about shoes, umbrellas, shawls, and handkerchiefs. Stein plays with these "female" objects to critique the ways in which they are involved in perceptions of gender and sexuality, teasing us with an association between female fashion accessories, diminutiveness, and nubility: "the least thing means a little flower and a big delay a big delay that makes more nurses than little women really little women."[17] A belated sexual awakening, Stein seems to suggest, may endanger a woman's chances of becoming a conventional wife ("really little women") but give her opportunities to become something else, such as a "nurse," which here might imply not servitude, but size and power.

The gloves in Mullen's poem "Tender" also seem to belong to "little women"; they are, punningly, "slight hand" and "a dainty", however, they are also like skin: some are white, some an off-white tan, and some are "black leather, second skin." The poem suggests, "Tight is tender, softness cured. Alive and warm, some animal hides. Ghosts wear fingers."[18] This is delicate, sensual, and erotic – but the (possibly) sexist implication that "softness" needs to be "cured" also suggests meat and thus animality, a racist trope historically used to "justify" the slave trade. This trope is emphasised in the double meaning of "some animal hides." The fact that "ghosts wear fingers" hints at something both haunted and disturbingly racist ("ghosts" may refer both to white people with their white hoods and to a pejorative term for black people).

However, whilst Mullen's deconstructions may go into intersectional areas far beyond Stein's, she emphasises that her use of "playful, punning, fragmented language" is a direct response to Stein's work: "I share her love of puns, her interest in the stuff of life, and her synthesis of innovative poetics with cultural critique."[19] What I am keen to highlight here is Mullen's explicit "recycling" of Stein's innovative poetics which, I suggest, make use of some of the particular characteristics of prose poetry.

One of these characteristics is prose poetry's tendency towards "dialogism," applying Bakhtin's discourse theory of dialogism – that is, of a multi-voiced text which is constructed in relationship with another's words.[20] Critics Jonathan Monroe and Margueritte Murphy have both applied a "Bakhtinian" approach to prose poetry and to Stein's work, arguing that her subversive use of these food and fashion discourses is "dialogic," working to keep surface meanings in play while simultaneously undercutting them or rendering them absurd.[21] In particular, the "tenderness" of Stein's buttons for Murphy is that they can simultaneously mimic and undo the very discourses they inhabit. Mullen explains in *Recyclopedia* how she is attempting something similar in her project to "recycle and reconfigure language from a public sphere that includes mass media and political discourse."[22] Stein's, and later Mullen's, love of the pun, irony, parody, and various kinds of "semantic or representational subversion" are examples of Bakhtin's "hidden polemic" in which "discourse is directed toward an ordinary referential object, naming it, portraying, expressing, and only indirectly striking a blow at the other's discourse, clashing with it, as it were, within the object itself."[23] This observation describes vividly what we see in both Stein and Mullen.

In "Breakfast," Stein plays with the reader's knowledge of what is likely to be found on an American–European breakfast table and the alternative frames of reference within which these words take on other meanings. She asks, "What is a loving tongue and pepper and more fish than there is when tears many tears are necessary," her move between culinary and psychological registers hinging on the pun "loving tongue" (*tongue* as cured meat as well as body part) so that "pepper" and "fish" hint a psycho-sexual struggle playing out within the cultural expectations attached to the breakfast meal.[24] In her poem "Tender," Mullen barely strays outside the linguistic boundaries of the marketing of gloves as a fashion or work accessory, but the wordplay of her ironic description "fits like a love" alerts the reader to the disruptive play of meanings within every short phrase of the poem.[25]

This leads to one of the central propositions of this study, that this duality or dialogism in Stein and Mullen's work is achieved primarily through their use of the prose poetry form. In the introduction to her recent book *British Prose Poetry,* Jane Monson suggests that there is an element of dialogism inherent in the form when she says,

> it is important to understand that the prose poem does not just cross literary boundaries, and neither is it simply a meeting between one genre and the next; it is a dialogue between a host of other disciplines and polarities.[26]

Paul Hetherington and Cassandra Atherton also draw attention to the way prose poetry "allows for the heterogeneous and heteroglossic."[27] Heteroglossia here refers to the ability of a literary text to include a plurality of voices and viewpoints. It is prose poetry's tendency to keep in play a variety of discourses, and thus multiple frames of reference, which makes it such a pertinent form for poets such as Stein and Mullen as they orchestrate their ironic play of meanings. Murphy is even more explicit, arguing that Stein's "subversive dialogism" propels her towards the choice of prose poetry as an inherently dialogic form. Although she is referring explicitly to Stein, this analysis applies equally to Mullen. Murphy suggests that prose poetry situates itself as poetry primarily by maintaining an ironic distance from those other prose discourses from which it borrows a rhetoric, a lexicon, and a register. She argues that "each prose poem is situated in a unique nexus of representative prose genres, absorbing and contesting them."[28] This resonates with poet-theorist Ron Silliman's contention that in prose poetry, poetic form has moved into the interior of prose, proposing it is the "torquing" of dialogism which activates prose into poetry.[29] The radical triumph of prose poetry is for Murphy located in the subtlety with which a poet such as Stein can keep the dialogism unresolved and in active play, orchestrating the echoes and tones of a subversive food and fashion discourse into a "polysemous discourse of great complexity."[30]

Such polysemy is equally apparent in Mullen. Her "handkerchief" poem "Hand in glove hankers" piles pun on top of cliché to keep alive the flirtatious language of advertising whilst signalling its complicity in maintaining race and gender stereotypes. The poem proclaims "Hand in glove hankers, waves a white flag. Hand to mouth surrenders, flirts with hanky panky."[31] The waving flag of the poem stakes a claim to white privilege whilst it faces the necessity of surrender. "Hand to mouth" suggests both this necessity and also a duplicity which reemerges as "hanky panky."

Whilst a tendency towards polysemy might be characteristic of all prose poetry, the deployment of the commonplace (the "prosaic") by the prose poetry of food and fashion makes apparent the particular play of tone and nuance achievable in this form. Another Stein food poem exemplifies this notion. Could there be anything more apparently bland and prosaic than writing about "pastry"? But Stein's poem of that title, whilst only a few words, can be read in many ways simultaneously: "Cutting shade, cool spades and little last beds, make violet when."[32] Is this a recipe for pastry, enlarging the domestic activity into a magnified act of digging and cutting? Is it gardening advice? The register partakes of both kinds of discourse but is neither, both gently mocking and utilising such language. The "cutting shade" and "cool spades" seem related more by rhyme and alliteration than sense, unless the "little last beds" are read as graves – and then they become gravediggers' tools. Domestic activity is subtly aligned with digging one's own tomb. But is it sweetened with violets, or is this the violet of the shade, or even of bruises? The polysemy of the word here makes it impossible to pin down its referent. Poignant, subtle, full of hints and echoes, this poem activates every part of language within it. It absorbs the instructional tone of domestic discourse ("make violet") and its paratactic freedom ("cutting shade, cool spades") whilst contesting its deadening and claustrophobic constriction ("little last beds") by leaving it open-ended. The unfinished gesture of the rhetoric "make violet when" leaves the poem ungrounded and incomplete (or open-ended), all its elements floating in a loose association away from their possible place in a conventional domestic discourse.

The proposition that prose poetry is a dialogic form suggests that Baudelaire's poem "Soup and Clouds" is doing more than the ironic juxtaposition that Sorrell claims. Is there something more contested within the words themselves? Something more polysemous in its play of tones? Perhaps there is an unresolved dialogism at work here. There is a subtle but intense tonal play in Baudelaire's poem, heard in the self-mockery of the dreamer even before he is disturbed, and in the pile-up of ironies in his girlfriend's suggestion that he should try selling his "clouds," lending the material properties of the domestic realm to the immaterial world of the poet's imagination in order that they might earn money and provide the necessities of life such as the "soup" she is putting on the table. The poem refuses to resolve these ironies, acknowledging perhaps the poet's vacillation between the perfect but ephemeral imagined poems and the imperfect, fully realised poems which are debased as commodities. This is a debasement eroticised by the husky, wasted voice seducing the poet.[33] The poem remains uncertain, neither "soup" nor "clouds," but both simultaneously. Returning to Baudelaire's poem in the light of Stein and Mullen's heteroglossia, "Soup and Clouds" now seems to exemplify the capacity of prose poetry to orchestrate multiple registers and tones.

What enables this heterogeneity, I suggest, is prose poetry's access to the linguistic structures of both prose and poetry. This is made apparent by the way both Stein and Mullen exploit the form's duality to free themselves from the structural constraints of traditional grammar in order to develop new, open-ended linguistic structures that keep their dialogism and polysemy in play.

Stein is, of course, well known for her linguistic experimentation. Critics such as Marianne DeKoven, Lyn Hejinian, and Barbara Will have all drawn attention to the importance of Stein's experimentation with a "lively," interactive grammar.[34] For Will, Stein's decentred and fluid grammar, which demands active reader involvement in the construction of meaning, is fundamental to her notion of "genius." Will argues that Stein comes increasingly to take a radical view of genius as a capacity engendered in the reader by the interactive demands of the text, a capacity for "a decentred and dialogic, open-ended and collective mode of 'being'" triggered by the grammatical and linguistic demands of the text.[35] Of particular relevance here are Stein's experiments with "deixis," those aspects of grammar which establish the spatial and temporal co-ordinates of a piece of writing, such as pronouns, tenses, temporal and spatial adverbs, and prepositions. In conventional deixis, these co-ordinates tend to be organised around one subjectivity or a single "deictic centre."[36] This is the "canonical" deictic situation described by theorists such as Karl Bühler and John Lyons.[37] In her experimental grammar, Stein departs from this "subjective" or "egocentric" orientation of conventional deixis, decentring it in order to engage the reader in a deictic *activity* of orienting, placing, and adjusting.

Stein's poem "A Long Dress" demonstrates this idea dramatically. In my discussion of this poem above, it is clear that the dress is presented neither solely from the inside nor from the outside; rather, we are presented with multiple perspectives simultaneously. These multiple perspectives are made possible, in part, by the lack of any grounding pronouns in the poem. The poem's viewpoint(s) are not attached to any one perception or person. If we examine this poem's deictics further, it becomes apparent that its spatial and temporal coordinates are also left ungrounded and open. The poem poses the question "Where is the serene length" and replies with the deictic declaration "it is there." But where? We are given no anchor for this deictic. It seems that "there" is referring only to a positioning within the written text itself. This "impossible" inside/outside garment is only perceivable as it comes into being in language and is subject to the reader's active engagement with the text.

Stein's deixis works here as an additional strategy for keeping the poem, and indeed the garment, fluid and multiple. It is perhaps not surprising that the poet who declares, "Act so that there is no use in a centre" experiments with unmooring her deixis from its centre.[38] In another of her *Tender Buttons* poems, "A Method of a Cloak," the lack of deictic markers forces the reader to interrogate the grammar to locate its co-ordinates, only to find that the deictic centre and its "field" seems to expand in widening concentric circles to move the frame of reference so that, as with "A Long Dress," we seem to see the cloak from many perspectives, inside and outside. I quote this short poem in full:

A METHOD OF A CLOAK

A single climb to a line, a straight exchange to a cane, a desperate adventure and courage and a clock, all of this which is a system, which has feeling, which has resignation and success, all makes an attractive black silver.[39]

The "single climb to a line" seems to be an external view, whereas "an attractive black silver" could be referring to the surface or the lining of the cloak, another inside/outside conflation. There are no clear deictic directions to help us establish the point or points of view from which the cloak is being depicted, nor are there explicit temporal or spatial coordinates to ground the viewing. Instead, the poem situates the garment within various "systems," commercial, social, metaphorical, and metonymic. There is some kind of sexual/social/economic exchange hinted at in "a straight exchange to a cane," whilst, within a figurative use of language, the cloak might be a metaphor for "adventure" or metonymically (the hero's cape) represent "courage." The deictic openness of the poem allows the cloak to be unfolded like a Cubist painting in which all perspectives are presented simultaneously. And, of course, it also supports the ironic layers of meaning around the making and status of a fashion item we have already seen interrogated by *Tender Buttons'* dialogism.

Stein is experimenting here with the grammatical deixis conventionally associated with prose and prose literacy, illustrating Stephen Fredman's argument that one of the defining characteristics of prose poetry is the way that it "contends" with the conventions of prose, particularly its "embedded" deixis, by which deictic coordinates are established within a mutual grounding of discourses within a text.[40] However, the prose poetry form, with its dual allegiance to prose and poetry, allows Stein not only to experiment with the conventions of prose but also with those of poetry. And poetry has its own deictic conventions. This has been demonstrated convincingly by prose historiographers Jeffrey Kittay and Wlad

Godzich, and, more recently, by poet Denise Riley and critic Heather H. Yeung.[41] Yeung teases out this idea in her book *Spatial Engagement with Poetry*. For her, poetic deixis is rooted in the complex materiality of poetry.[42] Grammatical or prose deixis, such as Stein experiments with in the poems discussed above, draws on a poem's qualities as a written artifact. However, poetry also has aural and visual qualities, and Yeung points out that these can act as a "poetic deixis" grounding the poem back within the reader's own body. It is clear that Stein draws on this kind of deixis in *Tender Buttons,* exploiting in particular the "aural" aspect of her poetry. Many of the poems rely on sonic similarities to create connections between words or phrases. The poem "Apple," for example, starts "Apple plum, carpet steak, seed clam, colored wine, calm seen, cold cream, best shake, potato, potato and no no gold work with pet."[43] There is not much help here from conventional grammar. This isn't even a simple list as it develops into the repetition of "potato" and the declaration "no no gold work with pet." There are no grammatical deictic markers to enable us to establish spatio-temporal coordinates, nor to be confident about the relationship of these items to each other, or indeed to us. What Stein gives us is an intense play of sonic effects to create a network of connections between these words: the alliteration on the letter "c," the rhymes of "calm seen/ cold cream," "steak/shake," "potato/no," the sound echoes of "plum/calm/cream," etc. Connections and relationships are established at a bodily or sensory level through the visual and aural patterning of the words. The semantic co-ordinates of the textual elements may be impossible to pin down, but the language carries sonic and visual "meaning" beyond the semantic, and the deixis of these "meanings" orients them to the body performing or reading the text.

Stein's experimentation with deixis, then, is multiple: the open-ended nature of her prose deixis working with a poetic deixis that points the reader back to the body. Stein thus exploits the prose poem's linguistic allegiance to both prose and poetry, fusing and radicalising the grammar conventions of both to support her liberation of the domestic. The Stein prose poem engages the reader in a new and active remaking of domestic items, a refashioning in which the body and the intellect are given equal authority in making new connections and reperceiving the world. Albert Spaulding Cook has commented that Stein's experimental deixis not only engages the reader in dynamic deictic activity but also forces us into a "renegotiation" of our position in relation to the text at almost every sentence.[44] This constant grammatical renegotiation, involving us in repositioning, reevaluating, and reestablishing connections, is the underpinning of Stein's "lively" domestic world in which no "thing" is fixed, including those categories of gender and sexual identity conventionally associated with the domestic realm.

Harryette Mullen "recycles" Stein's deictic experiments to make a new grammar of her own. In her article, "Enclosure and Run: The Fugitive Recyclopedia of Harryette Mullen's Writing," Robin Tremblay-McGaw points out Mullen's interest in Ron Silliman's deictic experimentation – but of course Stein is a common source for both Silliman and Mullen.[45]

Trimmings offers a particularly pertinent comparison with *Tender Buttons*. Some of the poems in *Trimmings* seem to follow Stein's lead and dispense with deictic markers altogether. "Tender," discussed above, insists it "Fits like a love, an utter other uttered," but leaves us wondering whom does it fit? And what exactly is "it"?[46] Elsewhere, Mullen presents us with the elusive scatter of "Night moon star sun down gown"[47] or the strange mystery of "Body on fire, spangles."[48] We are given no grammatical indication of situation or person. Other poems in *Trimmings* initially appear to be organised around a pronoun – usually a she or her – but then the deixis shifts to leave its coordinates ambiguous. "Becoming," the first poem in the book, starts with "such a small waist" which appears to refer to a "her" wrapped around with a snake-like belt: "Becoming, for a song. A belt becomes such a small waist. Snakes around her, wrapping. Add waist to any figure."[49] A few lines later, the poem appears to confirm this, telling us that the cinched belt "Sucks her in." However, whether "she" refers to one specific she or her is made ambiguous by the generic "Add waist to any figure."

This ambiguity is further hinted at through the poem's reliance on indefinite articles. The specific belt becomes any belt, the waist any waist. The verb "snakes" can no longer be attached with any certainty to a belt, and perhaps belongs with "becoming," the construction of self. The openness of the grammar allows a poem, which initially appeared to be about a fashion item, to widen out into an exploration of the role of fashion and advertising in the construction of identity. And any belief we might have in a solid, organised, material world loses its stable coordinates, becoming loose and available for reorganisation by the reader. In "Becoming," even the sentences become slippery. A sentence that appeared to express conventional approval of a trim waist ("A belt becomes such a small waist") could be read as the belt itself *becoming* the small waist. And "Sucks her in" might not be referring to the corseting of the belt, but to the dangerous seduction of advertising and fashion rhetoric to which she submits or "buckles." This short poem unravels into multiple possible readings.

Moreover, as this poem demonstrates, what emerges from this deictic looseness is a slippage between garments and the body itself, the belt "becoming" the waist it encircles. In many of Mullen's poems, body parts and items of clothing seem to float in a strange assemblage, the open deixis of the poems leaving it unclear where items are in relation to each other.[50] In "Swan neck," for example, the female body and its adornments hover together, the face disconnected from its body: "Swan neck, white shoulders, lumps of fat. A woman's face above it all."[51] The disassembling of the body empties out its secrets and leaves an inhuman "bust" that is nevertheless politically significant, perhaps, in its whiteness; it is "paled into significance," the poem tells us. This is one of a number of poems in *Trimmings* in which Mullen seems to question whether the body is just wearing these clothes or is actually constructed from them, a commodity fashioned out of an assemblage of accessories. In poem after poem in *Trimmings,* the female body appears disaggregated, a mere collection of parts, suggesting the alienating impact of its commodification. A chilling example is "Harmless amulets arm little limbs with poise and charm."[52] This one-line poem is possibly about bracelets, but reads more as if we are opening a drawer of dismembered doll parts in a toy factory. The absence of deictic markers keeps us guessing to whom these "little limbs" belong, and we are unable to co-ordinate them into a coherent body.[53]

The fluidity of this deixis is reinforced by the intense punning which Mullen uses to elide further the female body and its clothes. In her poem "Cinderella highball cocktail frock," Cinderella hobbles home in a "lame dress," a pun playing between the ideas of lamé material and becoming lame.[54] The body is again shaped – or deformed – by its garments. It is a commodity formed by its clothes, the boundary between them increasingly unclear. Mullen's rendering of the body as a permeable territory, its "borders on edges where skin stops or begins,"[55] is both witty and profoundly disturbing.

Mullen's use of advertising and commercial register throughout these poems suggests there are commercial forces driving this "shaping" with a violence that threatens to dismantle the female body altogether. "Opens up a little leg" combines fluid deixis with puns on "tart," "gash," and "slashed" to hint at a conflation between the commodification of the female body and the violence of an assumed ownership that ensues: "Buy another peek experience," the poem puns, the "price is slashed."[56]

However, Mullen goes further than Stein in her interrogations of socially constructed categories of being. Her poems are not just about femaleness but address a racialised femaleness. Many of the poems in *Trimmings* are about a whiteness (or a rosy-white pinkness) that is constructed by linguistic and social forces in the text. "Girls in white" (white dresses? white skins?) is a recurring phrase throughout *Trimmings* and is associated with a particular socio-economic power. In "What's holding her up," the "girls in white" are affluent and leisured, they are "laced up, frilled to the bone."[57] Again, there is a brutality associated with this power, hints of gun violence in "Semi-automatic ruffle on a semi-formal gown." This is not only a socio-economic violence but a racial aggression. Mullen explains, in an interview quoted by Deborah Mix, "As a black woman writing this language, I suppose I already had an ironic relationship to [Stein's] pink and white femininity."[58] Mix emphasises how Stein's critique acts as a starting point for Mullen's more overtly political deconstructions.[59] Although Mullen recycles some of Stein's strategies for interrogating domestic female space and consumer fetishism, she develops them into a powerful, intersectional critique of her own.

Blackness, when it surfaces in Mullen's poems, is "othered," appearing as a shadow, or just glimpsed in the tears and gaps opened up in and around whiteness. Discussing Mullen's article, "Optic White: Blackness and the Production of Whiteness," Tremblay-McGaw reminds us that for Mullen, "the racial category of whiteness is predicated on the black."[60] In Mullen's poem "A light white disgraceful sugar," white and pink are only "pale" compared to a "shadow" which is situated "behind her."[61] If femaleness is produced as a commodity, *white* femaleness is constructed out of the exploitation of a blackness which is used as its foil. In another poem, blackness is described ironically as a "pearl" (also the name Pearl) constructed from tears and "a salted wound": "A mother's luster manufactured a colored other," Mullen tells us, "Pearl had a mother who cried."[62]

Like Stein, Mullen doesn't just experiment with the grammar of prose; she also mines the poetic conventions available to a writer of prose poetry. She too deploys the sonic effects of language to amplify the non-logical web of connections created by her puns and word play. In "Some panties are plenty. Some are scanty," for example, the "scant/scanty" pun is amplified by repetitions, the rhyme with "panties" and the alliteration and play of panties/plenty, plenty/scanty.[63] These sonic effects support a poetic deixis which emphasises the materiality of language and its relationship with an embodied reading of the poem. Juliana Spahr reminds us that, in Mullen's combination of grammatical and sonic play, readers are "invited to be constantly shifting locations, constantly struggling with a sampled and punned language, to talk back and to talk with."[64]

This ability to find a language to "talk back with" is crucial for Mullen. Some of her poems emphasise that, despite the perils of entering language and its constructions of race and gender, there are also dangers in silence. The final poem of "Trimmings," for example, crystallises the danger of naivety about the role of language in constructing the body: the "she" of this poem thinks she can retreat from language and becomes "veiled in silence."[65] But this is not an escape-route from the world's constructions but rather renders it more vulnerable to projection, exploitation, and colonisation: "A veiled, unavailable body makes an available space," Mullen tells us. Rather than silence, Mullen chooses the work of an active subversion of language, working through it to activate its gaps, overlaps, wrinkles, and obvious seams. Like Stein, she draws on the grammar and linguistic conventions of both prose and poetry, available in the prose poem, to expose the flux and malleability of language, grounding the reader not in the stability of conventional syntax and deixis, but in their own embodied reading experience. For Mullen, as for Stein, the multiplicity of the prose poetry form thus offers particularly rich strategies for subverting and remaking language.

It is, then, the linguistic plurality of the prose poetry form, drawing on the tones, registers, grammars, and conventions of both prose and poetry, that makes it such a rich form for writers such as Stein and Mullen, writers for whom linguistic experimentation is intrinsically linked with subverting those social, racial, and sexual constructs associated with the advertising and commodification of the domestic. Of course, they are writing from very different contexts, and Mullen's poetics are more overtly rooted in race and gender concerns than Stein's mainly language-based poetics. However, both Stein and Mullen exploit a dialogism inherent in the prose poem to orchestrate a complex interplay of discourses and frames of reference. Both keep this dialogism open and unresolved by experimenting with a decentred, multiple deixis. This radical deixis is made possible by prose poetry's divided tap root which draws on the traditions and literacies of both poetry and prose. Stein and Mullen develop the tonal polysemy of Baudelaire's form to engage the reader in an active reconstruction of domestic discourses whilst also exposing the linguistic basis for the distinctive characteristics and potentiality of the prose poetry form.

Notes

1 Harryette Mullen, "Trimmings," in *Recyclopedia: Trimmings, S*PeRM**K*T, and Muse & Drudge* (St. Paul, MN: Greywolf Press, 2006), 29.
2 Charles Baudelaire, *Paris Spleen,* trans. Martin Sorrell (London: Alma Classics, 2010), 88.
3 Sorrell, "Introduction," *Paris Spleen,* viii.
4 Gertrude Stein, *The Autobiography of Alice Toklas* (London: Penguin, 2001), 130.
5 Mullen, *Recyclopedia,* vii.
6 Mia You, "Sublime Deformations of Nature," *Poetry Foundation,* 4 April 2017, www.poetryfoundation.org/harriet-books/2017/04/sublime-deformations-of-nature.
7 Mullen, *Recyclopedia,* 1.
8 In the discourse theories of Mikhail Bakhtin, a dialogic discourse is one that engages with and is informed by other, sometimes contradictory discourses.
9 Margueritte S. Murphy, *A Tradition of Subversion: The Prose Poem in English from Wilde to Ashbery* (Amherst, MA: University of Massachusetts Press, 1992), 149.
10 Gertrude Stein, *Tender Buttons* (Mineola, NY: Dover Publications, 1997), 8. (Note: the edition used is an unabridged version of first edition.)
11 John Berger, *Ways of Seeing* (London: Penguin, 1972). The phrase "male gaze" was first coined by scholar and filmmaker Laura Mulvey, "Visual Pleasure and Narrative Cinema," *Screen* 16, no. 3 (October 1975): 6–18.
12 Gertrude Stein, "Breakfast," in *Tender Buttons,* 27–8.
13 Deborah Mix, *Vocabulary of Thinking: Gertrude Stein and Contemporary North American Women's Innovative Writing* (Iowa City, IA: University of Iowa Press, 2007), 4.
14 Harryette Mullen, "Interview with Harryette Mullen," interview by Cynthia Hogue, *Postmodern Culture* 9, no. 2 (January 1999).
15 Mullen, *Recyclopedia,* x.
16 Mix, *Vocabulary of Thinking,* 4.
17 Gertrude Stein, "Coloured Hats," in *Tender Buttons,* 14.
18 Mullen, *Recyclopedia,* 5. Please note that none of the poems in *Recyclopedia* are titled by Mullen but for ease of reference, I have adopted the first word/phrase of each poem as a working title here.
19 Mullen, *Recyclopedia,* x.
20 Bakhtin first introduced the concept of dialogism in his essay "The Dialogic Imagination" (1975), but continued to develop it throughout his writings.
21 Murphy, *Tradition of Subversion;* Jonathan Monroe, *A Poverty of Objects: The Prose Poem and the Politics of Genre* (Ithaca, NY: Cornell University Press, 1987).
22 Mullen, *Recyclopedia,* x.
23 Mikhail Bakhtin, *Problems of Dostoevsky's Politics* (Minneapolis, MN: University of Minnesota Press, 1963), cited in Murphy, *A Tradition of Subversion,* 157.
24 Stein, *Tender Buttons,* 26.
25 Mullen, *Recyclopedia,* 5.

26 Jane Monson, ed. *British Prose Poetry: The Poems Without Lines* (Cham, CH: Palgrave Macmillan, 2018), 11.

27 Paul Hetherington and Cassandra Atherton, eds. *Prose Poetry: An Introduction* (Princeton, NJ: Princeton University Press, 2020), 10.

28 Murphy, *A Tradition of Subversion*, 165.

29 Ron Silliman, *The New Sentence* (Berkeley, CA: Roof Press, 1987), 89.

30 Murphy, *A Tradition of Subversion,* 165.

31 Mullen, *Recylopedia*, 56.

32 Gertrude Stein, "Pastry," in *Tender Buttons*, 35.

33 The girlfriend's voice is described as "charming, raw … hysterical and brandy damaged." Baudelaire, *Paris Spleen,* 88.

34 Marianne DeKoven, *A Different Language* (Madison, WI: University of Wisconsin Press, 1983); Lyn Hejinian, *The Language of Inquiry* (Berkeley, CA: University of California Press, 2000); Barbara Will, *Gertrude Stein, Modernism and the Problem of "Genius"* (Edinburgh: Edinburgh University Press, 2000).

35 Will, *Problem of "Genius,"* 1.

36 The "deictic centre" might be understood as the anchor point of an utterance or text, enabling the listener or reader to make sense of relative spatial and temporal terms such as "here," "there," "now," "then," etc.

37 Karl Bühler, *Theory of Language*, trans. Donald Fraser Goodwin and Achim Eschbach (Amsterdam: John Benjamins, 1982); John Lyons, *Semantics*, Vol. 2 (Cambridge: Cambridge University Press, 1977).

38 Gertrude Stein, "Rooms," in *Tender Buttons*, 43.

39 Gertrude Stein, "A Method of a Cloak," in *Tender Buttons,* 6.

40 Stephen Fredman, *Poet's Prose: The Crisis in American Verse* (Cambridge: Cambridge University Press, 1983), 3. Fredman bases his argument on Jeffrey Kittay and Wlad Godzich's historiographic study of the development of prose and its authority derived from an "embedded" writing-based deixis as opposed to the "embodied," performance-based deixis of poetry. Jeffrey Kittay and Wlad Godzich, *The Emergence of Prose: An Essay in Prosaics* (Minneapolis, MN: University of Minnesota Press, 1987).

41 Kittay and Godzich, *The Emergence of Prose*; Denise Riley, *Words of Selves: Identification, Solidarity, Irony* (Stanford, CA: Stanford University Press, 2000); Heather H. Yeung, *Spatial Engagement with Poetry* (New York: Palgrave Macmillan, 2015), 44.

42 Yeung, *Spatial Engagement with Poetry*, 7.

43 Gertrude Stein, "Apple," in *Tender Buttons,* 30.

44 Albert Spaulding Cook, *Forces in Modern and Postmodern Poetry*, ed. Peter Baker (New York: Peter Lang, 2008), 20.

45 Robin Tremblay-McGaw, "Enclosure and Run: The Fugitive Recyclopedia of Harryette Mullen's Writing," *Multi-Ethnic Poetics* 35, no. 2 (2010): 71–94.

46 Mullen, *Recyclopedia,* 5.

47 Mullen, *Recyclopedia,* 19.

48 Mullen, *Recyclopedia,* 37.

49 Mullen, *Recyclopedia,* 3.

50 This resonates with sculptor Louise Bourgeois's hanging mobiles of female garments, hangers, and lumps of bone.

51 Mullen, *Recyclopedia,* 50.

52 Mullen, *Recyclopedia,* 42.

53 This image of the dismembered doll is explored in greater depth in Alison Benis White's prose poetry collection *Small Porcelain Head* (New York: Four Way Books, 2013).

54 Mullen, *Recyclopedia*, 38.

55 Mullen, *Recyclopedia*, 29.

56 Mullen, *Recyclopedia*, 49.

57 Mullen, *Recyclopedia*, 34.

58 Mix quotes this 1999 interview with Mullen in Deborah Mix, "Tender Revisions: Harryette Mullen's Trimmings and S*PeRM**K*T," *American Literature* 77, no. 1 (2005): 65.

59 Mix, *Vocabulary of Thinking*, 4.

60 Harryette Mullen, "Optic White: Blackness and the Production of Whiteness," *Diacritics* 24, no. 2/3 (Summer–Autumn 1994): 71–89, quoted in Tremblay-McGaw, "Enclosure and Run," 73.

61 Mullen, *Recyclopedia*, 11.

62 Mullen, *Recyclopedia*, 60.

63 Mullen, *Recyclopedia*, 23.

64 Juliana Spahr, *Everybody's Autonomy: Connective Reading and Collective Identity* (Tuscaloosa, AL: University of Alabama Press, 2001), 117.

65 Mullen, *Recyclopedia*, 62.

6

THE CONTEMPORARY VERNACULAR

Exploring Intersections of Architecture and Prose Poetry

Anne Caldwell

> The idea of a room becomes a moor; intimacy is as wide as a meadow. Alice doesn't know this place, or what she even understands by place. The pathway she finds leads back to the room. The room opens out and she finds herself next to a river.[1]

In this chapter, I aim to demonstrate how, from a multidisciplinary perspective, prose poetry can be used to develop a richer understanding of place by exploring connections between poetry and architecture, and to consider why prose poetry in particular benefits from being critically examined through this lens. I consider what features of the form can be exploited to help represent place/space within my own creative work, exploring the idea of braiding and use of the vernacular. This examination leads to a discussion on the form's characteristics of intertextuality, allusion, and compression, which are seen as key attributes of prose poetry by Paul Hetherington and Cassandra Atherton. To this end, I highlight examples from my poetry collection, *Alice and the North,* that demonstrate how my creative practice has been shaped by this enquiry, particularly in the light of reading Gaston Bachelard's *The Poetics of Space*.

My prose poetry collection *Alice and the North* seeks to celebrate, in a literary context, what I have termed the "contemporary vernacular." This term comes from new movements within the field of architecture and is used to describe buildings that utilise materials from their locality in a sustainable way to enhance a sense of community or regional identity.[2] The term resonates with my own thinking about place, space, and writing, which has a strong environmental context. This approach provided a useful focus to consider the similarities between architecture and poetry and to consider where these disciplines might intersect. The "contemporary vernacular" is a term that could be seen to combine a Modernist

DOI: 10.4324/9781003199533-7

architectural tradition, as proposed by Le Corbusier, and an appreciation of how the vernacular could inform a contemporary design that is environmentally sensitive. In this chapter, I will demonstrate that the concept of the contemporary vernacular can be used in a writing context to understand a sense of place and enable a writer to have what Brenda Miller (2001) has described as a "braided" conversation with the environment.[3] With its emphasis on environmental issues and ecology, I also investigate the idea of the contemporary vernacular in order to bolster my own framework of eco-poetics and therefore position my creative practice in a wider theoretical context.

Alice and the North is a sequence of prose poems that forms a love song to the North of England and is linked by the character of Alice who shifts and changes as she journeys through this landscape and beyond. I have used the lens of architecture in my creative process to shape an understanding of the urban and rural environments through which she travels. The fertile ground between the two art forms was the focus of a conference in London at The Courtauld Institute in 2011. As the conference introduction states:

> Poetry and architecture, brought together by Gaston Bachelard in his seminal investigation of lived-in space, are art-forms that nevertheless continue critically to be considered broadly apart from one another. The one concrete and three-dimensional, the other abstract and metaphorical, these two creative art-forms invite further comparison.[4]

Ian Seed's observations on prose poetry also chimed with my interests: "Each prose poem is like a little block … like houses all the same on the surface, but if you go behind the walls, the doors, and the windows, each house will have its own world."[5] His definition of prose poetry is clearly seen in architectural terms here. I took his metaphor and linked it to the notion of the "contemporary vernacular" when examining my own writing about place. The North has a venerable tradition of vernacular buildings that can be traced right back to Neolithic practices.

I first turned to the dictionary definition of "vernacular" to begin an investigation into the relationship between language and building design. *The Merriam Webster Dictionary* defines the word in these terms, as "using a language or dialect native to a region or country rather than a literary, cultured, or foreign language; of, relating to, or being the common building style of a period or place."[6] Here, we find the idea that the languages and architecture of a region are clearly interrelated, with the former being an expression of voice and the latter being an expression of its built environment and traditions. Delving a little deeper, within the field of sociolinguistics, we discover that the term "vernacular" is freighted with connotations of class, race, and level of education. As George Yule notes, "It is usually native, mostly spoken informally rather than written and usually seen as of a lower status than more codified forms."[7] A similar perspective informed the way that architects used to view vernacular buildings, namely, as being of less worth than professionally designed ones.

However, since the Arts and Crafts Movement (1880–1920), architects have begun to see the vernacular as worthy of more interest, and as I began to draft my own writing, I was curious to see how this focus could inform the way my work was shaped. As a result, I began to explore ways of honing my use of voice more carefully. I started by incorporating speech patterns, family sayings, and personal memories in the prose poetry form, as may be seen, for instance, in the following example:

> Her mother sterilises Kilner jars in the oven, purses her lips. She fills a larder with the summer's glut, slow-cooks meringue, brittle with resentment and love. *It can all happen in an instant*, she says, darkly. Alice has some idea of what this meant.[8]

I used a mix of fictional and autobiographical material from Congleton in the 1970s in this prose poem. This approach proved to be a rich imaginative seam that brought to life my own particular sense of place and "northernness," thereby placing the reader in a particular time frame and location which arises out of my childhood memories.

A similar interest in the specific use of place and time can be found in the way building design developed in the early twentieth century. Modernist vernacular architecture can be traced back to Frank Lloyd Wright, who coined the term "Organic Architecture" in the 1930s, seeing it as involving an "interpretation of nature's principles manifested in buildings that were in harmony with the world around them."[9] As the Guggenheim Museum website goes on to note, "Wright held that a building should be a product of its place and its time, intimately connected to a particular moment and site—never the result of an imposed style."[10] Wright's design for Fallingwater (1936–1939, Mill Run, Pennsylvania), for example, was radical in its site-specific approach, incorporating an existing waterfall into the building itself.

Currently, I see this notion of "organic" vernacular undergoing a renaissance in the art forms of both poetry and architecture, particularly in relation to new environmental movements. In her 2016 work, *Contemporary Vernacular Design: How British Housing Can Rediscover Its Soul*, Clare Nash highlights architecture across the UK and Europe that draws on vernacular principles but uses modern-day environmental building methods and adheres to eco-energy requirements.[11] For example, her principles can be seen in Assemble's regeneration of Granby Street in Liverpool, which includes an indoor winter garden and creative spaces for residents, and which won the Turner Prize in 2015.

Nash's definition of the contemporary vernacular was useful when I came to explore the links between architectural design and prose poetry, and led to a richer understanding of the relationship between language and place in relation to the North. The concept informed the shaping of my collection of prose poems as a whole. In the process of writing, I conceived the prose poems as a series of building blocks that would come together to form a complete, multidimensional structure. The poems can be seen to inhabit an organic, vernacular form of literary construction, located within its own psychogeographic boundaries.

Within the book-length structure of *Alice and the North*, I have explored the ways in which an intimate engagement with the North's geology, flora, fauna, and built environment can enable a writer to engage in a "braided" conversation involving place, history, and culture, revealing new strata that move away from more stereotypical ways of conceiving the region. Brenda Miller coins this idea, in relation to the lyric essay, when she talks about her writing process having "a sense of weaving about it, of interruption and continuation," like the braiding of bread, or of hair: "I had to keep my eye on the single strands that came in and out of focus, filaments that glinted differently depending on where they had been. At the same time, I had to keep my eye focused on the single image that held them all together."[12] She goes on to say that this approach allowed her essays, though still personal, "to expand more outward, taking on myriad facts and stories of the outer world as well as the inner."[13] I decided to investigate this idea within the framework of a prose poem, through the notion of a braided conversation with the vernacular and other language registers. I wanted to show how, in linguistic terms, this process could involve the interweaving of local idioms and idiolect, in this case associated with the North. However (and more crucially), it does not just involve bygone phrases: it is a conversation that is continually being recreated in a modern, playful way that deepens my own relationship to place. Simon Armitage has touched on this association between language and place, observing that his writing is another way of returning home:

> Living in Britain is an incredibly intense linguistic experience, and a lot of that relates closely to geography: your accent, your dialect, your background, your class. Many poems are expressions of that, even subconsciously. At some level I knew my vocabulary was a product of my landscape.[14]

His vernacular poetic voice is characteristically masculine in its blunt tone and often occurs in dialogue with a father figure. Armitage recognises the influence of Ted Hughes in his work and observes how "his poetry woke me up, not just to poetry, but fundamentally … because he came from the next valley. The house where he grew up looks almost identical to the house I grew up in."[15] Two key questions emerged in relation to my own poetics. First, was it possible to explore a northern contemporary vernacular that inhabited a territory beyond the voices of these two dominant, male poets and was more female in tone? Second, could I create a prose poetry sequence that drew on the language of the Brontës and Dorothy Wordsworth as much as William Wordsworth or Ted Hughes?

I agree with Armitage that a writer's vocabulary is partly the product of geography, but I was interested in taking a different approach to "northernness" in my own work, particularly as I see place in more fluid terms, and not just related to the idea of home. I began to explore how a feminist voice might characterise my prose poetry by the invention of a shape-shifting persona called "Alice," who, as stated earlier, ties the collection together and is not only transformed but also liberated as the work progresses and she starts to find her own, adult voice. As I drafted the collection's opening poems, such as "Ferns and Voles,"[16] Alice emerged as a Lewis Carroll character, looking in the mirror to discover her sense of identity: "Alice doesn't have a looking glass but there's a full-length mirror in her mother's room and a cat that refuses to smile. She's five and the world's full of wonder."[17] Carroll's Alice changes in shape and size as she tries the "Drink Me" bottle in order to fully explore Wonderland. My Alice is sometimes a child, sometimes a giantess, or longing for "a tea party or a game of croquet with flamingos."[18] This fluid sense of identity allows her to shift between landscapes that are both real and imaginary, thus deepening an understanding of the idea of the North. Carroll was chosen carefully as a source of inspiration. Bryan Talbot has celebrated Carroll's connections with the North in his graphic novel, *Alice in Sunderland* (2007).[19] His work interweaves the history of the city (and Britain) with myth, autobiography and scholarship on the work of Carroll. Talbot suggests that the northern city of Sunderland is the setting for the buried roots of Carroll's surreal masterpiece rather than the southern city of Oxford, which usually claims to be the inspiration for his writing. Bearing this notion in mind, I saw the potential of using Alice as a persona who could uncover the untold stories of the North and places that have been marginalised.

The Poet Laureates Armitage and Hughes are regarded as canonical figures in poetry and have a more established relationship to the landscapes of the North of England than Carroll. They have proved to be major influences on my work in the past. But I wanted to explore the North with fresh eyes and discover alternative ways of creatively imagining a sense of place. I therefore found it productive to turn to other branches of the arts, such as architecture, to explore how a creative person could take a familiar source of inspiration and make it her own. I also decided to write a full-length book of prose poetry for the first time, and this proved to be a fruitful line of enquiry as it enabled me to step outside the dominant confines of poetic literary tradition. The idea of stepping into another realm, just as Alice goes "through the looking-glass" and starts to see the world in a different light, was very appealing. Through the persona of Alice, I intended to create space for a more feminist language register to imagine the North. This process mirrored the notion of investigating the fruitful space between architecture and poetry. The enquiry enabled me to edit my work with a three-dimensional understanding of what the language of a prose poem could achieve, particularly when it came to exploring image and metaphor, which I will discuss later in this chapter.

Prose poetry in particular benefits from being critically explored through the lens of architectural theory, because of the cross-genre nature of the form itself that has been developing without the burden of a longer, formal tradition. The form does have its own cultural history, which Jeremy Noel-Tod traces back to Baudelaire, but his observation that neglected prose poets "comprise an alternative history of modern poetry, and an experimental tradition that is shaping its future"[20] is especially relevant to my exploration of "the contemporary vernacular." Like Clare Nash, to whom I have referred in the opening section of this chapter, Randall Thomas and Trevor Garnham argue that contemporary vernacular design can take inspiration from the natural world, striving to produce buildings that are not only carbon neutral but also produce their own energy. As Thomas and Garnham put it, "vernacular buildings were passive modifiers of the environment, whereas new technologies – in particular photovoltaic cells that convert solar energy into electricity – invite buildings to be active participants."[21] Thus, their definition suggests the methodology of looking both ways: back into an architectural tradition, and forward towards new ecological and sustainable building techniques.

As I noted earlier, my own writing does not just involve the longing for home that Armitage recognises, and a sense of fitting into a literary tradition; rather, it also looks to experiment, going beyond the established northern canon of writers. Through the medium of prose poetry, I wanted to be open to new possibilities in writing and had a desire to reinvigorate the traditional "building blocks" of both poetry and prose, as well as querying the supposed divide between them. I thought the form could offer the writer a way of doing both at the same time. The creation of the feminist persona of Alice became the voice in which I challenged the northern canon of writers such as Armitage and Hughes and presented alternative ways of perceiving the notion of the North, especially ones that recognised it as a region in flux. In my prose poetry sequence, Alice reflects on the literary traditions of the North but is also trying to find her own unique voice as a writer, mirroring the concerns of many contemporary architects in their design process.

I found this insight also influenced the way I began to handle time frames within my collection. My prose poems shift in and out of personal memory, present-day experience, and digital and future time frames, often juxtaposing them in one poem:

> And maybe the way forward is this unexpected winter sun and the cat asleep on her kitchen table; maybe the way forward is a kettle humming and peppermint tea, pale as longing in a cup; maybe forwards is all those Facebook good wishes, like kisses. And maybe it's an iPad with a broken screen that she can't afford to fix, but still works.[22]

Paul Munden recognises the concept of time operating in these fluid terms in my poem "Rust and Nettles," observing that "its twin prose-poetry consciousness [is] articulating flux, approaching time from multiple angles all within a very brief narrative that seems almost conventional in its telling."[23] As well as clarifying how time might operate in my work (and its intersection with space), the idea of looking backwards and forwards was emerging as an important way of interrogating the concept of "the contemporary vernacular." However, this notion might suggest a linear time frame wherein the vernacular was firmly rooted in the past, whereas I envisaged a vernacular use of language in poetry that was a non-linear, living, breathing process, one that was continually evolving.

This evolvement can be seen in the work of a poet like Patience Agbabi, who makes a pertinent observation about her own use of vernacular language in her reworking of *The Canterbury Tales*, commenting on how she "hoped to retain an earthiness and an otherness, that standard English would tame."[24] I see Agbabi as updating and re-purposing this iconic work for a modern audience. For example, the use of non-standard, Nigerian English for the character of the "Wife of Bafa" gives the voice its liveliness and power:

> My name is Mrs Alice Ebi Bafa
> I come from Nigeria.
> I'm very fine, isn't it?
> My nex' birthday, I'll be … twenty-nine.
> I'm business woman.
> Would you like to buy some cloth?
> I've all de latest styles from Lagos.[25]

Whilst re-drafting *Alice and the North*, I also wanted to retain this sense of a continual reinvention of language, to deploy the vernacular as sitting upon centuries of past usage; in short, I wanted to use the North as a palimpsest. This is where links with vernacular architecture are most strong, as I came to see that my own writing practice was an attempt at emulating the way that buildings are designed with a view to their provenance: their intimate, layered relationship with the local community and its ecological frame of reference, created over many years.

This approach seemed to provide a useful route into reflecting on writing about place within the form of the prose poem, for that form is one that is itself open, fluid, and amorphous, thus more receptive to such reinvention. It is a form that can accommodate the innovative juxtaposition of language registers, genres, and the use of palimpsestic techniques. I therefore experimented with this notion in drafting the following prose poem, "Sheep's Clothing," by taking the idea of place as both real and literary in nature. I began to build up the poem in layers, in a way similar to the creative process of constructing a building. The final draft drew on a range of adult and child-like language registers, alluding to *Alice's Adventures in Wonderland,* "Hansel and Gretel" and "Little Red Riding Hood" as my sense of place thickened and deepened:

A felled elm tree spreads out like a body on the ground before her with all its bare roots showing. Her father's music is scattered to the four winds. More storms roll in. She hears the words *Dutch elm disease* on the radio for the first time and senses the trees disappearing like old friends from the hedgerows.

Alice thinks of a huntsman out in the woods beyond Congleton Edge. She pictures a dark well somewhere in the Peak District. Would she drown in her own tears? Pools are brimming with ducks, dodos, a Lory and Eaglet.

She dreams of a wolf in sheep's clothing. She doesn't know what that means. But she knows about gingerbread houses. She knows you have to stick a chicken bone instead of a finger towards the grinning witch. She knows that much.

Will silence break into song? Things will never be the same again as she scatters bits of bread along the path and listens for a chaffinch or a blackbird or a coal-tit. Wind-blown nests and broken eggs are an arpeggio she practises in her head.[26]

In this prose poem, even the trees become characters, pictured as friends laid out across a field. Alice's sense of self is deeply entwined with her ever-changing environment, and I realised I could use this as a theme in the collection. The use of music and song adds to our understanding of the place being in flux, foreshadowing the environmental disasters to come. This sense of fluidity is also discussed by Hetherington and Atherton, who see "indeterminacy" as a key characteristic of the prose poetry form and trace its history back to the Romantic fragment:

> Prose poems are frequently characterised as fragmentary or incomplete in the way that they gesture to a larger, often unnamed frame of reference; present small, sometimes unfinished narratives, which are implied to be part of larger narrative structures; and are often characterised by considerable indeterminacy.[27]

By exploring prose poetry's flexibility, with its relative lack of a fixed, literary tradition, I have sought to re-invigorate my use of language and understanding of place and space. Like Anne Carson in her collection *Short Talks*, I was experimenting with writing small, contained rectangles of prose poetry and had begun to consider how this process is similar to the way a contemporary architect might design the rooms of a house in the vernacular tradition. My poem "Winter," for example, plays with the vernacular, re-inventing it for a contemporary audience, as this opening section shows:

This house been far out to sea all night
Ted Hughes, Wind.

Alice became Medusa – she was a line of Heptonstall venom, she was The Craggs spitting, hitting her house through all the fire and felt and flags.

Hair hissed Alice through the mullions, wind solid as stone walls. The roof
hurried inside, the Velux window turned to salt or was bent into a Lowry
figure. Hold on. She'd no coal. No outhouse nor barbecue with that promise
of a summer-filled bowl. Magpies chattered across the gimmer in their ash-
buzzard dive.[28]

The word "gimmer" is an old Yorkshire term for a ewe in between its first and
second shearing. The term gestures towards the county's rich sheep-farming
heritage and rural past, which formed a cornerstone of its pre-industrial identity. I am interested in the way that fragments of this identity linger in dialects,
so I have taken the word and modified it to suggest an imaginative passageway,
hinting at another vernacular northern term for an alley – a ginnel – which has
a similar sonic quality. The word "gimmer" was chosen because it encourages a
reader to take stock. For many readers, it might simply be an unfamiliar word but,
for others, it is a term that has been deliberately de-familiarised by being used in
a different context; some readers, indeed, might well confuse it with the more
familiar "ginnel." Similarly, while the magpies have been observed diving through
the landscape of ash trees, the latter have also been linked with buzzards, suggesting
the coinage "ash-buzzard," with its connotations of a predator lurking within this
copse. There is also a building mentioned in this poem, which features traditional
vernacular elements: "mullions," "stone walls," and an "outhouse." Yet, despite its
established qualities, the house itself is under siege, attacked by Hughes's strong
Yorkshire "wind," as the epigraph makes plain. For the wind is not merely literal: it
also operates as a metaphor for Alice's fury and anger. (Within the sequence as a
whole, Alice questions an older patriarchal tradition and, in particular, the North
of England's masculine stereotypes.) The layout of the poem tries to reproduce
this sense of bottled-up energy, suggesting, through its justified margins, that the
feeling of rage is caged up in a room.

It could be argued that the prose poem form itself gestures to a world beyond
this rectangle, by using intertextuality. Although this technique is a feature of all
writing, Hetherington and Atherton's own work in the prose poetry field frequently makes use of it. They regard it as a key feature of the form:

> A conscious intertextuality is a powerful tool for writers of very short forms,
> such as prose poems, because of its capacity to carry across meaning from a
> wide variety of other and more extended sources. It is a shorthand way of
> involving and transferring large ideas and wide frames of reference.[29]

This is partly achieved in my own work through the use of dialect words, as
detailed above, but also as a result of an imagined conversation with Hughes.
In the second paragraph, my prose poem further develops this idea: "Ted, she
thought, you'd scoff at drones, bombs and the Lycra men cycling." A wider sense of
northern identity and place is in flux. The location in West Yorkshire has become

gentrified. Once a mill village, producing the Victorian cloth fustian, it is now a tourist destination for, amongst others, "Lycra-clad cyclists," and it is a home for "incomers."

This sense of "northernness" in a period of social change, or in opposition to a dominant South, is a particular characteristic of the writing of Tony Harrison. His focus is on class distinctions, perhaps most explicitly in his poem "Them and [uz]," where he highlights the vigour of his northern idiolect and the way it was frowned upon by a teacher who describes Harrison as one of Shakespeare's comic characters, destined to speak prose rather than the language of "kings" – i.e. poetry.[30] There is a sophisticated narrative voice at work throughout this poem, one that can easily move between the world of classical references, Received Pronunciation, and a particular type of northern vernacular. A strong sense of place comes through the use of voice in a poem. The injustices, slights, disappointments, and what is left unsaid can lie just beneath the stories we tell ourselves about place, home, and belonging. Harrison's palimpsestic voice reveals an anxiety about straddling the two language registers, and I found I could relate to this sense of class injustice in his poetic voice, as I have had a career of 20 years in community arts/literature, working with the marginalised communities of Rochdale, Oldham, and Salford. But Harrison's work has a different tone to my own writing. There is more belligerence and gruffness in his work, more use of monosyllabic words; and, perhaps because of his masculine voice, I do not feel part of the "uz" he chooses to focus on.

I came from a different region of the North of England to Harrison and lost access to a local, northern dialect very early in my education. Like many writers, I have since travelled extensively and do not see myself as rooted in one community. The idea of place/home is therefore more complicated and palimpsestic. However, like Harrison, my local dialect was "bred" out of me by an education system which favoured Received Pronunciation as a way to "better oneself." Received Pronunciation enjoyed high prestige in the Britain of my youth, being thought of as the "southern accent of those with power, money, and influence."[31] Younger contemporary British poets like Liz Berry, based in the Black Country, have a more enlightened view:

> Choosing to write poems using dialect is like finding a locked box full of treasure. You know there's all sorts of magical things inside, you just have to find the key that will let you in. So put down your notebook, close your laptop, and start listening to the voices around you. For this is the way in, the place where the strongest dialect poetry starts: a voice you can hear.[32]

Berry, whom I also see operating within a contemporary vernacular framework, makes a direct link between a rediscovery of vernacular language and a stronger connection to a sense of place. She describes it as being like an archaeological process, like digging up her own Staffordshire Hoard of gold, with words, sounds, and phrases "glinting out of the muck,"[33] and out of the Black Country dialect spoken by people around her.

I considered whether this same process could be enacted in prose poetry and whether it resonated with my own writing methods. I have so little vernacular left within my own lexicon, but the notion of archaeology is very pertinent. When writing, I was looking for a few traces of long-forgotten dialect or sound rhythms and found them in the use of place names, speech patterns, and inflexions, as in my poem "City Short Cut":

> Alice and her cat set off for bread and milk, jaywalking through Manchester. Cars shave past on Princess Parkway, the tabby cat bristles, sensing the hot screech of rubber, but not tonight, not tonight.
>
> Alice buys cheap bread, pulls out slice after slice and tearing away crusts, rolling the sugary dough into balls, she slips them into her mouth. Remembers the feel of her best friend's skin. They were giggly on liquorice and Ribena, stroking each other in the hot gloom of the wardrobe.
>
> The cat growls and grins. Dreams of milk and silkiness on her tongue, a full belly, a gas fire spitting. She stares into the saucer of the moon. The cat begins to vanish.[34]

Alice is clearly located within the city of Manchester in this prose poem, but she is also situated in a parallel, dreamlike world with its grinning "Cheshire Cat" and her own "wardrobe" of childhood memories. The poem draws on Lewis Carroll's techniques of surrealism and play to juxtapose a real city and an imaginary one in close proximity. The writing is working with a number of language registers and compressed time frames. The use of repetition – "not tonight, not tonight," and "slice after slice" – mirrors the movement of her "jaywalking" across the city, and the rhythm of everyday, colloquial speech. My final sentence takes the reader back to Carroll and reflects a thematic strand that I exploit throughout the sequence. For example, at the end of the collection, I compare the idea of the North to an imaginary "Wonderland." Thus, Alice's North is somewhere that can be seen afresh, through poetry, with a child-like sense of delight. It is a place of re-enchantment.

This sense of enchantment also operates in the work of the Shetland-based poet, Jen Hadfield. She is also a writer who sees her North with a sense of wonder, but she has a slightly different approach to Liz Berry, and her techniques were ones I wished to emulate. Hadfield talks about how the Shetland dialect is "flitting" through her collection *Nigh-No-Place*.[35] Hadfield observes in the notes to her collection that she has taken inspiration from *The Shetland Dictionary*.[36] She suggests the position of prose poet as witness to the natural world through her close, observational style. I was inspired by this notion of dialect "flitting" through Hadfield's writing and used snippets of speech from Alice's family members in my work. I wanted a similar lightness of touch. For example, in the prose poem, "Nidderdale," Alice remembers this northern proverb: "Her father would have remarked, *it's raining stair rods, lass,* or *raining cats and dogs.*"[37] As noted earlier, the idea of "the contemporary vernacular" within architecture carries strong connotations of environmental awareness, and an ecological approach to building and design. This could be seen to mirror the way contemporary poets, such as Hadfield, have also risen to the challenge of considering how we are part of the more-than-human world, not separate from it:

> Two important traces of vernacular architecture can be resources for con-
> temporary architecture: the deep respect and perfect communion with the
> natural environment and the perfect relation and understanding of users'
> needs. The result of a complex balance between material, shape and natural
> context, vernacular architecture could become an extremely useful model
> of inspiration for the present.[38]

Inspired by Hadfield and other eco-poets' attention to ecology and attention to detail, in my own prose poetry collection, I considered the places where I have felt a strong emotional connection and understanding of the flora and fauna. I have therefore homed in on small, neglected towns in the North of England as well as overlooked parts of cities. I grew up in an all-female house-hold, in Congleton in Cheshire, and its semi-rural stories rarely feature in the more well-known narrative of the North as a region of industrial decline. My adolescence was instrumental in developing my identity as a writer who considers fleeting moments; what might be hidden in voices of quiet desper-ation, the secrets of family life and the interior world of women in particular. Andrew Forster, who provided a back-cover blurb for my last poetry collection, *Painting the Spiral Staircase,* remarked that, "for a poet who thinks maybe I'll just walk/out of my body altogether, these are poems of softly, intense, physical feeling. She takes the little moments of our lives and reinhabits them, making them resonate for us."[39] In order to create this resonance in *Alice and the North,* I decided to write from the body, rather than step "out of my body altogether," through a methodology that involved walking, photographing, and writing.[40] By walking, I have examined the in-between places – the hinterlands, county boundaries, and rural way markers of the North – to deepen my understanding of "northernness" and identity. I was inspired by Paul Farley and Michael Symmons Roberts' work, *Edgelands,* in my choice of focus, which features many hidden landscapes of the North. They visualise "edgelands" as a new "wilderness," between urban and rural, a debateable zone in a state of continual reinvention and ripe for poetic enquiry:

> The idea of edgelands does not just refer to parts of the physical environ-
> ment. It's a rich term for poetry too and can maybe help to break down
> other dualities. Poets have always been attracted to the overlooked, the
> telling details, the captured moment.[41]

Although I write about a wider set of locations in *Alice and the North* than those featured in Farley and Symmons Roberts' work, their reflections chimed with my notion of the contemporary North in a state of flux, difficult to define or pin down, and still characterised by outdated notions of its identity. Five of the prose poems in the first section of my sequence trace the possible borders of the North of England, including the county boundary of Staffordshire and the coastlines of Lancashire and East Yorkshire. Furthermore, my understanding of the geography of the North and how this shapes identity has come into sharper focus by mapping its pathways and littoral edges.

My prose poems reveal hidden stories of the North that exist beyond its urban centres and often focus on women's cultural histories. For example, in drafting the poem "Kippers," I focused on the village of Craster to see whether it could offer a microcosm of the identity of the North as a region, as opposed to other communities that have been dominated by homogenised housebuilding and identikit chains of businesses and shops.[42] Craster once thrived on herring fishing and has now lost this industrial function. Whilst fishing is still important, its main focus today is tourism and heritage, and a process of gentrification is taking place that I have already discussed in relation to the West Yorkshire villages known to Hughes. Craster's vernacular architecture is part of its status as the most northern "Area of Outstanding Natural Beauty."[43] The village is also at risk from climate change because of coastal erosion and flooding. The kippering of herrings once gave the coast of the North of England its identity, being one of the main sources of employment, especially for women, who gutted the fish. Now there is only one business remaining, L. Robson and Sons in Craster, which uses one-hundred-year-old smokehouses. Here is the first part of my poem, "Kippers" based on this location:

> These fishbones. They fill Alice's kitchen with the memory of the shore-line and the taste of kelp and salt. The memory of herring quines and kists. Some stick in the throat, or spread themselves out on her plate, sending her choking and running for the phone to dial 999. Some bones are so sweet she spends a Saturday making a fish bone and feather necklace to wear to a party. She sails out across the street in a blue silk dress and calfskin slippers.[44]

In my prose poem, the image of "fishbones" becomes a metaphor for memory, for the vernacular history of the village ("quines" and "kists") and its changing sense of northernness. Craster is the setting for early love, and is somewhere to preserve, in order to try to keep this memory alive. The metaphor of fishbones also carries connotations of choking and the painful nature of looking back into the past. The subject matter of this prose poem cuts through the idea of sentimentality or nostalgia for a previous time. Gutting fish may have emancipated the women who did it, allowing them to travel and giving them independence, but it was also a very harsh way of life. Salt cut into their fingers, and their hands were so lacerated that they would be wrapped in makeshift bandages. The prose poem form gestures towards this wider cultural history but leaves it implicit because of its slipperiness, use of allusion, and ability to move between the public and private spheres.

Whilst re-drafting this poem, I decided that, in order to mirror the collection's central theme, Alice needed to undergo a transformation. Alice becomes a boat, sailing out across the street. She is a fairy tale-like creature in silk and slippers. No Prince Charming is waiting. Alice is wearing a "fish bone and feather necklace," appropriating the signifiers of labour which could be metonymic for swathes of the North of England. Alice has also become a feminist character who can "free-wheel" or drive herself headlong towards the sea if she wants to do so. Through the writing of this piece, I was able to hint at this sense of a feminine, northern identity that escapes the shackles of the past in a nuanced way and forms the narrative backbone for the sequence as a whole. Her northern identity is also shaped by a growing awareness of the fragility of the North of England's edges and borders. Through the persona of Alice, my prose poems draw on contemporary eco-poetics, highlighting the environmental fragility of the North's coastlines. In the poem, "Spurn Point, Eastern Border," Alice observes: "If the planet continues to warm, this place will be a snake's tongue, swallowing itself once more."[45] A need for the return to a harmonious connection with the environment emerged as an underlying subtext in my exploration of the mutable borders of the North and the notion of a northern identity in flux. The process of redrafting my work made this subtext more apparent.

This insight introduced another poetic and architectural crossover. A deeper understanding of vernacular design and spatial characteristics could inform my enquiry. For example, Garnham and Thomas explore how, in the past, indigenous buildings were harmoniously suited to their particular landscape, such as igloos in the Arctic and stone houses in Orkney. They suggest that contemporary eco-architects can learn from this approach to design, arguing that "like plants and animals, a building must adapt itself to its habitat" and look to biology and indigenous cultures to inform superior contemporary design.[46]

How might these principles apply to poetry? The work of Bachelard provided a key. Garnham and Thomas echo the ideas of Bachelard, who observed that "man is laid in the cradle of the house," which is "the human being's first world."[47] Bachelard discusses how certain kinds of spaces – their shape, size, arrangement, and structure – resonate with the full depth of the developed psyche and allow for "well-being."[48] He clearly links the idea of the poetic image and principles of good design, citing poets' memories or dreams of built spaces that have significance and conjure up images of shelter or protection: "great images have both a history and a pre-history … every great image has an unfathomable oneiric depth to which the personal past adds space and colour."[49] When re-drafting my prose poetry sequence, I tried to bear in mind these ideas, envisaging it as an architectural, three-dimensional construct, using key images of buildings, stones, and place names as through-lines and extended metaphors.

Furthermore, Bachelard demonstrates how the metaphor of the cave and the hut recur in literature, illustrating our deep psychological need for shelter. For example, he talks of how Thoreau built his hut in the Walden woods in an attempt to reconnect with the essential roots of America. Was I trying, through the writing process, to reconnect with the roots of my "childhood" North? As part of the research process for my collection, I began to draft some starting points for prose poems to help me explore my personal history in the context of reading Bachelard. As the following extracts from drafts of two of my poems show, I attempted to focus on the significance of constructing a childhood den as well as engaging in a critical/creative conversation with Bachelard's theoretical ideas:

> When Bachelard talked of nests and shells, he spoke to our bodies, rather than brains, our instinctive need to curl up, safe from turbulence; our desire to shelter from the cyclones that life hurls when we are up on the moors without a coat, a flask of tea or a pair of good strong boots.

> I remember the warmth of my father's forearm, the bass-clef comfort of having him close as we listened to Bach on Sunday afternoons. Rain streaked down the conservatory glass and peach-coloured roses hung their heads in the borders. I built a den in the disused garage from a table, three blankets and a muffle of old coats. My skin smelt of wood-dust. I remember a canopy made of brooms and garden canes, spiders scuttling across a concrete floor. The disturbing delight of my sister's ghost-tales.[50]

I pictured the den in these drafts as both a physical setting for storytelling and as a portal for the imagination. One could argue that the prose poem is itself den-like, performing this function of containment, but the notion of a portal or TARDIS captures the open-ended nature of the form better. Creating an image such as this is like a psychic short-cut: a way of reconnecting with something lurking in the unconscious or the forgotten parts of the psyche. This notion of containment is developed by Hetherington and Atherton, who see "compression" as a characteristic of the prose poetry form:

> Prose poetry tempers the features of traditional poetry and prose in order to conjure ramifying and verbally suggestive tropes where unfolding narratives are present but largely implicit, and the condensations of poetry are able to fall naturally into paragraphs rather than truncations of poetic lineation. In this way, prose poems frequently open up, TARDIS-like, to reveal much more than their actual size on the page would appear to allow.[51]

Conclusion

Just as I have found Alice's North impossible to define in singular terms, I would also argue that there is no single version of a northern contemporary vernacular. I have discovered so many variations within the North of England (and its poetry) and see the region as more of a container of different versions of non-standard English that are changing all the time, in response to immigration, urbanisation, and our digital lives. But, by exploring the notion of the contemporary vernacular within architecture, my understanding of place and space has come into sharper focus. As a prose poet, I have examined the need to look not just forwards and backwards, but also laterally, to situate my poetry within the canons of contemporary writing. These insights provided the initial themes for the development of my poetics, helping me draw together key features of contemporary architecture and prose poetry and articulate how my persona operates within a prose poetry sequence.

Furthermore, I began to see the prose poem metaphorically in three dimensions, as an architectural space. The form has the potential to act as a series of passageways and doorways, or a container for intertextuality, allusion, and fragments of stories. I have discussed how *Alice and the North* can be pictured as a construct, where each poem can act as a building block and has an interrelationship with the whole. My collection gestures outwards to wider narratives of the North that lie beyond its boundaries, and the brevity and compression of the prose poetry form is suited to this notion. The process of drafting my work has taken inspiration from new developments in eco-architecture, where a complex balance between the material shape of a building and its natural context has become a guiding principle. Just as one can envisage a building as a dynamic process of recycling, weathering, and renewal, a prose poem can also be a space in flux, where a braided conversation between identity, the natural world, and the built environment can take place.

Bachelard believed we were heading towards a "bungalow" age (where there is limited access to space for our imaginations and dreams) and that we needed to reimagine the spaces that have special resonance for the psyche, such as cellars and attics.[52] I am hoping that my prose poems will create similar resonances for readers, deepening and thickening their awareness of place through the richness of the linguistic possibilities that the prose poem has to offer.

Notes

1 Anne Caldwell, "Storm Brewing," in *Alice and the North* (Scarborough, UK: Valley Press 2020), 19.

2 Maria Philokyprou, Aimilios Michael, Eleni Malaktou, and Andreas Savvidies, "Environmentally Responsive Design in Eastern Mediterranean. The Case of Vernacular Architecture in the Coastal Lowlands and Mountainous Regions of Cyprus," *Building and Environment* 111 (January 2017), 91.

3 Brenda Miller, "A Braided Heart, Shaping the Lyric Essay," in *Writing Creative Nonfiction: Instruction and Insights from the Teachers of the Associated Writing Programs*, ed. Philip Gerard and Carolyn Forché (Cincinnati, OH: Story Press, 2001), 41.

4 Ayla Lepine and Caroline Levitt, "Intersections: Architecture and Poetry (London, 3–4 June 2011)," *ArtHist.net*, 5 May 2011, https://arthist.net/archive/1337.

5 Ian Seed, interview by Ian McMillan, "New Towns," *The Verb*, BBC Radio 3, March 2016, quoted in Jane Monson, ed. *British Prose Poetry: The Poems Without Lines* (Cham, CH: Palgrave Macmillan, 2018), 8.

6 "Vernacular," *Merriam-Webster.com Dictionary*, Merriam-Webster, accessed 9 October 2021, www.merriam-webster.com/dictionary/vernacular.

7 George Yule, *The Study of Language*, 6th Edition (Cambridge: Cambridge University Press, 2016), 5.

8 Caldwell, *Alice and the North,* 14.

9 "Organic Architecture," Solomon R. Guggenheim Museum Teaching Materials, accessed 9 October 2021, www.guggenheim.org/teaching-materials/the-architecture-of-the-solomon-r-guggenheim-museum/organic-architecture.

10 "Organic Architecture."

11 Clare Nash, *Contemporary Vernacular Design: How British Housing Can Rediscover Its Soul* (Newcastle-upon-Tyne: RIBA Publishing, 2016).

12 Miller, "A Braided Heart," 48.

13 Miller, "A Braided Heart," 50.

14 Simon Armitage, "A Life in Writing: Simon Armitage," interview by Sarah Crown, *The Guardian*, 9 December 2011, www.theguardian.com/culture/2011/dec/09/life-in-writing-simon-armitage.

15 Simon Armitage, "Interview with Simon Armitage," interview by Lisa Allardice, *The Guardian*, 7 June 2019, www.theguardian.com/books/2019/jun/07/simon-armitage-poet-laureate-ted-hughes-came-from-the-next-valley.

16 Caldwell, *Alice and the North*, 12.

17 Caldwell, *Alice and the North,* 12.

18 Caldwell, *Alice and the North,* 24.

19 Bryan Talbot, *Alice in Sunderland* (Milwaukie, OR: Dark Horse Books, 2007).

20 Jeremy Noel-Tod, ed. *Penguin Book of the Prose Poem: From Baudelaire to Anne Carson.* (London: Penguin, 2018), xix.

21 Trevor Garnham and Randall Thomas, *The Environments of Architecture: Environmental Design in Context* (London: Taylor and Francis, 2007), 7.

22 Caldwell, *Alice and the North,* 26.

23 Paul Munden, "Playing with Time: Prose Poetry and the Elastic Moment." *TEXT Special Issue 46, Beyond the Line: Contemporary Prose Poetry* (October 2017): 12.

24 Patience Agbabi, "The Wife of Bafa – Analysis," *Writers on Writing*, accessed 9 October 2021, www.transculturalwriting.com/radiophonics/contents/writersonwriting/patienceagbabi/thewifeofbafa-analysis/index.html.

25 Patience Agbabi, "The Wife of Bafa," *Telling Tales* (Edinburgh: Canongate, 2015), 31.

26 Caldwell, *Alice and the North*, 18.

27 Paul Hetherington and Cassandra Atherton, "Like a Porcupine or Hedgehog? The Prose Poem as Post-Romantic Fragment," *Creative Approaches to Research* 9, no. 1 (2016), 19–38.

28 Caldwell, *Alice and the North*, 42.

29 Paul Hetherington and Cassandra Atherton, eds. *Prose Poetry: An Introduction* (Princeton, NJ: Princeton University Press, 2020), 187.

30 Tony Harrison, "Them and [uz]," in Tony Harrison, *Selected Poems* (London: Penguin, 1979), 122.

31 David Crystal, "Language and Time: RP and Its Successors," *BBC*, 29 October 2014, www.bbc.co.uk/voices/yourvoice/feature2_4.shtml.

32 Liz Berry, "Using Dialect in Poetry," *The Poetry School*, 2016, https://poetryschool.com/assets/uploads/2016/01/Liz-Berry-Using-Dialect-in-Poetry.pdf.

33 Berry, "Using Dialect in Poetry."

34 Anne Caldwell, "City Short Cut." An earlier version of this prose poem was published in *Slug Language* (Fife, UK: Happenstance, 2008), 28.

35 Jen Hadfield, *Nigh-No-Place* (Tarset, UK: Bloodaxe Books, 2008), 64.

36 John Graham, ed., *The Shetland Dictionary*, 3rd edition (Lerwick, UK: Shetland Times, 1993).

37 Caldwell, *Alice and the North*, 36

38 Emil Creangă, Iuliana Ciotoiu, Dragoş Gheorghiu, and George Nash, "Vernacular Architecture as a Model for Contemporary Design," in *Eco-Architecture III*, ed. Santiago Hernández (Southampton, UK: WIT Press, 2010), 157.

39 Anne Caldwell, *Painting the Spiral Staircase* (Cardiff: Cinnamon Press, 2016), back cover notes.

40 Caldwell, *Painting the Spiral Staircase*, 37.

41 Paul Farley and Michael Symmons Roberts, *Edgelands, Journeys Into England's True Wilderness* (London: Jonathan Cape, 2011), 6.

42 Caldwell, *Alice and the North*, 56.

43 Northumberland County Council, *Northumberland Coast AONB Management Plan*, accessed 9 October 2021, www.northumberlandcoastaonb.org/management-plan/.

44 Caldwell, *Alice and the North*, 56.

45 Caldwell, *Alice and the North*, 23.

46 Garnham and Thomas, *The Environments of Architecture*, 7.

47 Gaston Bachelard, *The Poetics of Space*, trans. Maria Jolas (Boston, MA: Beacon Press, 1994), 7.

48 Bachelard, *The Poetics of Space*, 7.

49 Bachelard, *The Poetics of Space*, 33.

50 Caldwell, early drafts of prose poems. Some of these ideas were incorporated into "Ferns and Voles," *Alice and the North*, 12.

51 Paul Hetherington and Cassandra Atherton, "'Unconscionable Mystification'? Rooms, Spaces and the Prose Poem," *New Writing* 12, no. 3 (2016): 279.

52 Bachelard, *The Poetics of Space*, 33.

7

"IMAGE MACHINE"

Gaspar Orozco's *Book of the Peony* and the Prose Poem Sequence as Perceptual Trick

Helen Tookey

In this chapter, I shall focus on the prose poetry collection *Book of the Peony* by the Mexican writer Gaspar Orozco, translated by Mark Weiss, and published with the Spanish and English in facing-page translation by Shearsman Books in 2017. In the first part of the chapter, I shall explore my own reader-response to the book, in particular the way in which it struck me as acting like an "image machine," to borrow a term from Charles Simic.[1] I shall consider what aspects of this book in particular, and then the prose poem sequence more generally, contribute to this effect. By way of comparison, I shall also look more briefly at Orozco's previous collection of prose poetry, *Autocinema*. In conclusion, I will suggest that – much like that other classically modernist form of representation, the cinema – the prose poem (and the prose poem sequence) can be understood as a fundamentally paradoxical form that plays a kind of perceptual trick on the reader.

Reading *Book of the Peony*

Book of the Peony could be described as a book-length sequence of prose poems, divided into two numbered parts: there are 22 poems in Part 1 and 19 in Part 2. (It could therefore also be considered as containing two sequences, but the topic – the peony – is the same in both.) In the Shearsman edition, the Spanish text of each poem is printed on the left-hand page and the English translation on the facing right-hand page, in short text blocks justified left and right (see Figure 7.1). I shall return later in the chapter to the question of layout and typography, because it is relevant to the ways in which we as readers – or, we might say, viewers – respond to the poems. The whole book, as the title suggests, is structured around the idea, or the image, of "the peony," which is explored in various aspects and takes on a number of symbolic roles or forms.

DOI: 10.4324/9781003199533-8

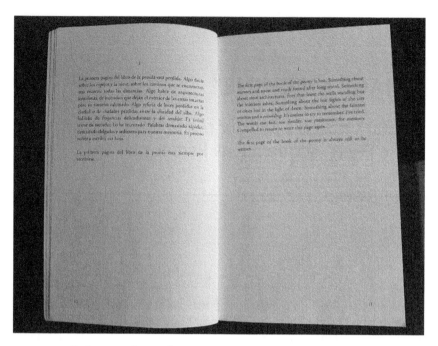

FIGURE 7.1 Facing-page layout from *Book of the Peony*, reproduced by permission of Shearsman Books

I discovered the book through Shearsman's website (I was not familiar with any of Gaspar Orozco's previous work) and found it extremely compelling. As a writer of poems, including prose poems, I was interested in trying to analyse what exactly I found so engaging about the book, and in thinking about this, I realised there were two things that it reminded me of. The first was Joseph Cornell's assemblages in boxes, which (like many people) I also find compelling; I shall return to Cornell, and expand on this connection, later in the chapter. The second, perhaps more unlikely, association was with an object from my childhood, or rather with my memory of this object: a small plastic souvenir that my grandmother brought back as a present for me from a trip to Liechtenstein in the late 1970s, when I was perhaps eight or nine years old.

The object is moulded in the shape of an alpine chalet and is an example of the "viewmaster" type of image-display toy popular in the 1970s. Inside, there is a circular plastic disc with tiny reproductions of photographs of Liechtenstein tourist attractions, which you as the viewer click through by pressing the chimney. My sister and I loved the way this gadget simultaneously mimicked both an alpine chalet and a camera, like a spy camera pretending to be something else. We were also puzzled and amused by the fact that almost all the images were captioned "Something Vaduz" or "Vaduz Something" – Vaduz Gardens, Castle Vaduz, Palace Vaduz, and so on. This created the impression in our minds that there was really only one thing in Liechtenstein – "Vaduz" – which presented itself in many different aspects. I mention this because I think it partly accounts for the association in my mind between *Book of the Peony*, when I first read it, and the memory of this viewfinder toy.

For me as a reader, the experience of reading *Book of the Peony* felt similar to that of clicking through a sequence of images; the book as a whole seemed to me to work similarly to a magic lantern or a slide projector. And although I initially thought this was perhaps an odd response, I realised quite quickly that it fitted very well with the wider context of prose poetry. For example, David Lehman quotes Martha Kinney, with reference to Rimbaud's *Illuminations*, describing "the prose poem as a lantern, an illuminated container, casting images and phrases needed but barely understood."[2] In his preface to his translations of *Illuminations*, John Ashbery describes the book as being "like a disordered collection of magic lantern slides"[3] – and of course the title *Illuminations* already suggests something along those lines. I shall consider below some of the specific elements of the prose poem, and particularly the prose poem sequence, that might serve to enable that effect. First, though, I want to look in more detail at *Book of the Peony*, and how Orozco uses the idea or the image of the peony.

"The Endless Enigma Locked in That Flower"[4]

The first poem, as we might expect, establishes a number of the key tropes in the book:

> The first page of the book of the peony is lost. Something about mirrors and snow and roads found after long travel. Something about slow architectures, fires that leave the walls standing but the interiors ashes. Something about the lost lights of the city or cities lost in the light of dawn. Something about the faintest aromas and a *trembling*. It's useless to try to remember. I've tried. The words too fast, too slender, too passionate, for memory. Compelled to return to write this page again.
>
> The first page of the book of the peony is always still to be written.[5]

The text sets up from the beginning the idea of a circular structure or process (so already something like the carousel of a slide projector). We feel from the outset that we are held, perhaps trapped, within a cyclical, endless process, that when we get to the end we will be compelled to return to the beginning – along with the writer/speaker, who is "compelled to return to write this page again." There is also the sense here of a recursive text – another layer, a pre-existing text, which can never quite be tracked down ("The first page of the book of the peony is lost") and yet has somehow left traces in the speaker's memory. And those traces themselves deal with traces, with fragmentary remains – ruins, ashes, lost lights, faint aromas. We are given from the outset (even from the title, which is both the title of *this book* we are holding in our hands and, at the same time, appears to refer to another, pre-existing book) the sense of endless layers, of something always receding before us – which is, of course, similar to the structure of the peony flower itself, with its very tightly folded layers. The flower, like the text, creates the sense that you could keep peeling open layer after layer but the "centre" itself would always elude you.

The sense of layering, and of a recursive, receding, mode of representation or narration, comes across particularly in Orozco's incorporation of references to various Chinese and Japanese texts and artworks focusing on the peony. For example, in Poem 11 of Part 1, we read:

> They asked him the colour of the peony. He didn't answer. The conversation turned to other things. A little later, the man—of whom nothing is known, except the power of his pen—quietly retired from the place. They saw him set out on the stony path towards the southern mountains. Nothing more was heard of him. On the table was found a wrinkled piece of paper on which these words were written: *The color of the thin wound that the eclipse may open in the water only once. And it remains in the gaze.*
>
> The invention of this minor incident is attributed to the poet Meng Haoran. It would appear on a page of his "False Memories of Hanshan," an album that brings together drawings, stories and poems. The only known copy was lost in 1864 in the fall of Nanjing, the final incident of the Taiping War.[6]

Here, we have a story involving a disappearance (of the unknown man), a trace left behind (the paper) which itself refers to a trace (the "thin wound" which "remains in the gaze"), and then the statement that the story itself was an invention, "attributed to" a poet who writes a book called *False Memories*, the only copy of which is then lost. The story is a *mise en abyme*, a piece of text into which we keep falling and falling, a flower made up of endless layers with no solid centre.[7]

This idea of the peony as representing something essentially elusive, transient, and impossible to pin down, recurs throughout the book. Words used to describe it include "Arcanum," "enigma," "mystery," "labyrinth"; it is "the flower that never stops unfolding, never stops fading."[8] In Poem 5 of Part 2, we have a particularly striking representation of the peony as trace, this time as a kind of signature; what remains after violence, madness, or the collapse of systems:

> You will find its outline scratched on the wall of the furthest cell of the empty madhouse, on the only image rerun on the blind television. Its diagram burns on the smoky mirrors of the leprosarium, on the x-ray of the inferno that hides in your entrails, on the garden tattooed on the corpse's fingers.[9]

It is notable that all the images here are connected to the realm of the visual, and more specifically to various technologies of visual imaging: a scratched outline on a wall, a diagram somehow "burned" onto the surface of a mirror, a television image, an X-ray, a tattoo. In other words, the peony is *itself* here presented as a kind of image machine, or at least as an entity that is somehow able to project itself onto a variety of surfaces using a variety of imaging technologies. This explicit reference to types of image machine occurs at other points in the book, too. For example, in Poem 3 of Part I, the speaker turns his room into a *camera obscura*:

> I cover the windows of the room facing the river with black paper. No light, except for what comes through the small tear that I made in the paper. *Camera obscura*. The weightless film of the world seeps through a pinhole.[10]

In the next poem, the peony "duplicates its domain" in the mirror;[11] in Poem 6 of Part I, meanwhile, the peony is imagined as projecting itself inside the head of the observer, making of the skull a kind of cinema:

> The idea of *that* peony unfolds fully-formed in the mind. Then the brightness comes forth, the unimaginable energy breaks free. Touched and overcome by so great a discharge, the skull becomes transparent and is filled with light—a vessel overflowing with the singular glow of that image.[12]

(This image of an image projected inside the skull, along with a reference to that most intriguing of image machines, the magic lantern, is also found in Orozco's previous collection, *Autocinema*: "It was already written that, in the period of total clarity, she would project on my skull's thinnest wall the tiny illuminations of her magic lantern."[13] I shall consider this collection later in the chapter.)

In addition to this emphasis on transience and on visuality, the peony is also described in terms of paradox, the unstable conjunction of opposite forces: "There is a violent stillness in the petal, an immobile turbulence" (Poem 8, Part 2).[14] Because it represents change and transience, the peony is associated with time: "Time changes from snow to flame and flame to clotted blood. […] Time, like the peony. Like the peony that melts within our eye" (Poem 8, Part 2).[15] There is again here a specifically visual aspect, the peony linked to the idea of a visual sequence, a flicker of images melting one into the next, in our "eye" or in our imagination (our "mind's eye"), the way we might see snow as flame and flame as "clotted blood." The peony is cinematic, in this sense, and inherently unstable, one version of it disappearing into the next in an endless progression, or perhaps regression, a gradual melting-away towards an implied end-point which, paradoxically, can never be reached: "There's no conclusion. No end" (Poem 21, Part I).[16]

The very last poem in the book simply states "You call it peony. I call it emptiness" (Poem 19, Part 2).[17] Given the relevance of the Chinese and Japanese contexts, which Orozco draws on throughout the book, it seems likely that this refers to the Buddhist concept of *sunyata*, commonly translated "emptiness" or "voidness."[18] This is a complex concept but fundamentally relates to relinquishing attachment to ideas of permanence, of things, of the self. In Mahayana Buddhism, once a person seeking enlightenment (a bodhisattva) has progressed through the first six stages or "perfections," he or she then understands *sunyata* and the true nature of reality and can progress to Buddhahood; it is the understanding of *sunyata* that marks the distinction, and once it is understood, the understanding cannot be lost – the person cannot, as it were, "fall back" through the earlier stages.[19] The concept of emptiness, *sunyata*, fits with the emphasis throughout the book on the paradoxical, transforming, endlessly receding nature of the peony. Having shown us all these different views of the peony but ending with the statement that the concept of the peony is in a sense *empty*, the book sends us back to its beginning – "the first page of the book of the peony is lost," is "always still to be written."

The Prose Poem Sequence as Paradoxical Form

Why then did the experience of reading this book feel, to me, similar to that of clicking through a series of visual slides – why did it remind me so strongly of the little image machine remembered from childhood, the miniature chalet with its circle of tiny photographs?

The first reason, I think, is that this book is so clearly structured as a sequence of different presentations of the same thing (the peony). Reading the sequence, it is as though we are looking at the same object from different angles or with different filters or levels of magnification – an impression enhanced by the explicit references, scattered throughout the book, to various types of visual imaging. Of course, a sequence of slides or images need not all depict the same object, but we can easily imagine a series of images being used in this way – to give us different angles, to zoom in and back out, to show the object from above or behind or in other lights. And in the particular case of the Liechtenstein souvenir, as mentioned above, the repetition of the name "Vaduz" did create precisely the effect of being shown different "angles," or versions, of the same thing.

The second reason is that, as I have already indicated, *Book of the Peony* has a circular structure, in which we are always brought back to the beginning, back to the mysterious "first page" which is somehow always "still to be written." For me, this recalled the disc of images in the chalet viewfinder; it also recalled the circular carousels of slide-projectors, the (not infrequent) experience, as a child in the 1970s, of sitting in relatives' darkened sitting-rooms, watching the holiday slides click through the carousel, hearing that familiar rattle as the machine clicked round, wondering how many more slides to click through before we came back round to the beginning again.

Both of those aspects are quite specific to this particular book, but I now want to argue that there are further aspects contributing to this "image machine" quality and that these aspects are more characteristic of prose poetry as a form in general. The first of these is to do with the relative speed at which we read prose, compared to lineated poetry. This in turn is connected with our expectations of prose, as a genre or mode of writing, but which in the case of the prose poem turn out to be misleading. A lineated poem forces us to read it relatively slowly because it works by setting up tensions between line and sense: it may not be written in conventional syntax or complete sentences, and even if it is, it breaks that sense over the lines in various ways, creating a deliberate mixture of pause and flow. But a prose poem tricks us into reading it more quickly because it is structured as continuous prose. As David Lehman comments on Charles Simic's *The World Doesn't End*, "This succession of sentences, not lines, moves at a speed faster than verse."[20] Or as Anthony Howell puts it, "There is a 'throughness' to conventional prose. With it, we travel on through one sentence to the next, and we are building something by going towards it. The writing may well feel 'transparent' – we are simply looking through it at the sense."[21]

The power of prose poetry comes in large part because of its ability to exploit our expectations of prose – we read it quickly, as though it were "transparent" to sense, but we then find ourselves puzzled, not sure in fact what we have just been shown, having to go back and look at it again. As Jeremy Noel-Tod says in his introduction to *The Penguin Book of the Prose Poem*, "our habitual expectation when we see a passage of prose is that it will explain, not sing."[22] With a sequence of prose poems, then, there can be an experience of reading through them quickly, much like clicking through a series of images. Compared to the slow process of reading lineated poems, we feel as though each individual prose poem can be seen and taken in almost "at a glance." But we may well then realise that this is not actually the case at all: in a sequence of prose poems there is a tension or paradox, created by the apparent "throughness" or transparency of prose set against the density and poetic intensity of the prose poems' language. In *Book of the Peony*, this tension is particularly generated by means of the recessive and recursive aspects of the text, our sense of the peony as constantly receding before us, ungraspable, presented in text that often itself takes on the structure of a *mise en abyme*.

As an inherently paradoxical form, the prose poem (and the prose poem sequence) might seem the perfect vehicle for a paradoxical mode of representation – the attempt to capture, and frame, something that is essentially fleeting and contingent. Sima Godfrey analyses this aspect of the prose poem sequence in her article "Baudelaire's Windows." She suggests that Baudelaire's *Petits poèmes en prose* "represent the subjective aestheticization of Paris into a gallery of anecdotal scenes [...] a series of pictural *tableaux*."[23] What drives the creation of these *tableaux*, she argues, is "[the] tension that the modern poet feels, between the personal need to confront the real temporal world of contingency and the poetic need to frame it in art."[24] She goes on to stress the importance, and paradoxical nature, of the *frame* as both supplemental to and partly creating or defining that which is framed: "The frame and the window pane function analogously, creating energy and containing it. The depth and infiniteness of the framed object is ironically intensified by the limitations imposed upon it by a frame."[25]

"The Small Model Room of the Box"

At this point, I want to return to Joseph Cornell's assemblages, which gain their affective power precisely from this structure of being "framed" or contained. As many commentators on Cornell's work have noted, it is exactly the act of bringing together apparently disparate objects and *putting them inside a box* that gives his work its uncanny power – that, in Godfrey's terms, both "creates energy and contains it." As Mary Ann Caws puts it, Cornell's assemblages work by creating "correspondences" – associations, juxtapositions – among their various components, but it is the act of compressing these within a box that sets them working, or in Caws' term *animates* them: "For Cornell, the prime place for the animation of correspondences is the small model room of the box."[26] Similarly, Diane Waldman notes that in his use of boxes Cornell was drawing on the use of construction and boxes by Dada and Surrealist artists, including Duchamp, Schwitters, and Dalí. As Waldman states, these artists in turn were drawing on the already familiar concept of the cabinet of curiosities, the *Wunderkammer* so beloved of the Victorians, and behind that the whole historical trope of treasure-chests, jewel-boxes, caskets, and so on: "The box is a treasure chest, one containing many of life's secrets and mysteries."[27]

Visually, the box heightens and intensifies the associative connections we make between the objects; our eye and our attention are corralled within the space of the box, which in Cornell's pieces often seems to take on an almost infinite depth, the endlessly recessive quality I identified earlier in *Book of the Peony*. This is perhaps most the case in those boxes in which Cornell uses dark blue – the colour we associate most with distance and the unreachable. Rebecca Solnit analyses this emotive quality of the colour blue in *A Field Guide to Getting Lost*:

> For many years, I have been moved by the blue at the far edge of what can be seen, that color of horizons, of remote mountain ranges, of anything far away. The color of that distance is the color of an emotion, the color of solitude and of desire, the color of there seen from here, the color of where you are not. And the color of where you can never go.[28]

Waldman argues that Cornell's box constructions both reflect his particular view of, or stance towards, the world, and create in themselves a world or realm with very specific affective qualities:

> Cornell's deeply reverential attitude towards the universe as a mirror of mysterious truths is conveyed in each and every one of his box constructions.

The distillation of all these interests into the spare but poetic fantasy of his boxes transformed the box construction into a realm of both precise and enigmatic existence.[29]

This description – "a realm of both precise and enigmatic existence" – maps remarkably well onto *Book of the Peony*, in which the peony is repeatedly redescribed or re-presented in precise, specific ways, but also remains essentially enigmatic, subject to "perpetual transformation"[30] and, as we have seen, to a kind of eternal receding-from-view. This *mise en abyme* structure is replicated throughout the text and sometimes refers to objects that feel as though they would be perfectly at home in one of Cornell's boxes: for instance, the egg in Poem 12, Part II, on which is drawn "with the tip of a hair" the outline of a map of a secret garden "known to a few for the rarity of its peonies,"[31] or the cage in Poem 14, Part II, made for the favourite fighting cricket of a Chinese prince, "delicately carved out of red wood" and which "fits in the hollow of your hand."[32]

Where Cornell's boxes are physical boxes, prose poems of course create their box-like effect by means of shape and layout on the page – typically, a block of text, justified at both sides, surrounded by white space. This is where even apparently minor aspects of typography and page layout can make a considerable difference to the visual effect of prose poems and (therefore) to the way in which we read them. Certainly, one of the elements of *Book of the Peony* which contributed to my sense of the book as an "image machine" is the presentation of the text in short blocks, justified left and right, and rarely longer than they are wide. As a comparison, the prose poems in the Harcourt Brace edition of Charles Simic's *The World Doesn't End* are set ragged-right, and with a first-line indent – both of which elements, I would argue, detract to some extent from the satisfying *block* or *box-like* shape of justified text.[33]

Autocinema: "The Films of the Mind"

By way of comparison to *Book of the Peony*, I would like to look briefly at Gaspar Orozco's previous collection of prose poems, *Autocinema*, also translated into English by Mark Weiss, and published in the US, although not in the UK. Interestingly, this book is *explicitly* constructed around the idea of an image machine. In his translator's note, Mark Weiss notes that *autocinema* is the ordinary Spanish term for a drive-in cinema; here, though, as he says, the suggestion is more "a filmography of the self."[34] As Gaspar Orozco put it in an email to me, *Autocinema* was "thought not so much as a book of poems about cinema but conceived as a collection of poems as films themselves. Each poem as a film projected into the page. The films of the mind."[35]

Autocinema is constructed around the controlling idea of each prose poem as a film projected onto an unlikely surface: for example, "Film seen on a piano key," "Film seen within an amber bead," "7 films seen in the holes in a telephone receiver." In this sense, there is an overall connectedness throughout the book. But the "content" of each film is different. Although certain topics recur and thread through the book (including the idea of the city, the theme of looking, and to some extent the same preoccupation with receding and disappearance that is so central to *Book of the Peony*[36]), the "films" (the prose poems) deliberately draw on a wide range of settings and images. This is very different from *Book of the Peony*, where the conceit is that we are looking throughout at different versions/images of the same object.

There is also a difference in layout between the two books which feels significant in terms of the reading experience. In *Autocinema*, the English translation sits underneath the Spanish original so that each page is fuller than in *Book of the Peony*. Furthermore, some of the pieces are longer than one page in the original, such that the English text has to follow the Spanish on the next available page. For both of these reasons, and ironically despite the explicit visual metaphor, *Autocinema* as a reading experience does not, for me, conjure the impression of an "image machine" in the same way that *Book of the Peony* does. This is created by the various elements I have explored above: the tightness of focus, the obsessive returns to the same object, the sense of recursiveness and circularity in the text, the actual references to forms of visual imaging, and the contrast of text block against white space, producing the effect of a small screen or an image projected against a white wall. In Sima Godfrey's terms, "the energy of contained space is intensified by the limitations imposed upon it by framing constraints."[37] Paradoxically, *Book of the Peony*, while lacking *Autocinema*'s explicit framing in terms of an image machine, makes particularly good use of these framing constraints (alongside its imagery and textual tropes) to create the *effect* of an image machine.

Conclusion: Image Machines and Perceptual Tricks

In the quotation from Simic with which I began, it is the city itself – that quintessentially modern setting – that is being described as an "image machine." The city acts like a gigantic projector, continually bombarding us with its flicker and frenzy, its seductive and ever-changing sights. The fundamental challenge for modern art is to find the means by which to adequately represent and convey this experience. For many writers and cultural critics in the first decades of the twentieth century, it was cinema that seemed to hold the most promise in this respect. Wyndham Lewis, Dorothy Richardson, H.D., Anaïs Nin, and Virginia Woolf all wrote of cinema as the quintessentially modern art form, the form most capable of capturing the constantly changing, fleeting nature of "modern life."[38] Indeed, in some ways, the two can be seen as causally connected. In her 1926 essay "The Cinema", Woolf describes the "chaos of the streets" as "a scene waiting a new art to be transfixed"; this new art, of course, is cinema, by means of which "[the] most fantastic contrasts could be flashed before us with a speed which the writer can only toil after in vain."[39] This, suggests Raymond Williams, is no coincidence: in his essay on the emergence of new "metropolitan" forms of perception, he argues that cinema not only utilised but was "an art form created, in all important respects, by these perceptions"; indeed, he argues more broadly that the elements we think of as most characteristic of modernist art and literature (such as fragmentation, collage, or "stream of consciousness" techniques) were driven by the nature of the modern city itself: "the key cultural factor in the modernist shift is the character of the metropolis."[40]

Sima Godfrey makes a similar point in her article on Baudelaire. The prose poem sequence, the *Petits poèmes en prose*, develops formally from the artist-poet-*flâneur*'s experience of the modern city: "The voyeuristic artist glimpses moments of the 'eternal' in the elusive rhythms of the city and frames them into *tableaux* of modern life which he can step back to read."[41]

In both cases, there is an interesting paradox at work. Cinema operates by means of a perceptual trick: it convinces us that we are seeing continuous motion by means of the projection of a series of still images. The prose poem, as argued above, similarly tricks us, playing on our expectations of prose (as opposed to lineated poetry) as something we can read quickly, text that is "transparent" to sense, as Anthony Howell puts it; or to go back to Jeremy Noel-Tod's phrase, a prose poem can trick us into thinking it's explained something, when really what it's done, in a much more mysterious way, is to "sing." The prose poem sequence draws us in, pulls us through, with its appearance of short, easily digested blocks of text; yet we realise that we have in fact been drawn into something quite different, a puzzling space of ramifying associations, much like a Cornell box. *Book of the Peony*, with its eternally receding, ungraspable subject, makes particularly brilliant use of this paradoxical effect, leaving the reader as the speaker himself seems to be left, inside a space that is continually disappearing and a moment that is always in process of passing away:

> Here I leave the flaming peony, burning in its transparent flame. Unfolded in the darknesses of its scent. Wounded. I leave the peony in the disarmed water of this night. I entrust it – like a light that may never be seen again – to the time of this blind moment that melts away as I write. I leave it here, illuminating you.[42]

Notes

1 Charles Simic, *Dime-Store Alchemy: The Art of Joseph Cornell* (New York: New York Review Books, 1992), 30:

> "In murky corners of old cities where everything—horror, too—is magical," Baudelaire writes. The city is a huge image machine. A slot machine for the solitaries. Coins of reverie, of poetry, secret passion, religious madness, it converts them all. A force illegible.

Simic's phrase here felt very resonant, for me, in thinking about Orozco's text, for several reasons. A city can be understood as an "image machine" on several levels: cities are full of created images such as advertising posters, and they also continually present us with fleeting "images" as we, and other people, move through them. Somewhat similarly, a text can be seen as an "image machine" in the sense that it presents us with textual images; but also, as I'm arguing here in relation to Orozco's text, it may have qualities that remind us of a physical "image machine" such as a magic lantern or slide projector. It also feels very relevant that Simic uses the phrase in the context of writing about Joseph Cornell, whose work was one of the first things that came to my mind when I started to reflect on *Book of the Peony* – and also that he here quotes Baudelaire, the key figure in the modern Western history of the prose poem.

2 David Lehman, "The Prose Poem: An Alternative to Verse," *The American Poetry Review* 32.2 (March/April 2003): 46.

3 John Ashbery, Preface to *Illuminations*, by Arthur Rimbaud, trans. John Ashbery (Manchester, UK: Carcanet, 2011), 16.

4 Gaspar Orozco, *Book of the Peony*, trans. Mark Weiss (Bristol, UK: Shearsman, 2017), 77.

5 Orozco, *Book of the Peony*, 11.

6 Orozco, *Book of the Peony*, 31.

7 The term *mise en abyme*, meaning "put into [an/the] abyss," or as we might say rendered abyssal, originally derives from heraldry, and was first used by André Gide in his journals to refer to recursive structures in paintings (such as Velázquez's *Las Meninas*) or in literature (such as *Hamlet*, with its "play within a play"); Gide, *Journal I: 1889–1912* (Rio de Janeiro: AmericEdit, 1943), 44–5. The concept was elaborated at greater length by Lucien Dällenbach in *Le récit spéculaire: essai sur la mise en abyme* (Paris: Seuil, 1977) and subsequently used in post-structuralist literary theory and film theory.

8 Orozco, *Book of the Peony*, 49.

9 Orozco, *Book of the Peony*, 65.

10 Orozco, *Book of the Peony*, 15

11 Orozco, *Book of the Peony*, 17.

12 Orozco, *Book of the Peony*, 21.

13 Gaspar Orozco, *Autocinema*, trans. Mark Weiss (Victoria, TX: Chax Press, 2016), 46.

14 Orozco, *Book of the Peony*, 71.

15 Orozco, *Book of the Peony*, 71.

16 Orozco, *Book of the Peony*, 51.

17 Orozco, *Book of the Peony*, 93.

18 See e.g. John Bowker, ed., *The Cambridge Illustrated History of Religions* (Cambridge: Cambridge University Press, 2002), 83.

19 Bowker, *The Cambridge Illustrated History of Religions*, 83.

20 Lehman, "The Prose Poem," 45.

21 Anthony Howell, "The Prose Poem," *Fortnightly Review* (1 April 2016), http://fortnightlyreview.co.uk/2016/04/prose-poetry.

22 Jeremy Noel-Tod, "Introduction: The Expansion of the Prose Poem," in *The Penguin Book of the Prose Poem: From Baudelaire to Anne Carson*, ed. Noel-Tod, Jeremy, (London: Penguin, 2018), xxi.

23 Sima Godfrey, "Baudelaire's Windows," *L'Esprit Créateur* 22, no. 4 (Winter 1982): 83.

24 Godfrey, "Baudelaire's Windows," 83.

25 Godfrey, "Baudelaire's Windows," 91.

26 Mary Ann Caws, *Joseph Cornell's Theater of the Mind: Selected Diaries, Letters, and Files* (New York: Thames and Hudson, 1993), 30.

27 Diane Waldman, *Joseph Cornell: Master of Dreams* (New York: Harry N. Abrams, 2002), 23. The image of the *Wunderkammer* (or *Wunderkabinet*) appears in Orozco's collection *Autocinema*, in the prose poem titled "Film seen in a *wunderkabinet* made by Ulrich Baumgarten (1600–1652)"; Orozco, *Autocinema*, 20.

28 Rebecca Solnit, *A Field Guide to Getting Lost* (Edinburgh: Canongate, 2017), 29. Cornell, whose boxes can be seen precisely as expressions of "solitude and desire," the fantasised journeyings through space and time of a person who never in fact travelled beyond New York City, was clearly working with this peculiarly affective capacity of the colour blue in many of his boxes. It is striking that the image chosen for the front cover of Diane Waldman's large-format book *Joseph Cornell: Master of Dreams* is that of the 1952–1954 "blue" version of *Untitled (Medici Princess)*.

29 Waldman, *Joseph Cornell*, 13.

30 Orozco, *Book of the Peony*, 51.

31 Orozco, *Book of the Peony*, 79.

32 Orozco, *Book of the Peony*, 83.

33 These typographical deviations from a more strictly box-like format seem all the more surprising since Simic is, of course, so strongly inspired by Cornell (though, of course, he may have had little or no say in the matter).

34 Mark Weiss, "Translator's Note," in Orozco, *Autocinema*, 13.

35 Email to the author from Gaspar Orozco, 26 May 2019.

36 All of these elements are brought together strikingly in the poem "Another": "Behind the film is another film. Behind the actors others lurk. There's another city within this city. Within the depths of light, another brightness flickers. Beneath the words are other words, intoned by other voices. Beyond the shadow drips another shadow. Behind the music another music quietly advances. Other eyes are seen behind your eyes." Orozco, *Autocinema*, 75.

37 Godfrey, "Baudelaire's Windows," 92.

38 See in particular H. D.'s text "The *Borderline* Pamphlet," written in 1930 to accompany the release of the film *Borderline*, directed by Kenneth Macpherson, in which H. D. starred alongside Paul Robeson. In this text, H. D. praises "film art" as "the synthesis toward which we have been striving" and describes film as "the modern attempt to synchronize thought and action, the inner turmoil and the outer." H. D. (Hilda Doolittle), "The *Borderline* Pamphlet," in *The Gender of Modernism*, ed. Bonnie Kime Scott (Bloomington, IN: Indiana University Press, 1990), 121, 123.

39 Virginia Woolf, "The Cinema," in *The Crowded Dance of Modern Life*, ed. Rachel Bowlby (Harmondsworth, UK: Penguin, 1993), 58.

40 Raymond Williams, "Metropolitan Perceptions and the Emergence of Modernism," in *The Politics of Modernism: Against the New Conformists*, ed. Tony Pinkney (London: Verso, 1989), 46, 45.

41 Godfrey, "Baudelaire's Windows," 83.

42 Orozco, *Book of the Peony*, 89. I am grateful to Anne Caldwell and Oz Hardwick for inviting me to take part in the Prose Poetry Symposium at Leeds Trinity University in July 2019, and for subsequent discussions and suggestions on this chapter. I am also grateful to Tony Frazer at Shearsman Books for permission to quote from *Book of the Peony* and to use the illustration; to Charles Alexander at Chax Press, and to Mark Weiss, for permission to quote from *Autocinema*; and to Gaspar Orozco, for being willing to discuss his work, and prose poetry generally, with me by email and generously granting me permission to quote from our correspondence.

8

WRITING THE PROSE POEM

An Insider's Perspective on an Outsider Artform

Ian Seed

In an act of self-examination, this essay will investigate my own development as a writer of prose poetry, including the tracing of literary ancestry and the ways in which I have been inspired by the prose poem specifically as an outsider art form. In the course of this investigation, I will analyse different literary techniques deployed in prose poetry, for example: the way in which the prose poem in all its brevity is especially well placed to create an alternative world in just a few sentences; the use of an unreliable yet credible narrator; and the rapid way in which perspective on a situation, object, or psychological state can suddenly change within the space of a small paragraph in a manner which forces us to suspend our belief in the reality we thought we knew. This will lead into a brief discussion of why the prose poem as an outsider art form offers an inimitable perspective on the world we live in, and why it may be more important than ever now.

With the recent publication of anthologies of the prose poem, such as *The Valley Press Anthology of British Prose Poetry* and *The Penguin Book of the Prose Poem*, and critical anthologies such as *British Prose Poetry: The Poems Without Lines* and *Prose Poetry: An Introduction*, the prose poem seems to be finally entering mainstream consciousness in the United Kingdom.[1] This was not the case until recently, even if the prose poem has been practiced as an art form in the UK by a number of prominent and less prominent authors since the 1890s.[2] David Caddy describes the prose poem as a "hidden" form, as "part of a counter-discourse through its lack of general visibility within English mainstream poetry."[3] This is not the case in the United States, where a number of notable anthologies of the prose poem have been published since the 1970s.[4] Patricia Debney tells us that when she moved from the USA to the UK, it did not even occur to her that "the prose poem was a form that no one – not one – in my classes of adult students in the UK would ever have seen or thought about making themselves."[5] When I was taking my MA

DOI: 10.4324/9781003199533-9

in Creative Writing at Lancaster University in 2003–2004, almost none of the tutors or my fellow students on the course had heard of "prose poems." (Ironically, a couple of years later, I would go on to create and teach a course on prose poetry for the Department of Continuing Education at Lancaster University.)

Yet my own discovery of the prose poem came decades before that. It started with my discovery as a sixth-former of alternative poetry in the mid-1970s and in the early 1980s. My first encounter with small square blocks of prose presented as poetry was in the winter of 1974–1975.[6] My mother owned a few unusual books. One of these was *Love and War Poems* by the pacifist American poet Kenneth Patchen (1911–1972), published in 1968 in a stapled, but high-quality edition as "Whisper & Shout No. One." It sold for 2s 6d, or 1 dollar.[7]

What I found so affecting was not only Patchen's passionate language, or his rich, sensory imagery, or his playfulness (often forgotten), or his utterly uncompromising style – which, granted, can at times result in terrible writing – but also the different *shapes* of the poems on the page: short lines, long lines (which like Whitman's do not stop before the right margin), poems written in a mixture of prose and verse, titles written vertically down the left side of the poem, and *those* poems written as small square blocks of prose, such as the following:

> Red grapes shielded from the sun by thick, velvety leaves. Vines strong with the strength of the loved earth, grapes like huge shiny drops of blood on the undersides of those green fingers. The air is rich with the smell of growing, womb-warm under the sun of the noon-day …
>
> Down the rows walk three men in single file … heads bent … hands tied behind them … A few yards back a fourth man in the cab of a truck sprawled high with bodies listens to instructions over a two-way radio and yawns nodding at something said by a fifth man who is squinting wearily down the sights of a heavy rifle mounted in the cowling. … After a time the voice of the two millionth man gives the awaited order and the finger of a two-millionth and first man tightens on the trigger. And under the sun of the noonday the air is rich with the sweetish smell of the harvest.[8]

One thing that struck me here – although I would not have framed it in such terms at the time – was the way in which the poetic is contrasted with a more objective, documentary style to heighten the obscenity of the atrocities being committed off-camera. The poem ends where it began, with the sensory description of the air "rich with the sweetish smell of harvest." The lyricism of the language only reinforces a sense of horror, disgust, and shame.

I was impressed by what could be achieved in so few words. And finally, there was the fact that this was called a "poem," but in terms of shape, it did not resemble any of the poetry that I was studying at school, although I had read and enjoyed Blake's *Marriage of Heaven and Hell*, which I had picked out on my own from the school library. Blake was in fact an important figure for Patchen. (In a short

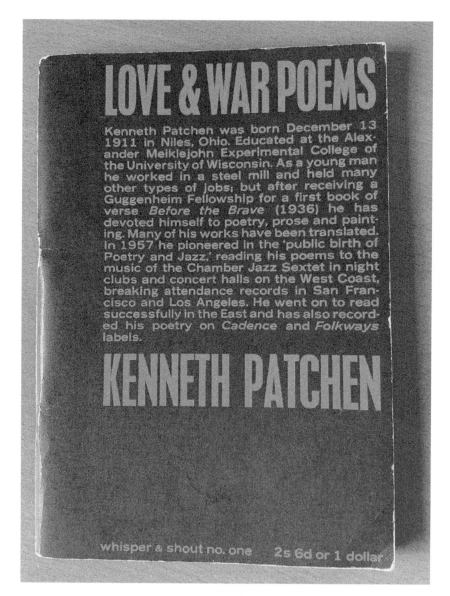

FIGURE 8.1 Kenneth Patchen, *Love and War Poems.* "Whisper & Shout No. One" (1968)

essay in the *Love & War Poems*, he memorably declares: "Thank God for William Blake! And thank William Blake for a very great deal of God!"[9]). Patchen's political prose poems presage Carolyn Forché's widely anthologised "The Colonel" and the prose poems of Claudia Rankine.

The fact that I discovered prose poems through editions like this meant that for me they quickly became associated with a literature which was underground and subversive. Prose poems were outsiders. In spite of their square shape, they would not be boxed in by academic labels or commercial interests. Throughout the years, and through many a move from country to country, I have shed most of the books I have owned and read. However, I have hung onto my small press publications for dear life, always making sure they were safe somewhere.

However, while Patchen's work widened my sense of the possibilities of language, it never occurred to me that I too could write poems – if that's what they were – in square blocks of text, even if I was, of course, like many teenagers, trying my hand at lyrical free verse. The first prose poems that made me want to write my own were those of Pierre Reverdy, which I first read in 1979 as a third-year undergraduate student at Nottingham University. As with the poems of Patchen, I discovered them in a small press publication. It was simply titled "Pierre Reverdy," had a plain white card cover, and contained 16 unnumbered pages of poetry on flimsy paper.[10] Unlike the Patchen book, there was no introduction, no afterword, no table of contents. Beyond the poems themselves, there was only the information that the translator was Vivienne Finch and that the pamphlet was published in an edition of five hundred by "The X Press."

I was immediately enchanted by the writing of Pierre Reverdy, and indeed remain so to this day.[11] The prose poems in these translations by Vivienne Finch subtly evoke the atmosphere of Montmartre in the years just prior to the First World War. They also conjure up another, alternate world somewhere between dreaming and waking. Reverdy uses a language which is elliptical yet simple and vivid, and always hauntingly beautiful. Take, for example, "Mascot":

> Little doll, good luck charm, is struggling at my window, at the mercy of the wind. The rain has soaked her dress; her face and hands are fading. She has even lost a leg. But her ring remains, and with it, her power. Winter knocks her against the glass, her little foot blue-shoed, and she dances, dances with joy, and with cold, to warm up her heart again, her wooden heart, the good luck charm. At night, she lifts up her arms beseechingly towards the stars.[12]

I tried several times to write something like this, but the results were almost always self-consciously poetic. It was in 1980 when I had left university and was working in series of menial jobs that I discovered the prose poems of the British poet and editor, Cory Harding, who remains one of underground poetry's best secrets. It was Harding who had brought out Vivienne Finch's Reverdy translations. He also used his X Press to publish his own work, for example, the A4-chapbook, *Blue Yellow & Green*, which was, in the poet's own words:

> Typed on an Olympia portable typewriter (pudding face type) and dooplicated [Harding often played with spellings] on Armageddon (cheap & nasty) paper using ex-army stencils run off on a Roneo-Vickers 865 machine one rainy Sunday afternoon at the Cats Meat Warehouse, Tooting

FIGURE 8.2 Pierre Reverdy, *Pierre Reverdy.* Translated by Vivienne Finch (Croydon: X-Press, 1980)

in a special limited edition of 75 copies only with a silk-screen cover by the author.[13]

The title is perhaps unusual for a poetry collection, but it is an apt one. The prose poems (many titleless) make frequent references to colours and tell surreal stories that can be visualised as a painting, or as a series of paintings. Like many prose

FIGURE 8.3 Cory Harding, *Blue, Yellow & Green* (Croydon: The X Press, 1980)

poems, Cory Harding's convey strong feelings of estrangement and a loss of identity, employing an inseparable mix of pathos and absurdity, and have an oddly biblical quality:

> I would like to ascend into that little blue hole in the sky until I no longer remember how I was once human and how my body once consisted of spare parts that have now become obsolete. I would like to float up into that hole

> at the back of the sky until small clouds enter my body and I forget how my voice once consisted of thousands of wires that burned and sparkled in the dark, and how my body was once controlled by electricity, and how my feelings were ruled by magnets, and my thoughts by poisonous chemicals. You had promised me I would see the beautiful birds beneath the water and the fish swimming thru the blue sky and the clouds floating beneath the ground. But after you gave me this new face it dissolved into a pool of water on a road bordered by high trees where I lay breathing into a rubber tube that sighed like the passing of clouds across my chest.[14]

For better or worse, Cory Harding's work compelled me to try my hand at writing something similar. One early evening in January 1981, when I was walking home in the snow, the draft of a prose poem formed itself in my head:

The final version came out like this, with the title "Insect":

> Walking by the council houses in the falling snow, I thought I saw someone waving to me from a downstairs window. Yet when I got close enough to press my face against the frosty glass, I realised I had been mistaken; there was only a family watching television. Looking more closely still however, I saw myself walking on the screen. The youngest daughter was crying because the way I dragged my crushed leg behind me reminded her of an insect.[15]

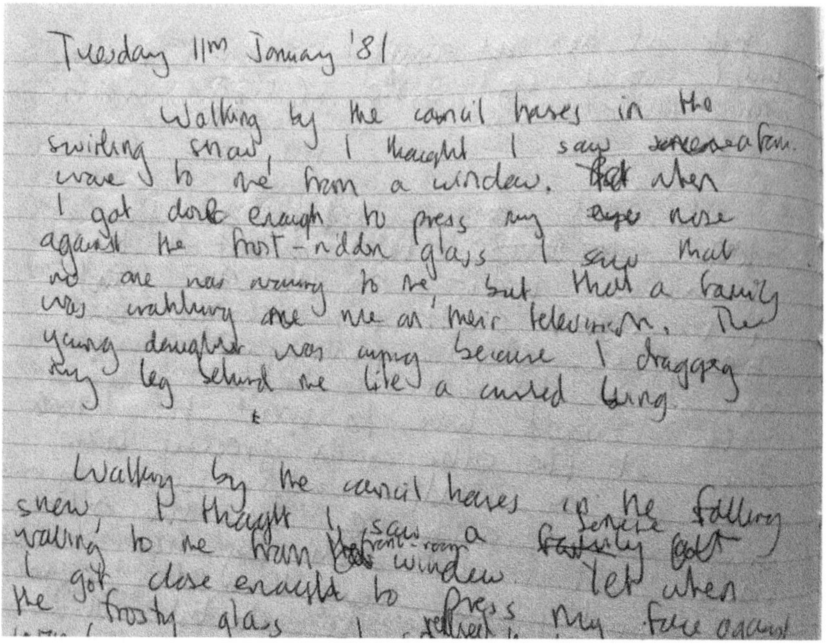
Tuesday 11th January '81

Walking by the council houses in the swirling snow, I thought I saw someone wave to me from a window. But when I got close enough to press my nose against the frost-ridden glass I saw that no one was waving to me, but that a family was watching me on their television. The young daughter was crying because I dragging my leg behind me like a crushed thing.

Walking by the council houses in the falling snow, I thought I saw a girl waving to me from a front-room window. Yet when I got close enough to press my face against the frosty glass, I realised

FIGURE 8.4 Ian Seed, "Insect" first draft

The language here is very different from that of Reverdy or Harding, far less "poetical." It is stripped down to a minimum. The po-faced narrator does not express any emotion. Nevertheless, loss (perhaps grief), estrangement, and disorientation are conveyed through the storyline, the imagery, and the way the prose poem changes perspective, continually replacing one reality with another. It is clear that the narrator is very much on the outside of what is happening, both in a psychological and physical sense. The world with its falling snow and frosty glass is a cold, inhospitable place. The marginalised narrator is an unreliable one, unsure whether what he sees corresponds to reality: "I *thought* I saw someone waving to me from a downstairs window." But when he approaches the window, he sees that *no* one is waving. Or is that, too, a misperception? Perhaps someone *was* waving, even if now the family appears to be gathered round a television. And then – impossibly, or almost impossibly – he sees himself on the screen and realises that the youngest daughter is crying because the way he drags his crushed leg behind him reminds her of an insect. It is as if it is only now that he realises that he *has* a crushed leg. And yet how could he have *not* realised? The situation raises several unanswered questions: why is our protagonist walking through a council housing estate in the falling snow? Why does he think he sees someone waving to him when in all probability no one is? Why does this family who does not seem to know him care about him one way or the other? What is he doing on television? He seems to have no knowledge of how this can be so. How was his leg damaged? Why does he not seem to know about it until he can see himself through the eyes of "the youngest daughter"? What is actually going on here? Can it be said that anything is really going on at all? It is as if some kind of trick has been played upon the reader, not unlike those pictures which play with perspective and make the impossible seem possible.

Perhaps the narrator, or at least the author *behind* the narrator, is simply, in a well-worn phrase, pulling the wool over our eyes. And all this happens in the space of just 81 words. The poem works, I would say, because it hits us before we know we have been hit. I would argue that with a longer piece it would be difficult to pull off the same effects because we would have time to start to doubt what we are being told, and we would have to begin to look for evidence in the form of "reality" details.

I sent "Insect," alongside some much weaker work, to Pete Mortimer, editor of the prestigious *Iron*. He had always rejected my writings in the past, but his rejections were kind and encouraging enough for me to keep trying him. He accepted "Insect," jokingly asking me if he should publish it under the name Franz Kafka.[16] Astonishingly, I had not thought about Kafka when writing "Insect," even though in my 19th year, I had soaked myself in his work, and I now realise that his influence has lasted to this day. It is worth noting that Kafka's very short stories, written around the same time that Reverdy was writing his early poetry, have been published both as fiction and as prose poems.[17]

A figure I feel even closer to, in some respects, is Max Jacob (1876–1944), friend and mentor to Pierre Reverdy, although I don't believe I had read any of his work back in 1981.[18] While Kafka builds an alternative universe through the accumulation of seemingly realistic detail, Jacob is a writer who, with just a few brushstrokes, plunges us into a world we create for ourselves.[19] His language is plain, pared-down, and almost conversational, like that of someone telling a jokey anecdote in a bar. Yet many of the pictures he paints are astonishingly beautiful, filled with a sense of mystery and loss, which is in no way diminished by their comic absurdity. Here is "The Beggar Woman of Naples," taken from Jacob's groundbreaking collection of prose poems, *Le Cornet à dés* (The Dice-Cup), like Reverdy's *Le voleur de Talan*, published in 1917 and at the author's own expense:

> When I lived in Naples, there was a beggar woman at the entrance to my palace, to whom I'd toss a coin or two before getting into my carriage. One day, surprised she'd never thanked me, I looked at her more closely. It was then I saw that what I'd taken for a beggar woman was a wooden crate painted green, containing some red soil and a few half-rotten bananas.[20]

What makes us do a double-take here is the way Jacob makes us believe in the impossible, or at least the highly improbable. Even when afterwards we realise that at one level we have been tricked, at another level we have absorbed and internalised the prose poem's fictive logic. However unreal, it has become part of the reality of life.

I attempted something similar, many years later, in my own prose poem "Town Centre":

> A thin youth with tousled hair and a wispy beard was walking from car to car stuck in the traffic. He tapped on each window and held out his hand for money. One driver, perhaps to show off in front of the woman next to him, jumped out of his car. Shouting and shaking his fist, he ran after the beggar all the way up the crowded high street. I thought he would catch him, but the beggar, turning a corner, ducked unseen into an Italian restaurant. I found him sitting at a table there, looking at a menu. The tablecloth was piled high with coins he'd taken from his pockets. He invited me to join him.[21]

Like my earlier poem "Insect," "Town Centre" plays with perspective, and yet establishes a reality effect through its twists and turns. With the first two sentences, it appears as if the story is being told by an omniscient narrator. In the third sentence, the narrative voice becomes more hesitant with that word "perhaps," which indicates that in fact the scene is being played out in front of someone who is watching. It is only in the fifth sentence that we realise that in fact this is a first-person narrative: "I thought he would catch him." Like a short film, the narrative jumps from one shot to another until the narrator is suddenly and unexpectedly face to face with the beggar in an Italian restaurant, although we are not told how the narrator got there. We then see that the beggar is a kind of trickster, almost a magician, as he piles high the coins he has taken from his pockets. The invitation that the beggar/trickster/magician makes to the narrator is most unlikely and yet seems somehow entirely logical within the context of the prose poem, where almost anything can happen, and which possesses its own truths.

Coins are, of course, a symbol of luck. In dreams, they are said to represent positive feelings about things that have been or can be achieved. They may indicate the birth of a relationship with the person who shows or gives them to you. There is the sense in this poem of some kind of reconciliation taking place, perhaps even a metaphysical one. When I read this poem back to myself, it brings a sense of reassurance, whereas I am chilled by the earlier prose poem, "Insect."

A colleague of mine has said that "Town Centre" reads like a secular version of the work of George Herbert, and I can see what he means by that. Think, for example, of Herbert's poem, "Love (III)," a three-stanza narration of the healing power of God's love, which concludes: "You must sit down, says Love, and taste my meat: / So I did sit and eat."[22] Herbert is a long way from preaching in his poetry. Rather, as Hannah Brooks-Motl has observed, he is interested in seeing how "moods and […] psychological states [play] out in multiple ways"; and in "Love III," a "reader looking for a tidy – or happy – ending […] might end up troubled by the poem's surprising and insistent ambivalences."[23] Herbert was not writing in prose poetry, but rather employing a variety of forms, including visual poetry, to investigate the complex nature of his (and our) relationship with God. However, prose poems with their suppleness of form, their blurring of the boundaries between prose and poetry, their ability to encompass shifting registers of language within a small space, combining the lyrical with the banal, for example, and with their interest in what is "other,"[24] can offer an ideal vehicle for investigating universal questions in a personal, specific, and concrete manner. Often, as in "Town Centre" (or in Herbert's "Love (III)"), this questioning of what it means to be human will be embodied in stories of chance encounters. Moreover, as outsiders, prose poems offer a different kind of space where what is strange can be welcomed in.

Although I am (at least intellectually) an atheist, I believe that many of my prose poems, like those of Max Jacob, in their explorations of chance encounters, frequently in the most banal of circumstances (for example walking in the park or sitting in a train carriage), contain a yearning to transcend empirical reality in the search for a deeper metaphysical one.[25] At the same time, there is a mistrust of the possibility of truly ever transcending the here-and-now, as if it were only a kind of mirage produced by a sense of loneliness or alienation, or of having been abandoned, albeit temporarily:

> It had been a long journey. While I was waiting outside the chapel for the others to arrive, a woman asked me if I could look after her dog for a few minutes. After some time, she had still not returned. What, I wondered, was

I going to do with this shaggy black creature she had left me with? I decided to go and look for her. The village was so small that I soon reached its edges. Here there was a river, and on the other side another chapel, similar to the first, but situated in a heathland of the softest green and purple hues I had ever seen. It felt familiar and yet like another world. I wanted to cross the river and touch the softness, but there was no bridge. Besides, the dog was starting to bark as if suddenly realising that I was not his real owner.[26]

There is perhaps a hint of Max Jacob's beggar woman of Naples in the woman who asks the narrator of "Baptism" to look after her dog for a few minutes. Dogs are sometimes associated with a depression one cannot shake off. (Winston Churchill famously spoke of his own "black dog" of depression.) The narrator is unwittingly stuck with the "shaggy black creature." A different, perhaps more real, or perhaps illusory, world is just out of reach on the other side of a river he cannot cross, a river that, as I was writing "Baptism," brought to my mind the River Lethe in which Dante is dipped so that he can be purged of his sins, at the top of the mountain in Canto XXXI of *Purgatorio*, the second volume of the *Divine Comedy*. There is always the possibility that one can at least learn something from such encounters and be given the opportunity for some kind of reconciliation, as in "Town Centre" (above) and "November" (below). The prose poem is perhaps uniquely adaptable enough to contain many possibilities in just a few short sentences.

After "Insect" in 1981, I only wrote intermittently for a couple of decades: the odd poem, the very occasional short story, and around a dozen or so prose poems. The Italian writer Natalia Ginzburg has somewhere said that up until the age of around 25, writers can rely on a kind of innate lyricism. After that, if we are to write at all, we have to make writing an integral part of our everyday lives. Absurdly, it took me until my early 40s to realise that. Even when I returned to writing, most of that was in the form of a more realist poetry and longer short stories.[27]

I occasionally wonder why I abandoned the prose poem for so long. Perhaps some part of me believed it was somehow not a valid form of writing. What brought me back to the prose poem in late 2004 was an increasing interest in abstract, rather than narrative poetry; for example, the work of Gertrude Stein, John Ashbery, Rosmarie Waldrop, Sheila E. Murphy, Rupert M. Loydell, and Jeremy Over.[28] Murphy's prose poetry, which I only came across because I was asked to review her wonderfully titled *Proof of Silhouettes*, was of special significance to me.[29] What I admired about her work was its sheer delight in sounds, and the associations of language and imagery it ignites. Murphy's writing has a potent stream-of-consciousness, "automatic" element, which takes the reader into an alternative primitive and magical world, the world of "nonsense," which, for its effectiveness, must play off sense. At the same time, Murphy's prose poetry can assume an intensely lyrical quality. What fascinated me here was the strange beauty of Murphy's writing, the way it worked precisely because of its lack of narrative while at the same time hinting at the possibility of narrative (we as readers can if we wish try to imagine what that narrative may be). I was also engaged at an emotional level by the tone of the poems, which is at once absurd, humorously self-deprecatory, exuberant in its delight at its own musicality, curious (one feels as if the author herself does not know where she is going next on her journey), and yet also brimming with a strange, poignant yearning. Here as an example is Murphy's prose poem (which takes the form of a *haibun*, i.e. a short section of prose, followed by a haiku in prose form, without a full stop at the end, thereby implying an openness to the unstated possibility to a more extended story and world around it), "How Partial Therefore Lovely":

> How partial therefore lovely from afar the leaves, the colour tour from a gray boat. Her company seemed sterling in white humour capable of being shared. Earth would mist away some of our tantrums. Would rigidify formed aftermath. A clause of sponge weighted and blond. The iffiest of turns leased to margins popular as a comeuppance.
>
> Rigour shift, a tourist in possession of completed rose that numbers fourteen.[30]

The short sentences and the "s" sounds create a kind of whispered urgency here. We are presented with a series of odd, at first seemingly disparate, and yet quite compelling images, such as the "clause of sponge weighted and blond." Phrases such as the "iffiest of turns" and "popular as comeuppance" make us smile. There is a satirical element, here, too, in phrases such as "the colour tour from a gray boat" and "her company seemed sterling." At the same time, we start to sense that perhaps there is a story of a disintegrating relationship underneath all this ("Earth would mist away some of our tantrums"), with one person who is committed to the relationship now finally coming to realise the superficiality of the other, a "tourist in possession of completed rose." And yet this relationship is also in some sense "lovely" precisely because it is only "partial" and still offers the possibility of wholeness. What is also interesting here is the way in which distances are collapsed and landscapes merged in such a brief piece of writing.[31] We have the distant prospect of the "leaves from afar," the sudden close-up of the personified "clause of sponge," and the imagery of both sea and land. And all this is in the space of 7 sentences and 73 words (including the title). Of course, we can't be sure about anything. The poem remains open to the reader's interpretation. Whatever way it is understood, it remains a mystery at its heart, which is one of its strengths, for it is a poem which continually entices us back to reread to enjoy its sounds and imagery, and to construct our own story around it.

After reading the abstract, experimental prose poems of Sheila E. Murphy and others, I began with a series of my own, which depended mainly for their effect on rhythm and sound, and on the accumulation of disparate imagistic fragments.[32] I began by setting myself my own Oulipo assignment. Every morning, apart from

Sunday, I would wake to my alarm at 5.30 a.m., and then write, as fast as I could, over three A4, wide-lined pages. In the evening, when I returned from my temporary office job of the time, I would go through the three pages, underlining any phrases, or words, or images that struck me as being potentially interesting. After that, I would sit down at my computer and join the phrases, or words or images into a prose poem, feeling free as I did so to alter, cut and re-order. This did not take a huge amount of my day – around 20 minutes in the morning, and then an hour or so (sometimes less) in the evening. I always wrote with a delicious feeling of liberation. How wonderful to be freed from the obligation to "make sense," or to tell a story. One of these prose poems, "Recount," written in the autumn of 2004, has some affinity with Murphy's "How Partial Therefore Lovely" in its hint of a portrayal of a relationship in need of repair:

> The first green. Crows squawk away from treetops. In the river, a replica of the branches we walk under, but colder, without colour. A dog wanders, indifferent to rain. You question that "finally" once more, the husk of our lives swept away by one casual encounter too many. Wine on the terrace. I've been dreading the moment, too terrified to turn, but they are all smiling, glad to see us. What has changed is hardly perceptible. The work is ours.[33]

As with Murphy's poem, a psychological, interior landscape predominates over a physical one. There is a mystery at its core. Readers, as well as the protagonists, are challenged to make the necessary effort to create a story if they wish to do so: "The work is ours." However, "Recount" is arguably less static than "How Partial Therefore Lovely," conveying a sense of possible death and rebirth with its imagery of a river, and of a "husk," which, as Jill Eulalie Dawson points out in her commentary on the poem, "suggests the vulnerability of a seed (new growth) when its protection is swept away."[34]

After about a year, I felt I'd written this kind of prose poem out of my system. Stuck for ideas, I turned to cut-up and collage, producing both lineated and prose poems in this way, with varying degrees of success.[35] And then, in 2010–2011, almost without any intention on my part, I began writing narrative prose poems on a daily basis. Or rather, it was as if they were writing themselves.[36] What surprised me was how similar they were in spirit to the few prose poems I had been writing 30 years before, as if they had just been waiting for me to open the door to let them out. It feels like cheating. I have not had to struggle with my narrative prose poems in the way that I do with other kinds of writing, and yet I believe that the best of them are the only writings of mine that are somehow genuinely themselves.[37] They have needed just a little nurturing from me in order to make their own way in the world. Perhaps, like the friend in my prose poem "November," they were simply waiting for me to recognise them:

I was sitting on a park bench, thinking of an old friend, of how I had never embraced him. I hadn't seen him for years, and yet as I was wondering about him, I saw him pass by in the light rain that had started to fall. He turned and stared as if he could not believe it was really me. He seemed to have hardly changed, while I had aged almost beyond recognition. I got up and ran to take him in my arms, to hold him so close I could stop his eyes from wandering over my face.[38]

Coming up to the third decade of the twenty-first century, which has shown itself willing to embrace a number of new and hybrid literary forms, the prose poem, in both its narrative and its more abstract modes, is likely to flourish.[39] My own hope is that the prose poem will continue to remain an outsider form, will continue to undermine our expectations of literature, and in order to open up new possibilities, will continue, as the poet Jeremy Over puts it, to throw "authority figures off the scent – pretending to fish for the moon so that they can be left alone to pull up the nets and see if they have snared any real fish."[40] In this essay, I have examined different life situations – real or imagined – which the outsider form of the prose poem is uniquely suited to navigating. A comparative analysis has been conducted of the differences in starting point and effect between prose poems which lean more towards narrative and those which are more abstract and seek to subvert the act of storytelling. I hope I have shown that prose poems, both those written over a century ago and those being written today, will continue to offer a vital alternative space in which what is awkward, strange, and exiled can find a home and thrive in new, unexpected ways.

Notes

1 Anne Caldwell and Oz Hardwick, eds. *The Valley Press Anthology of Prose Poetry.* (Scarborough: Valley Press, 2019); Jeremy Noel-Tod, ed. *The Penguin Book of the Prose Poem: From Baudelaire to Anne Carson.* (London: Penguin, 2018); Jane Monson, ed. *British Prose Poetry: The Poems Without Lines.* (Cham, CH: Palgrave Macmillan, 2018); Paul Hetherington and Cassandra Atherton, eds. *Prose Poetry: An Introduction* (Princeton, NJ: Princeton University Press, 2020).
2 See Margueritte S. Murphy, "The British Prose Poem and 'Poetry' in Early Modernism," in *British Prose Poetry*, ed. Monson, 29–45.
3 David Caddy, "'Hidden' Form: The Prose Poem in English Poetry," in *British Prose Poetry*, ed. Monson, 20.
4 Most notably, Stuart Friebert and David Young, eds., *Models of the Universe: An Anthology of the Prose Poem* (Oberlin, OH: Oberlin College Press, 1995).
5 Debney, "Wrestling with Angels," in *British Prose Poetry*, ed. Monson, 320.
6 For a discussion of what a prose poem might be, see Anthony Howell, "The Prose Poem" – What the hell is it?", The Fortnightly Review, 1 April 2016, https://fortnightlyreview.co.uk/2016/04/prose-poetry/, or Monson, introduction to Monson, *British Prose Poetry*.
7 Kenneth Patchen, *Love and War Poems* (Derby, UK: Whisper & Shout, 1968).

8 Kenneth Patchen, "Vines with Their," in *Collected Poems* (New York: New Directions, 1952), 445.

9 Kenneth Patchen, "Blake," in *Love & War Poems*, 33.

10 Pierre Reverdy, *Pierre Reverdy*, trans. Vivienne Finch (Croydon, UK: X-Press, 1980).

11 See, for example, Pierre Reverdy, *The Thief of Talant* (Cambridge, MA: Wakefield Press, 2016), my translation of Reverdy's 1917 self-published "novel in verse," *Le voleur de Talan*. This is the first translation of *Le voleur de Talan* into English.

12 Pierre Reverdy, "Mascot," in *Pierre Reverdy*, n.p.

13 Cory Harding. *Blue, Yellow & Green* (Croydon, UK: The X Press, 1980).

14 Cory Harding, "The Mystery of the Blue Sky (part 2)," in *Blue, Yellow & Green*, n.p.

15 Ian Seed, "Insect," in *Shifting Registers* (Exeter, UK: Shearsman, 2011), 31.

16 Over the decades, "Insect" has taken on a life of its own, appearing in various journals and anthologies. For example, in 1987, it was featured on BT's *Dial-a-poem* series. More recently, it was discussed in Sally Cline and Midge Gillies, eds., *Literary Non-Fiction: A Writers' and Artists' Companion* (London: Bloomsbury, 2015). It appears in my collection *Shifting Registers*.

17 See, for example, Friebert and Young, *Models of the Universe*.

18 I am currently working on a translation of Max Jacob's 1917 groundbreaking book of prose poems, *The Dice Cup*. My translation is due to be published by Wakefield Press (Cambridge, MA) in 2023.

19 Max Jacob was of course also a painter and art critic, but it was Picasso who persuaded him that his true vocation was that of poet.

20 Max Jacob, *The Dice Cup*, in my own translation, due for publication by Wakefield Press (Cambridge, MA) in 2023.

21 Ian Seed, "Town Centre," in *Makers of Empty Dreams* (Exeter, UK: Shearsman, 2014), 15.

22 George Herbert, "Love (III)," in *George Herbert and the Seventeenth-Century Religious Poets*, ed. Mario A. Di Cesare (New York: W. W. Norton, 1978), 69.

23 Hannah Brooks-Motl, "George Herbert: 'Love (III)': A 17th-Century Poet's Project Invites Its Reader to the Table," *Poetry Foundation*, 24 August 2012, www.poetryfoundation.org/articles/69843/george-herbert-love-iii.

24 As Delville puts it, the prose poem can work as a "self-consciously deviant form [. . .] calling into question the naturalness of accepted boundaries between prose and poetry, the lyric and the narrative, or the literal and the figurative." See Deville, *The American Prose Poem*, 11–18.

25 Although gay and, in his own words, an "atheist Jew," Max Jacob had a religious vision in 1909 and eventually converted to Catholicism in 1916. This did not prevent him from being arrested and transported in February 1944 to Drancy, a transit camp for Jewish deportees, where he died three weeks later.

26 Ian Seed "Baptism," in *New York Hotel* (Bristol, UK: Shearsman, 2018), 32.

27 See, for example, my long short story *Amore Mio* (Lancaster, UK: Flax Books, 2010).

28 Perhaps I also felt that now that I had completed my MA in Creative Writing at Lancaster University, for which I had written a series of interlinked realist short stories, I had in some sense "paid my dues" and was free to experiment and write whatever the hell I liked.

29 Sheila E. Murphy, *Proof of Silhouettes* (Exeter, UK: Stride Books, 1996). My review, which expresses my ambivalence at that time about linguistically-innovative writing, was published on Martin Stannard's *Exultations and Difficulties* blog, 31 October 2004, https://exultationsanddifficulties.blogspot.com/2004/10/. It was really only after I'd written the review that I allowed myself to take a "leap of faith" and surrender to Murphy's writing.

30 Sheila E. Murphy, "How Partial Therefore Lovely," in *A Curious Architecture: A Selection of Contemporary Prose Poems*, eds. Rupert M. Loydell and David Miller (Exeter, UK: Stride, 1996), 115.

31 The ways in which "TimeSpace" can be uniquely intensified in the prose poem is insightfully investigated in detail by Hetherington and Atherton, "Prose Poetry and TimeSpace" in *Prose Poetry: An Introduction*, 128–50.

32 The best of these were eventually gathered in my first-full length collection of poetry, *Anonymous Intruder* (Exeter, UK: Shearsman, 2009).

33 Ian Seed, "Recount," in *Anonymous Intruder* (Exeter: Shearsman, 2009), 49.

34 Jill Eulalie Dawson, "A Brief Introduction to the Prose Poem," in *Twelve Rivers* 8, no. 2 (Autumn/Winter 2017), 6.

35 On occasion, I still turn to cut-up and collage now, but I believe that there are other poets who use this technique to much greater effect than I could ever hope to. However, I did get lucky on occasion. Here, for example is my prose poem "Exile," in *Makers of Empty Dreams*, 73, which begins with a quotation from John Clare, "There's the path if you chuse it":

> I pursue him for years through spattered streets. One morning I abandon the chase and take the road out of town. Puffs of cloud keep pace with me. I am nothing, and alone, and everything is possible. I walk until the air grows brown, weaving dreams around trees. Their branches brush my face like fingers, or tear as if their stories would draw blood.

36 I should add that my prose poems of that time were considerably enriched by my reading of contemporary authors of the prose poem, such as Linda Black and Lucy Hamilton. See, for example, Linda Black, *Root* (Exeter, UK: Shearsman, 2011), and Lucy Hamilton, *Stalker* (Exeter, UK: Shearsman, 2012).

37 Diane Athill, in her memoir, *Instead of a Letter*, expresses a similar sentiment about her short stories which she began writing in her 40s, after several failed attempts during her life at other genres (travel writing, poetry, newspaper articles):

> As soon as that story was finished, another one began, and by the end of the year I had written nine. I did not think about them in advance: a feeling would brew up, a first sentence would occur to me, and then the story would come, as though it had been there all the time.
>
> *Instead of a Letter* (London: Granta Books, 2001), *205*

38 "Ian Seed, November," in *Identity Papers* (Bristol, UK: Shearsman, 2016), 88. Oddly, I think another influence here is the poetry of Edward Thomas, which is permeated with a sense of regret at roads not taken, and which made me want to start writing in the first place when I was in my late teens.

39 See, for example, Hetherington and Atherton, *Prose Poetry: An Introduction*, 4.

40 Jeremy Over, "Fishing for the Moon: Some Recent Prose Poetry in the US," *Hard Times: Contemporary British Poetry Issue* 80, (2006), 39–44.

9

"A FORM OF HOWLING. A FORM OF CHANTING. A FORM OF LOOKING OUT FOR EACH OTHER"

Poetics and Politics of the Contemporary Indian-English Prose Poem

Divya Nadkarni

In this essay, I examine the prose poem as a form and genre category in the context of Indian-English poetry. To date, the prose poem as a distinct form has received little systematic attention in the field of Indian poetry in the English language. In contrast to its burgeoning popularity in Western Anglophone literary contexts, as seen in the numerous anthologies and critical collections appearing in the past few years,[1] the scene in India might seem oddly bare. Not only are there as yet no exclusive anthologies of prose poetry, but collections by individual poets in the form also appear to be scarce. Yet, beneath the surface, beneath inclinations to look for and valorise that which is systematised, the picture is quite different: open any collection of poems, and one is likely to encounter at least a few prose poems, weaving always in and out of conversation with verse poems. In translated collections, one often finds the prose poems outnumbering the verse poems, or at least having a conspicuous presence.[2] In literary journals – for example, *Almost Island, nether,* or *The Bombay Literary Magazine,* among others – the prose poems published are comparable in number to those in verse. In practice, prose poems appear to be flowering. Only, they are hardly ever named as such, and if there is a category distinction at all, it is remarkably faint. Where they exist, they do so in fluid continuity with verse poems, thriving side by side, often inextricably intertwined. One could say, we (Indian readers, as it were) have not yet begun to make a distinction in our practices of reading between prose and verse poems. One could say the category distinction is too foreign; it reeks of imported goods. Decolonial scholars have after all pointed out that theoretical and critical scholarship on Indian-English poetry continues to be largely derivative,

DOI: 10.4324/9781003199533-10

often serving primarily to reinforce Eurocentric "universalist" assumptions by tracing stylistic and formal developments solely in terms of developments taking place in the Western, Anglophone literary scene. As Tabish Khair would have it, "it appears that the old colonial discursive relationship of the native informer and the colonial historian has continued in other shapes."[3] Would a genre category of prose poetry thus applied not pose a similar risk? What theoretical pursuits could ensure that we don't merely apply categorical determinations upon a body of practice that is as ever struggling to free itself from its colonial inheritance while doing justice to the particularities of "every day Indian reality"?[4]

From another position, we might look at Indian-English poetry in the twenty-first century, in the context of the global literary marketplace, of the all-pervasive MFA, that appears to suggest that it is time to let go of the category of Indian-English poetry in its entirety. In today's context, such a category serves only to "otherise," reinforce, in Rankine and Loffreda's words, "a sensibility that champions the universal while simultaneously defining the universal, still, as white [Anglo-American]."[5] For instance, Indian-English poetry is largely absent from the Anglophone mainstream, except in the odd suspiciously hustled "special issue"[6] that brings with it its thematic constraints (are these poems Indian enough?) and allied market-oriented demands.[7] Going with this second scenario, one would take issue not with the term "prose poetry," but the term "Indian-English."

Without taking a position in this discussion, however, I would like to suggest that even in their continuity with verse poems, prose poems do demonstrate certain qualitative differences that are worth attending to: not only in their appearance on the page, but also in the ways they demand to be read, and the kind of meanings they make possible. When we use the term prose poetry now, we assume a category – a formal and/or genre-category – with certain attributes and an accruing body of practices. We also claim certain lineages and reject others (lineages that break from verse traditions, or establish specific kinds of continuities), in order to develop specific modalities of interpretation.[8] Prose poems, as scholars like Hetherington and Atherton have argued, demand different modes of attention and call for different registers of understanding than the typical "lyric." It is precisely this difference *in* continuity that is of interest to this chapter.

Subsequently, I suggest that in the Indian context, reading a prose poem *as* a prose poem entails a crucial hermeneutic responsibility, namely, attending to the inherent multilinguality of the Indian context. Where the poem in English often sits at the intersection of multiple vernacular and Western Anglophone poetic traditions, it becomes important to ask what theoretical dis/continuities an exploration of prose poetry as a category could lead us to. In the light of the thematic and theoretical concerns of this volume, this essay thus seeks to make a contribution to discussions around the conceptualisation of prose poetry as a formal category within the Indian-English poetic landscape, and in the larger socio-political context where the place of English poetry on the whole is relentlessly questioned. The prose poem, I would argue through my case studies, carries the potential to forge a bridge between multiple genres and traditions (poetics), and the capacity to push at the limits of lyric subjectivity towards intersubjectivity, or what the poet Nandini Dhar has called the "lyric we" (politics).[9]

Here then is a map of the chapter: in the following section, I attend to the historical distinction between prose and poetry in Indian literature, aiming to set the stage for how we might conceptualise the distinctions and continuities between prose and verse poetry. I position the prose poem as a form that establishes distinct continuities with the classical Indian literary traditions of the *kavya* and *bhasha* literatures while facilitating critical emancipatory innovations in the contemporary. This is followed by close readings of poems by Vivek Narayanan and Nandini Dhar in order to demonstrate how attending to prose poetry as a formal category might help us to understand anew the immense emancipatory political potential the form carries.

Contextualising Indian-English Prose Poetry

Indian-English poetry as a particular linguistic/aesthetic cultural practice is no longer new, even though as English language literature it is widely regarded as one of the "new literatures" to emerge only in the mid-twentieth century towards the end of the colonial period.[10] In the light of its colonial inheritance, it continues to occupy a fraught terrain in the broader Indian literary field, criticised as it is for "its slavishness to a foreign tongue," its "audacious mimicry," and its inability to capture the reality of post-independence Indian social life.[11] While these criticisms have continued well into the turn of the twenty-first century, scholars like Mehrotra and King have argued that the development of a unique Indian-English poetry is unquestionable. English can no longer simply be considered a language to accrue Western capital. It is indelibly "linked to the same processes of modernisation, which for historical and political reasons, have become wedded to the spread of the English language and the evolution of an English language culture alongside Hindi and the regional languages."[12]

Yet, even the strongest defences of Indian-English literature reveal lacunae. I would like to address two of those here. The first concerns what Mehrotra identifies as the inadequate recognition of multilinguality as an inextricable part of Indian-English poetry. As I mentioned earlier, nearly all roads in post-independence poetic criticism lead back to British modernism. Most fail to cast even a sidelong glance at literary traditions in other (Indian) languages that form a part of its development as well. Many Indian poets writing in English are at least bilingual and typically inhabit a "prismatic interlingual space"[13] that goes beyond mere references or symbolic allusions to Indian traditions or folk materials. Indian-English poetry's very sensibility, Mehrotra argues, is multilingual; it is "mottled," "osmotic"; its lineages are so thickly entwined that readers may never quite succeed in tracing these multiple inflections. But, says Mehrotra, neither can the poet. It is no simple or transparent exchange. Mehrotra quotes the poet A. K. Ramanujan's crucial observation:

> English and my disciplines (linguistics, anthropology) give me my "outer" forms – linguistic, metrical, logical and other such ways of shaping experience; and my first thirty years in India, my frequent visits and fieldtrips, my personal and professional preoccupations with Kannada, Tamil, the classics and folklore give me my substance, my "inner" forms, images and symbols. They are continuous with each other, and I no longer can tell what comes from where.[14]

India is a country of many languages, and perhaps most Indian writers speak, think, dream, and maybe even write in at least two languages. Yet theoretical developments have only insufficiently acknowledged the extent to which innovation in form and syntax in Indian-English literature is indebted to this multilinguality and is co-constituted by a continuous process of interaction with a multilingual literary and social context.

Through the framework of multilinguality, Mehrotra counters simplistic attributions of Indian-English as being alienated from "everyday Indian reality" merely because it is the language of a small, urban, frequently foreign-educated elite. However, he doesn't quite get to one crucial nuance in this critique: the issue of India's caste, religious, and racial/geographical exclusions. Anti-caste scholars have long been pointing out that the "elitism" of Indian-English literature is fundamentally linked to its invisibilising of deep-rooted caste, religious, and racial discriminations in the country.[15] For instance, Naskar and Mandal have argued that though the English language "has firmly consolidated its place with other Indian languages"[16] and has even come to be considered by many as the language that promises "the annihilation of caste,"[17] literary practices in English have consistently failed to realise this promise. Tahir points out that as a language of an urban elite, caste has problematically come to be a scene of (mis)representation, and reification of caste hierarchies.[18] Furthermore, as anti-caste scholar Yogesh Maitreya has observed, English literary practices have failed to "visibilise the [all-pervasive] truth of caste in Indian society"; they have been unable to "recognise and problematise the privileges of the aesthetic and literary traditions they've inherited."[19] So long as Indian literature in English does not systematically question its literary inheritances as well as engage with issues of caste and geographical exclusion, it will only perpetuate these discriminatory practices and fail to contribute to any truly emancipatory project in the country. With the few exceptions of twentieth century fiction and poetry originally in English that do take up caste as a subject matter of the work, there is a lot wanting when it comes to actually rethinking an entire literature's traditional inheritances. In this sense, many would argue, the English language in Indian literature has a long way to go to actually capture "Indian reality" and truly facilitate emancipatory change.

Bringing these two concerns together in this chapter, I would like to suggest that an engagement with prose poetry as a form shows us a way to formally engage with linguistic multiplicity while paving a road to a critical engagement with literary tradition and a commitment towards an inclusive and caste-critical public culture.

Kavya or Poetic Literature: Contextualising the Prose Poem in Indian Literature

In locating the place of Indian-English prose poetry at the intersections of multiple traditions, it is helpful to turn to the concept of *kavya* as known in the context of classical literatures from the subcontinent. *Kavya* is today characterised broadly as "poetry." However, as classical literary scholars have argued, the genre classification of *kavya* as poetry is not inherent to the practice. It is largely a consequence of the colonial encounter and a universalisation of the genre distinctions between prose and poetry.[20] To quote Lienhard's understanding of *kavya* as poetic literature,

> if artistic values are not dependent on outer form, but on the manner in which a work is structured, it follows that practically any sort of text – a gnomic or didactic verse, an inscription or even a treatise – may be regarded as a poetic work.[21]

Whatever the (formal) nature of the works ascribed to *kavya* traditions, they share among them a particular *quality* of emotional expressiveness, a quality of newness.[22] As Vinay Chari observes:

> The test of a *kavya* was taken to be the quality of delight or emotional thrill (camatkara) that poetry communicates … The definition of the nature of kavya varied from school to school, but the criteria adopted fall roughly into three categories. First, literature is defined by some speciality or deviancy in its use of the linguistic medium, whether it is figurative expression, or stylistic patterning, or foregrounding of some sort. The second type of definition was one based on the claim for a special poetic semantics consisting in oblique or implicative expression, as opposed to the literal manner… The third…was a view that was based on the quality of the meaning itself, which in poetry is emotive meaning, or rasa—this term being understood not as the affective response of the reader but as the cognitive content of the work itself, determined contextually by the presented situation or thought and by the type of discourse that the work purports to be.[23]

Similarly, Bronner, Schulman, and Tubb identify several characteristics of *kavya* that resonate closely with what we might call prose poetry in today's context: (i) a "tremendous vitality" and inclination to innovation and change;[24] (ii) an awareness of socio–political change and flux that prompts "novelty" to become the touchstone of its quality;[25] (iii) "readable, but not too heavy, inventive and imaginative, centred around a story … cutting edge … and deeply significant";[26] and (iv) with a balance between "extreme" linguistic and cultural complexity and intelligibility.[27]

The observations above resonate abundantly with recent theories of prose poetry. Hetherington and Atherton, for instance, have noted prose poetry's formal slipperiness and abiding continuity with oral and epic poetic traditions that are passed down in "unlineated form,"[28] locating in precisely this slipperiness its "potential to cross the divide between the urge toward poetry – its capacity to articulate what is otherwise unsayable – and the more discursive and narrative-driven prose of novels, biographies, and the like."[29] Similarly, theorists like Mark Irwin and Margueritte Murphy have written about prose poetry's expressive reach in its fundamentally dialogic and heteroglossic character; its openness "to sudden changes that might appear histrionic or cloying in verse."[30] Most importantly, they talk about how the prose poem as a form can unsettle readers:

> It is only upon reading them that surprises happen, and what appears to be a standard paragraph is outed as a prose poem – at which point poetry asserts itself over the idea of the prosaic. This unsettles the experience of reading because the familiar (the usual assumptions that attend on reading prose [and poetry]) is made strange.[31]

The prose poem has thus come to be recognised not as a fixed form, but as a *quality* of expression that has the capacity to unsettle genres and push against their communicative limits.

Taking these similarities in hand, we can begin to get a sense of how the concept of prose poetry might open up particularly invigorating continuities with classical vernacular literary traditions from which English language poetry seems to have long been severed. Furthermore, in line with Bronner et al.'s observation about the *kavya* tradition's commitment to innovation, the prose poem in the twenty-first century appears not just as a site of continuity, but also of renewal. However, in this context of renewal, it becomes important to take note of the problems of *kavya*. Anti-caste scholars have argued that the *kavya* tradition has been an active participant in the marginalisation of vernacular (*bhasha*) literary practices,[32] speaking for the maintenance of a hierarchical status quo, fundamentally pitted against "literary diversity and the principle of literary equality."[33] Under the umbrella of *kavya* literature as *the* classical Indian literature, literatures in other languages and across class and caste divides, that speak back to and subvert *kavya* traditions, have been systemically invisiblised, or merely read as derivative.[34]

Following Bronner et al.'s case for innovation as "the organising principle by which to structure the history of *kavya* literature,"[35] I suggest that what we call prose poetry in the Indian-English poetic context presents a "vigorous site of literary innovation"[36] and political reimagination, in which the precolonial and caste-dominant heritages of *kavya* literature can be questioned. With the levelling force (or potential) of the English language, the prose poem is in a unique position to forge progressive continuities with the traditions of both the *kavya* and *bhasha* poetic literatures, and in doing so, both challenge colonial or anglophone theoretical frames, while also serving as a site where the very idea and historical narrative of *kavya* can be renewed. Moreover, as a formal practice, prose poetry presents a productive site of multiplicitous and layered interaction between literary traditions and the processes of translation that are often integral to an Indian writer's imagination. As such, it is worthwhile exploring prose poetry as a distinct formal category for precisely these reasons. With this in mind, I will now consider two examples which help us theorise the poetics and politics of prose poetry in English in India.

Aspects of the Indian-English Prose Poem

In what follows, I take up two aspects of prose poetry in the Indian context, as manifested in two book length collections: *Life and Times of Mr S* by Vivek Narayanan and *Historians of Redundant Moments* by Nandini Dhar.[37] Through Narayanan, I will look at how the prose poem facilitates the reinterpretation of the epic (*mahakavya*) tradition in Tamil. With Dhar, I will take a close look at how the prose poems facilitate *inter*subjective forms of understanding, thus moving beyond lyric subjectivity, towards a "lyric we." While the two collections are by no means representative of the wide variety of prose-poetic practices, they are exemplary in highlighting the dialogic and genre-bending potential of the form in conversation with verse poems. Both collections include prose and verse poems, thus showing different ways in which both forms cohabit the poetic space, where they differ, and what kinds of understanding they facilitate. Both tell stories with central characters and narrators, thus visibilising the processes of lyric subject formation and de-formation. While I treat the collections separately, the concerns overlap, ultimately demonstrating key operational aspects of the poetics and politics of Indian-English prose poetry.

Narayanan, *Life and Times of Mr. S*

shaken up from within by the re-detonation of the always finished[38]

Vivek Narayanan, in *Life and Times of Mr S*, takes up the Tamil classical epic tradition and attempts to work out ways to make this tradition compatible with both the traditions of Indian-English writing and the peculiar contemporary socio-political scramble that marks our current information age. Mr S resembles an anti-epic hero; his greatest adventures, his most difficult trials are performing/ surviving an everyday cast into what he calls a "pluriverse." He seems nervous and beleaguered and is inclined towards frequent and crushing self-flagellation. He has a pressing poetic impulse; he'd like to think of himself as a poet, but language overwhelms him; the very question of identity – who are you? where do you come from? – terrifies him. He is worried by politics but politically ineffectual; his mind is but "a soggy wafer ... scrambled by all registers."[39] He is disgusted by the legacy of his Tamil-Brahminical roots but doesn't quite know how to question them. It is in this context that he reads a translation of the *Cilapattikaram* (A Tamil epic from the first century CE), wondering if the past has any bearing on his present, if there is some kind of connection he might make with that ancient text. And with that reference point, the narrative kicks off. S's "pluriverse" is created by language and his life's greatest undertaking is to break out of its prison.

Through the *Cilapattikaram*, the poems in the book take up the epic tradition both in form and content:

> And yet my total memory torments me oh that I might
>
> like Kannagi
>
> chuck my burning breast at the untrue city
> in the meter of sweet-mango-fruit, sour-mango, sweet-mango,
>   sweet-mango-fruit –
>
> ...
>
> rein in the true political   bring out weak and spineless testicularly
>   encumbered man your truer Kannagi   your inner kanmani
>   your truest courage   your missing breast   step by step
>   minute by minute   stand turn back   look   look hard and
>   devour my dear sir   the sweet mango fruit of that vision.[40]

Mr S, internet-scrambled and politically ineffectual, with the aspirations simultaneously of an epic hero and an epic poet, takes apart the very notion of the epic (*mahakavya*) genre, and with it the colonial legacy of genre writing. As we've seen before, the *Kavya* tradition did not carry genre distinctions in its context of production. Critics such as Ramanujan have argued that a subset of *kavya* has been reinterpreted in generic terms, and specifically as "epics," in the nation-building project under colonial influence.[41] Through Mr S, the poems pose the question of how an "epic" comes to be, and through what interactions certain texts come to be constituted as epics. S's globalised internet-ravaged present appears altogether unconducive to epic creation. The poems not only manage to put the classification of Mr S as an epic hero at stake but also call to question the genre of the epic, and the concept of "genre" itself.

Let's take a look at what happens to the concept of the epic invocation once S has read the *Cilapattikaram* and embarked on his journey. In "Short Prayer to the Economy":

> prayers for fishes, tossed each to each in translucent glue prayers for the hairier beasts, roistering in rolling tundra if we are to conceive a world, let us conceive it—at all risk—one
>
> . . .
>
> I've found I don't know I need I to know who can I talk to who can I call what must I do where must I put it how can I use it what is your number who will you call where will we go how will we make it where will we put it who can I finger how will they take it where is the button how can I find it how did he get there who does he know what can it do where does it go how do you work it what will it work take what it will work it you do how does it where what can it do who does he know who did he get there how did he find it how is the button where will they take it how can I finger who will we put it where make it how we will go where call you what who number how how must I put where do I must what call I can who talk to I who can to know I need I know I don't I found I feed
>
> > prayers for the musical crow, the intimate mosquito,
> > > whose kisses are here to say
> > prayers for the contract killer, the contractual signer, unspeakable
> > > unimpeachable bond
> > and our shared godless theology that hooks the day to day[42]

The poem taps into the historical archive in which genre properties are delineated while also establishing a relation to vernacular Tamil literary traditions and to the processes of translation. Pitting the language and metrical rhythms of the Tamil epic against bits of technobabble and internet-era distraction, along with the inevitable prose-ness that enters into any situation of translation, the poem seems to trouble the very project of writing poetry in English and in genre today.

I have mentioned earlier that not all the poems in the collection are prose poems. As we read through, we begin to see the circumstances in which they appear. After a somewhat flattering "lyric" beginning, we see S starting to flounder. He doubts his lyric voice; he doubts his accent; he doubts his nationality: where he belongs and whom he can represent; he doubts his familiarity with his classical literary roots; he can't decide which pen to buy and which muse to invoke; he doubts his very identity as a poet. And it is in these moments of heightened existential conflict, we see the text opening into prose. It is quite literally the dam of the lyric bursting. The poem above begins as a verse poem, but only to explode into prose when the epic meter can no longer be contained, where no form in the English language can carry the content, when the grand-eloquent becomes a mere redundancy. Note, in the first example, the voice switching from the first to the third person, the prose rescuing S from "his own obsolescence,"[43] and letting him carry on speaking. Where the very lyric subjectivity of S threatens to become obsolescent, the prose-poem finds voice and comes through as a last resort, showing us in its very composition a glimpse of the polyphonic voice of intersubjectivity.

Dhar, *Historians of Redundant Moments*

> No one warned us against more unified versions of ourselves. No one warned us of the dangers of confronting ourselves as one unbroken word.[44]

The prose poems in Dhar's *Historians of Redundant Moments* challenge the time-worn notion of the *lyric I* – the very constitution of lyric subjectivity as singular in poetry – through the characters of twins. The book traces the stories of Toi and Tombur growing up in post-1977 Kolkata (India), in the aftermath of the 1967 armed-peasant uprising in Naxalbari (known now as the Naxalite movement).[45] The poems show us how any subjectivity is constituted only in and through a "community of experience,"[46] in an evolving process of sharing feelings, bodily sensations, and expressions. In a concert of evolving commitments through a continuous communication of difference, the twins constitute a *we* only as "plural subjects."[47] In this play of the "lyric we," we can see a model analogy for how the prose and verse poems come to form, precisely in interaction with each other.

As the twins show us, the only way to understand them is as a *we* constituted by distinctive perspectives on their world, thus posing a direct challenge to the concept of a singular poetic speaker, the *lyric I*. As Sophie Loidolt argues, following Hannah Arendt, the *we* of a genuine political intersubjectivity is not a *we* that subsumes the individual. There is no *we* without the interaction of "singular world accesses,"[48] just as there is no subject without the *inter*action with others. No *I* without *we*, and no *we* without *I*. Through Dhar's prose poems, we can go a step further. There is no *I* without *we*, and there is no *I* that is as complete, stable, unchanging, or fixed in time. Any attempt to fix the *I* results in a loss of the *we*, and consequently, a loss of *I* too.

If, as readers, we see theirs as one story, we see merely a word, *Toitombur*,[49] a book "full of small small writings/ No pictures";[50] a thing, a nesting doll, with a "plastic torso: useless."[51] We see one of the sisters as dead, gone, and the other "on [her] way to a cryptic closure . . . like obsolete poems."[52] Or we could say not a poem at all, but a "text," a textbook.[53] A reader who does not wish to fix this *I* only as loss, takes on an ethical responsibility. If we wish to imagine any future for and with Toi *and* Tombur, a future that can right past wrongs, if we desire any (more just, more free, more communicative) world to be possible at all, we must take recourse in the *I* that is ever unformed, ever moving, and ever oriented with and as a *we*.

The multiplication of the *I* comes at the behest of a multiplication of the very forms of (poetic) expression that claim to constitute subjectivity. Recognised poetic traditions, forms, and ways of the text existing on the page are equally multiplied, challenged, immersed in the life world of other forms of expression. Through the prose poems amidst verse, we begin to see an approach to poetic traditions and poetic subjectivity that shows us a way to reflect on the processes by which we become (political) subjects, even as we subject(ify) and characterise others. Traditions, in being thrown into states of flux, become the ground for movement, coming together not as pure or singular but as exercises in intersubjectivity and interlingual dialogue. The prose poems are located in the long and (largely) globally invisible vernacular traditions of Bengali women's writing and the relatively newer tradition of poetry in the English language. In interaction, they pose a challenge to the Anglo-American poetic influences inherited along with the latter,[54] as well as the contemporary traditions of the American creative writing industry.[55] The couplets that appear ever so often throughout the collection pay homage not only to the twoness of the twins, but to the ghazal form in Urdu poetry, and particularly the ghazal form as it gets adapted into the English language. For instance, several lines from the poem "Naxalbari is not the name of a village only" are almost verbatim reproductions of lines from several of Agha Shahid Ali's poems. Ali is perhaps one of the most prominent proponents of the Ghazal form in English language.[56] Yet, we can see clearly that Dhar's couplets are not ghazals. They hint at the form, but they shy from it; they do not associate wholly with it and also stay clear of "appropriating" it.[57] The narrative arc, facilitated in part by the dense weave of prose and verse poems, ensures that literary traditions don't become artefacts but remain dynamic processes, coming to be constituted always in conversation with each other.

Conclusion: "Casting Yourself Across, Casting Yourself Anew"

I would like to conclude with the question: so, what constitutes the politics of prose poetry? Current global understandings of the political value of poetry can be broadly seen as taking one of two directions: poetry as activism, or poetry as facilitating critique through its formal autonomy. Despite the irreconcilability of the two positions, they cohere in one second important respect: both have been conceiving of poetry as centred upon a subject, with the subject being either outside of politics (autonomist) or inside of politics (activist). The activist model relies heavily on the "I" as hermeneutic friend, at times necessitating a total identification with it in order to stake a political claim.[58] The autonomy model on the other hand, seeks to dispense with this subjectivity altogether. As one might recognise in some of the more contemporary conceptualist practices of poetry, there is a push to erase the writer's ego; to use anonymity as an instrument of power, as the ultimate sign of autonomy, to turn poetic forces against notions of subjectivity and subjective expression that are to this day dominant conceptions of poetry.[59] Interpretations of poems under this framework are often invested in demonstrating how the subject can be done away with altogether, or in evincing the (infinite) struggle for a relevant subject position. Either way, to borrow Loidolt's words, both positions hold on to "the ontology of the individual." However, if politics is what goes on *between* people,[60] such a focus on the subject in poetry cannot be satisfactory. As I hope to have shown in this chapter, prose poems, in their resolute transgression of singularity, be it of language, subjecthood, or literary tradition, show us a way towards a genuine intersubjectivity and interlinguality. They become the ground for movement, coming together not as pure or singular form but as exercises in community, dialogue, and hybridity.

Both in Narayanan's *Life and Times of Mr. S* and Dhar's *Historians of Redundant Moments*, we have seen that the prose poems offer the (Indian-English) poem a way to defy absolute identification with any one form, genre, or tradition. Rather, they serve as a bridge between traditions. It is on the threshold of the prose poem that, for instance, the lyric romantic tradition can cohabit with the tradition of Bengali women's writing; or the tradition of the Tamil epic with anti-caste consciousness[61] and the fragmented languages of the internet. They also serve as places to incubate, to plot out new poetic forms and expressions,[62] new resistances and defiances, and new political subjecthoods. Where Mr S is dwindling into obsolescence in lyric, prose restores communicability to his language and a certain visceral materiality to his presence. Where within the binds of the lyric, it can be either Toi or Tombur but not both, prose offers a space where the *lyric I* can expand to become a *lyric we*, offering us the possibility of an intersubjective and interlingual plurality without sacrificing subjecthood or the particularity of different forms of expression. It is in this fundamental dialogical political plurality that I would like to locate the politics of prose poetry in the Indian-English context.

Notes

1 Two of the more recent theoretical volumes exploring the development of prose poetry as a form are Paul Hetherington and Cassandra Atherton, eds. *Prose Poetry: An Introduction* (Princeton, NJ: Princeton University Press, 2020), and Michel Delville and Mary Ann Caws, eds. *The Edinburgh Companion to the Prose Poem* (Edinburgh: Edinburgh University Press, 2021). For a short but exhaustive glance at the numerous recent anthologies and collections of prose poetry, see Hetherington and Atherton, *Prose Poetry: An Introduction*, 4.
2 See, for instance, Manglesh Dabral, *This Number Does Not Exist: Selected Poems 1981-2013*, trans. Nirupama Dutt, Sarabjeet Garcha et al. (Mumbai: Paperwall Poetrywala, 2014); Joy Goswami, *After Death Comes Water: Selected Prose Poems*, trans. Sampurna Chattarji (New Delhi: Harper Perennial, 2021). Goswami's prose poetry collected exclusively is the first of its kind.
3 Tabish Khair, "Artist in Action: On the Lack of an Adequate Critical Vocabulary," in *The Routledge Companion to World Literature and World History*, ed. May Hawas (London: Routledge, 2018), 36.

4 A phrase oft used by the poet R. Parthasarthy; quoted in Arvind Krishna Mehrotra, "The Emperor Has No Clothes," in *Partial Recall: Essays on Literature and Literary History* (Ranikhet, India: Permanent Black, 2012), 184.

5 Claudia Rankine and Beth Loffreda, "On Whiteness and The Racial Imaginary," *Literary Hub* (9 April 2015), https://lithub.com/on-whiteness-and-the-racial-imaginary/.

6 A prime example would be *Poetry Magazine* 214, no. 4 (July/August 2019). Themed under "Global Anglophone Indian Poems," the issue carried an apparently arbitrary and non-representative collection of poems that raised a number of eyebrows.

7 I recall the words of the poet Reginald Shepherd, who has argued that while it is due to its fundamental social otherness that poetry's political project is shaped, it often tragically ends up fixing its "others," reifying otherness, reinforcing those exclusionary categories that it sought to escape. While an encouragement to use "poetry as a means to assert or claim social identity" is a big step in poetry's ethical project of inclusion and social justice, it becomes, as Shepherd argues, incumbent upon minority writers to become its forbearers, to evince their political stance and identity in every instance of poetic expression. Reginald Shepherd, "The Other's Other: Against Identity Poetry," *Michigan Quarterly Review* XLII, no. 4 (Fall 2003), http://hdl.handle.net/2027/spo.act2 080.0042.407.

8 See, for instance, Nick Admussen, "The Chinese Prose Poem: Generic Metaphor and the Multiple Origins of Chinese SANWENSHI," in *Edinburgh Companion*, ed. Delville and Caws, 247–61. Admussen notes that a genre is constituted not by "an ideology, a lineage of influence, or even a set of formal restrictions, but a web of hermeneutic methods, a habit of grouping similar works that allows readers to understand the texts they read," 247.

9 Nandini Dhar, "Interview with Nandini Dhar on Historians of Redundant Moments," interview by Julianna DeMicco, Agape Editions (20 March 2017), https://blogging thenuminous.com/2017/03/20/interview-with-nandini-dhar-on-historians-of-redundant-moments/.

10 Bruce King, *Modern Indian Poetry in English* (New Delhi: Oxford University Press, 2001), 2–3.

11 Mehrotra traces this history and critical lacuna in his essay, "Towards a History of Indian Literature in English," in *Partial Recall*, 205–7.

12 King, *Modern Indian Poetry*, 3–4.

13 Mehrotra, "The Emperor Has No Clothes," 170.

14 A. K. Ramanujan, quoted in Mehrotra, "The Emperor Has No Clothes," 177.

15 Another key area when speaking of the exclusions wrought by literary practices in the English language is the issue of literatures of the Indian North East or Kashmir, both politically contested regions. Writing from the North East has hardly found import in literary narratives of the "mainland," and especially writing in English from the region faces a double marginalisation. This topic, however, is too vast in scope and thus will not be covered here. However, while I begin to highlight the caste-related exclusions of classical *Kavya* and *Bhasha* literatures, it would be important to keep in mind that literature from the North East finds almost no place in the classical literary traditions of the "mainland." For literature on the topic, see Kailash C Baral, "Articulating Marginality: Emerging Literatures from Northeast India," in *Emerging Literatures from Northeast India The Dynamics of Culture, Society and Identity*, ed. Margaret Ch Zama (New Delhi: Sage Publications India, 2013), 3–13; and Tillotama Misra, "Speaking, Writing and Coming of the Print Culture in Northeast India," in *Emerging Literatures from Northeast India*, 14–28.

16 Goutam Naskar and Ranjit Mandal, "Casteist Language/s: Situating English and Vernacular Languages in Indian Educational Context," in *Caste, Gender and Media: Significant Sociological Trends in India*, ed. Srabanti Chodhuri and Chandan Basu (Kolkata: Netaji Subhas Open University, 2017), 431–42.

17 Taken from the title of what is regarded as the foundational text of anti-caste praxis, Bhimrao Ramji Ambedkar, *Annihilation of Caste: The Annotated Critical Edition* (London: Verso Books, 2014) (originally written in 1936). For a detailed examination of the emancipation promised by the English language, see also Chandramohan S, "Claiming the English Language as a Dalit Poet," *The Indian Express* (17 April 2021), https://indianexpress.com/article/opinion/columns/claiming-the-english-language-as-a-dalit-poet-7277032/. S argues that "denting the discourse of the nation could be easier in English," thus creating "springboard for [a new] anti-caste linguistic and cultural praxis."

18 Abu Tahir, "Indian English Literature and Its Caste Discrimination; A Great Blow on Cultural Diversity, with a Special Reference to Mulk Raj Anand's 'Untouchable,'" *The Literary Herald* 1, no. 4 (2016), 59–64.

19 Yogesh Maitreya's call for submissions for issue 4 of *nether Quarterly*, accessed 18 August 2021, https://netherquarterly.com/about/.

20 A similar contention against the "universal distinction between fiction and non-fiction" in classical Indian literature has been posited by C. Rajendran, "The Actual and the Imagined: Perspectives and Approaches in Indian Classical Poetics," in *Approaches to World Literature*, ed. Joachim Küpper (Berlin: Akademie Verlag, 2013), 121–32.

21 Siegfried Lienhard, *A History of Indian Literature: A History of Classical Poetry Sanskrit – Pali – Prakrit* (Wiesbaden, Germany: Otto Harrassowitz, 1984), 3.

22 In Bronner et al.'s interpretation, the words, "there is something different about your speech," mark the beginning of the Sanskrit *Kavya* tradition. Yigal Bronner, David Dean Schulman, and Gary Alan Tubb, *Innovations and Turning Points: Toward a History of Kāvya Literature* (New Delhi: Oxford University Press, 2014).

23 V. K. Chari, "The Genre Theory in Sanskrit Poetics," in *Literary India: Comparative Studies in Aesthetics, Colonialism, and Culture*, ed. Patrick Colm Hogan and Lalita Pandit (Albany, NY: State University of New York Press, 1995), 64–5.

24 Bronner et al., *Innovations and Turning Points*, 3.

25 Bronner et al., *Innovations and Turning Points*, 5.

26 Bronner et al., *Innovations and Turning Points*, 12.

27 Bronner et al., *Innovations and Turning Points*, 18.

28 Hetherington and Atherton, *Prose Poetry: An Introduction*, 5. Further in the chapter, they note:

> Prose poetry may be a relatively new part of this tradition but, like the Sumerian lyric, it connects to a long-established human need to speak in ways that defy mundane and commonsense assumptions about the world, and that depart from the time-centred narratives and the discursive modes of most forms of storytelling.

29 Hetherington and Atherton, *Prose Poetry: An Introduction*, 9.

30 Mark Irwin, "Distortion and Disjunction in Contemporary American Poetry," *The American Poetry Review* 40, no. 6 (November/December 2011): 39, quoted in Hetherington and Atherton, *Prose Poetry: An Introduction*, 10.

31 Hetherington and Atherton, *Prose Poetry: An Introduction*, 16.

32   A relationship in which, as mentioned earlier, literatures from the North East are doubly marginalised and excluded, finding no place in those "defining" literary traditions of India.
33   Purushottam, for instance, traces emancipatory traditions back to the little literatures that sought to subvert the caste and class practices of major Sanskritic or Bhasha literatures. See K. Purushotham, *Dalit Literature: Emerging Trends* (Warangal: DRS I Kakatiya University, 2018), 77.
34   This domination was only further entrenched by the constitution of the canon of Classical Indian Literature in the nation-building project under colonial influence. While scholars like Sheldon Pollock have suggested that "the hegemonic hold of Sanskrit-centered kavya tradition" ended in the eighteenth century, others like Ramakrishnan have argued that this shift has nevertheless left unaffected the dominance of Sanskrit *kavya* as *the* classical Indian literary centre on the global stage. See E. V. Ramakrishnan, "Language, Power and Ideology: The Changing Contexts of Bhasha in India," in *Language Policy and Education in India*, ed. M. Sridhar and Sunita Mishra (London: Routledge India, 2016), 57–69.
35   Bronner, Schulman, and Tubb, *Innovations*, 3–5.
36   Hetherington and Atherton, *Prose Poetry: An Introduction*, 14.
37   Vivek Narayanan, *Life and Times of Mr. S* (New Delhi: HarperCollins India, 2012); Nandini Dhar, *Historians of Redundant Moments: A Novel in Poems* (Los Angeles: Agape Editions, 2016).
38   Vivek Narayanan, "His Own Obsolescence: 2," in *Life and Times of Mr. S*, 18.
39   Vivek Narayanan, "Mr S, On First Looking into Parthasarthy's Cilapattikaram," in *Life and Times of Mr. S*, 10.
40   Vivek Narayanan, "Mr S, On First Looking into Parthasarthy's Cilapattikaram," in *Life and Times of Mr. S*, 10.
41   A. K. Ramanujan, *Speaking of Śiva* (Harmondsworth, UK: Penguin Books, 1973).
42   Vivek Narayanan, "Short Prayer to the Economy," in *Life and Times of Mr. S*, 14.
43   Borrowed from the title of the subseries in the collection.
44   Nandini Dhar, "Spider Girl," in *Historians of Redundant Moments*, 44.
45   For a concise history of the uprising, its political allegiances, and its consequences on following generations in West Bengal, see Amitabha Chandra, "The Naxalbari Movement," *The Indian Journal of Political Science* 51, no. 1 (1990), 22–45.
46   I borrow the term from John Dewey, *Art as Experience* (New York: Penguin, 2005), 109.
47   Much like taking a walk together, as Margaret Gilbert argues in "Walking Together: A Paradigmatic Social Phenomenon," *Midwest Studies in Philosophy* 15 (1990), 1–14. In the article, Gilbert argues that "sharing actions" doesn't imply sharing a collective goal, but rather constituting "plural subjects" or *inter*subjects of certain principles of action and acting together; "participating in an activity . . . whose goal is the goal of a plural subject, as opposed to the shared personal goal of the participants" (p. 9). Such an "our goal" involves a continuously evolving narrative; a mutual responsiveness and a shared commitment to an activity, to communicating its principles, conventions, and beliefs, especially when the participants reach a "fork in the road" (p. 10).
48   Sophie Loidolt, "Hannah Arendt on Plurality, Action, and Forms of the 'We,'" paper presented at Shared Commitment in Crisis: Social Ontology, Engagement, and Politics, Institute for Philosophy and Social Theory, University of Belgrade, September 2018.
49   Dhar derives the names of the twins from the Bangla/Bengali word *toitombur*, which means *full to the brim*.
50   Nandini Dhar, "In My Noonday Dreams," in *Historians of Redundant Moments*, 97.

51 Nandini Dhar, "Historying," in *Historians of Redundant Moments*, 1.
52 Nandini Dhar, "Teaching This Syllabic Landscape to Dance," in *Historians of Redundant Moments*, 107.
53 I refer to a poem in the book titled "This is how Tombur became a History Textbook." In making the distinction between poem and text, I also refer to Louise M Rosenblatt, "Towards a Transactional Theory of Reading," *Journal of Reading Behavior* 1, no. 1 (1969): 31–49: "The text is a necessary, but not a sufficient, condition of the poem. For this, a reader or readers with particular cultural and individual attributes must be postulated."
54 Rajeev S. Patke, *Postcolonial Poetry in English* (Oxford: Oxford University Press, 2006).
55 Christopher Beach, *Poetic Culture: Contemporary American Poetry between Community and Institution* (Evanston, IL: Northwestern University Press, 1999), 54.
56 Nishat Zaidi, "Center/Margin Dialectics and the Poetic Form: The Ghazals of Agha Shahid Ali," *Annual of Urdu Studies* 23 (2008): 55–66.
57 Dhar also observes at the end of the book that her reference to Ali serves as a marker to another kind of political resistance in post-independence India: Kashmir's struggle for freedom. To quote:

> As a holder of the Indian passport, who also supports Kashmir's right to self-determination, I want to use Ali's lines as a mark of my solidarity to the Kashmiri struggle. Yet, that solidarity is precarious, precisely because my use of these lines possesses the danger of replicating the very same occupation I am speaking against.
> *Nandini Dhar, Historians of Redundant Moments, 109*

58 See Christopher Soto, "What Constitutes Political Poetry?" *Poetry Foundation*, 5 September 2017, www.poetryfoundation.org/harriet/2017/09/what-constitues-as-political-poetry.
59 See Robert Fitterman, "Does American Political Poetry Have a Future?" *Vice*, 8 July 2014, www.vice.com/en_us/article/9bznvp/does-american-political-poetry-have-a-future-707; Kenneth Goldsmith, "Flarf Is Dionysus. Conceptual Writing Is Apollo," *Poetry* (July/August 2009), www.poetryfoundation.org/poetrymagazine/articles/69328/flarf-is-dionysus-conceptual-writing-is-apollo.
60 As Hannah Arendt has convincingly argued in Hannah Arendt, *The Human Condition* (Chicago: University of Chicago Press, 1998).
61 As seen in Vivek Narayanan, "On the Necessity of Speaking of Caste," in *Life and Times of Mr. S*, 63–6: "casting yourself across, casting yourself anew – with your English in your secret pouch – but that's no escape."
62 Here, I follow Michael Clune, who in his essay argues that a prose poem is "a virtual poem. Its way of ending, its closure lies outside of poetry, outside of aesthetic form. The prose poem is a quasi-form, a way to plot out a form that works, that makes something happen." It serves as a "formal instruction," a blueprint as it were, for making the finished poem, but it never quite is the finished poem. See Michael W. Clune, "Theory of Prose," *NO: A Journal of the Arts* 6 (January 2008): 48–62.

10

COLLABORATION, CONVERSATION, AND ADAPTATION

The Prose Poetry Project and Renga Attitude

Jen Webb

Mary Oliver opens the foreword to her 2004 volume of essays by writing, "Prose flows forward bravely and, often, serenely, only slowly exposing emotion . . . Poems are less cautious, and the voice of the poem remains somehow solitary." In this, she distinguishes prose from poetry in terms of their "personal" qualities – courage, serenity, and restraint.[1] However fully one accepts this characterisation, it is certainly the case that poetry – or the poet performing the craft of poetry production – is widely considered to be "somehow solitary."[2] Prose too is often "somehow solitary"; but though there are examples of routine collaborative practice – scriptwriting teams, or journalist/sub-editor pairs, or academic co-authors – it is difficult to come up with many examples of collaboratively written poems. When poets write, we write alone.

Except when we don't. In this chapter, I discuss what is now a well-established multi-person collaboration called the Prose Poetry Project, which involves extensive prose poetry "conversations," co-optations, and collaborations. The Project emerged quite spontaneously in late 2014, when Paul Hetherington emailed a draft to several colleagues, who responded in kind. The University of Canberra (UC) then housed a group of lecturers and PhD candidates who were enthusiastic both about creative practice and about working with each other. This was fertile soil for the Project; and what began in an entirely ad hoc manner quickly became an event *cum* group *cum* game. Over the coming months, new poets from UC and elsewhere were invited to participate, and a year later, the project had 17 contributing poets from Australia and the UK, who had between them produced some 700 prose poems. Now, in 2021, there are 24 poets, 5 of them still located at UC, the other 19 located across Australia, in Singapore, Israel, and the United Kingdom, and with connections to New Zealand, Africa, and the United States.[3] The steady – several times a day – flow of posts to the Project members' inboxes

DOI: 10.4324/9781003199533-11

is testament to the energy, productivity, and enthusiasm for collaborative writing that continues to animate the group.

Collaboration in poetry has a long history in literary culture, but the practices collected under the term "collaborate" have a wide range of meanings. Antonia Pont and Cassandra Atherton outline a taxonomy of meanings in their discussion of what they term the "triangle of collaboration."[4] Along one side of the triangle are two or more "self-sufficient subjects" working together to achieve a desired aim in a relationship that is "akin to a professional or craft configuration." The second side involves collaborators working more closely on their increasingly interwoven identity, resulting in a relationship "that creates at the level of artefact but also foreseeably at the level of category itself" – which is to say, the individuals begin to lose their sense of independent being. On the third side of the triangle is the sort of "collaboration" where only one party is aware of and in control of the process: an approach Thomas Leitch describes as intertextuality or adaptation rather than collaboration *per se*. He dryly makes the point that "the dead make perfect collaborators, because they're never in a position to demand the credit the living feel should be ours alone,"[5] an attitude Geraldine Monk acknowledges, humorously excusing her "collaborations" on the grounds that "if there is an afterlife, my requisitioned collaborators will have all eternity to wreak their anger upon my celestial being."[6]

In this chapter, I ignore this category of "collaboration" in favour of the other two sides of the triangle. Side two, the collaborative mode that risks the dissolution of discrete individuals into a new ontological formation, is characterised by a famous nineteenth-century example known as "Michael Field." Katherine Harris Bradley and Edith Cooper, two people so utterly connected through their relationship of love and poetry that they claimed a single voice and name, effectively – at least textually – became one identity, and they utterly rejected the notion that either poet's work could be distinguished from the other.[7] Nearly a century later in 1944, a hemisphere apart and driven by a very different impulse, the Australian dyad of James McAuley and Harold Stewart co-authored a sequence of poems under the name of Ern Malley. Theirs was a spurious use of this ontologically disturbing mode of collaboration, since they did not subsume their two identities into one, though they did produce a new identity in the form of one of Australia's most famous poets. Their literary hoax achieved part of their objective – to fool the editor of *Angry Penguins* journal, Max Harris, into believing that these were authentic poems. But it did not achieve their underlying objective: to debunk the modernist form and demoralize its supporters, since "Ern Malley" remains recognised more than half a century later as a poet of quality.[8] "Malley" has achieved international recognition and has been anthologized, including in Kenneth Koch's 1961 special edition of *Locus Solus*, where Koch writes, "Though Harris was wrong about who Ern Malley 'was' (if one can use that word here), I find it hard not to agree with his judgment of Malley's poetry."[9] This is perhaps not surprising because whatever the motivation to collaborate, it frequently generates quite remarkable outcomes, and "the strangeness of the collaborating situation . . . might lead them to the unknown, or at the least to some dazzling insights at which they could never have arrived consciously or alone."[10]

The more commonly adopted mode in Pont and Atherton's taxonomy – where the collaborators work together to achieve an artefact but not to risk the loss of their identity – is seen in many of the 192 pages of collaboratively written fragments of novels, lineated lyrics and prose poems published in Koch's *Locus Solus*. It opens with several examples of Chinese and Japanese collaborations, showcasing traditional forms, including *renga*. Given the long history of creative collaboration in those cultures, and the supple ways in which haiku can operate, it is not surprising that many poet-collaborators look to Japanese forms for at least a starting point. I think, for example, of Yoko's Dogs (a.k.a. Jan Conn, Mary di Michele, Jane Munro, and Susan Gillis), whose first collection relies on the Japanese traditions of linked verse.[11] I think too of long-term collaborators poet Ken Cockburn and artist/writer Alec Finlay, who over 2010 and 2011 undertook a Scottish version of Matsuo Basho's seventeenth-century opus *Narrow Road to the Deep North* (1689–1691). Like Basho, Cockburn and Finlay travelled through the north of their country, and like Basho, they visited and wrote poetry at each of 53 stations. Following Basho's lead, Cockburn says, they had planned to write "a renga for each place we visited – a two-handed renga, not a formal one":

> we did that for the first couple of places that we went to, but then we thought, *this is not really what we want to do*. The form was too limiting. The blog became much more interesting, we could add whatever we wanted to it: photographs, small poems written in situ, descriptive prose, longer poems.[12]

Still, it retained the traces of Basho's model, and like him, they produced a book a few years after the journey was completed, titled *the road north*.[13] Though finally Finlay and Cockburn wrote neither *renga* nor prose poems, their effective reaching beyond the boundaries of form and tradition provides an example of how far collaborative creative play can take writers in the continual development and reinvention of voice and self.

Denise Duhamel and Maureen Seaton, another long-term creative pair, have been co-authoring poetry for many years using the model of a poetry cycle, or poetry chain. This is loosely related to the Japanese *renga* form in that it involves a composition process where one poet writes a few lines, then sends them to the other, who adds new lines, edits others, and returns the new draft to the first poet. They describe as "spontaneous and wonderfilled" this process of call and response until there is a completed poem that is truly, line by line, the work of each.[14]

As well as co-authoring poetry, Duhamel and Seaton are also co-editors, and with David Trinidad they produced the 2007 anthology *Saints of Hysteria*.[15] While much of this is lineated poetry, several prose poetry collaborations are included, one of these an excerpt from Olga Broumas and Jane Miller's *Black Holes, Black Stockings*.[16] Broumas and Miller note that their collaboration approach is based on "two rules: write every day . . . and don't look back til it's done" – very different, therefore, from either the Duhamel/Seaton or the Cockburn/Finlay dyads. Miller continues, noting that their collaborative process takes them to "the wonderful world of self-effacement . . . Everyone should consider disappearing for a while into another voice!"[17]

What is referenced in many of the notes appended to the *Saints of Hysteria* or the *Locus Solus* poets, in the diaries kept by the Michael Field duo, as well as in Pont and Atherton's description of the second side of the triangle is that alongside the delight and the generative dynamism of working with another is the problem, and risk, of having to compromise one's individual and independent voice in the interests of the collaborator's individual and independent voice. Michel Foucault's work suggests that what is at risk is one's stable self-identity as "author," an identity that is the product of the Enlightenment and offers what Foucault describes as "the privileged moment of individualization."[18] Collaborate, and you may lose your identification with the writing you have produced and become simply one part of a larger whole. Pierre Bourdieu, more pragmatically, outlines the economic loss a creative practitioner risks when subsuming their discrete identity within a group: "For the author, the critic, the art dealer, the publisher or the theatre manager, the only legitimate accumulation consists in making a name for oneself, a known, recognized name": *a* name, not a pair or group of names.[19] Yet the very long history of Japanese co-authored poetry shows that there is no real risk of loss when engaging in a collaboration with other creatives. In fact, there is possibly as much or more gain as there is loss in collaborating *as* a prose poet *with* other prose poets.

Here is a possible alignment between Western and Japanese poetry. I look particularly to *renga*, because an important underlying aspect of that form is the Buddhist logic of *muga* (self-forgetting), or, as Tadashi Ogawa puts it, self-abandonment, "the acknowledgement of seeing something with the other person's eyes."[20] Octavio Paz, who collaborated with three other poets on a major *renga* cycle published as *Renga: A Chain of Poems,* noted that this project required them to adopt the *muga* attitude: "The practice of the *renga* implies the negation of certain cardinal Western notions, such as the belief in the soul and in the reality of the I," an attitude that emerges in some, but not all, Western poetry collaborations.[21]

Japanese poetic forms have had a strong influence on twentieth-century poetry, as Rosy Saikia points out in elaborating the role haiku played, particularly in the development of twentieth-century imagist poetry, as evidenced for example in many of Ezra Pound's poems.[22] Prose poetry too has an established "family" relationship with Japanese poetry: Hetherington and Atherton cite the seventeenth-century Duc de la Rochefoucauld's belief that haiku had a role in the development of the prose poem, and they note the continuing influence of Japanese poetry in the practice of *haibun*, which comprises, effectively, prose poems punctuated by haiku.[23] Koch too observes that "Japanese poets wrote together as naturally as Shelley wrote alone"[24] and, given the increasing familiarity of (adapted) Japanese forms among Western poets, it is likely that not only the form but also the openness to co-authorship is why it is so often adopted for contemporary practice. And this delivers very productive outcomes: because collaboration not only changes the thinking and practice of the poets involved but, by instantiating a change from self-contained poem to a linked sequence, it also changes the reader's experience. As Nobuyuki Yuasa suggests, such sequences offer "a kind of kaleidoscopic beauty with infinite variety revealed to the reader in a slowly evolving movement."[25]

While traditional *renga* is culturally specific, precise, and directive, the *idea* of *renga* can translate very well into contemporary collaborations. The rules, Konishi Jin'Ichi explains, include not just the mode but also the context for practice, which holds that a traditional sequence must be produced by "an assembly of renga enthusiasts who are both the poets and the audience" and who are, ideally, "persons who share a degree of friendship as well as similar levels of technical competence" and who will hold "regular gatherings for the enjoyment of renga."[26] Replace "*renga*" with "prose poetry," and this is precisely what emerged, albeit spontaneously and without conscious reference to *renga*, within the Prose Poetry Project. Shared email exchanges provide the required "regular gatherings"; participants all have "technical competence," and they "share a degree of friendship" – which is necessary to ensure the group possesses the levels of trust required to expose what are often early drafts to the scrutiny of others. The regular poem exchanges, along with the appropriation of phrases and concepts from each other's drafts – which often become "slowly evolving" sequences of images and ideas – provide the impetus to stay connected to the Project. Though the extent of individuals' engagement waxes and wanes over the years, there are always at least half a dozen people contributing new work and sparking new lines of thought on pretty much a daily basis.

Ogawa expands on the social complexities incorporated in the rules of *renga*. These include the absence of control by any one poet (the "master" sets the theme of a *renga* sequence but does not regulate how or what the other poets write); the openness that is necessarily inherent when more than one subjectivity is involved in the making of a work; the sense of complementarity when one poem responds to those that preceded it and inflect those that follow; the uncertainty, since other participants are always likely to introduce unexpected elements; and the incompleteness of each poem, because it is only one part of a much larger corpus.

"One can say," Ogawa writes, "that this sense of incompleteness opens up a freely moving space or the possibility of a horizon of satisfaction."[27] This is very distinct from the Wordsworthian notion of poetry as emotion recollected in tranquillity, rather than a conversation between poets who reflect on, and respond to, the work of each other more than the promptings of one's personal and individual concerns.

These complexities are largely encompassed by the operations of the Prose Poetry Project, and one outcome is the production of substantial numbers of poems, most of which are close to publishable standard, and many of which have been published either as stand-alone works, as collaborative artefacts, or as interwoven collections. The latter are evidenced in a trilogy of anthologies of early Project work, edited by members of the Project. Titled *Seam* (2015), *Pulse* (2016), and *Tract* (2017), each volume showcases aspects of the "kaleidoscopic" effect that, for Nobuyuki Yuasa, emerges from this mode of collaboration.[28] Shane Strange, who edited the first volume, identified mirrorings and shadowings of topic or voice across the poems and arranged them into pairs that reflect the shimmering of thought and image. Monica Carroll joined Shane Strange to edit the second volume, and they elected to weave together selections from a year of work that reflect the flow of images that runs through series of posts. They also made the decision to present the poems without either author's name or page numbers, writing:

> We wanted to show that the collaborative vigour of the Project didn't arise from any individual or select group of voices, but from the broad mixture of contributors, whose voices intermingle, reflect and amplify each other.
>
> . . .
>
> We wanted to concentrate on the way these pieces wove threads through each other into longer fabrics: resonating images, themes, narratives, motifs, ideas and connections. We hope you can feel a "pulse" of meaning through the book.[29]

While the contributors were pleased to be part of this publishing experiment, the reviewers found it a bit problematic. Chloe Wilson observes that "the arrangement of *Pulse* is curious . . . to discover the author of any individual poem, a reader is obliged to consult the list at the back of the anthology."[30] Lucy Alexander (who has since become a member of the Project) found it both more challenging and more open to challenge. While she writes positively about the experience of reading these connected fragments, and what she terms the echoes and reverberations across the collection, she is not as impressed by the de-identification of the poems' authors. "While it's interesting for a collaborative project to be so collaborative that the individual is lost within the project itself," she asks, "is this what the published volume of finalised work should reflect?" and points out:

> This raises interesting questions about the nature of publication and how contributors might be paid and acknowledged for their work. As Paul

Munden seems to bitingly remark in the closing poem of the collection: "The author would / like to recall one of his recent prose / poems. Sadly, he cannot identify which."[31]

Certainly, as noted earlier, Mode 2 of Pont and Atherton's taxonomy is often uncomfortable for Western poets, and indeed for their readers who may struggle to engage with writings that refuse the Western privileging of individualisation. Still, for the third collection, *Tract*, the editors bowed to the need to include page numbers but remained unmoved by those concerns and again excluded the authors' names from the body of the book. Their aim in doing this was to present "an interwoven sequence" that showcases "the extraordinary narrative and reflective capabilities of the prose poem form,"[32] and means the collection presents as though authored by all 22 poets.

This is probably as closely aligned as the Project's operations are to traditional *renga*, since the formal rules of practice are far less applicable – indeed, barely applicable at all – to current ways of being or writing. Those rules include the presence of a master and a scribe; the requirement that at each sitting, the *renga* group will produce a hundred verses of 17 syllables and that the themes, lexical categories, and the use of repetition and seriation are both prescribed and restricted.[33]

The Project poets break all these rules but retain a clear alignment to the *renga attitude* in an approach to appropriation that is aligned with many adoptions and adaptations of form over the centuries. There are, in fact, genealogical traces of poetic thought that run right through the corpus of poetry, as ideas and experiments shift and morph between cultures and decades. Eighteenth-century French poets' experiments, for example, were adopted and adapted by nineteenth-century French poets,[34] whose resistance to the strictures of the academy are likely to have informed the post–World War I surrealist poets, who themselves advanced modes of collaborative writing and rule-breaking that were adopted and adapted by the 1950s New York School poets,[35] who subsequently influenced prose poets like Simic and Strand and Waldrop.[36]

Renga itself had changed significantly from its traditional form well before westerners began considering its affordances. By the seventeenth century, it had shed much of its formality and become what was now simply considered a type of *haikai* (linked verse). This formal change was accompanied by a change in status, from poetry of and for the elites, to poetry of and for the people; and by changes in history and culture. As Haruo Shirane writes:

> *Haikai* . . . emerged from the interaction of socially and temporally disparate worlds, from the intersection of a seemingly unchanging, idealized past (that included China) with a constantly, rapidly changing present, the centripetal

force of the former serving to hold in check the centrifugal force of the latter.[37]

These two forces animate a productive tension in seventeenth-century Japanese poetry, where the self of the poet is simultaneously part of a post-traditional present, and a tradition that belongs in history. What is evident in this poetry is a seethe of interweaving voices, accents, languages, and discourses, where urban elites rub shoulders with commoners and provincial poets, and where the ordinary issues of everyday life receive attention alongside formally approved themes.[38]

A similar interweaving is seen in contemporary Anglophone poetry. Consider the New York School poets who, as Allen Ginsburg notes, had a shared interest in "the transformation of the diction and the rhythms into vernacular rhythms and/ or spoken cadences and idiomatic diction."[39] Consider too the present rise in the popularity and commercial (if not critical) success of instapoetry[40]; or spoken word poetry which does not comfortably find a fit in an art form that depends so much on publication.[41]

Prose poetry too has until recently been hovering on the edges of approved forms. When it (re)appeared in its Anglo twentieth-century mode, it was largely rejected by the American academy on the grounds that it was not really poetry. Famously (or notoriously), Mark Strand's collection of "short prose musings," *The Monument*, was shortlisted for the 1978 Pulitzer Prize in poetry but was not awarded the prize because one of the three judges, Louis Simpson, objected that it was primarily prose and thus not appropriate for a prize "designed expressly to honor verse."[42] Lehman quotes Charles Simic as saying, "The prose poem has the unusual distinction of being regarded with suspicion not only by the usual haters of poetry, but also by many poets themselves" and suggests that it is "poetry that disguises its true nature."[43] The conflation of prose and poem in one name is, perhaps, why Michael Riffaterre describes it as "the literary genre with an oxymoron for a name."[44] Billy Collins too questions its status, saying: "Poems are supposed to look a certain way. Prose is like water – it'll fill any vessel and take any shape that you pour it into. But a poem is more like a piece of sculpture, and it has a structural shape to it."[45] He expands on this more generously later in the interview, when he identifies rhyme and meter as the trainer wheels of poetry and notes that with the trainer wheels removed, and when done well, such poems – prose as well as free verse – "have a beautiful acoustic system of sonic reverberation and vowels echoing . . . the poem becomes a musical system."

Nonetheless, prose poetry has still not comfortably found a home in the authoritative spaces of poetic practice; and John Taylor's discussion of the origins of prose poetry in fifth-century BCE Greece seems to imply that this outsider status is built into the DNA of prose poetry. He identifies the *mimos,* or "the imitation of the everyday," as the ancestor of this form because of its dependence on demotic speech and its celebration of quotidian objects and events.[46] He also points to Aristotle's uncertainty about what *mimos* actually is, since Aristotle introduces "an art which imitates by language alone, without harmony, in prose or in verse . . . This form of imitation is to this day without a name."[47]

Because it begins as an unknowable outsider, because it rejects the strictures of line, and because it is simultaneously arcane *and* pedestrian, taking the familiar, comfortable form of the paragraph, prose poetry remains a "rebellious" form.[48] But in these refusals, and in its capacity to combine poetic music and imagery with narrative impulse, it offers opportunities to expand language and its uses. Russell Edson's "The Taxi," for instance, starts:

> One night in the dark I phone for a taxi. Immediately a taxi crashes through the wall; never mind that my room is on the third floor, or that the yellow driver is really a cluster of canaries.[49]

This surreal set of images and events captures something of the uncertainty of everyday life. As Edson says in a later article, prose poetry is "a statement that seeks sanity while its author teeters on the edge of the abyss. The language will be simple, the images so direct . . . "[50] And the use of the comic mode, along with the deployment of accessible language in the accessible form of the paragraph, results in a clear-eyed representation of the fragility of social life.

Fragility is exemplified again in the prose poem "Film shoot," by Australian poet John Kinsella, which begins: "A friend rang to see if it was okay for a mate to take his film crew up to Wheatlands for an on-location shoot."[51] While here Kinsella avoids both the comic and the surreal, his poem effectively adopts the vernacular and demotic voice, focusing on quotidian issues that are world shattering – the impacts of the Anthropocene on the natural world. In its concision, imagistic construct, and (when read out loud) poetic rhythms, it shimmers as poems do. In this, it complies with the prose poetry conventions as articulated by editor of *Amaranth Poetry Journal* Becky Rodia: that is, it may "*look* like prose," but it does not "*read* like prose" because there is in prose poems "a hidden-yet-logical system" that holds together the wilder, more arcane images and statements such works often contain.[52]

Like Edson's "The Taxi," Kinsella's "Film shoot" has a strong sense of story, beginning *in medias res*, incorporating character, location, and a sort of plot, and unscrolling to articulate a narrative of environmental disaster. There is frequent uncertainty about when a paragraph-length work is flash fiction and when it is prose poetry, as found in any number of blogs, editorials, or commentaries. Vaughan Rapatahana devotes a column of *jacket2* to the issue but asserts that "There is often no clear-cut distinction between prose poetry and flash or short fiction."[53] While some commentators make the point that fiction is about story, and poetry about image and rhythm, Brian McHale argues against this view on the grounds that poets do not ignore narrative.[54] Arguably, prose poems have the capacity to tack closer to story than do lineated poems because they are constructed via sentences rather than lines. But poems of any form should not entirely eschew stories because narrative matters. As Australian novelist, poet, and medical practitioner Peter Goldsworthy says:

> I always thought poetry and short stories were in our DNA. Those things are part of us; the deeper structures of language, the deeper structures of rhyme, rhythm and assonance, the music; they serve a necessary evolutionary purpose of making ideas memorable.[55]

Prose poetry, in its capture of fragmentary narratives of the everyday, captures attention, as has Basho's poetry – over several centuries – very likely for the sorts of qualities Goldsworthy lists: its attention to "making ideas memorable"; accommodating the quotidian; featuring the lives of fishermen, beggars, and housewives; storying the countryside in which they lived; and creating images of the most ordinary of lived places and pursuits. Portraits of community, in effect. Certainly, post-traditional *renga* focused on a broader community than the "persons of technical competence" privileged in the early form. This presented affordances for developing points of connection and building harmony and also introduced a playful element in the ways each poet responded both to the rules of the form and to what other poets in the group had delivered.[56] This new attention to collectivity is what Ogawa describes as the "trans-subjective" – in distinction to what he calls "the prevailing European view … [that] grounds the essence of literature, especially lyricism, in the self".[57]

Post-traditional *renga* is therefore not so much co-authorship as a sort of Bakhtinian dialogism: the concept that life is a shared event; that to live is to participate in a continuing process of dialogue; and that it is in engaging with others that meaning is given form and life is given meaning.[58] Or, as Ogawa says, "What matters most is to abandon the 'funk hole' or 'dugout' of the self and enter into the ocean of a shared life with others."[59]

Abandoning the dugout in favour of dialogism has been very effective in the case of the prose poetry collaborations *cum* conversations practiced over the past half-dozen years by members of the Project. The rules of this group are few and simple: each member should contribute at least three poems in a year; poets should exchange their work via group email; and "fast writing" is expected. What are exchanged, therefore, are not polished poems, but fresh drafts – what Billy Collins refers to as poems "with the paint still wet."[60] There are no requirements as to topic, voice, or content. Nor is individual ownership a strong feature; frequently, one or more members of the group will respond to someone else's post in an antiphonal manner, or by "stealing" phrases and ideas – to the point that we began, early on, to describe this practice as "authorised theft" – in a model that recognises the linked-verse patterns of *renga*.

Of course, theft is a part of poetry; in his "Advice to poets," Kevin Brophy warns "Show them nothing. They steal everything. / They are thugs and desperately / short of ideas."[61] But not only does the Project accept, and indeed expect and encourage such thefts; the form in which we work facilitates it. The *renga* tradition similarly expects an antiphonal engagement and an unfolding of the idea being pursued, but it requires precise structures for each poet to adopt. Prose poetry, perhaps more than other contemporary poetry forms, and more than traditional *renga*, is characterised by what Project member Oz Hardwick describes as "inherent shareability" because, unlike formal poetic structures, it is open as to form.[62] Prose poetry has no rules controlling the use of line or syllable count (cf. cinquain, haiku), rhyming pattern (cf. sonnet, ballade), stanza structure (cf. epic, sestina), or repetition (cf. pantoum, villanelle). All prose poets need do is capture a word, phrase, image, or idea from another's work and then take it into any context they choose. This allows for the speed with which members can respond to one another, and significantly expands the type, tone, mood, and content of the works produced, while allowing the Project members – who are widely diverse in terms of age, cultural tradition, national identity, gender, and interest – to produce poems that are distinctively their own, while comprising part of a greater whole.

During December 2014, the first month of the Project's life, there were just three poets involved. Several more joined in January, and the record of postings that month and from then on shows a distinct tendency to weave in and out of other's posts; to reconsider issues raised by others; to view the key object under consideration as through a prism, casting different perspectives in different lights. I include below a sequence of excerpts of poems worrying at the problem of absence and loss, the posts following rapidly on each other's heels, providing an example of the flow of thought and the speed of response:

> Poet 1, *25-Jan-2015 10:17 PM*
> Their childhood had been sent to the tip: photographs, tools, mementos, gifts their father had given—emblems of fond gestures and his strange way of talking—old teddy bears, childish drawings they'd left for safekeeping. A truckload of loss; decades of erasure, as if a blank sky had fallen . . .
>
> Poet 2, *26-Jan-2015 10:52 AM*
> From what he saved of his parents' things, he finally carted a few treasures halfway around the world, wanting to see them in a new light. But the light proved harsh, more fond of its own glitter . . .
>
> Poet 3, *26-Jan-2015 12:54 PM*
> . . . The phone rings briefly, then stops; his house pauses, a moment's silence for the incompleteness of things. The cat cries at the door to be let in. He would cry too, but there is no one to open the door, no cushion where he can curl himself, and sleep.

Poet 4, *26-Jan-2015, 01:33 PM*

A trace of your home in the China-man statues and snapshot assortments. Brass and glass. The blood cannot move around your body. All there, but for that missing. One of everything as a token marking the habits, so the absent cannot swell . . , I want the weeping from when I was ten and grasping you were old, even then, and one day I would lose you.

Poet 1, *26-Jan-2015 01:49 PM*

What he lost was not what he believed he had lost. He had believed that loss lay chiefly in the absence of things that they might make and share—small trays inlaid with mosaics, piles of clean washing, elaborate salads in large bowls. And in the loss of conversation. But something else was missing . . .

Poet 3, *26-Jan-2015 02:04 PM*

When I mislaid the diamond you gave me, you were unexpectedly serene. Not so when I lost the car keys, the book you were reading, your mother's phone number. Not so when I mislaid the map, dropped the fishing rod overboard, fell through the glass. For months we grappled with the inconstancy of things . . .

At this point the poets seemed to lose interest in loss; and a few days later, another poet entered the game and changed the parameters, shifting from absence to presence and from external objects to bodies and their pleasures:

Poet 5, *29-Jan-2015 02:28 PM*

He thought of his grandfather forcing him to help build a concrete driveway when he was ten: grey powder and gravel and sand being mixed. He thought of the heat in summer. The beautiful way the gravel felt when it fell through his fingers . . .

Poet 6, *02-Feb-2015 04:56 PM*

what we'll do is remove the dusty fly-spotted umbrella light-shade from over the bed, and we'll put there something that catches the will of the leaves outside the windows and holds it in the centre of the room . . . your blood is of that language, tipping and will be so while your hands find the way to your mouth. mouth wet and working in joy's animation of hunger . . .

Poet 4, *07-Feb-2015 07:25 AM*

Hands in the dark bag. Working by touch and contour . . . Don't tap. Use black force. The pop tops and film sets itself free, in a tangle, in a twirl, in an exhale. Take those clean fingertips and catch the cross spliced start . . .

Poet 7, *07-Feb-2015 12:09 PM*

They'll take my old words and put them on the easel. They won't know the meanings in their head but they'll find them in paint, or chess moves . . . that's the shared genetic meal, shared many times around the campfire, and everyone knows it and relates to it and sees the magic and stares happily into the fire, finally happy to say nothing.

These snatches of poetry, written individually but in threaded conversations, indicate the affordances of a community of practice. The same modes of collaboration, conversation, and appropriation between the members have continued and expanded over the years. Sometimes pairs of poets will rework several of their drafts into one multi-paragraph poem attributed to both; sometimes groups of poets will collaborate on a theme, and each independently write a set of poems that address that theme from separate perspectives; sometimes the poets construct their own sole-authored collections of works that found their genesis in this collective space. The Project, which began in a context of considerable trans-subjectivity and openness to conversation, has continued to operate in that mode. What we are doing is not *renga*, but – we hope – it honours the logic and the impulse of *renga*: to form and maintain a community committed to experiments, to the making of poems, and to their pleasures. This experiment in play, prose poetry, and creative collaboration has continued for some 7 years and involved 30 poets from across Australia and across the globe. It attests to a model of practice that allows a wide range of voices, vision, aesthetic taste, and cultural interests to steep together and to galvanise a remarkably sustainable and shareable approach to poetry practice. The indications from the past years suggest that the structure of prose poetry, which provides a supple and highly variable form in which to shape poems, and a hint of narrative traction that sparks new lines of address, is the key element in the success of this project. We add to that the *renga* attitude of collaboration, mutual respect, and respect for the demands of poetry and practice, alongside an attitude that encourages play, risk-taking, and a continual adjustment of the poet's self to the idea of the poem. What we have found is that this approach engenders both poetry and a rich seam of connection to a community of practice.

Notes

1 Mary Oliver, *Long Life: Essays and Other Writings* (Boston, MA: Da Capo Press, 2004), xiii.
2 Jen Webb and Monica Carroll, "A Seethe of Poets: Creativity and Community," *TEXT Special Issue 40* (April 2017): 1–15.
3 Australians: Lucy Alexander, Cassandra Atherton, Eugen Bacon, Monica Carroll, Jen Crawford, Martin Dolan, Ross Gibson, Stephanie Green, Charlotte Guest, Dominique Hecq, Paul Hetherington, Penelope Layland, Maggie Shapley, Shane Strange, Jen Webb, Jordan Williams. Internationals: Anne Caldwell, Carrie Etter, Niloofar Fanaiyan, Oz Hardwick, Rupert Loydell, Andrew Melrose, Paul Munden, Alvin Pang. In 2015, its first full year, there were 15 members, who were joined over the years by a further 15, bringing the total active members from January 2015 to August 2021 to 30. Of the original 15 members, 12 are still active members of the Project.
4 Antonia Pont and Cassandra Atherton, "Poetics of Collaboration: Introduction," *Axon: Creative Explorations* 6, no. 1 (March 2016), www.axonjournal.com.au/issue-10/introduction.

5 Thomas Leitch, "Collaborating with the Dead: Adapters as Secret Agents," in *Adaptation Considered as a Collaborative Art,* ed. Bernadette Cronin, Rachel MacShamhráin, and Nikolai Preuschoff (Cham, CH: Springer, 2020), 20.

6 Geraldine Monk, "Collaborations with the Dead," in *The Salt Companion to Geraldine Monk,* ed. Scott Thurston (Cambridge: Salt Publishing, 2007), 181.

7 See Holly Laird, "Contradictory Legacies: Michael Field and Feminist Restoration," *Victorian Poetry* 33, no. 1 (Spring, 1995): 116.

8 David Rainey, *The Hoax and Beyond* (Melbourne: Heide Museum of Modern Art, 2009).

9 Kenneth Koch, *Locus Solus II: A Special Issue of Collaborations* (Summer 1961): 203.

10 Koch, *Locus Solus II*, 193.

11 Yoko's Dogs, *Whisk* (Toronto: Pedlar Press, 2013).

12 Ken Cockburn, personal communication to the author, 15 June 2014.

13 Alec Finlay and Ken Cockburn, *The Road North* (Swindon, UK: Shearsman, 2014).

14 Denise Duhamel and Maureen Seaton, "Featured Selection: A Poem Cycle," *Plume* 26 (August 2013), https://plumepoetry.com/featured-selection-a-poem-cycleby-denise-duhamel-and-maureen-seaton/.

15 Denise Duhamel, Maureen Seaton, and David Trinidad, eds., *Saints of Hysteria: A Half-Century of Collaborative American Poetry* (Brooklyn: Soft Shell Press, 2007).

16 Olga Broumas and Jane Miller, *Black Holes, Black Stockings* (Middletown, CT: Wesleyan Poetry Series, 1985).

17 Duhamel, Seaton and Trinidad, *Saints of Hysteria*, 96.

18 Michel Foucault, "What Is an Author?" trans. Josué Harari, in *The Foucault Reader*, ed. Paul Rabinow (New York: Pantheon Books, 1984), 141.

19 Pierre Bourdieu, *The Field of Cultural Production: Essays on Art and Literature* (Cambridge: Polity, 1993), 75.

20 Tadashi Ogawa, "The Trans-subjective Creation of Poetry and Mood: A Short Study of Japanese Renga," *Comparative and Continental Philosophy* 1, no. 2 (2009): 202.

21 Octavio Paz, "Introduction," in *Renga: A Chain of Poems*, by Octavio Paz, Jacques Roubaud, Edoardo Sanguineti, and Charles Tomlinson (New York: George Braziller, 1972), 21.

22 Rosy Saikia, "Image and Beyond: A Re-reading of Basho's Haiku," in *Consciousness, Theatre, Literature and the Arts 2015*, ed. Daniel Meyer-Dinkgräf (Newcastle-upon-Tyne: Cambridge Scholars Publishing, 2016), 133.

23 Paul Hetherington and Cassandra Atherton, eds. *Prose Poetry: An Introduction* (Princeton, NJ: Princeton University Press, 2020), 18, 91–2.

24 Koch, *Locus Solus,* 193.

25 Matsuo Basho, *The Narrow Road to the Deep North and Other Travel Sketches*, trans. Nobuyuki Yuasa (Harmondsworth, UK: Penguin, 1966), 12.

26 Konishi Jin'Ichi, "The Art of Renga," trans. Karen Brazell and Lewis Cook, *The Journal of Japanese Studies* 2, no. 1 (Autumn, 1975): 33.

27 Ogawa, "The Trans-subjective Creation," 196.

28 Shane Strange, ed., *Seam: Prose Poems* (Canberra: Recent Work Press, 2015); Shane Strange and Monica Carroll, eds., *Pulse: Prose Poems* (Canberra: Recent Work Press, 2016); and Monica Carroll and Paul Munden, eds., *Tract: Prose Poems* (Canberra: Recent Work Press, 2017).

29 Strange and Carroll, *Pulse,* n.p.

30 Chloe Wilson, "A Shrine to the Fragment. Review of *Pulse: Prose Poems*," *TEXT: Journal of Writing and Writing Courses* 20, no. 2 (October 2016), http://www.textjournal.com.au/oct16/wilson_rev.htm

31 Lucy Alexander, "Reading in an Undiscovered Library: *Pulse – Prose Poems* as Collaboration," *Verity La* (23 June 2017), https://verityla.com/2017/06/23/reading-in-an-undiscovered-library-pulse-prose-poems-as-collaboration/.

32 Carroll and Munden, *Tract,* n.p.

33 Jin'Ichi, "The Art of Renga," 37.

34 Fabienne Moore, *Prose Poems of the French Enlightenment: Delimiting Genre* (Farnham, UK: Ashgate Publishing, 2009).

35 Mark Silverberg, ed., *New York School Collaborations: The Colour of Vowels* (New York: Palgrave, 2010).

36 Cassandra Atherton and Paul Hetherington, "The Ordinary and the Unreal: American and Australian Prose Poetry," *Axon: Creative Explorations* 7, no. 2 (December 2017), www.axonjournal.com.au/issue-13/ordinary-and-unreal.

37 Haruo Shirane, *Traces of Dreams: Landscape, Cultural Memory, and the Poetry of Basho* (Palo Alto, CA: Stanford University Press, 1998), 5.

38 Shirane, *Traces of Dreams,* 8.

39 Anselm Berrigan, ed., *What is Poetry (Just Kidding, I Know You Know): Interviews from the Poetry Project Newsletter (1983–2009)* (Seattle, WA: Wave Books, 2017), 43.

40 Kate Kovalik and Jen Scott Curwood, "#poetryisnotdead: understanding Instagram poetry within a transliteracies framework," *Literacy* 53, no. 4 (November 2019): 185–95.

41 Javon Johnson, *Killing Poetry: Blackness and the Making of Slam and Spoken Word Communities* (New Brunswick, NJ: Rutgers University Press, 2017).

42 David Lehman, "Introduction," in *Great American Prose Poems: From Poe to the Present,* ed. David Lehman (New York: Scribner, 2003), 11.

43 Lehman, "Introduction," in *Great American Prose Poems,* 13.

44 Michael Riffaterre, *Semiotics of Poetry* (Bloomington, IN: Indiana University Press, 1978), 117.

45 Laurence Léveillé, "Collins Shares Thoughts on Shift in Methods of Writing Poetry," *The Chautauquan Daily,* 28 June 2012, https://chqdaily.wordpress.com/2012/06/28/collins-shares-thoughts-on-shift-in-methods-of-writing-poetry/.

46 John Taylor, "Two Cultures of the Prose Poem." *Michigan Quarterly Review* 44, no. 2 (Spring 2005). http://hdl.handle.net/2027/spo.act2080.0044.223.

47 Aristotle, *On the Art of Poetry,* ed. Gilbert Murray, trans. Ingram Bywater (Oxford: Clarendon Press, 1920), 8.

48 Anne Caldwell, "Reawakening Wonder: How Cartography Can Act as Creative Research for Prose Poetry," *New Writing* 15, no. 4 (2018): 401.

49 Russell Edson, "The Taxi," in *The Reason Why the Closet-man Is Never Sad* (Middletown, CT: Wesleyan University Press, 1977), 67.

50 Russell Edson, "Portrait of the Writer as a Fat Man: Some Subjective Ideas or Notions on the Care and Feeding of Prose Poems, 1975," in *Claims for Poetry,* ed. Donald Hall (Ann Arbor, MI: University of Michigan Press, 1983), 103.

51 John Kinsella, "Film Shoot," in *Anthology of Australian Prose Poetry,* eds. Cassandra Atherton and Paul Hetherington (Carlton, AU: Melbourne University Press, 2020), 112.

52 Becky Rodia, "Comments – Editorial and Otherwise," in *Always the Beautiful Answer: A Prose Poem Primer,* ed. Ruth Moon Kempher (St Augustine, FL: Kings Estate Press, 1999), 247.

53 Vaughan Rapatahana, "Bending Genres: Flash Fiction/Prose Poetry in Aotearoa New Zealand," *Jacket2*, 26 March 2018, https://jacket2.org/commentary/flash-fictionprose-poetry-aotearoa-new-zealand.

54 Brian McHale, "Beginning to Think about Narrative in Poetry," *Narrative* 17, no. 1 (2009): 11.

55 Peter Goldsworthy, personal communication to the author, 7 March 2014.

56 Shirane, *Traces of Dreams*, 152.

57 Ogawa, "The Trans-subjective Creation," 197.

58 Michail M. Bakhtin, *The Dialogic Imagination: Four Essays*, trans. Caryl Emerson and Michael Holquist (Austin, TX: University of Texas Press, 1981).

59 Ogawa, "The Trans-subjective Creation," 200.

60 This is a term Billy Collins frequently used during his The Poetry Broadcast sessions (held on Facebook from the start of the 2020 pandemic) when he read one of his own new and unfinished poems.

61 Kevin Brophy, *Portrait in Skin* (Wollongong, AU: Five Islands Press, 2002), 41.

62 Oz Hardwick, personal communication to the author, 18 July 2021.

11

FRAMING CATASTROPHE

The Ekphrastic Prose Poem

Patrick Wright

This chapter will explore how the subject of grief can be mediated by way of the ekphrastic prose poem. Rather than discuss the latter more generally, I am particularly interested in how the prose poem is able to accommodate a profound sense of loss or catastrophe. Moreover, with reference to my own poems, I will show how J. M. W. Turner's late paintings, which can be seen as abstract or formless, are a screen through which my personal grief can find a representation and be articulated. In so doing, I further recent work by Paul Hetherington and Cassandra Atherton, among others, where the prose poem is understood as a form that is recursive and circular and lends itself to themes such as trauma or disaster. I have also been inspired by Gilles Deleuze, who interprets Turner's paintings in terms of catastrophe: not as representing catastrophe but rather as "catastrophes in themselves and for those who view them."[1] The analogy I present is between these features of the prose poem identified by Hetherington and Atherton and the swirls of light and fog that mark Turner's art. Both poem and painting, word and image, can then be seen as forms that contain, each in their own way, what cannot be reduced to narrative.

Recent developments in ekphrasis, as noted by Camille Guthrie, owe a debt to Classical strategies. Rather than follow James Heffernan's critique of ekphrastic poets who write of a still and silent image or partake in a verbo-visual contest for authority,[2] Guthrie recommends an ekphrastic mode of "stepping into the aura." With Barbara Guest's "Roses" and Kevin Young's "Cadillac Moon" in mind, she talks about how "the relationship between poet and artist in these examples is not adversarial; it's a response based on enthusiasm and engagement. A poetics that suggests permeability *and* difference: an interaction that doesn't require a winner."[3] This mode has encouraged me to nurture a dialogical rapport with the artwork, in which it can be celebrated and re-imagined while, at the same time, holding sway

DOI: 10.4324/9781003199533-12

in shaping my poem in both content *and* form. In this way, with a poetics that as Guthrie declares "revels in the image," "asks," "reveals," and "wonders," I also employ the rhetorical ploy of *energeia* (vividness). This means rendering an absent image present in a way that produces a new image(s) in the mind of the reader and transforms my poem on the page.[4]

My ekphrasis thus counters what I observe as a tendency, from the mid-nineteenth century, for experiments in poetic form to ensure their techniques constrain visual form and what, through Modernism, was coveted as the immediacy of the image (suggested though contended by Frank O'Hara's poem "Why I Am Not a Painter").[5] This is more overt when ekphrasis becomes a sub-genre and centres upon a pre-existing artwork where the picture or prompt is usually figurative, characterised by mimesis, narrative or iconography.[6] W. H. Auden's "Musée des Beaux Arts" (his response to Bruegel's *Landscape with the Fall of Icarus* and other works) is emblematic here. That is to say, there is a bias towards images with referents or that may be read like a text: where "everything turns away / Quite leisurely from the disaster" (where the disaster refers to the dissolution of the sign).[7] It is telling then that Bruegel's painting can be perceived as an allegory of Matthew Gumpert's proposal that

> the catastrophe is both that which resists incorporation into the larger totality of events . . . and that which, even as it happens, dissolves instantaneously into that totality, which disappears, like Icarus, into the great sea of events, with barely a splash.[8]

This evasion of the formless is evident even when the ekphrasis of modern art strays beyond the descriptive, as identified in Guthrie's examples; likewise, the ekphrastic prose poem, on the verge of amorphousness and identity crisis, needs the reassuring buttress of figures. This is also apparent in recent examples, which, despite innovations in other areas, continue to privilege the content (rather than the form) of the visual field.[9]

With this bias in mind, in a sequence of poems on Turner's late seascapes, I have focused on *formlessness*. Intrigued by these puzzling artworks, predominantly light and colour, I ask: What is an appropriate formal response for a poet engaged in ekphrasis when a painting has no discernible signs? After attempts to describe the surface (limited to colour, traces, or marks), I found that the formal elements of the image were generative of what became, in the end, poetic form. After my re-reading of Lyn Hejinian (for whom "form is not a fixture, but an activity"), Charles Olson (who argued that "form is never more than an extension of content"), and Michael Davidson's "painterly poem" (which, unlike a poem "about" a painting, "activates strategies of composition equivalent to but not dependent on the painting"), I arrived at the idea that my ekphrasis must allow the painting to produce a form which is, at the same time, indicative of the formless.[10]

So what form *is* fitting? One answer, proposed by Owen Bullock, is that when poets respond to the form of the artwork, what can occur is a "radical ekphrasis" that re-invigorates the writing process.[11] I understand this mode as writing with the formal properties of the image. This is distinct from bringing a still or silent image under the rules of language and craft, as epitomised by Keats's "Ode on a Grecian Urn."[12] With Turner's paintings, this could have meant counteracting the expansiveness: to impose a form (with, say, the use of metre) and thus keep the catastrophe in check. After all, these paintings are immersive, their sublimity asking to be reined in by *poiesis*. Rather than obey the impulse to shore up the ruins and gain mastery over the image (an approach as reactive as it is conservative), I invite the formlessness to shape my poem, as Bullock suggests. This also means participating *in* the disaster and constructing a form that, to follow catastrophe's more abstract definition, "[subverts] a system of things."[13]

While not seeking a mimetic engagement, as suggested by Simonides's pronouncement that "poetry is a speaking picture, painting a silent poetry" or Horace's well-cited dictum *ut pictura poesis* ("as is painting, so is poetry"), my poetic forms bear some correspondence to visual form, as I will illustrate. Furthermore, rather than transcribe the painting's *semiotics* – storms, vortices, indistinct fish, and so forth – and proceed around the canvas metonymically, so to speak, I prefer to forge a metaphorical bond between painting and poem. In other words, rather than include visual cues in my writing, I am inclined to parcel out thoughts and affects which I see as prefigured in Turner's art. In so doing, rather than meet the task with denial of my subjective investments, I cultivate attention towards how his pictures resonate. For example, a painting such as *Sunrise with Sea-monsters* (1845) articulates latent material suitable for the lyric. First, its significance is registered as a simultaneity (it "speaks" to my unconscious) and then becomes an armature around which I construct my poem.

In seeing Turner's paintings this way, as representing, in a nascent state, my inflected biography or personal feelings around grief, I also see the prose poem as an apt container. Just like a frame can hold apocalyptic scenes within limits, I see the prose poem as another potential frame that can hold my sense of disarray. The form is fitting in that, like the process of grief, it suggests recursion and circularity as opposed to linear narrative progression. I have been persuaded here by Oz Hardwick's argument that "the prose poem . . . provides the ideal arena to express the elegiac mode in a manner that reaches beyond the lyric or confessional."[14] The prose poem is therefore instrumental in enabling a mode of ekphrasis which is, essentially, a re-mediation or means of refracting (in the manner of a lens) a lyric impulse, one that gives form to formlessness.

I am aware of a congruent distrust of the prose poem as a legitimate form (since it is not written in the kind of line associated with what is traditionally called "the poem") and a distrust of abstract paintings that to some may seem vacuous or inscrutable. I read these two anxiety-inducing forms, prose poetry and abstraction, as a potential marriage: the prose poem ("the slipperiest of genres" for David Wheatley) coupled with the slipperiest of canvases.[15] More specifically, it is possible to observe a correlation between the English-language disapproval of the prose poem and a similar disapproval towards Turner's late paintings, voiced by Ruskin and others in the late nineteenth century: each form signifying a confusion around genre (poetry or prose, finished or unfinished?) and an ensuing fear of collapse into formlessness.[16] Just as the prose poem unsettled traditional poetic prosody, images where form predominates troubled prevailing notions of art's moral purpose; and while a reading of the literary form may affirm, as Jane Monson does, "a dialogue between a host of other disciplines and recognised polarities,"[17] each can just as easily be disparaged.

How I remodel the prose poem ekphrastically involves then, as its basis, my proposal that an inter-artistic kinship exists between these two domains. At the same time, this is not to avoid the paradox that they are forms *and* formless. Just as Michael Riffaterre sees prose poetry as "the literary genre with an oxymoron for a name" and Kevin Brophy acknowledges its "defiant formlessness," while making my comparison to Turner's paintings, it is important to see them as similarly problematic: as paintings, yes, but also as liminal and next to nothing.[18]

For David Caddy, the prose poem is

> without line breaks [and] retains the tension between line and sentence structure without the use of line endings. It has the potential to build pace, rhythm, music and produce meaning as much as free verse, only it has to generate tension, drama and crises through sentence structure, relationship and language use alone. It is . . . a freedom to open possibilities and to move away from stultifying rigidity and closure.[19]

Turner's late seascapes are likewise open-ended, have no clear edges, and like the prose poem are a modern form that resists definition: they are avant-garde and *terra incognita*. Both exist outside of linear time: for Deleuze, Turner's paintings are "ageless," while for Hetherington and Atherton, the prose poem underlines "what *has happened* and *will always be happening*."[20] Alternatively, we can read such images in the way in which Monica Carroll and Jen Webb see the prose poem: as resistant to form and emphasising process.[21] Jeremy Noel-Tod also characterises the prose poem in terms of "expansiveness," which is how I regard Turner's final paintings.[22]

The viewer's position is also relevant: how the eye *reads* the painting in a similar way to how Carrie Etter *sees* the prose poem:

> While a lineated poem's development requires some sort of progression as it moves down the page, most reductively a movement from point A to point B, a prose poem develops without "going" anywhere. It simply wants to inhabit or circle A.[23]

This idea of the prose poem as a circumlocution aligns it with the flatness or dispersal of Turner's paintings. The poem has layers with no solid centre; or, for Helen Tookey, the form is like a lantern or illuminated container, "casting images and phrases needed but barely understood." Tookey advances her case that, especially when read in a sequence, the prose poem has a "lantern-like effect" and manifests a "cinematic or filmic quality" suggestive of the visual arts.[24] It is also worth noting that prose poems are often brief (rarely more than a single page), and this is analogous to a painting's entirety on a rectangular plane.

However, Paul Hetherington's model of the prose poem as offering "resistance to closure," including attention to the unconscious and a visionary thrust, is particularly relevant here. This is because the movement of the eye in front of Turner's seascapes can be circular and non-progressive, in a similar fashion to the way in which, in Hannah Stone's words, "[the prose poem] lends itself to a spiral, meditative process rather than a linear narrative locution."[25] This continual overturning of narrative (from the Greek, *katastrophē*, "overturning," or "sudden turn") can mean that, in the prose poem and painting alike, interpretation is recursive; meaning is elusive or polysemic. While prose moves forward (from the Latin, *prōsa*, "straightforward"), verse *turns* (from *vertō*, "to turn around"), and the prose poem keeps turning, where its inner elements revolve around each other as Turner depicts light and shade in a swirl of interaction. Could there be a resemblance, then, between the "unfinished" Turner paintings (which some critics regard as finished) and the prose poem, which also evokes the Romantic fragment or vignette, while being just as composed as other poems?[26]

Before addressing this, though, it is important to consider how these paintings and the prose poem serve the lyric. Indeed, Elizabeth Bergmann Loizeaux sees ekphrasis as a "sub-genre of the lyric," and I agree with her opinion that "the prevalence of ekphrasis indicates continuous and ongoing efforts across the twentieth century to break open the possibilities of lyric poetry."[27] This is the case in my poems, especially in mediating grief (too difficult to confront in itself) through an artwork which can filter, distort, or disguise, like frosted glass. Turner's paintings thus serve as a visual analogue for overwhelming loss, while the prose poem confers a set of formal conventions that contain the "subject" of both the lyric and artwork, which is catastrophe.

Though I respect the historical motivations for a shift away from free verse and lyric or Romantic modes of expression (as many postmodern poets of the 60s and 70s show), my poems are not just machines or systems of production. They are self-reflexive and experimental while still in the tradition of the lyric, defined by T. S. Eliot as "the expression of the poet's own thoughts and feelings."[28] With Loizeaux's argument in mind, my poems develop an oblique, partial, and tenuous relationship with the artwork that is also lyrical. In my poem "Seascape" which follows, for instance, beyond the title and reference to "the sea," "God" and "one immense field of consciousness," I make little reference to the content; instead, I focus on the "I"/"she" relationship. My prose poem is formally produced by traces or vague inscriptions in the Turner, which help to warp themes that would be too stark otherwise (for myself and also possibly the reader). This poem also performs a more contemporary version of what Loizeaux claims: that ekphrasis "[expands] lyric subjectivity into a field that includes at least one other, the artist/ work of art, with a third always present and sometimes active in the exchange, the audience."[29] While discussion of the latter is beyond the scope of this chapter, in "Seascape," I invoke three others, through the pronouns "she" and "you," and the "sea": the artist/artwork. This exudes an air of mystery (who is "she" and "you"? and is the "sea" the actual sea or Turner's sea?).

"Seascape" is based upon my recollection of the artwork. This temporal detachment left the image unclear and my imagination was free to roam beyond its actuality. It shone in my mind's eye like a hologram, an ember, an after-image. Writing at a distance, I take advantage of misperception: allowing myself to see things in the image while bypassing more informed ways of looking (filtered, say, through art criticism). This can also mean disregarding the artist's intent: my notional ekphrasis conjuring up not so much Turner's picture but rather how I mis-remember it. I also recall pareidolic forms in the lower left of *Sunrise* (monsters or mere atmospherics?). Given that such images speak to me, they prefigure the lyric. In other words, I am under the illusion that my poem already exists in *symbolic* form, that it incubates within the image, or that my poem foreshadows the seeing or re-seeing of the artwork.[30] In "Seascape," this is implied by my subversion of the usual epigraph: my poem emerged before seeing the painting. It began as a freewriting exercise within the frame of my notebook. Soon my memory of the painting led to my poem, and the shape of the canvas suggested a prose poem. This was further adapted through my reading of Michael Symmons Roberts's "A Mancunian Diorama," which is a full-page spread and evokes a cinematic landscape.[31] I associated this with the expansiveness of Turner's seascapes, borrowing from film the technique of the wide-angle shot:

Seascape

The sea has no reply—& I'm devastated. The sea is easily equated with God. It ushers the waves towards me. I want to know why the sea is reticent. Even the sea won't accept my roses. Each year at Perranporth it's the same. I lay out the roses & the waves don't seem to care. I can't say which way the tide is turning. My fingers are dinted by thorns. No, even the sea won't accept my roses. It keeps giving them back, each wave returning the gift—like she often did. Was that generosity gone too far or a kind of self-hate? A dozen roses on the sand. A grief unresolved since God has refused to bear witness. *Are you not yet ashamed?* I am stood Canute-like. I am a dolt. How can I expect to shame the sea with my tears? The sea is making me wonder if the sky & stars are really the inside of my brain. In which case *she's out there,* I think. Why do we say the sea is blue when it's really grey? It recedes now—one immense field of consciousness. I ask the sea again to *give her back, please.* The plea of mortals in their millions. It's familiar to the sea. I believe the sea will make an exception. The only way to know for sure is to wade out & find a rip current, evade lifeguards between flags. The surfers are souls having a near death experience. They've risked jellyfish & sharks, joyous in wetsuits, halfway towards the empyrean. A friend says my only hope is immanence. I am privy to the knowledge of what's happened. Ashes in the mica. While she's in everything—from beach huts to kayaks to Alsatians on leads—while the sea is a sadist & says: *now it's time to leave.*

FIGURE 11.1 Patrick Wright, "Seascape. Before J.M.W. Turner".

Like the painting, I justify the text (stretching it from the left-hand margin to the right), fashioning a taut canvas. I also accentuate gaps where contemplation is apt (between lines and phrases). This slows the pace and calls to mind an artwork that needs time to be fully appreciated. The painting is able to re-frame subject matter that is barely speakable. Rather than write about grief, my poem mediates it, gives poetic form to catastrophe, which is always formless before it can be rendered. I also include disparate lexicons, fusing post-apocalyptic writing, art history, and the elegy. These are clashed together for dramatic effect and re-present the centripetal force that marks the painting.

So, rather than reproduce in words Turner's painting, I re-imagine it and make an absent artwork present (*energeia*). Visions that come to mind are idiosyncratic, for both me and the reader. In this way, my ekphrasis could be said to involve "double vision" as Hetherington and Atherton call it:

> In presenting an image that interprets an actual or notional work of visual art . . . at least two different perspectives are being given. The first . . . is that possessed or embodied by the artwork, and the second perspective is that provided by the poem.

Moreover, they clarify that "Poem and painting . . . create a third perspective, which results from the complex admixture of perspectives that painting and poem provide when viewed/read simultaneously."[32] Although having painterly and poetic perspectives is possible with "Seascape" (multiple perspectives arising in the literary alchemy that occurs when picture and poem are read or seen together), it is meant to stand alone, where my ekphrasis, potentially read intertextually or as a palimpsest, is more simply a lyric poem seen through the lens of a painting.

My most prescriptive rule in writing "Seascape" was that I wanted to use the repetition of a phrase (here, it is "the sea") that would, simultaneously, anchor my initial phrase of freewriting and signal that the speaker is returning to the same place, seemingly outside of linear time. Only later did the form of the prose poem suit my themes and lyric mode. This was because my style and diction began to evoke recent paintings I had been drawn to (Turner's); and I noticed that, by positioning the phrase "the sea" at different points across the line (and other rhymed phrases), it effected an undulating, wave-like motion. My ekphrasis is formally generated where the arrangement of lines was revised with the frame of the canvas in mind and the artist's point of view (the same as the speaker's in the poem: at the edge of the waves). The orientation of the page is landscape: finding correspondence with the visual medium. The sentences are digressive and recursive: just as a narrative is advancing, it stalls, gets interrupted and returns back to "the sea." I do this through line breaks, short sentences, and punctuation. I read the latter, like an artist's use of line and brush-strokes, as a way for a poem to draw attention to its artifice and materiality. Just as Turner captured fleeting effects of light, I give "Seascape" a look of the unfinished (with, for example, the use of ampersands and lacunae).

In looking to elicit a swirling motion I had in mind Hardwick's observations on the prose poem's tendency to disrupt the expected narrative structure of "the Aristotelian beginning-middle-end."[33] I explored ways where I could, like Hardwick, give rise to an opening within the mind of the reader without arriving at narrative closure. To move towards my ending, I pause in using "the sea" as a refrain. In my answer to grief, I allow the poem to travel elsewhere (out to sea). At this point, I make my sentences longer, using em-dashes to suggest agitation. In the final line, I return to the sea and end with "now it's time to leave": the sea finally speaking (making what was absent present, through prosopopoeia) and gesturing back to the start of the poem.

In making use of a frame to influence formal decisions, I draw on a well-recognised convention in prose poetry.[34] Examples that have influenced my poems tend to utilise a rectangle of text (such as Anne Caldwell's *Alice and the North* and Anne Carson's *Short Talks*).[35] My practice is comparable, then, with poets who draw attention to the prose poem's edges and what they suggest: in Caldwell's words, "that sense of the littoral, whether literal or more metaphorical."[36] The prose poem becomes a kind of place, one with edges.

With "Seascape," I adjusted the margins to fit the shape of the canvas. The waves in Turner's image, after all, disappear into the blind field and sky. The visual experience is sublime, where the only marks are waves and streaks of cloud, indicative of a poetic line which runs from the left-hand margin to the right. One unexpected effect of this isomorphism was that the words then carried similar weight across the line. Just as Stiliana Milkova notes that "the physical border of the picture frame operates as a demarcating device in the ekphrastic text," my tendency was to integrate this element into my poems, and do so concretely.[37] In "Seascape," the text is justified and the margins draw attention to the edges of the page and limitations of my poem. Moreover, I juxtapose two time periods and subjects in the one box, where the final line returns the reader back to the start, implying a temporal loop. Here, as Sima Godfrey writes, "The depth and infiniteness of the framed object is ironically intensified by the limitations imposed upon it by a frame." Tookey sees likewise how this approach intensifies associative connections; the reader's eye and attention are "corralled within the space of the box."[38]

Does the horizon imply a stanza break? And do the darker hues in the lower half of the painting suggest less space between the words, with the words written above double or triple spaced? And does the proportion of sky and sea inside the frame lead me to consider the line length for each stanza? I had these questions in mind while working on my poem "The Sea." Here, I have two stanzas: the first spatially evocative of the sky and the second evocative of the sea, while the white space that separates them is suggestive of the horizon. The result, as Hetherington and Atherton observe about such poems generally, is a poem that appears to hang on the page like art on a gallery wall:[39]

The Sea

After J. M. W. Turner

The sea is teal, like blood in a mortuary. The canvas is scentless, nothing
but an exquisite arrangement of colour, the complex pulse of water.
Becalmed, the mind is like this in yoga, churns with the waves, breaths
slowing almost to a stop. Nerves alert to perturbance. From my seat,
mounds are breasts, curves lining up like matryoshka dolls, decreasing
in size to the horizon.

The sea below—the sky a degree lighter in shade, opalescent. Waves seek
quiescence, the flatline of an encephalograph. The expanse of seeing
through cataracts. The sea is rhythm, the timbre of her voice, echolalia
in response. On this side is ebullience, fullness; on the other is jouissance—
loneliness and mourning a dead mother, the shore drawn with nonchalance.

FIGURE 11.2 Patrick Wright, "The Sea. After J. M. W. Turner"

With the idea of association or multiplicity in mind I have also examined how
the prose poem's frame can be evocative of the larger "box" of an exhibition
space of several artworks, and the so-called white cube of the gallery setting.
Inspired by Hetherington's collection *Gallery of Antique Art* and Ágnes Nemes
Nagy's ekphrastic prose poem "A Walk Through the Museum,"[40] I have elsewhere
presented my movement around the gallery by writing in stanzas (*stanza* might
translate as "room"). My lyric impulse led me to view artworks in a sequence,
either within the walls of the gallery or the pages of a book, as reproductions.
Using poetic form as a container in this way is not, in itself, innovative. For instance,
one could look to the inter-artistic encounter in Derek Mahon's "Courtyards in
Delft," "The Studio," and "New Space" in response to three-dimensional objects
and architectural space.[41] However, the prose poem is distinctive in representing
the morass of sensation which can occur in a gallery; one that includes blurbs,
visitors, and curators. I also wonder if movement through a gallery is (like the prose
poem) often recursive; a doubling back on ourselves, trying to find our bearings
in rooms characterised by estrangement. In which case, stanzas might collapse into
ekphrastic compartments within a larger box: how images are approached, moved
away from, and returned to. The poem could also re-present a journey through
the exhibition or monograph (taking on the characteristics of the *haibun*) or amal-
gamate the whole visit into a word collage or *gestalt*.

So far, I have shown how my sense of catastrophe came first and my later
viewing of Turner was useful in giving shape to it. I have also presented the prose
poem as a form close to the formless – as a form that the formless is able to
produce – and how this form can serve as a means of containment. In a similar
way, Atherton considers how the prose poem is well placed to represent trauma,
referring to Mariko Nagai's *Irradiated Cities*: his poems marked by a stalling of

narrative or incompleteness; expectations are defied, especially with regard to a lack of a forward movement.[42] I am reminded of Mark Wallace's reading of the prose poem as "a disorientation that orients while reminding us of a need for disorientation."[43] Moreover, like Hardwick, I see prose poetry as having the capacity to "address a subject such as loss without directly addressing it at all, or provide consolation while acknowledging, in form as well as content, that grief knows no consolation." Hardwick alludes to Alexander Long, who, in his attempt to write a lined verse poem about a friend's suicide, had failed "because lines, meter and rhyme somehow simplified the terrible gravity of the event." Long writes how: "Not until I encountered the prose poem did I realise what kind of space was available to me."[44] My experience of the prose poem is similar, especially in how I see it as a way to represent trauma through the use of recursion and circularity.

In my poem "Shade and Darkness," for instance, I started with the template of the sestina, a set of repeating words that would be gradually brought together to resemble an envoi:

Shade and Darkness

Before J.M.W. Turner

Before any rainbow arrives, I learn how your grandparents survived the Holocaust, how they were put in a nuthouse for exposing the truth. I learn the kernel of abuse can be traced to your dreams of deluge. Such madness we couldn't see through, opaque as your eyes, this surface steeped in Goethe's frozen music. Before any rainbow arrives, I follow murmurations. Over waves, shore birds glide, spiralling, threatening a tailspin. I wonder which camp they were in, whether it was Auschwitz. In your eyes, I saw the first abuse. I tried to trace the madness back, to patch over the abyss—like finding sense in this, abstract and opaque. I tried to thaw your frozen music, release the birds from their circular trance.

FIGURE 11.3 Patrick Wright, "Seascape. Before J.M.W. Turner".

In having a loose sestina in mind, I had an organising principle and set of constraints around which my writing could revolve. This can be understood in terms of "procedural form," which refers to a poem that is composed with predetermined rules. As Marjorie Perloff explains, the rules which can at first seem restrictive are enabling; the constraint, which she links with postmodern poetry, "is a *generative* device: it creates a formal structure whose rules of composition are internalised so that the constraint in question is not only a rule but a thematic property of the poem as well."[45] But such rules would not be visible in the final poem, and the acts of composition and revision might render them indistinct. Thus, as Perloff clarifies, "there are as many possible constraints as there are poems, and the constraint is not an external form that is readily recognised but may be a rule that remains largely hidden to the reader."[46]

For me, such procedures were generative and helped to prevent me from subverting things to such an extent my poem was itself a disaster. My constraints were sufficient in how my poem could be a lyric poem *and* tied to an image; how it could be ekphrastic while description of content was minimal. In "Shade and Darkness," my tether to the image includes the title: I use apocalyptic imagery, allude to the Deluge (in keeping with Turner's biblical motifs), and indicate opacity and abstraction; otherwise, my dynamic is formal. Similarly, my first draft was written as a single sentence. With Michael Longley's "The Butchers" as a catalyst,[47] I joined separate clauses with conjunctions. The result was a lyric poem, though it was also ekphrastic in formally re-presenting Turner's catastrophe.

In most of my poems, the painting came first, and this determined formal devices which in turn produced my poem. Nevertheless, with "Shade and Darkness," my rules were decided on in advance and then discovered in an image that seemed to bear these out. In this case, as with "Seascape," my epigraph suggests this genesis with the word "before" rather than the more commonplace "after." Once the poem and image were matched, another phase occurred during which I harmonised my poem with Turner's image. My relationship with the artwork is thus one of mutuality. The poem lies at the site of mediation. I do not write "about" the picture; the poem is instead drafted in anticipation of the image; the later experience of looking then determines my revision. I then have a refraction in the form of a prose poem.

Although the lines in "Shade and Darkness" seem to be caught in a loop and disrupt narrative progression, they are not inconsequential, nor do they overlook the properties of the poetic line as discussed by Katy Evans-Bush.[48] The final word and first word carry additional weight: our eyes are meant to linger on the final word, move down and back to the left. It suggests physical and temporal movement. This is the case even if the right margin is "ragged," which some might assume is an arbitrary word-wrap. Consequently, Noel-Tod's idea of the prose poem as "a poem without line breaks" is problematic given that the right margin can be a distinctively *visual* marker.[49] Though not a hard return, I would not want a typesetter to print my poem differently, just as an artist might object to a new frame without consultation.

Adopting the conventions of the prose poem while looking to develop them is part of my wider project. Indeed, I have been eager to encourage myself away from free verse, which I believe at times (again following Perloff) "has become . . . little more than linear prose, arbitrarily divided into line lengths."[50] I investigated ways to distinguish my second collection from my debut, which was predominantly marked by free verse, and, aside from its relevance to prose poetry, I enjoy how procedural form has the capacity to force me away from my usual routines and functioning. As a result, I looked at Hejinian's avant-garde and experimental modes along with French Oulipo work, including Georges Perec and Raymond Queneau. I also dabbled with lipogrammatic writings (the abstention from the use of a given letter, word, punctuation mark, and so forth). Later, I limited myself to basic restrictions; otherwise, my poems became too contrived or mannered. For instance, while I admire Christian Bök's univocalic "Chapter A" (for Hans Arp) from his collection *Eunoia*, in following this approach, my poems became game-like or lost their emotional centre.[51] This was also true when I tried redaction, strike-throughs, footnotes, or broke lines syllabically.

Perhaps settling for the prose poem as a basis for what I develop is a way to guard against words becoming *too* visual, or, in other words, my ekphrasis giving credence to the mimetic fallacy or the fantasy that the word-image relationship could be anything other than infinite. Some forms I have referred to help in keeping my poems meaningful, lyrical, and distinctive as *poems*; though in more finished versions I have pushed the prose poem one stage further, and (while working with the margins, as demonstrated) given it a more "exploded" appearance. In my reading of Carson, I am looking at how subversion of punctuation and grammar might be analogous to the image. Just as modern art often makes use of incongruity and fragments, I am employing dependent clauses, parataxis, word collage, and tabulation. I associate prose with lineation and figuration in visual art; and if there are no lines in the artwork, I am inclined to subvert linguistic conventions, again as a procedural strategy.

To conclude, in my own poems, if the image is abstract or formless, the whole page, margins, spaces, and punctuation often take on meaning and become framing devices. It is fitting for such images to generate poetic form. In most cases, then, I ensure that the relationship between the poem and the image has a formal correspondence. Procedural form is a tactic for generating such poems, where the rules are rendered opaque or nested in another (more identifiable) form. It is a form only because it retains some trace of the procedure used to generate it, one that is often invisible to a reader, but nevertheless present as a formal consideration. My poems are first and foremost lyric poems; though the use of form and modes of ekphrasis allows me to reconfigure my voice and re-mediate content that would be too difficult for me to convey otherwise. I am thus more cognisant that my use of "free" verse is in no way free when it pertains to the lyric. Indeed, these are not formless poems; they are poems that re-present the formless.

Notes

1 James Williams, "Deleuze on J.M.W. Turner: Catastrophism in Philosophy?" in *Deleuze and Philosophy: The Difference Engineer*, ed. Keith Ansell-Pearson (London: Routledge, 1997), 233–46.

2 James A.W. Heffernan, *Museum of Words: The Poetics of Ekphrasis from Homer to Ashbery* (Chicago: University of Chicago Press, 2004).

3 Camille Guthrie, "Writing Poetry about Art," *Poetry Foundation*, 12 April 2013, www.poetryfoundation.org/harriet/2013/04/writing-poetry-about-art.

4 Ruth Webb, *Ekphrasis, Imagination and Persuasion in Ancient Rhetorical Theory and Practice* (Aldershot, UK: Ashgate, 2009), 87–106.

5 Art Berman, *Preface to Modernism* (Chicago: University of Illinois Press, 1994), 49; Rebecca Beasley, *Ezra Pound and the Visual Culture of Modernism* (Cambridge: Cambridge University Press, 2007), 52.

6 James Francis, "Metal Maidens, Achilles' Shield, and Pandora: The Beginnings of Ekphrasis," *American Journal of Philology* 130, no. 1 (Spring 2009): 1–23; Ruth Webb, "*Ekphrasis* Ancient and Modern: The Invention of a Genre," *Word & Image* 15, no. 1 (1999): 7–18.

7 W. H. Auden, "Musée des Beaux Arts," in *Selected Poems*, ed. Edward Mendelson (New York: Random House. 2007), 87.

8 Matthew Gumpert, *The End of Meaning: Studies in Catastrophe* (Newcastle-upon-Tyne: Cambridge Scholars Publishing, 2012), xxxiv.

9 Paul Hetherington and Cassandra Atherton, "Double Vision: Ekphrasis as a Way of Looking Twice," paper presented at *Art and Soul Symposium*, University of Winchester, 2019.

10 Lyn Hejinian, "The Rejection of Closure," *Poetry Foundation*, 13 October 2009, www.poetryfoundation.org/articles/69401/the-rejection-of-closure; Charles Olson, "Projective Verse," in *Collected Prose*, ed. Donald Allen and Benjamin Friedlander (Berkeley, CA: University of California Press, 1997), 239–49; Michael Davidson, "Ekphrasis and the Postmodern Painter Poem," *The Journal of Aesthetics and Art Criticism* 42, no. 1 (Autumn 1983): 72.

11 Owen Bullock, "Fresh Modes: Towards a Radical Ekphrasis," *Axon: Creative Explorations* 9, no. 1 (May 2019), www.axonjournal.com.au/issue-vol-9-no-1-may-2019/fresh-modes.

12 Heffernan, *Museum of Words*, 107–14.

13 Williams, "Deleuze on J. M. W. Turner," 234.

14 Hardwick, "Shaping Loss." See also Mark Wallace, "Split: Seam and Abyss in the Prose Poem," in *The Rose Metal Press Field Guide to Prose Poetry: Contemporary Poets in Discussion and Practice*, ed. McDowell, Gary L., and F. Daniel Rzicznek (Brookline, MA: Rose Metal Press, 2010), 74–8.

15 David Wheatley, "By Soft Return." Review of *The Penguin Book of the Prose Poem: From Baudelaire to Anne Carson*, edited by Jeremy Noel-Tod. *The Poetry Review* 109, no. 1 (Spring 2019). https://poetrysociety.org.uk/review-by-soft-return/.

16 Hetherington and Atherton, "'Unconscionable Mystification'?" 265–81; Sam Smiles, "Unfinished? Repulsive? Or the Work of a Prophet? Late Turner," *Tate*, 1 January 2009, www.tate.org.uk/tate-etc/issue-15-spring-2009/unfinished-repulsive-or-work-prophet.

17 Jane Monson, "Introduction," in *British Prose Poetry*, ed. Monson, Jane, *British Prose Poetry: The Poems Without Lines*. (Cham, CH: Palgrave Macmillan, 2018), 11.

18 Monica Carroll and Jen Webb, "'Defiant Formlessness': Prose Poem as Process," *TEXT Special Issue 46, Beyond the Line: Contemporary Prose Poetry* (October 2017): 1–15; Michael Riffaterre, *Semiotics of Poetry* (Bloomington, IN: Indiana University Press, 1978), 117; Kevin Brophy, "The Prose Poem: A Short History, a Brief Reflection and a Dose of the Real Thing." *TEXT: Journal of Writing and Writing Programs* 6, no. 1 (April 2002). www.textjournal.com.au/april02/brophy.htm.

19 David Caddy, "'Hidden Form': The Prose Poem in English Poetry." In *British Prose Poetry*, ed. Monson, 21.

20 Gilles Deleuze and Félix Guattari, *Anti-Oedipus: Capitalism and Schizophrenia* (London: The Athlone Press, 2000), 132; Paul Hetherington and Cassandra Atherton, eds. *Prose Poetry: An Introduction* (Princeton, NJ: Princeton University Press, 2020), 26.

21 Carroll and Webb, "'Defiant Formlessness,'" 1–15.

22 Jeremy Noel-Tod, "Introduction," in *The Penguin Book of the Prose Poem: From Baudelaire to Anne Carson* ed. Noel-Tod, Jeremy (London: Penguin, 2018), xxxiii.

23 Carrie Etter, "The Prose Poem," in *The Portable Poetry Workshop*, ed. Nigel McLoughlin (London: Palgrave, 2017), 72.

24 Helen Tookey, "'Image Machine': Gaspar Orozco's *Book of the Peony* and the Prose Poem Sequence as Perceptual Trick," Chapter 7 of this volume.

25 Cassandra Atherton and Paul Hetherington, "Breaking Boundaries and Crossing Lines: English-language Prose Poetry Today," keynote address at the Prose Poetry Symposium, Leeds Trinity University, 2019; Hannah Stone, "'In the Eye of the Beholder': Prose Poetry in Dialogue," Chapter 3 in this volume.

26 Paul Hetherington and Cassandra Atherton, "The Prose Poem's Post-Romantic Inheritance," in *Prose Poetry: An Introduction*, ed. Hetherington and Atherton, 28–50.

27 Elizabeth, Loizeaux, *Twentieth-Century Poetry and the Visual Arts* (Cambridge: Cambridge University Press, 2008), 1–9.

28 T. S. Eliot, "The Three Voices of Poetry" in *The Lyric Theory Reader: A Critical Anthology*, ed. Virginia Jackson and Yopie Prins (Baltimore, MD: John Hopkins University Press, 2014), 197.

29 Loizeaux, *Twentieth-Century Poetry*, 5.

30 John Hollander, "The Poetics of Ekphrasis," *Word & Image* 4, no. 1 (1988): 209.

31 Michael Symmons Roberts, *Mancunia* (London: Cape Poetry, 2017), 16–7.

32 Hetherington and Atherton, "Double Vision."

33 Oz Hardwick, "Prose Poetry and Resistance to Narrative," Chapter 2 in this volume.

34 See Hetherington and Atherton, *Prose Poetry: An Introduction*, 58, 88, 110–11.

35 Caldwell, *Alice and the North*; Anne Carson, *Short Talks* (London: Brick Books, 2015).

36 Anne Caldwell, "Reawakening Wonder: How Cartography can Act as Creative Research for Prose Poetry." *New Writing* 15, no. 4 (2018): 405.

37 Stiliana Milkova, "Ekphrasis and the Frame: On Paintings in Gogol, Tolstoy, and Dostoevsky," *Word & Image* 32, no. 2 (2016): 153x.

38 Godfrey, "Baudelaire's Windows," 91; Tookey, "Image Machine," Chapter 7 in this volume.

39 Hetherington and Atherton, "Double Vision."

40 Paul Hetherington, *Gallery of Antique Art* (Canberra, AU: Recent Work Press, 2016); Ágnes Nemes Nagy, "A Walk Through the Museum," in *Penguin Book of the Prose Poem*, ed. Noel-Tod, 189–91.

41 Bridget Vincent, "Object Lessons: Derek Mahon's Material Ekphrasis," *Interdisciplinary Literary Studies* 20, no. 3 (2018): 371–84.

42 Cassandra Atherton, Jane Monson, and Ian Seed, "Insiders on and 'Outsider' Artform," paper presented at Prose Poetry Symposium, Leeds Trinity University, 2019; Nagai, *Irradiated Cities*.

43 Wallace, "Split: Seam and Abyss," 77.

44 Alexander Long, "Something Like a Meditation," in *Rose Metal Press Field Guide*, ed. McDowell and Rzicznek, 43–4.

45 Marjorie Perloff, *Differentials: Poetry, Poetics, Pedagogy* (Tuscaloosa, AL: University of Alabama Press, 2004), 208.

46 Perloff, *Differentials*, 208.

47 Michael Longley, "The Butchers," in *Selected Poems* (London: Cape Poetry, 1999), 101.

48 Katy Evans-Bush, "The Line," in *Stress Fractures: Essays on Poetry*, ed. Tom Chivers (London: Penned in the Margins, 2010), 191–212.

49 Noel-Tod, *The Penguin Book of the Prose Poem*, 20.

50 Perloff, *Differentials*, 205.

51 Christian Bök, *Eunoia* (Toronto, ON: Canongate Books, 2008), 12.

12

"AN INTERLUDE SUSPENDED"[1]

Historical Biography Through the Lens of Prose Poetry

Edwin Stockdale

The contested category of prose poetry is, for many, something of a mystery, representing a dubious point of paradox at which ostensible literary opposites somehow meet and combine. In this chapter, I shall not attempt to solve this mystery. Rather, in investigating the possibilities afforded by the uncertainty, instability, and "openness" (in the sense of Umberto Eco's idea of "the open work") of the prose poem, I shall discuss the ways in which the form – and its inherent mystery – particularly lends itself to certain aspects of historical biography. In doing so, I shall make specific reference to my current project, *Alchemy in the Tower*, a collection of poems – both lineated and prose poems – focusing on King Richard III and the Princes in the Tower. I take as my starting point Paul Hetherington and Cassandra Atherton's recent landmark study of prose poetry, in which they suggest that:

> Prose poetry has the potential to cross the divide between the urge toward poetry – its capacity to articulate what is otherwise unsayable – and the more discursive and narrative-driven prose of novels, biographies and the like. Prose poetry understands prose's conventions and its constituent parts – its sentences and paragraphs – while also being conspicuously a form of poetry, and sometimes even lyrical in its inflections.[2]

The key word here is "unsayable," a term meaning that which cannot be expressed through the conventions of formal prose, but which I broaden out to also embrace that which cannot with certainty be known.

I shall begin by examining prose poetry as a distinct form and its relation to lineated verse, in order to demonstrate the way in which it gains its distinctive energy from what I term the "dissonant harmony" of its parts, the apparently oxymoronic conflation of freedom and formality. I will then explore the ways in which

DOI: 10.4324/9781003199533-13

this energy engenders both movement and stasis, and the way in which the prose poem allows for the simultaneous expansion and compression of time. In the light of these discussions, I will analyse the ways in which this dissonant harmony of conflicting impulses within the form prompted me to adopt it for my prose poem "Old Year's Night," a poem that illuminates an unknowable, "unsayable" moment in the boyhood of the future king, whose character and reign remain a mystery which is more vigorously debated than any British monarch before or since.

Old Year's Night
Sandal Castle
31 December 1460

The young Richard restless in his four-poster bed. His spine aching. His bones cold. Outside, flakes fall large as lilies.

He is fraught with news of his father's death. His horse skids on ice; he crumples on the ground. In his fitful bed he arches his spine, but his frame doesn't settle.

Calder dark. Sky dark. Castle stone dark. Mist surges from the river. His father caught by fog: hushed, still.

Richard starts as his father is stabbed, stabbed again. His father's stoat-brown eyes follow him. Richard Plantagenet, Duke of York, beheaded in Wakefield snow. Eight-year-old Richard shivers awake.

Snow covers the landscape but can't bury those forked bodies. Out in the Wolds, wolves stir.[3]

From a critical viewpoint, prose poetry as a form is both contested and constantly mutable. As Monica Carroll and Jen Webb explain, "Attempting to define the prose poem is an ongoing occupation of critical scholarly discourse while, in contrast, the practice of poetry and prose as writing is rather more nomadic and flexible,"[4] suggesting that the writer is unfettered by the need for categorisation, possessing the freedom to cross boundaries at will in their practice, wandering where they like. Likewise, Owen Bullock, too, questions the usefulness of categorical definitions, noting that:

> We are challenged as readers and writers to look at concepts such as "prose poetry" to see, ultimately, whether they are helping or hindering us. Perhaps the designation "prose poetry" is more useful to readers and critics. . . . It is the writer who is more able to work in the liminal space that does not need a name, and innovative writing, which is of its times, is often nameless or in defiance of these categories.[5]

In questioning the need for demarcation and naming of categories, Bullock homes in on the "liminal space" between clearly defined states, to which the term "prose poetry" is applied, but which is actually something "other" to both of the categories to which this name gestures.

In simple terms, the main defining characteristic of the prose poem is that, unlike most other poetic forms, the prose poem is not arranged in discrete lines. As Bronwyn Lea notes, "Whenever we see, or more importantly hear, language arranged in lines we know we are entering the gallery of the poem. White space and silence frame the poem and alert us to its language."[6] Lea asserts that listeners, as well as readers, are attuned to "language arranged in lines," thereby recognising it as poetry. In such a formulation, the line break is an essential aspect of the poem's rhythm and phrasing, the "white space and silence" at the end of each line a choice on the part of the poet in order to guide the reader or listener by providing a pause to catch breath, reflect, anticipate, or even be deliberately disrupted in order to intensify the effect of the poem's language. Although prose poetry eschews the line break, the rhythm of sentences remains of paramount concern and the pauses which contribute to this dynamic are provided by punctuation. While the "white space and silence" around the commonly regular form of the prose poem is less immediately apparent to the reader, and possibly the listener, than that which surrounds the ragged right-hand margin of lineated verse, it is no less vital an aspect of the poem. As Paul Munden observes, the "brief space" occupied by a prose poem is "not only a *brief* space, but a *tightly framed* space,"[7] which derives its energy, unlike prose narrative, in no small part from the space within which it occurs.

Addressing this dimension of prosody, Sean O'Brien suggests the following exercise: "Ask a colleague to supply two anonymous pieces – one a free verse poem printed as prose, the other a prose poem. Decide which is the conventionally lineated poem and supply the line-endings."[8] O'Brien argues that, in undertaking this exercise, one would not be able to discern which piece was originally lineated verse and which was conceived as a prose poem, as their effects are so similar. Addressing lineation, Alan Wall describes prose poetry as: "Prose which has the intensity of poetry, but whose lines go to the end of the page, beyond the control of the writer."[9] In recognising this, we may be reminded of the "defiance" noted by Bullock and see the line of the prose poem journeying to the edge of the page "in defiance" of the categorical expectations of poetry.

Glyn Maxwell, although referring to lineated poetry, sees line and form as having "a direct effect on the silence beneath it, which is to say on the whiteness before and after it and where the lines end."[10] Like Lea, Maxwell sees line endings as being where language interacts with "the silence" – that is, the white space – both around and underneath the form in which it is arranged. Maxwell and Lea are both referring specifically to lineated poetry. However, as I have suggested, "white space and silence [also] frame" the prose poem, albeit in a slightly different manner. This difference may be thought of as pertaining to the negotiation of space. As Luke Kennard asserts, for example, "Prose poetry is more spacious; it tends to contain complete sentences; it allows for more incongruity and complex yet visible patterns."[11] The dynamic between the protean prose poem and the surrounding white space is thus more mutable, for although the neat-edged form appears more contained, it is effectively more volatile, the arrangement of its parts ever-changing on different pages and with different voices. This difference creates what may be thought of as dissonant harmony of unsettled elements. In the same vein, David Caddy argues that this difference is a defining characteristic of prose poetry:

> The prose poem, seen here as a poem without line-breaks, retains the tension between line and sentence structure without the use of line-endings. It has the potential to build pace, rhythm and music, and to produce meaning as free verse, only it has to generate tension, drama and crises through sentence structure, relationship and language use alone. It is, in a sense, a freedom to open possibilities and to move away from a stultifying rigidity and closure.[12]

In Caddy's view, the prose poem's evasion of the line break – that "defiance" again – grants the writer "freedom," even as the box-like rectangle of the poem appears closed. It is from this oxymoron of formality and "freedom" that the prose poem is forged.

Turning to these ideas in action, in Sarah Corbett's prose poem "Migraine," the speaker addresses Dorothy Wordsworth as she takes a long walk in order to try and dispose of her migraine:

> you try and out-walk it, walk all day pushing on, pushing on . . . the rain a percussive *te*-dum *te*-dum on your neck, your scalp, . . . the sparse cobbles of your spine where the cord tightens; you cannot stop it, you cannot; . . . the fat pulse in your crown where once the plates were soft and open; if only they would un-fuse now[13]

Here, the tension created by Corbett allowing the line to run on mimics the unyielding nature of her subject's migraine. The effect is further enhanced by the absence of full stops throughout the poem, with the pauses introduced by commas and semi-colons, suggesting relief which is only fleeting, articulating for the reader the nagging, unending insistence of the ailment. While presented as a block of continuous prose, however, the poem is suffused with the formal devices of lineated poetry, most notably in the rhythmic repetition of "pushing on, pushing on," "*te*-dum *te*-dum" and "you cannot stop it, you cannot."

The formal requirement of prose poetry – that is, creating a block or blocks of text, in which all the demands of poetry must be met, but in which the poet's most distinctive tool of the line break is forbidden – may appear to restrict the poet; but it is the form's apparent restriction which lends itself to heightened engagement with space and time. As discussed above, Kennard has noted that the prose poem is "more spacious." Paul Munden sees the prose poem's block of text as encapsulating a "single moment,"[14] which is most usually set out as a single paragraph, although, as I shall go on to discuss, the same can be said of a prose poem containing multiple paragraphs. In approaching a "single moment" in my poem "Old Year's Night," I was cognisant of Paul Farley and Michael Symmons Roberts' observation that, "Poets have always been attracted by the overlooked, the telling details, the captured moment."[15] In my poem, I wished to focus on a single, captured moment while simultaneously illuminating the "telling details" which history has not recorded, in order to negotiate the intricate gaps in the written record of a key moment in Richard's life. The prose poem provided a perfect form in which to do this as, in the words of Linda Black, "the prose poem encourages thoughts to be continuous, to twist and turn, hold themselves up short, or open out into a broader perspective."[16]

In "Old Year's Night," the single moment I focus upon is when the young Richard finds out that his father is dead. The poem takes in the wintry land-scape in order to both set a scene and foreshadow Richard's possible depression and Seasonal Affective Disorder. In search of a wider perspective, I incorporate John Ashdown-Hill's observation that, "One possible cause of scoliosis [a condi-tion from which Richard suffered] is a physical trauma of some kind – such as a fall from a horse."[17] The poem, along with the rest of my book-length sequence, draws upon diverse sources, including historical records, visual art, fiction, drama, poetry, and histories, and the prose poem provides here the ideal form in which to combine these varied – and sometimes contradictory – materials, providing a nexus in which time and narrative possibilities are condensed and, simultaneously, expanded.

Umberto Eco, in *The Open Work*, argues that,

> The author offers the interpreter, the performer, the addressee, a work *to be completed*. He does not know the exact fashion in which his work is to be concluded, but he is aware that once completed the work in question will still be his own.[18]

I suggest that prose poetry, with a formal openness born of its urge, in Caddy's terms, to "move away from a stultifying rigidity and closure," provides an ideal place for juxtaposition, in which indeterminacy can be explored without privileging one particular reading. With this openness of text in mind, Andy Brown suggests that, "In a prose poem, . . . the lack of context on the page (a decontextualized 'spot of time') sends readers off in search of it."[19] This "spot of time" may itself be the site of further openness. Paul Munden, for example, argues that the form of the prose poem makes it ideal for enacting startling shifts in time:

> If a lineated poem can handle a vast yet instant time-shift, then it might be concluded that the lineated form is ideal for the task. . . . The answer, I believe, has something to do with the prose poem's casual poise, its

appropriation of prose for poetic purpose, where swift and brief fluidity of syntactical movement blurs the radical time shifts. . . . The equivalent of the *volta* may sometimes be present in the prose poem in the form of a time shift – not occupying a specific *position* within the poem, or turning point more associated with the turn of line, but a time shift that exists within the elastic, single moment of the paragraph-poem, charging the whole work.[20]

In the prose poem, then, it is how the time-shifts function that is important. The key word in Munden's discussion, I suggest, is "charging": it is the energy of the lines as they push beyond the usual constraints of the line break that facilitates the fluidity of time within the poem, allowing sometimes dramatic time-shifts to occur. For example, Helen Ivory's "The Story of the City" begins conventionally enough, but then what Munden terms "the radical time shifts" happens:

> It all began a long time ago as stories are wont to do. It began with wolves, but wolves were too fierce, so they were written out of the story. The story really begins when some of the cast-out wolves turned their coats inside-out and called themselves dogs.[21]

Ivory's poem begins like a traditional fairy story but, almost as soon as they are introduced, the wolves are explicitly discarded from the narrative. Then, there is a different turn, in that some of the wolves become dogs by inverting their fur. This demonstrates that, through there effectively being three separate beginnings to this prose poem, it is these time-shifts which "charge" the poem.

A different approach, yet still employing time-shifts, may be found in Helen Tookey's poem "Halb Null":

> It occurred to me to ask the time . . . How did it get so late? We had done nothing . . . There were road blocks, long queues of traffic out of the city. At a standstill alongside a wide flat field, we watched circus performers rehearsing . . . It was late and they were only rehearsing, there was no sense of urgency or concern among them. But for us, time had slipped through our fingers, it seemed that we might never get back.[22]

Tookey's poem uses time-shifts to move constantly forward between discrete and apparently random recollections, a tension growing between urgency and stasis. A very different approach, displaying a more complex engagement with time, may be seen in Mary Jean Chan's "Dress":

> The same uniform for twelve years. . . . You washed it every single day . . . You began wearing that dress at the age of six, your skin haunted by the British flag, so you could be *Chinese with English characteristics*. Each time you wore it, you shut your body up. . . . Most mornings you see the face of a boy in the

mirror. You expect to fall in love with him. Meanwhile, your fingers brush the wrist of another girl as you jostle into the assembly hall . . . One night, you find yourself kneeling beside the pond. You dream. . . . You slip into the blue water, stripped of the glowing dress you wore for thousands of days.[23]

What Chan articulates here is time moving forwards and backwards in a loop and the medium of prose poetry provides the ideal space in which to do so. Through these three poems, then, we may see different ways in which the prose poem embraces and fosters time-shifts within its unbroken line.

As Munden notes, the prose poem "blurs" these shifts, even as it blurs the categorical distinctions between poetry and prose. In discussing the form, Michael O'Neill observes that, "The prose poem contains within itself the ghost of a more evidently rule-governed poetry in the process of freeing itself from more traditional forms."[24] In these ghost-like qualities which haunt the text, we may see also the hazy fringes of shifting time to which Munden refers, and it is at this point of unresolved mutability and otherness that we may unearth the mystery which lies at the heart of the prose poem. Alluding to this otherness, Paul Hetherington and Cassandra Atherton point out that:

> Prose poems . . . inhabit an open space that begins where there is no particular beginning and concludes without resolving any particular narrative. They open questions and scenarios . . . The linguistic space of prose poetry tempers the features of traditional poetry and prose in order to conjure ramifying and verbally suggestive tropes where unfolding narratives are present but largely implicit, and the condensations of poetry are able to fall naturally into paragraphs rather than truncations of poetic lineation.[25]

Here, Hetherington and Atherton observe the prose poem's tendency towards the "open work," rather than providing narrative closure. Formally, this is achieved by its location within the "white space and silence," to return to Lea's formulation, surrounding the block(s) of text in the prose poem. By adopting such an apparently rigid frame, the prose poem paradoxically moves beyond this frame. For example, Mona Arshi's poem "Barbule" starts: "An opening or an opening of an opening."[26] Here, the prose poem is looking ahead and behind, asking questions and not answering them. This poem talks about openings, then retreats, qualifying the initial "opening," and almost closing itself down. The grammatical status of the first "opening" is ambiguous, whereas the second is probably a verb and the third a noun. Arshi's play of language opens up possibilities upon possibilities while almost collapsing in on itself.

Anne Caldwell, though writing specifically on landscape, could equally be referring to time when she notes that, "The prose poem's indeterminacy and fluid status *between* genres give the writer a flexible, linguistic space to reveal the complexity of this terrain."[27] This "fluid status" is intimately bound up with the

"liminal space" to which Bullock refers: prose poetry, I suggest, contains "an interlude suspended." In this, I acknowledge Hetherington and Atherton, who observe
that, "prose poems usually yield for the reader a complex textual engagement in
which ideas and motifs frequently fold back on themselves, or present unresolved
issues for consideration."[28]

On movement and stasis in the prose poem, Hetherington and Atherton also
say that prose poetry is,

> looking forwards and backwards, understanding transitions, providing
> passages and doorways. Space opens before and behind it, sometimes like
> closed rooms, sometimes like expanding fields. It understands both prose
> and poetry, and it comfortably inhabits the space between them.[29]

However, while prose poetry "comfortably" occupies the space between prose and
poetry, at the same time, prose poetry is *un*comfortable, thriving, as we have seen,
on tension, and charged with the dissonant harmony of its clashing elements. The
core of this dynamic tension is encapsulated in Hazel Smith's observation that,
"Prose poetry . . . by its very nature . . . questions the division between poetry and
prose."[30]

I suggest that the prose poem's energy is, then, born in this space in which uncertain, sometimes contradictory, divisions are interrogated. It is precisely this which
recommends the form so perfectly for aspects of my poetic sequence relating to
events surrounding the life of Richard III and the Princes in the Tower, with both
its action and its main protagonist drawing layer upon layer of conflicting interpretations around an enigmatically unknowable centre. Interpretations of Richard
III's character are themselves fraught with contested divisions. Chris Skidmore, for
example, outlines the Richard of popular belief:

> The Richard we have ourselves inherited through historical tradition is one
> that has been shaped and moulded by that convenient fiction, of viewing
> Richard as the personification of evil, a child-killer, a man whom nothing,
> or no one would stop from obtaining his ambition of wearing the royal
> crown.[31]

Here, Skidmore acknowledges the Shakespearean villain who has so shaped
popular perceptions of Richard's character for five hundred years. Alison Weir, for
example, is one such proponent of this view, being convinced of Richard's guilt,
and even going so far as to accuse him of uxoricide, suggesting that, "The man
who had murdered two children would not have hesitated to dispose of an ailing
and unwanted wife, especially when she was known to be dying anyway and there
was little chance of anyone proving his guilt."[32]

However, as A. J. Pollard observes, this popular image is far from universally
accepted, and he notes that, "There remain two Richards of tradition: a noble

Richard and a monstrous Richard – a northern Richard and a southern Richard. Which of the two is correct is, of course, another question."[33] Likewise, moral considerations aside, the debate also remains ongoing as to whether Richard may be considered a good or bad king. According to Desmond Seward, "The reign of Richard III [was] a nightmare, not least for the king himself."[34] On the other hand, Matthew Lewis points out that, "The sense that Richard was a good lord and a fair king has lingered in the north . . . as though they saw something that the rest of the country and all of history has missed. Their Richard was not a murdering, usurping, cruel tyrant."[35] David Hipshon acknowledges the difficulties of taking an objective view when he points out that, "It is impossible to judge Richard III as a ruler because his reign was too short to allow him to show what he could do."[36] These divergent, contradictory perspectives on the man and his actions are succinctly summed up by Charles Ross: "In the end, any 'contrariety of character' of Richard stems not from what we know about him, but from what we do not know about him."[37] It is with this acceptance of the unknowable that I aim in my prose poems such as "Old Year's Night" to approach my subject "without," in Hetherington and Atherton's words, "resolving any particular narrative."

As we have seen, prose poetry dwells in a mutable space in which poetry and prose simultaneously both interact and assert their own identities. It is thus a form which is perfectly suited to a historical period in which, as Terry Breverton explains, "The snarled skeins of the familial rivalries of the Wars of the Roses, of the claims to the kingship between and within the great noble houses of York and Lancaster, form the backdrop to an understanding of the events of Richard's life."[38] I am writing my poems about the small, intimate moments into which these "snarled skeins," intrude upon the lives of Richard III, the Princes in the Tower and their families. Inevitably, some of these poems feature complex and contested narratives, and one such is "Old Year's Night," which moves between Richard in London and his father in Yorkshire. David Horspool, writing of the young Richard, notes that, "He was born into, and died in, a time of violence, uncertainty,"[39] and it is this sense of uncertainty, in particular, that I wished to foreground in the poem.

Initially considering lineated verse, I considered a number of options regarding where to place the line breaks, initially looking at very short lines, intended to represent Richard's curved spine:

In bed
he arches
his spine,
but his frame
doesn't settle.
His sleep
is fitful.

The short, broken lines articulate the unsettled subject, while the layout itself is aesthetically pleasing. Ultimately, however, I decided that the lineation was too neat and ordered. Following this, I tried slightly longer lines:

> In bed he arches his spine,
> but his frame doesn't settle.
> His sleep is fitful.

The alignment of punctuation with line endings creates an emphatic pause at the end of each line, thus forcing the reader to stop and consider each image in turn before moving on, thereby creating an accumulation of discrete images. This, however, created a different kind of neatness, with images too distinctly demarcated. Consequently, I re-lineated the poem in order to introduce enjambment, thereby giving the impression of images effectively toppling over the line break and into each other:

> In bed he arches
> his spine, but his frame
> doesn't settle. His sleep
> is fitful.

This unstable, unstoppable progression across enjambed lines reflects Richard's physical and psychological trauma, its broken syntax enacting his fitfulness for the reader. However, I wondered if this may consequently guide the reader down one particular interpretation of Richard at this moment, at the expense of historical uncertainty, so tried a further revision:

> In bed he arches his spine, but his frame doesn't settle.
> His sleep is fitful.

I hoped that the long line followed by a short line would introduce suggestions of conflict and fragmentation, while at the same time gesturing towards the "insecure world" in which Richard grew up.[40] However, as with my second approach, I felt that the punctuation at the end of the line stopped the reader or listener and did not carry them through the shifting physical and temporal spaces of the poem.

While considering these drafts and their relative merits and demerits, I was also reading Josephine Wilkinson's *Richard, The Young King to Be*, in which she writes:

> In the hushed, numbed days following the death of his father, as the winter snows buried the dead and the icy winds whispered to the living, did Richard silently contemplate the beautiful Yorkist badges with which he was surrounded? For everywhere he looked during those dark and lonely days, Richard's eyes fell on the badges of the House of York.[41]

Wilkinson's book is popular history, a biographical study of Richard growing up, but it occurred to me that this passage could also stand as a prose poem, in which the prose, to return to Wall from earlier in this chapter, possesses all the "intensity of poetry," as it ventures beyond the historical record and enters Richard's thought processes. As Hetherington and Atherton observe, "Prose poetry makes a virtue of brevity, absence, and gaps in narrative, and fills in missing details with its various poetic figures,"[42] something which Wilkinson observes in her quoted passage, and which suggested to me the adoption of the form as a possible alternative to the various patterns of lineation, all of which I had found lacking in some respect.

The prose poem on which I settled takes inspiration from the black-on-white blocks of text common to the form, but increases the sense of fleetingness and dislocation through breaking it into shorter prose stanzas. Within this prose structure, it employs all the tools associated with poetic craft, such as alliteration ("Richard restless"), assonance ("snow covers," "forked bodies," "wolds"), and onomatopoeia ("skids," "crumples"). There is also in places a deliberate avoidance of expected prose norms, such as the absence of verbs in: "Calder dark. Sky dark. Castle stone dark." This lack of verbs removes indications of agency or time, thereby creating an impression of the static moment while simultaneously facilitating instant switches in both time and space.

Referring back to Munden's consideration of prose poetry and time-shifts, he asserts that,

> prose poems reflecting on the passage of time, or incorporating time-shifts as a significant part of their content, do so with remarkable *abandon*, the effect at once casual and extreme. It is as if the expected parameters of time are thrown to the wind, and the gesture is all the more striking on account of the brief space in which it happens; not only a *brief* space, but a *tightly framed* space, with no line or stanza breaks or other spatial elements to assist in the temporal stretches and shifts.[43]

This notion is key to my adoption of prose poetry in this case. I see the prose poem as a nexus, wherein time and possibilities are condensed and, simultaneously, expanded. In "Old Year's Night," I employ "*tightly framed*" verse paragraphs in order to move almost instantaneously between different times and locations, sometimes even within the same verse paragraph. The lack of "spatial elements" that Munden notes can be seem as part of the challenge to the page which Maxwell articulates thus: "Poems must be formed in the face of time, as we are. Whatever the whiteness is to you it's *also* time."[44] In "Old Year's Night," I have sought to express the simultaneous expansion and compression of uncertain time and space within the expansion and compression which occurs within the uncertain and debated form of the prose poem as it confronts the reader on the page.

On considering the key characteristics of this paradoxical form, Hetherington and Atherton note that, "where works of microfiction emphasize the movement of narrative through time – focusing on what happens, albeit in very few words – prose poetry tends to emphasize what *has happened* and will *always be happening*."[45] While specifically invoking microfiction here, the same urge for linear narrative is widely characteristic of both fiction and non-fiction. In treating the subject of Richard III's contentious reign, historians, novelists, playwrights, and poets are bound by the expectations of story – in its broadest form – to privilege interpretations of events and motivations for which no definitive evidence survives. In contrast, the prose poem offers a charged space in which a moment – an "interlude suspended," which not only "*has happened*" but will "*always be happening*" – may be stretched, compressed, and inspected from all angles. As Jane Monson explains, "the prose poem does not just cross literary boundaries, and neither is it simply a meeting between one genre and the next; it is a dialogue between a host of other disciplines and recognised polarities."[46] Drawing on the prose poem's uncertain definitions and its easy ability to incorporate fragmentation and disjunction, both spatial and temporal, I suggest that it is a particularly apt form with which to approach the contested details of unknowable history: an "interlude suspended" for observation, its every surface sharp and bright, but open to interpretation.

In his prose poem "Orientate" John McCullough asks: "What can you say when you ask the world for space to frolic and acres appear on every side, carry on to the horizon? No walls or barriers, only there are, just not where expected."[47] Prose poetry, I suggest, offers the writer just such a space, existing between, within and through different genres and forms. And it is in this room, in which physical, formal, and temporal walls may not be quite where we expect them to be, in which we may encounter the silent or ambiguous truths – the interludes suspended – of unknown and unspoken histories.

Notes

1 Colm Tóibín, *The Master* (London: Picador, 2004), 10.
2 Paul Hetherington and Cassandra Atherton, eds. *Prose Poetry: An Introduction* (Princeton, NJ: Princeton University Press, 2020), 9.
3 Edwin Stockdale, "Old Year's Night," *Dream Catcher* 42 (2020): 48.
4 Monica Carroll and Jen Webb, "'Defiant Formlessness': Prose Poem as Process." *TEXT Special Issue 46, Beyond the Line: Contemporary Prose Poetry* (October 2017): 12.
5 Owen Bullock, "The Successful Prose Poem Leaves Behind Its Name," in *British Prose Poetry: The Poems Without Lines*, ed. Monson, Jane (Cham, CH: Palgrave Macmillan, 2018), 243.
6 Bronwyn Lea, "Poetics and Poetry," in *The Cambridge Companion to Creative Writing*, ed. David Morley and Philip Neilsen (Cambridge: Cambridge University Press, 2012), 68.
7 Paul Munden, "Playing with Time: Prose Poetry and the Elastic Moment." *TEXT Special Issue 46, Beyond the Line: Contemporary Prose Poetry* (October 2017): 2.
8 Sean O'Brien, "Introduction to Poetry," in *The Handbook of Creative Writing*, ed. Stephen Earnshaw (Edinburgh: Edinburgh University Press, 2007), 195.
9 Alan Wall, "Questioning the Prose Poem: Thoughts on Geoffrey Hill's *Mercian Hymns*," in *British Prose Poetry*, ed. Monson, 170.

10 Glyn Maxwell, *On Poetry* (London: Oberon, 2012), 18.

11 Luke Kennard, "'Man and Nature in and Out of Order': The Surrealist Prose Poetry of David Gascoyne," in *British Prose Poetry*, ed. Monson, 253.

12 David Caddy, "'Hidden' Form: The Prose Poem in English Poetry." In *British Prose Poetry*, ed. Jane Monson, 21.

13 Sarah Corbett, "Migraine," in *A Perfect Mirror* (Liverpool: Liverpool University Press, 2018), 34.

14 Munden, "Playing with Time."

15 Paul Farley and Michael Symmons Roberts, *Edgelands, Journeys into England's True Wilderness* (London: Jonathan Cape, 2011), 6.

16 Linda Black, "Begin with a Hook," *Magma* 54 (2014): 2.

17 John Ashdown-Hill, *The Third Plantagenet: George, Duke of Clarence, Richard III's Brother* (Brimscombe Port, UK: The History Press, 2014), 57.

18 Umberto Eco, *The Open Work*, trans. Anna Cancogni (Cambridge, MA: Harvard University Press, 1989), 19.

19 Andy Brown, "'I Went Disguised in It': Re-evaluating Seamus Heaney's *Stations*," in *British Prose Poetry*, ed. Monson, 184.

20 Munden, "Playing with Time," 8.

21 Helen Ivory, "The Story of the City," in *Maps of the Abandoned City* (Dublin: SurVision, 2019), 10.

22 Helen Tookey, "Halb Null," in Caldwell, Anne, and Oz Hardwick, eds. *The Valley Press Anthology of Prose Poetry*. (Scarborough: Valley Press, 2019), 70.

23 Mary Jean Chan, "Dress," in *Flèche* (London: Faber and Faber, 2019), 10.

24 Michael O'Neill, "Marvellous Clouds: Reflections on the Prose Poetry of Woolf, Baudelaire and Williams." In *British Prose Poetry*, ed. Jane Monson, 82.

25 Paul Hetherington and Cassandra Atherton, "'Unconscionable Mystification'? Rooms, Spaces and the Prose Poem." *New Writing* 12, no. 3 (2015): 272.

26 Mona Arshi, "Barbule," in *Small Hands* (Liverpool: Liverpool University Press, 2015), 46.

27 Anne Caldwell, "Reawakening Wonder: How Cartography can Act as Creative Research for Prose Poetry." *New Writing* 15, no. 4 (2018): 414.

28 Paul Hetherington and Cassandra Atherton, eds. *Prose Poetry: An Introduction*, (Princeton, NJ: Princeton University Press, 2020), 128.

29 Hetherington and Atherton, "'Unconscionable Mystification'?" 279.

30 Hazel Smith, *The Writing Experiment: Strategies for Innovative Creative Writing* (Crows Nest, AU: Allen & Unwin, 2005), 183.

31 Chris Skidmore, *Richard III: Brother, Protector, King* (London: Weidenfeld & Nicolson, 2017), 7.

32 Alison Weir, *The Princes in the Tower* (London: Pimlico, 1997), 210.

33 A. J. Pollard, *The Worlds of Richard III* (Brimscombe Port, UK: Tempus, 2001), 50.

34 Desmond Seward, *Richard III: The Black Legend* (London: Penguin, 1997), 255.

35 Matthew Lewis, *Richard III: Loyalty Binds Me* (Stroud, UK: Amberley, 2018), 387.

36 David Hipshon, *Richard III* (Abingdon, UK: Routledge, 2010), 247.

37 Charles Ross, *Richard III* (New Haven, CT: Yale University Press, 1999), 229.

38 Terry Breverton, *Richard III: The King in the Car Park* (Stroud, UK: Amberley, 2015), 12.

39 David Horspool, *Richard III: A Ruler and His Reputation* (London: Bloomsbury Continuum, 2017), 24.

40 Alison Weir, *Richard III and the Princes in the Tower* (London: Vintage, 2014), xv.

41 Josephine Wilkinson, *Richard, The Young King to Be* (Chalford, UK: Amberley, 2008), 78–9.

42 Hetherington and Atherton, *The Prose Poem*, 197.

43 Munden, "Playing with Time," 2.

44 Maxwell, *On Poetry*, 54.

45 Hetherington and Atherton, *The Prose Poem*, 26.

46 Monson, "Introduction," in *British Prose Poetry*, 11.

47 John McCullough, "Orientate," in *Reckless Paper Birds* (London: Penned in the Margins, 2019), 30.

13

WHO ARE THE CONTEMPORARY SYMBOLISTS?

The Prose Poem and the Decorative-Subjective Approach

Ruth Stacey

In 1891, the Symbolist poet Stéphane Mallarmé, interviewed by Jules Huret, was quoted as saying,

> To name an object is to remove three-quarters of the enjoyment of a poem, which derives from the pleasure of gradually perceiving it; to suggest it, that is the dream. It is the perfect use of that mystery which is the symbol: to evoke an object little by little [. . .][1]

This chapter will discuss contemporary examples of the prose poem in reference to its origin as a symbolist poetic form that allows a space for specific poetic techniques such as musicality, decorativeness, and subjectivity. It will examine the work of contemporary practitioners who are utilising this particularly symbolist approach in their work, with a focus on the poets Cassandra Atherton and Paul Hetherington. It will discuss the prose poem as a symbolist poetic space that prioritises a decorative-descriptive experience for the reader, and contrast its immediate density on the page, often typeset as a square, with the expansive potential the unlineated sentences of prose allow for playfulness and experimentation. Furthermore, the original symbolist poets also sought to combine emotional expression and a surfeit of feelings and sensory experience within their writing, and this chapter discusses how intertextuality and memoir are used by poets I identify as contemporary symbolists in order to achieve similar ends. This chapter examines the ways in which deliberate ambiguity in the use of symbolic imagery, and unsettling subjectivity in the narrative "I," result in a layering of voices and movements through time periods which creates the suggestion of meaning but no certainty. Based on this critical understanding, the chapter will conclude by reflecting upon this symbolist approach in my own practice.

DOI: 10.4324/9781003199533-14

A Provocation

Posing the question *Who are the contemporary symbolists?* is a provocative beginning to this chapter, adopting a confrontational approach which sits well with the original symbolist poets who were famed for their rebellion against the traditional poetics of their age. I believe the challenging aspect of this question is the application of a categorical label to twenty-first-century poets, which may appear to be limiting them within the confines of a particular *-ism*, rather than being free to define themselves. No poet likes to be contained. However, my intention is not to limit, but to view the poets discussed through a particular lens in order to illuminate a commonality they share and identify certain techniques that may be utilised in creative practice by other poets to write contemporary symbolist poetry for themselves. The question is also provocative because symbolist poetics were not abandoned and forgotten in the nineteenth century, but rather became the foundation of the literary movements that followed, thereby being both influential and enriching for the poets of the twentieth century, with aspects integral to contemporary poetics. Its legacy may be observed in, for example, neo-surrealism, the use of *vers libre*, and the prose poem form. Therefore, suggesting that certain poets are doing something *more* than this and are more specifically "symbolist" requires focus on other aspects of symbolist poetics; most significantly, musicality, subjectivity, and decorativeness. Third, it is a provocation, because the first symbolist poets, after flaring into popularity in the *fin de siècle* era for their rich use of language and idealism (which contrasted with the practical, brutalist, industrialised society surrounding the poet practitioners), latterly became viewed as using a kind of sickening opulence of language, with the symbolists becoming interchangeable with the decadents, and the term "decadent" altering signification from pleasing to insulting. In short, symbolists were viewed as "too much" and their style of poetry an affectation.

To take one example, Lisa Goldfarb notes that, "For Auden it is hard to imagine a worse outcome for a poet than to endorse a symbolist aesthetic and 'to retreat from rhyme and reason into a Mallarmesque / syllabic fog,'"[2] and this conjured image of symbolist poetics as a fog (something damp and annoying, or worse, something negative and frightening to be lost within) articulates why twenty-first-century poets may not wish to be assigned thus. Yet, it is precisely this opulent-sensual approach, combined with playfulness, musicality, and subjectivity to create an all-encompassing fog of symbolist poetics, that certain poets are employing in their approach to prose poetry; not merely in their use of the form, but by fully embracing symbolist practice in all its "Mallarmesque" profusion.

Defining Symbolism

In order to define the poets who are working as contemporary symbolists, I must first explain that my purpose is not to provide an in-depth history of the symbolist movement here but move swiftly to define the language through which I will discuss contemporary practitioners. Symbolist poetics is often associated with, and has greatly influenced, other movements such as decadence and aestheticism, imagism, and surrealism and could be considered the bedrock of modernism. Baudelaire initiated the symbolist aesthetic movement when he published *Les fleurs du mal* in 1857, and it would become a huge influence on the French poets who followed him and rebelled against realism and descriptive preciseness. These poets included Paul Verlaine, who published a collection of essays in 1884 defining symbolism and discussing poets (himself included), who he named as "cursed poets" – *poètes maudits* – those who were at odds with society, including Arthur Rimbaud, Stéphane Mallarmé, and others. Verlaine did not see the poets' curse of suffering as tragic, but as vital to produce art, and this myth (that a poet must suffer), perpetuated by Rimbaud's fierce poetry of revolt and subsequent rejection of the life of a poet at a young age, lingers in the perception of symbolist poets. However, although there was an aspect of rebellion and rejection of society norms within the movement, it was also about striving for something, through imagination and dreams, greater than ordinary perceptions. As Rosina Neginsky observes of Schopenhauer, "pessimism [. . .] played an important role in the evolution of the symbolist worldview,"[3] and she quotes Schopenhauer's view that, "Fine art can give us temporary relief from ceaseless striving by making us forget our desiring individuality in the aesthetic act of rapt contemplation,"[4] positioning the production of art as providing a refuge from the everyday. It is this aspect of symbolist poetics on which I shall focus.

Despite the *Manifesto of Symbolism* by Jean Moréas, published in *Le Figaro* in September 1886, the symbolist movement, in sympathy with the manifesto's aims perhaps, is difficult to pin down, as may be indicated by its range and influence mentioned above. The manifesto itself, although aiming to consolidate the movement, is itself poetic and subjective and open to interpretation. In it Moréas writes that, "Symbolic poetry seeks to clothe the Idea in a sensual form [. . .] because the essential character of Symbolic art consists of continuing until the concentration of the Idea in itself."[5] Building upon this, Nathalia Brodskaya defines how "Symbolism opposed society's ideas of science, aspiring to return art to the priority of the spiritual over the material,"[6] and thus represented a desire for the ineffable rather than the certain, and goes on to describe the symbolists' pursuit of the "dream" space as, "a demonstration and even a symbol of their exceptional imagination, capable of transcending reality."[7]

My interpretation of this focuses on the ideas of clothing and continuing, dream and transcendence. The image Moréas conjures of "clothing" an "Idea" could suggest clothing to mean covering (to make enigmatic) or clothing as saturating by layering words like fabric sheets, wrapping words on words (to make rich and dense). Combined with the concept of continuing (to denote expansiveness), this definition of symbolist poetics can be seen, as many scholars agree, to be exemplified or perfected in the poetry of Stéphane Mallarmé. As a poet myself, who sees words in a very visual way with an image forming in my mind, I picture Moréas' description of "clothing" and "continuing" as a statue wrapped in layers of fabrics, becoming more remote and enigmatic with each layer. This idea could be described as a technique of veiling, with the veil both obscuring and tantalising the reader. I call this approach to writing poetry not simply a symbolist approach, but a kind of decorative ambiguity, with the intention of layering, saturating, and overwhelming the poem with imagery and symbols to actually reveal, as Moréas defined it, "the primordial idea."[8] To write poetry with a decorative-subjective approach, one can return to Mallarmé and his definition of certain working principles that define the idea of the dream state in the poem as central to the transcendence of reality. In the same 1891 interview with Jules Huret with which I opened the chapter, Mallarmé is quoted as saying,

> The contemplation of objects, the images that soar up from the reveries induced by them, are the song; the Parnassians grasp the object in its entirety and show it. In doing so they lack mystery; they remove from minds the delectable pleasure of believing that they are the ones creating.[9]

What is striking in Mallarmé's description of his poetic practice is how unapologetic he is in his use of sensual description and recognition of the bodily experience of making and reading poetry. It produces reveries; it is delectable and creates pleasure. Writing of Mallarmé in 1899, Arthur Symons asserted that he lived a life of "persistent devotion to literature" and that all his poems "are the evocation of a passing ecstasy, arrested in mid-flight [. . .] It is a mental transposition of emotion and sensation, veiled with atmosphere, and becoming, as it becomes a poem, pure beauty,"[10] describing both the process of making and of reading Mallarmé's poetry in language that could be describing a romantic experience. However, Mallarmé is not invoking longing for a lover or retelling romantic encounters within the poems to create sensual scenarios. As Henri Peyre observes, "the elegies and the invocations to women, the tenderness of relived memory [. . .] cease with Mallarmé to be one of the central motifs of poetry,"[11] emphasising that it was pursuit of suggestion and idealism, above everyday superficialities, that directed Mallarmé's poetic practice.

Mallarmé's poems were crafted to leave things unsaid in order to allow the "delectable pleasure" of inviting the reader to "believe they are the ones creating." Peyre quotes a "youthful article" written by the 20-year-old Mallarmé in *L'Artiste* (15 September 1862), which states in its first line, "Everything sacred that wants to remain sacred envelops itself in mystery,"[12] and this links neatly to the image of the veiled statue described previously as a way to begin thinking about creating decorative ambiguity within one's own poetic practice today. Taking a somewhat mysterious and ineffable concept and turning it into a practical first step by creating a visual expression of it has been helpful in my own practice. Discussing Mallarmé's practice, Symons wrote:

By the time the poem has reached, as it seems to him, a flawless unity, the steps of the progress have been only too effectively effaced; and while the poet, who has seen the thing from the beginning, still sees the relation of point to point, the reader who comes to it only its final stage, finds himself in a not unnatural bewilderment.[13]

This focus on removing any certainties through the process of crafting the poem, on suggesting, hinting, and "clothing" the original idea or inspiration within the poem, is expressed by Mallarmé in the Huret interview as "enigma." In this interview, Mallarmé states that, "In poetry there must always be enigma, and the goal of literature, there is in fact no other, is to *evoke* objects,"[14] showing once more his absolute devotion to his aim; this goal or *no other*. As Symons observed, "Pursue this manner of writing to its ultimate development; start with an enigma, and then withdraw the key of the enigma; and you arrive easily, at the frozen impenetrability of [Mallarmé's] latest sonnets,"[15] and a frozen poem may suggest something glacial, off-putting, and ultimately unreadable. However, it could also be intriguing, and not having the key to unlock the enigma will in Mallarmé's view create the intended "reveries." For Mallarmé, this idea of suggestion as the aim of the poem, to be deliberately enigmatic, will elicit the "delectable pleasure" response in the reader. I suggest this could be described as flirting or teasing the reader, a pleasurable experience, and one which I shall shortly explore in the contemporary prose poems of Cassandra Atherton.

By returning to the source of symbolist poetics and its most devoted practitioner, and by distilling certain elements from Mallarmé's practice – namely the evocation of enigma above all things, and the creation of images that stimulate reverie – we can, as working poets ourselves, implement this pursuit of veiling in our own practice and identify it in others. I shall now turn to consider the work of poets who I believe may be considered contemporary symbolists; those who are not only working in the prose poem form, but saturating their ideas and clothing them in sensual imagery, thereby effacing the original form so the reader can no longer follow, as Symons expressed it, the poet's process "point to point,"[16] presenting instead a seemingly disparate connection of images. How to create reveries is something I will explore in the latter part of this chapter when I consider practice.

There are many contemporary practitioners of the prose poem form and many utilise methods such as fragmentation, collage, or surreal insertions to unbalance the reader and layer meaning. Others are, I suggest, using a more specifically symbolist approach to create enigmatic, expansive spaces within a confined space (the text block of the prose poem) to make, as David Lehman has described it in relation to another original symbolist, Rimbaud's practice: "dream landscapes and journeys, visionary fragments."[17] Consequently, this chapter could expand indefinitely in order to examine those who are doing so, to a greater or lesser extent. For example, I would name Gasper Orozco's *Book of the Peony* (2017), discussed at length by Helen Tookey in the present volume, as a contemporary symbolist collection that is suffused with a decorative-subjective approach, employing sensual clothing of an idea in order to create an enigma; something that is layered and saturated through repeated meditations on the peony. However, I shall focus on two poets who collaborate a great deal and have also written extensively about the prose poem form in numerous articles and a recent book, *Prose Poetry: An Introduction* (2020): Cassandra Atherton and Paul Hetherington. Both create the decorative ambiguity I am seeking, and I am honing in on particular examples here, namely Atherton's sensual use of breath and intertextuality, and Hetherington's use of ekphrasis to create a decorative, picturely quality to his poetry.

Hetherington and Atherton examine the contemporary expressions of symbolist poetics in relation to neo-surrealism in prose poetry, noting that, "Symbolism values dream imagery and often addresses aspects of external reality through giving emphasis to more or less abstract symbols over 'realistic' description."[18] They go on to discuss the ways in which symbolism influenced surrealism and how "The neo-surreal is a postmodern outgrowth of such preoccupations,"[19] with unconscious material. They note that contemporary neo-surrealist prose poems "tend to emphasize disruptive effects and narrative disjunction without turning inward to locate and articulate unconscious experiences and impulses."[20] Contemporary, mostly American, prose poets differ from their European forebears, the Symbolists and Surrealists, by their adoption of "different manners and methods," but their similar purpose is clear as they explore "the stuff of dreams and nightmares."[21] The original methods as articulated by Mallarmé and defined at the beginning of this chapter are a source of continued influence on contemporary poetry, as evidenced by the widespread use of neo-surreal approaches and the usefulness of the prose poem form to house these methods. I am turning the lens on Atherton and Hetherington as I appreciate their use of original symbolist poetic technique, making them my contemporary symbolists.

Playful Dalliance in the Poetry of Cassandra Atherton

As I was searching for poets who were contemporary symbolists, I began by identifying the form of the prose poem as a signifier. This led to researching both the history of the prose poem and attendance at symposia at which contemporary practitioners were discussing the form. As well as the prose poem form itself, I was seeking something more, namely further use of symbolist poetics; the dreamy, decorative ambiguity that I was aiming to write in my own work to express the life of the symbolist artist Pamela Colman Smith (1878–1951). Smith, a prolific artist and illustrator who worked with Bram Stoker, William Butler Yeats, and Ellen Terry, is largely forgotten despite producing one of the most famous sequences of artworks in the world, the Rider-Waite tarot deck. My poetry collection aims to create an imagined set of memoirs by Smith using symbolist techniques, which requires embedding the decorative-subjective approach throughout. In the work of Cassandra Atherton,[22] I found a pure example of the style I was seeking: a playful dalliance of language and structure that produced the "delectable pleasure" response as the poet held the reader in a flirtation of suggestion. This is achieved in the use of musicality through rhyme and word associations, building layers of imagery without revealing the "point to point" process, but rather effacing to leave enigmatic connections. Her work is inherently playful and literary, gesturing towards and citing diverse artworks – books, films, paintings – whilst gleefully erotic in places, as she uses direct address to create intimacy, constantly suggesting and hinting at other works. These references in the poems to other texts are a vital aspect of a decorative-subjective approach which creates a sensual breathlessness; a reverie of perplexing action as the reader actively participates in the poem. If only you, the reader, can connect the references, you might unlock the key to the greater picture.

Elsewhere, Hetherington and Atherton have discussed the nature of intertexts:

> The choice and use of intertexts allows for insight into the writer's internal libraries, webs, interests and imaginations. When an intertext is used, it is placed in a new context and thus, reframed and reworked, it grows in meaning [. . .] prose poetry is markedly extended by its intertexts.[23]

This idea that the intertext "grows in meaning" echoes Moréas in *The Symbolist Manifesto* when he called for the poetry to continue. The prose poem form, in contrast with a constrained form, allows expansiveness with the use of unlineated poetic sentence and no capped length; but combined with intertexts, the potential for expansion and for the poem to continue outside the space on the page is immeasurably increased. Further, Hetherington and Atherton have discussed how intertexts are "subversive and playful" and expand meaning from various sources: "Intertextuality is thus a powerful tool for writers of very short forms such as prose poems because of its capacity to carry across meaning from a wide variety of extended sources."[24]

This ability to expand outwards into texts and references beyond the poem is demonstrated in both Hetherington's and Atherton's poetry. In "Modi," from her collection *Exhumed* (2015), Atherton focuses her attention on the painter Amedeo Modigliani (1884–1920).[25] The poem opens with a first-person voice employing sensual imagery: "I melt into his canvas. Fibres prickling my back as I search for a theme." The use of the word "melting" displays the layered meaning that is distinctive of Atherton's work, suggesting both an image of paint melting onto a canvas as a painter works, and imagery of a body's response to sexual desire. This is amplified by using the word "prickling," which conveys the tactile sensation of the paint being applied or a body being stroked, but which also carries an echo of the slang word for the penis. As the poem unfolds, Atherton layers references to Amedeo Modigliani's life and circle, including his lover Jeanne, and expands outwards through references to other painters and poets. Keats' "La Belle Dame sans Merci" is quoted, and by describing imagery that could be associated with late Pre-Raphaelite John William Waterhouse's paintings *Miranda* (1916) from Shakespeare's *The Tempest*, and *A Mermaid* (1900), Atherton moves outwards in playful, sensual associations to create a rush of wetness at the end of the poem, signifying climax perhaps after the foreplay at the beginning of the poem. This exuberance and the bold references to desire and sex – "Poking me with the wooden end of the brush, I climb onto its wooden tip" – invite the reader to take part in this reverie of associations and expansive dialogue about artist and muse. With transformative slippage in the space of the prose poem, the reader can become the narrative "I" and, in searching for meaning, the key, becoming active in the poem. This puzzling out of enigmatic intertextuality is, I suggest, the way in which reveries are created. What Mallarmé described as the "delectable pleasure," a trance of suggestion, is the reader actively participating in the poem. Atherton is bolder than Mallarmé, who created ethereal and lofty reveries; she is a contemporary symbolist, in her dalliance with the reader, referencing much more direct sensuality.

In one sense, I have discussed this poem in particular as I did understand the key – the references to the artist and his life, the wider allusions – and understanding the intertexts allows one a feeling of figuring out the puzzle. Sometimes Atherton is direct in her referencing, using a quotation, a title, or even an epigraph. But the poems are never straightforward and leap like little fish, slippery and hard to hold as different images accumulate and continue to linger, requiring re-reading. However, I find there is as much, if not more, delectable pleasure in the poems in which I do not immediately understand the intertexts or connections. The images instead layer to create a sensual evocation of some deeper feeling and the desire to understand creates the reverie intended, as I actively puzzle out a line or an image and wonder what it reminds me of. This, in turn, draws my experiences into the space of Atherton's poem.

Atherton likes to move from one image to another, describing it vividly and then moving rapidly on as another image is suggested. This results in sense of breathlessness as, even though she often eschews complex or compound sentences, the poem gathers momentum as one simple sentence follows another. Mallarmé, in contrast, had an expansive style in his poetic prose, as described by one of his later translators, Evlyn Gould: "And as one reads, so many of Mallarmé's sentences dance on, puffing themselves up with relative clauses, that the relatives become more captivating than the sense of the whole they mobilize and detail in fractions, infinitely."[26] I think it is telling that Mallarmé's writing is described as becoming more captivating in fractions, as I believe this is what is intended in Atherton's and Hetherington's poetry. The layering of imagery and intertexts, whether the reader can find the key to unlock them or not, becomes, as a whole block of text, a captivating sensual experience. For example, in *Trace* (2015), the poem "Vitamin D" demonstrates Atherton's playful way of by employing homophones, associations or sideways slips in the mind through connections utilising the look or sound of a word – like pasty/pastry in the following extract – or through homonyms that create associated tangents, as demonstrated by the playful use of the word "solar," referencing both the sun and the body.

> I went looking for the sun. One morning. Pasty. Undercooked pastry. Looking for the golden brown glow. I needed to feel the weight of the sun on my shoulders. On my solar plexus. I took a glass of milk and a paint brush to baste myself.[27]

Atherton makes great use of internal rhyme through assonance and consonance to add a sense of musicality, combined with sibilance to emphasise certain images. It is, as with much of Atherton's poetry, both unfathomable and seemingly almost in reach; the meaning is buried under layers. As one thing seems to make sense, it retreats and something else is brought to the foreground. There is a neo-surreal or magical-realist quality in the image of a body being prepared as food – something surreal, unsettling, or uncanny – but this is more, I suggest, symbolist poetics at work. The enigma created by Atherton creates the active reader response needed to find the key to unlock it, resulting in a state of reverie, or puzzling on it, when reading. The references to the body are at the centre of the poem – skin as undercooked pastry, the weight of the sun on the skin and the milk basting it – yet despite being grounded in bodily imagery, there is something out of reach in the playful associations concerning the mind. In the latter part of the poem, Atherton writes, "My stripy banana lounge, / too long ago to unfold from my memory. For a while I/ thought I was well again."[28] The image of a striped sun chair that can no longer be unfolded acts as an image of containment and, contrasted with the imagery of light that permeates the poem, it hints at something darker. Atherton and Hetherington detail the prose poem form as having the "capacity to articulate what is otherwise unsayable,"[29] and this aspect of layering and evoking, but without creating any certainty, elicits a sense of things unspoken, of things that happen outside the boundary of the poem. This places Atherton's work within Mallarmé's outline for his poetics.

The Space as a Decorative Picture in Paul Hetherington's Poetry

As already mentioned, Hetherington and Atherton work in ways that are similar, and there are many intersections within their work. Not only do they regularly collaborate in scholarly articles and publications, but they are also both concerned with embedding within their work references (intertexts) to art, literature, and history. Hetherington can be as playful as Atherton at times, though perhaps not as directly sensual and intimate, as Atherton's use of direct address to the reader is often provocative and elicits a sense of intimacy that draws the reader into the sexual and bodily experience of the poem. In contrast, Hetherington's symbolist space leans towards a more contemplative and distanced experience for the reader, which is often more enigmatic and puzzling. Hetherington slips between the inner and outer world of the poem so that viewpoint is sometimes located within the moment, and at others outside the space of the poem, considering what is being observed from a distance. It is a different kind of sensual intimacy and allows things to be evoked and almost grasped, but then lost. Rather than a dalliance of teasing, Hetherington's poems evoke the sensation of a curtain being lifted but then quickly dropped again; offering a brief glimpse, with no assistance for the reader to make sense of what they have seen.

Discussing Hetherington's poetry in terms of pictures not only responds to his frequent use of ekphrasis, which will be discussed shortly, but also recognises that his text boxes appear to layer images in a way that focuses on the decorative in order to create ambiguities. The prose poem is a contained space, fenced, bordered, held – or, in terms of this discussion, framed. Each description of the containment of the block of text that makes the prose poem have slightly different feelings to them and changes the perception of the poem being in the white space. Mallarmé wrote in the 1897 preface to his experimental work *Un Coup de Dés Jamais N'Abolira Le Hasard* (*A Roll of the Dice will Never Abolish Chance*) that,

> The "blanks" indeed take on importance, at first glance; the versification demands them, as a surrounding silence, to the extent that a fragment, lyrical or of a few beats, occupies, in its midst, a third of the space of paper.[30]

This idea of surrounding silence (or contemplation) is palpably present in Hetherington's poems, even as they "continue" in their imagery and intertexts. Like pictures mounted on walls, the poems hang in space that forces focus on the decorative layering happening within the frame.

In his collection *Gallery of Antique Art*, Hetherington visits an imagined gallery and utilises ekphrasis, which results in a meandering between viewpoints and contemplations, with the prose poems acting as framed artworks in the gallery space.[31] Ekphrasis is a useful working technique for poets seeking to use a symbolist approach, as the subject is veiled from the beginning by the other artist who created the artwork. Consequently, it can allow transformation of image into words whilst describing an already enigmatic subject, creating an immediate layering effect. In the collection, the gallery presents a space to travel through and an ending (leaving the gallery), but the reader is encouraged to deviate from the prescribed route, to turn back to puzzle out the mysteries that are created through the subjectivity of the poems. That Hetherington closes with a question, "Who is he? you gestured/as he stepped left and out of sight,"[32] emphasises the ambiguities present in the text, and the inherent unknowing that is left in the reader as imagery and slippage between observer and observed is played out.

The poems are ordered in this collection to replicate passing through certain rooms and spaces so that the reader can journey through the gallery.

However, Hetherington does not just clinically reproduce what is on view like a tour guide, standing at a distance from the paintings. The viewpoint is constantly moving through the present moment, back in time, and forward into unanswered questions. Images encountered are observed, or the history depicted is discussed, or the context of the painter's life pondered upon. Always, the curtain is lifted and dropped over the frame of the prose poem, so that a painting in the poem "Tenth Room" can contain both the historical subject and the suggestion it depicts the narrative voice's daughter. This enigmatic approach makes each poem expand further than the frame of poem, into layers of history, allusions, and perplexing moments. There are also descriptions that remind the reader of the experience of being in the gallery in a bodily way, standing quietly, stumbling on flagstones. The gallery in the poem "Main Corridor" becomes a warning metaphor for the pursuit of "depictions of the ideal,"[33] with the meandering corridors articulating the expansiveness with no end that idealist art might demand or inflict.

The "interludes" poems, the café and garden, are constructed to be framed in a thinner block on the page in contrast to the others and are formatted in italic. Unlike the main poems from the gallery, which slip between observation and experience, the thinner poems are more permeable in the way Hetherington depicts layered spaces and involves the reader in the text. The painting or sculpture described absorbs the narrative voice and the reader in a more demanding way, as if speaking to the reader or a particular "you" to create intimacy and inclusion, and the streams of images are more enigmatic as they blend historical, mythical, and artistic facts. For example, in "Statues," "Rooms possessed us, their statues/ walking with hundreds of stiff-/gaited farewells. History gathered/ us into Penelope's loom."[34] Here, as in other poems, Hetherington acts as a perplexing and distant guide and provides information but confusion which the reader will have to actively seek to understand.

Both Hetherington and Atherton utilise intertexts and layering, fragmentation and montage, to create the symbolist poetic space of suggestion and decoration. In the *Gallery of Antique Art*, the reader is an invited visitor within a public setting. By contrast, in *Palace of Memory: An Elegy*, Hetherington brings the reader into a personal memoir. Rather than observing art, it is memory that is placed on the walls of white space; portraits of remembered things, hauntings of childhood. The first poem begins with the line, "Worn stones support facades/ with the cold press of forgetfulness – so much moss and/ lichen-covered ruin,"[35] establishing the atmosphere for the journey through the collection; a sense of crumbling time passing, slipping through the mind. Throughout the collection, memories are, I suggest, addressed like pictures, so that the aspect of using ekphrasis as a method to create described (or interpreted) artworks for the reader works in the same way as in the art gallery. The poem titled as Number 3 lists elements of a scene as if setting the picture in the mind of the reader with little fuss, making it clear for them. Yet it slips into enigma: "A dim way. Tall, curtained/ windows rising, like my father. Every shadow's an adhesive/stain [. . .]"

The collection is permeated with an air of lamentation for things slipping, in keeping with the "Elegy" of the book's subtitle, and a sense of not being able to hold on to or pin in place the memories that are uncovered for the reader: "Gates and alleys of the mind/ are open. In this dusk silence holds the moon as if it's a / chunk of something broken— it might be love [. . .]"[36] Like the art gallery and its endless rooms and corridors, surrounded by art to view and absorb, in this collection, Hetherington displays memories on the walls as the reader has to open gates and move through the alleys of the mind. The reader can traverse and get lost in here, faced with uncertainties, seeking understanding.

In Poem 26, Hetherington writes that, "Memory says we were never/ together there,"[37] personifying memory and adding to the sense of unease. There is something uncanny about the image of memory speaking to one directly, an unreliable yet persuasive commentator destabilising prose poems built upon layers of history, misremembering, and a sense of trespass. The veiling created by using the technique of ekphrasis in the art gallery poems, with the subject already veiled by the artist who created the work, is now veiled through time and the personal nature of the memories. Memories can be fallible, withheld from the reader, or revealed through suggestion. The recollections are particular and personal, yet also written in a way to be intimate for the reader to slip into these memory rooms, with the sense of imposing or domestic spaces – "Columns, hallways, the room where they'd waited [. . .]"[38] – allowing the reader, too, to travel back in time. These examples highlight Hetherington's use of symbolist techniques in order to focus on the decorative and ambiguous, painting specific ekphrastic memory pictures, replicating them for the reader but deliberately using suggestion in order to remain enigmatic. The poems contain hints, echoes, and edges, almost revealing, but then the curtain is dropped over the frame once more.

Conclusion and Suggestions for Finding the Decorative-Subjective Space in Practice

This chapter has explored the use of different methods to convey a sense of "continuing" for the reader, reaching beyond the space of the poem into a wider, almost endless, space of suggestion and allusion. Using intertexts and ekphrasis, the poet can layer and fragment images to create depth, condensing meaning and suggestion within the prescribed, limited space of the prose poem. The reader is invited into active engagement with the poem as they attempt to find the key to unlock the puzzle and what it suggests. Whether it is a playful dalliance with the reader or contemplative hiding and revealing, the poets are using symbolist techniques to create a sensual space that results, in Mallarmé's terms, in a reverie, as the reader seeks to understand what is being hinted at. As Hetherington and Atherton use direct address or slip between points of view, they engage the reader in being both clinical observer and sensual voyeur. Both poets in the collections discussed utilise intimate use of pronouns to create a sense of inclusion for the reader, with layers that are nonetheless uncertain, so that reader remains continually off guard and disorientated, negotiating the anxiety of space generated by symbolist techniques.

The prose poem form, as an original symbolist space, can be layered with the techniques discussed above, namely, decorativeness and subjectivity through the methods of ekphrasis and intertextuality, resulting in a decorative-subjective contemporary symbolist approach that goes beyond merely employing the prose poem form. By employing this approach, these contemporary symbolist poems engender the intended reverie of enigma as the reader seeks the key to understanding.

Within my own practice, as I worked on the imagined memoir of the life of the symbolist artist Pamela Colman Smith, I experimented with the methods I have identified in Atherton's and Hetherington's work. I found that defining these methods as contemporary symbolist practice and viewing them through this particular lens in order to illuminate a commonality between them was a way of taking the ineffable qualities of symbolist poetics and transforming them into a practical, craftsperson approach. These became my tools. Layering history and memoir and utilising intertextuality and ekphrasis as my main techniques engendered a "Mallarmesque" fog to envelop my poetry; but far from this being, as it was for Auden, a negative characteristic, it provided a vital means of evoking the point of view of a symbolist artist and encouraging the reader to take an active part in the poems as they seek out the key to the glimpsed and suggested meaning. Perhaps the reader will find the key, or perhaps not, yet I hope that the engagement will provide a delectable pleasure nonetheless.

> Asleep, I can hear the spider walking across the ceiling. The legs patter, louder than the percussion section of the orchestra. It is not the anecdote I wanted to begin with. Who is leading the spider? Does it wear a collar, a velvet girdle? If you keep a velvet ribbon in your pocket it is ready for any occasion: a garter to tie around a plump thigh or a noose to attach to the bar of the window. I can hear you thinking, what is the colour of the ribbon? Why does it always come back to colour? Ariadne's hair was black as soot scraped from the hearth. Elaine's skin was white as she lay back in her boat to die. Iseult's lips were naturally red, not tinted with rose petals. Olivia, dear one, beneath the terracotta sheet of our makeshift tent your veins stood out in blue lines; rivers racing to the sea. Ursula prowls the forest for honeycomb, growling her brown vowels.

Notes

1   Stéphane Mallarmé, *Interview with Stéphane Mallarmé*. Interview by Jules Huret, in *Enquete sur l'evolution litteraire* (Paris: Bibliothèque Charpentier, 1891), trans. Aaron Robertson, www.aaronrobertson.co/translations/mallarme-interview/.

2   Lisa Goldfarb, *Unexpected Affinities: Modern American Poetry and Symbolist Poetics* (Brighton, UK: Sussex Academic Press, 2018), 48.

3   Rosina Neginsky, "Introduction," in *Symbolism, Its Origins and Its Consequences*, ed. Rosina Neginsky (Cambridge: Cambridge Scholars, 2011), 3.

4   Arthur Schopenhauer, *The World as Will and Representation* (New York: Dover, 1969), 52, cited in Neginsky, *Symbolism*, 3.

5   Jean Moréas, "The Manifesto of Symbolism," in *Symbolism: Art of Century*, ed. Nathalia Brodskaya (New York: Parkstone Press, 2007), 9.

6   Nathalia Brodskaya, *Symbolism: Art of Century*. (New York: Parkstone Press, 2007), 30.

7   Brodskaya, *Symbolism*, 34.

8   Moréas, *Manifesto*, 10.

9   Mallaremé, *Interview*.

10   Arthur Symons, *The Symbolist Movement in Literature* (London: Lightening Source, 1899), 72.

11   Henri Peyre, *What Is Symbolism?* trans. Emmett Parker (Tuscaloosa, AL: University of Alabama Press, 2010), 67.

12   Peyre, *What Is Symbolism*, 69.

13   Symons, *The Symbolist Movement*, 72.

14   Mallarmé, *Interview*.

15   Symons, *The Symbolist Movement*, 72.

16   Symons, *The Symbolist Movement*, 72.

17   Lehman, "Introduction," in *Great American Prose Poems: From Poe to the Present*, ed. Lehman, David (New York: Scribner, 2003), 16.

18   Paul Hetherington and Cassandra Atherton, eds. *Prose Poetry: An Introduction*, (Princeton, NJ: Princeton University Press, 2020), 104.

19   Hetherington and Atherton, *Prose Poetry: An Introduction*, 105.

20   Hetherington and Atherton, *Prose Poetry: An Introduction*, 105.

21   Hetherington and Atherton, *Prose Poetry: An Introduction*, 127.

22   Cassandra Atherton, *Trace* (Braidwood, AU: Finlay Lloyd, 2015); Cassandra Atherton, *Exhumed* (Wollongong, AU: Grand Parade Poets, 2015).

23   Paul Hetherington and Cassandra Atherton, "'Unconscionable Mystification': Rooms, Spaces and the Prose Poem." *New Writing* 12, no. 3 (2015): 9.

24   Paul Hetherington and Cassandra Atherton, "An Intertextual Poiesis: The Luminous Image and a 'Round Loaf of Indian and Rye,'" *New Writing* 17, no. 3 (2020): 259–71.

25   Cassandra Atherton, "Modi," in *Exhumed*, 33.

26   Evlyn Gould, "Penciling and Erasing Mallarmé's 'Ballets,'" *Performing Arts Journal* 15, no. 1 (1993): 97–105.

27   Cassandra Atherton, "Vitamin D," in *Trace*, 23.

28   Atherton, "Vitamin D," 23.

29   Hetherington and Atherton, *Prose Poetry*, 9.

30   Stéphane Mallarmé, *Un Coup de Dés and Other Poems*, trans. A. S. Kline (Poetry in Translation, 2004), 77.

31   Paul Hetherington, *Gallery of Antique Art*. (Canberra, AU: Recent Work Press, 2016).

32 Hetherington, *Gallery of Antique Art*, 47.

33 Paul Hetherington, "Main Corridor," in *Gallery of Antique Art*, 11.

34 Paul Hetherington, "Statues," in *Gallery of Antique Art*, 21.

35 Paul Hetherington, *Palace of Memory: An Elegy* (Canberra, AU: Recent Work Press, 2019), 1.

36 Hetherington, *Palace of Memory*, 52.

37 Hetherington, *Palace of Memory*, 26.

38 Hetherington, *Palace of Memory*, 27.

14

ONE FOOT; MANY PLACES

The Prose Poem's Art of Standing Still While Travelling

Jane Monson

Typically discussed among terms that pertain directly or indirectly to duality, paradox, and contradiction, the prose poem has been frequently packaged as a confused or unsure thing, form, or genre. Charles Simic, in his renowned essay on the prose poem, said it was composed of fundamentally opposing forces and instincts; static and in motion at the same time within the same space:

> prose poetry is a monster-child of two incompatible impulses, one which wants to tell a story and another, equally powerful, which wants to freeze an image, or a bit of language, for our scrutiny. In prose, sentence follows sentence till they have had their say. Poetry, on the other hand, spins in place.[1]

These impulses have principally been deemed incompatible when the prose poem is – for obvious reasons – measured in literary terms, because broadly speaking, we continue to associate the sentence unit and story with prose and the (broken) line and image with poetry. Critics and creative writers, notoriously in the United Kingdom and America, have frequently asked the "is it poetry or prose?" question that has both dogged and raised the profile of the prose poem throughout history. As the editors of one of the earliest and most turned to prose poem anthologies, *Models of the Universe*, point out: "these works 'upset the makers of categories.' But if there is an upset here, the problem is not with the prose-poem as a form, but rather with too-rigid definitions of what poetry is or isn't."[2] If we stepped outside of this constructed dilemma, we would come across less frequently cited monstrous offspring analogies and far more fully-formed, relatively grounded angels. Conversely, poetic prose, short fiction, or any equivalent hybrid or blurred genres are comparatively unchecked across theory and practice. At this stage, even as the prose poem is far more accepted and celebrated now worldwide, do we need to

DOI: 10.4324/9781003199533-15

rethink our literary-based approach to the form? In other words: are there alternative spaces, practices, and disciplines that are far more conducive to an appreciation and understanding of the prose poem's many paradoxes and impulses? Arguably, literary evaluations that keep falling into fixed or even loose ideas of poetry and prose have potentially run their course when it comes to defining and framing the prose poem. This chapter seeks to open creative and critical debates further by looking at visual-based practitioners who have recently discovered the prose poem, and references poets and sources that locate the form's potential in other contexts outside of traditional notions and assumptions around the form.

Artists in a range of practices have found the prose poem invaluable for explaining and exploring their work when theory, terms, and language particular to their own disciplines have fallen short of either accepting or explicating their work appropriately. With less focus on the long-standing historical relationship between visual arts and the prose poem (which is typically concentrated around comparative critiques of nineteenth and twentieth century European and American painting from Baudelaire through to Stein's Cubist poems), this chapter is interested in late twentieth and twenty-first century examples. By focusing on the recent global bloom of the prose poem in parallel to developments within modern artistic practices (photography and film, for example), I hope to draw attention to the inter-relevance, if you like, of today's prose poem's role and structure and the visual and physical world of framed or boxed art around us. As the prose poem opens up critically and creatively, so it diversifies and continues to diverge from purely text-based and Western or European-centric notions of the prose poem. In a range of other spaces, the prose poem can not only thrive, but be used as a model to query and interrogate key questions around long-standing, traditional, and institutional rules around form and genre, and open up relevant conversations around marginalisation, acceptance, and paradox more broadly.

Several poets working today have illuminated these issues and helped move the conversation forwards, not backwards. Claudia Rankine, for example, personally and publicly identifies with the issues and limitations of fixed ideas around genres and boxes. After she wrote *Don't Let Me Be Lonely*, her publisher rejected her and in an interview for *The White Review* with Kayo Chingonyi, Rankine recalls that

> when they got the manuscript they said, "this is not poetry." It was one of those moments where I thought, "I'm disappointed about this, but this is what I need, I'm not gonna change anything to conform to somebody's idea about what the market needs."[3]

Rejected as poetry and received as "sociology," Rankine's experience is similar to other knee-jerk reactions when poetry neither looks nor sounds like verse, free or otherwise. Rankine's clarity and sure-footed conviction that form and content need to be at the inclusion, not exclusion of each other, is at the heart of the prose poem itself:

> I think people get into these boxes in terms of what the form should be, and I really believe that form and content should always be in dialogue . . . It's not that I have anything against traditional form, it's just that in thinking about race, you're thinking about people's lives. A book like *Citizen* was dependent on stories of people, and so one wanted to find a form that could hold that. In *Don't Let Me Be Lonely* I felt the sentence helped me more than the line, so I went to the sentence. These are questions one has every time you walk into the making of a poem.[4]

Rankine draws attention to inherent conflicts between theory and practice that often get caught in the muddle and crossfire at the border of writing and publication. As with every form of practice, the prose poem should be first and foremost an individual choice and one that simply befits the writing's content, subject, and topic more than other forms and genres. It gives people agency and room to combine erstwhile contradictory impulses. As with Rankine, this dialogue can happen fluidly within literature, but equally the prose poem can operate as successfully across literary divides as it can outside of them altogether. Today, we have several examples of where the prose poem is discussed closely in relation to art, all of which are fertile conversations to be maintained and continued. Adrian Wanner, in his groundbreaking book on the Russian prose poem, for example, investigates the prose poem in relation to minimalism in American visual arts.[5] Cassandra Atherton and Paul Hetherington in their diverse and thorough resource, *Prose Poetry: An Introduction*, dedicate a substantial amount of research to eye-opening ways of re-seeing the prose poem in relation to visual art.[6] Michel Delville and Mary Ann Caws likewise in their *Edinburgh Companion to the Prose Poem* include a host of critics and writers on its historical and cultural affinity to art, with Caws herself focusing on Cubism, via Gertrude Stein and Pierre Reverdy.[7] Donna Stonecipher's *Prose Poetry and the City* is essential for those curious about prose poetry and urban spaces, its possibilities and affinities within architecture, inner-city movement, and design.[8]

Evidently, the affinities between the prose poem and visual arts are both stable and actively in progress across the world. However, since the late twentieth century, their shared narrative is not so exclusively anchored in painting and ekphrastic discourses. Recently, British and international artists, architects, filmmakers, and photographers alike are beginning to engage with the prose poem as a form that is not only fitting of their practice but is helping them make sense of it. Paradox, density, concision, juxtaposition between the everyday and surreal, interrupted and distilled narratives, and compressed, encircled moments are all ways the prose poem operates best, particularly within the frame or box shape. In non-literary contexts, the prose poem helps artists ascertain a new language and perspective which focuses more closely on possibility and progress, rather than limitations or logical categories. Moving the prose poem into other spaces outside of written practice and theory also diversifies the ways that practitioners and theorists alike can keep breaking down the black and white, binary-based values which continue to dictate our everyday perceptions and judgements in art and life.[9] Baudelaire in his famous essay "The Painter of Modern Life," said that "the duality of art is a fatal consequence of the duality of man,"[10] and the prose poem was where he reconciled this dire consequence. As Sima Godfrey notes of Baudelaire's critique and unbridled admiration of Honoré Daumier as a modern artist and French caricaturist: "that doubleness of the image and the word strives towards a nostalgic unity of expression that parallels his own desire to integrate vision and language in poetry and, specifically, in that ambiguous poetic genre, the *poème en prose*."[11] Today, this can be succinctly paraphrased in Maxine Chernoff's: "I linger in the shadows. I learned how to do that by writing prose poems."[12]

The specific duality I want to focus on – between stillness and movement; standing still while travelling – is particular to the prose poem's tension between the narrative flow and momentum of prose rendered in sentence and paragraph and the intense stopping and scrutiny of a single moment, image, or object, effectively held by concise fragments of verses and broken lines. Suspended narration and tension between image and story is perfectly well explored in literary terms and theory, but our understanding and appreciation of the prose poem can change dramatically when these temporal and spatial contradictions are investigated in other arenas, also dependent on tensions between stillness and movement within framed margins. Photography and film are key examples here because of their reliance on vertical and horizontal borders to still narration or extract from life and render it uniquely within the limits of a frame. The tension or paradox between image/moment and narrative is all the more felt for being contained inside the box's parameters and in turn more relevant for those visual practitioners creating art within the screen, frame, and photograph. As Atherton and Hetherington point out in their chapter on image, memory, and prose poetry, "the prose poem – so frequently presented as a rectangular box on a page – is the literary form that most often resembles a photograph,"[13] and further to this, note the symbiotic relationship between form and handling of content: "the frame and the prose poem contain box-like images within defined spaces while simultaneously tearing a moment from an experience or narrative."[14] Prose poems that fall outside of these physical dimensions and go beyond a page or break their sentences into lines can lose their grip on visceral dynamics of suspended narration, upheld by contained brevity, economy of space, and closely connected, herded pathways. As Tung-Hui Hu asserts in his contribution to the *Rose Metal Press Field Guide to Prose Poetry*:

> as with the white space of a postcard that restricts the writing surface, a prose poem is fragmentary. Nothing stops a lyric poem from going on indefinitely . . . But a prose poem has to stop; too long and it turns into a short story.[15]

In front of these boxes, therefore, movement and stillness can co-exist and suspended narration can work intentionally, rather than be a source of confusion and disappointed expectations. We can sit or stand still suspended by what we see, and then travel through what they evoke or conjure, similar to experiences in a gallery, theatre, cinema, TV screen, or window. Whereas in literature, approaching what looks like prose for it to reveal itself as poetry can be confusing, unsettling, or contradictory, in visual arts of architecture, for example, this play upon or defiance of expectations has the potential to settle and inspire, rather than alienate or upset.

The film *Paterson*, directed by Jim Jarmusch, is an important example of cinematic prose poetry in the way it exploits this sense of narrative suspension.[16] Typical of the director, whose films consistently diverge from traditional narrative, the film is more concerned with close observation, rather than action developed through plot, time, and character. Over seven consecutive days, the film follows the daily repetitions and subtle shifts embedded into Paterson's routine afforded by the bus's route and his personality, as he wakes at the same time each day and visits the same bar each night. There is a circularity and feeling of containment set up in the repetition of Paterson alone: the name of the poet, the name of the city in which he works, and the 1927 poem, *Paterson* by William Carlos Williams is referenced directly in the film, as Jarmusch takes inspiration from "no ideas, but in things" and "a man like a city."

Akin to the bus's journey – continual were it not for bus-stops, lights, crossings – Paterson's writing takes place in snatches and at different points in time and space within the confines of routine. The film explores several dualities that work harmoniously, from the poet's relationship with his wife Laura (he, reliable patterns; she, spontaneity and surprise) to the set route of his daily life and job, while freely taking poetry from everyone and anywhere. Paterson carries his notebook in his pocket and jots lines in his head, sitting still in the driver's seat with his eyes on the road. The poet's ears are constantly alert to what is being said by passengers, his thoughts transcribing some of what they say to the page when the bus is stationary. Laura stays home but is in constant movement manifest in energetic conversation, continual generation of new ideas, and dexterous forays into art and music (Paterson rarely knows what to expect when he comes home). Paterson is out, moving through the city, albeit seated, and each day is modelled on the next. Less driven by time progressing, the film is about quiet, understated dramas, rendered in poems that emerge from moments in the gaps between acts of repetition.

This film encapsulates visually not just the poem *Paterson*, but how film and poetry can dovetail the contradictory nature of time and space in the prose poem: brief narrative moments that do not develop as traditional story in time and space, but as a protracted image or moment. The coexistence of movement and stillness is summed up in Williams's *Paterson*: "Inside the bus one sees/his thoughts sitting and standing. His thoughts/alight and scatter."[17] In the same way that juxtapositions within the prose poem are stitched together and made seamless in sentences within the framed limitations of the box, Jarmusch brings several elements of the city, otherwise separate from each other by fading images, together. As culture journalist James Prestridge observes,

> at one point, the Passaic Falls, Paterson and the Ohio Blue Tip matches all populate the frame. It gives the impression they are all connected, at least floating around in Paterson's mind, fuelling his poetic vision of the city – and life.[18]

Indeed, Jarmusch, when interviewed, makes a point about using film specifically as a form, to enable the "film to float past you"; the architecture of the film is built on "imagery floating by Paterson as he observes things in the world from his bus driver's seat."[19] As interviewer Leonard Quart surmises: "Paterson is a man whose mind drifts back and forth from what is in front of him to the words and images in his mind."[20] Likewise, this is our experience of watching the world unfold through Paterson's eyes looking through a bus window, as we take in the experience from the seat of a cinema or living room, within the screen's frame. The film moves forward and into itself within the focus of the central character as bus driver and poet; it is non-hierarchical in nature, achieved by investigating what happens in spaces made of unassuming, everyday opposites and the frames or boxes that hold them.

In 1953, the highly influential and controversial American filmmaker, poet, and critic, Maya Deren presented a paper entitled "Poetry and the Film" at a Cinema 16 Symposium.[21] In this paper, she argued that film works on two axes: the horizontal, including narrative, character, and action, and the vertical, characterized by the more ephemeral elements of mood, tone, and rhythm. Deren (and historically countless film makers in both Hollywood and, more surprisingly, independent cinema) draws clear distinctions between poetry and prose and illustrates the problems of using literary terms and differences within a non-literary space. Jarmusch shows, however, how they can work together by unifying and creating a suspended narrative where vertical and horizontal are not in tension but fused and utilised as one movement. *Paterson* works at the point where the vertical and horizontal meet; where neither narrative nor image dominates the other so that narrative is guided and informed by imagery and thought, rather than plot and action.

This tension or awareness between verticality and horizontality is not only an age-old argument in film, but in architectural (window) history.[22] Epitomised during 1920s Paris in the debates among two particular architects, Le Corbusier argued for what become the horizontal strip window, while Auguste Perret was invested in the traditional verticality of the French window. Essentially, their infamous disagreement came down to light and movement; glass versus concrete; panorama versus the up and down sweep of the eye. There are parallels here between the eye's landscape experience of the prose poem's sentence and block, versus the traditional portrait-orientated poem as it breaks the line and leads the eye downwards, theoretically at a much faster rate than the prose poem's steady pull across the page. As Gary Young puts it in his essay "The Unbroken Line", "The prose poem's democratic itinerary, its horizontal rather than vertical trajectory engenders a resistance to hierarchy and to inflation."[23] Bechir Kenzari – one of the few critics to explore the window as a specific architectural feature through which to draw parallels between prose poetry and architecture – notes in his article "Windows":

> In these poems, Baudelaire and Mallarmé tend to stress verticality, framing, interiority as conditions of a genuine poetic experience; whereas Apollinaire, through the concept of simultaneity, leans toward the themes of freedom, simultaneity, openness, panorama and exteriority. The nature of these poetic differences calls to mind Perret's apology of the strip window, symbol of exclusion, verticality and contemplation, and Le Corbusier's defence of the bay window.[24]

Similarly, N. Santilli notes of the prose poem's relationship to the urban window: "to read Baudelaire's 'Les Fenêtres' with its square of black text in a white surround is itself an act of looking through a window":[25]

> Windows prevent the complete detachment of an enclosed space. A transparent wall, the window paradoxically divides and conjoins two spaces: excludes and includes, separates and continues. The interior claims equality with that which it excludes. In other words, the binary system which the urban setting appears to establish is actually *a trompe-l'oiel*. The privileged text of the prose poem concurs with its architectural analog by registering a similar obfuscation of the room and street dialectic. When Baudelaire's narrators find themselves in a room, they are often looking out of the window. Consequently, the play between private and public spaces, facilitated by the window motif, breaks down the apparently rigid polarization of what is internal or external to the text – a distinction arising from a strong sense of closure which the prose poem exhibits but resists.[26]

Baudelaire's prose poem elegantly considers how a frame can make a scene profound. Where he saw the prose poem as key to capturing the essence of urban living, its rhythms, impulses, and undulations, Gaston Bachelard in his leading text, *The Poetics of Space,* on viewing the same city, saw its box-like composition as an infringement on movement:

> In Paris there are no houses, and the inhabitants of the big city live in superimposed boxes ... Elevators do away with the heroism of stair climbing so that there is no longer any virtue in living up near the sky. *Home* has become mere horizontality. The different rooms that compose living quarters jammed into one floor all lack one of the fundamental principles for distinguishing and classifying the values of intimacy.[27]

Architecturally and symbolically speaking, the window's role in prose poetry can be read in several ways, anywhere along the spectrum of enclosure/intimacy and hostility/constriction. It can operate as much as a held or contained space offering a way in as it can present a more hostile environment and permanent way out. In his collection, *A Portable Paradise*, Roger Robinson writes between pain and joy, injustice and passion about Grenfell, the city, racism (covert and violent), and the thresholds of physical and mental torture that play out daily in lives and memories of lives lost, horrifically and needlessly. Prose poems feature in each section, and many of them use the window as a symbol to illustrate the way it can break down people inside and outside, where the glass and its view serve as cold reminders of exclusion, alienation, and entrapment. In under half a page, Robinson's prose poem "Woke" encapsulates the physical pain of being beaten (relentlessly over generations), and the nightmarish and circular psychological pain of trapped vision and insight: "I woke up on/ the 16th floor of a tower block looking out the window with a clear/ view of the land that does not belong to me."[28] In "Ghosts," screams, fire, and prayers surround the subject, a "you" who sits "in the darkness for a while clasping your knees, looking out/ your extra large window at the view you've paid so dearly for."[29]

The image of the man here, but not here, being made to feel he does not belong either side of the window, recalls a line from André Breton's highly influential 1924 Surrealist Manifesto: "Il y a un homme coupé en deux par la fenêtre," (there is a man cut in two by the window).[30] Windows as symbols are reminders of structural and literal paradoxes throughout time and particular to Robinson's poems, violent systemic injustices are bred in paradoxes that construct and underpin society, literally cutting people in two: belonging/exiling, inside/outside, black/white, detachment/empathy, and life/death. Understanding the relationship between the prose poem and the window, particularly in cities, is a key resource for prose poetry studies where stillness and movement are in constant tension, where framed fragments of space appear everywhere in your line of sight; where intersections between horizontal and vertical lines are how the urban environment is carved up. In the city's blocked spaces, Baudelaire's romantic "undulations of reverie" today takes place behind more and more blocks of straight lines meeting at right angles, repeated as comic strips; where people exist in contained situations, as claustrophobic and unsafe as they are insulated and protected places.

Several contemporary studies explore these fundamental contradictions in relation to key issues and questions around marginalised people. Holly Iglesias's important creative and critical study, *Boxing Inside the Box*, is one of the few devoted resources we have on women's prose poetry, for example, and views the box as a constricted setting and construct that represents oppressed narratives around the female voice and body, and mirrors more broadly the marginalisation of cultures.[31] Similarly, poet Gretchen Henderson mentions the prose poem in *Beauty is a Verb: The New Poetry of Disability*, as a form that is at odds with free movement: "the prose poem, boxed as it is, for me seems to embody a want of movement – physical, aural or otherwise, made apparent by the limitations and liminality of its boxed-in body."[32] In both physical and mental spaces within gender, disability, and race, the prose poem can be used as an entirely applicable form to emulate individual and cultural experiences and narratives of restriction, patriarchy, disability, and racism.

Box and frame alike have several sides and points of view. From the outside and at a distance, prose poem and window alike appear as a framed block, a paragraphic section of a larger story separated by a boundary, with the glass obscured by reflection. All these contradictory and co-existing elements of what the window symbolises are concomitant with the prose poem's ability to draw you towards a world you were not expecting from the outside. Prose poem and window alike resemble riddles: ambiguous experiences of something both seen and unseen; language as an act that hides and reveals at the same time, like the function of the window, or the photograph. As David Lehman says of John Ashbery's prose poem "A Nice Presentation," the piece enacts a "mazy motion," saying and unsaying, leading then erasing the footprints:

> the sentences embody reversal and hesitation; they suggest a kind of logic but mostly they reveal that logic is an illusion. They enact a paradox; that one can be in perpetual motion while remaining stationary, as the mind of a perennial fence-sitter may race from one thought to the next.[33]

Robinson acknowledges that the prose poem's balancing of focus and circumspection, its riddle-like quality is where paradox and contradiction are reconciled. In an interview for *bath magg* poetry magazine with Gboyega Odubanjo, he sums this up perfectly as he recontextualises and moves the riddle-like quality of the prose poem from a predominantly European tradition to an African and Caribbean one, locating the form's propensity towards a riddle-like sensibility within Black thought and culture:

> Prose poems come from a revolutionary tradition of French poets from the late 19th century. Writers like Rimbaud and Baudelaire, and the whole idea that they were trying to rebel. So it is a form based in rebellion. But it is also a form based in ironic humour and surrealism and lots of different things. But the irony of it is when you start to read the prose poem you realise it is how Black people think . . . There is a paraphrasis, talking around something without telling you exactly what it is. And that comes from African and Caribbean traditions. What I was trying to do was use a form to try to get to what Black people's thoughts are like . . . Even though I may talk about prose poetry and prose poetry is perceived as being of the European traditions, in my mind this is all Black people things.[34]

The talking around something, the riddle-like movement and stasis of the prose poem – as Robinson identifies – is borne out of surrealism and irony, typically rooted in a European tradition post-Breton's manifesto, but the joint magic and truth that emerges from juxtaposing two things that do not typically exist in the same space is timeless with roots around the world. Jeff Wall, a leading contemporary Canadian photographer who revolutionised the traditional understanding and practice of photography, visually manifests much of what Robinson encapsulates and synthesises in his poetry and thought process. Wall is a master of juxtaposition, and in his method and style, this is manifest in crossing boundaries between disciplines and merging aspects of painting, photography, "cinematography"/"near documentary" (Wall's terms), advertising, and literature (novels and prose poetry). Inspired by the back-lit advertisements at bus-stops, he became famous for scaling the image up to giant electronic canvases – lightboxes – of a Renaissance grandeur, while depicting everyday urban or rural occurrences, all with a twist that turns them from what you may find on any street to surreal and dramatic riddles of reality:

> Wall describes his work as "cinematographic" re-creations of everyday moments he has witnessed but did not photograph at the time. "To not photograph," he says, "gives a certain freedom to then re-create or reshape what I saw." He takes months to stage and direct each of his "occurrences." "Something lingers in me until I have to remake it from memory to capture why it fascinates me," he says. "Not photographing gives me imaginative freedom that is crucial to the making of art. That, in fact, is what art is about – the freedom to do what we want."[35]

Akin to magical realism, his pictures depict then kink everyday scenes from modern urban settings, predominantly featuring marginalised, frequently overlooked subjects, places, and people, but always with a narrative or momentary slant on the familiar, achieved by introducing into the scene something Wall has read or witnessed. Thereby the image teeters on the edge of possible and impossible. With his magnificent light-boxes as the physical apparatus of his photographs, he brought what was otherwise considered the lowly photograph into the museum space, for the first time.

"Museum photography," until recently, was as paradoxical a term as prose poetry, for similar reasons around status, rules around tradition, and distinctions between their separate languages. As critic Julian Stallabrass points out in his article on Wall's instrumental role in bringing photography's form and the hallowed museum space together, "the museum's historic suspicion of the photograph had rested in its reproducibility and mechanical character."[36] Digitisation, however, became the bridge between snobbery around the snapshot and apparent lack of the artist's hand (versus time and effort in painting) and acceptance of photography as a recognisable and accepted art form. Wall showed how reworking the picture digitally "allowed detailed control over every element of the photographic scene and broke the ironclad association of photography with the recording of contingency."[37] As Wall puts it, writing of his first digital picture, *The Stumbling Block* (1991), digitization furthered a "visual poetry or prose poetry" which conflicts with the indexical aspect of photography."[38] In his dramatized recreations of a scene, he chooses to capture later, rather than deliver instant shots. With them, in practice and theory, he contorts our ideas and definitions of photography as snapshot, spinning their spontaneity into something closer to rehearsed theatre. Wall utilised to fantastic visual effect the prose poem's suspension of narrative and fine balancing between what you see and what you do not see; the riddle that comes from the possibilities of an interrupted, or highly distilled narrative and the brief space and paradoxical images and thoughts that conflate there:

> Wall calls his photographs, after Charles Baudelaire, "prose poems," a description that emphasises how each picture should be experienced rather than used to illustrate a predetermined idea or a specific narrative. His pictures may depict an instant and a scenario, but the before and after that moment are left completely unknown, allowing them to remain open to multiple interpretations. The prose poem format allows any truth claims of the photograph – the facts we expect from journalistic photography – to remain suspended, and Wall believes that in that suspension the viewer experiences pleasure.[39]

Wall describes his photographs in several ways that at the time challenged the orthodox world of photography and the common idea or ideal of photographer as instant witness; shooting there and then whether for reportage or snapshot, amateur or professional. He may well see the image he would like to photograph in any given situation but does not photograph it spontaneously; instead lets it work in the memory and develop internally. Over days, months, or years, he then recreates it, using non-professional models, taking them to the setting itself or using studios to replicate the setting and situation as closely as possible. The riddle or magical twist often comes from sources in painting (Hokusai and Manet, for example) and novels, like Ralph Ellison's *Invisible Man*, another major influence. In *A Sudden Gust of Wind (after Hokusai)* (1993), four people by a river and field near the city's edge react separately to the surprise of wind, blowing papers from someone's hands into the sky, passing over or getting caught at their heads. Two men are in suits, and the scene is a dramatic almost-possible reality, made intentionally incongruous to keep us in the space between conceivable story and improbable moment. In a recorded interview by Marc-Christoph Wagner with Wall for the Louisiana Museum of Modern Art, Wall states:

> pictures can't tell stories because they are still, so they step away from the flow of time and they step away from what we do with time which is narrate, but pictures can only give you a pattern that is recognisable as an

image that is excerpted from that narrative and cancels it out, but everything in that picture suggests its narrativity but it cannot give it to you, so
when you are experiencing the picture as a picture ... I believe that you the
viewer then are writing it, you're writing the story.[40]

Instead, Wall wanted the narrative to come together through moments, thoughts,
and memories that grew out of the picture when faced or experienced by the
viewer, rather than the picture imposing a narrative. For example, *Pair of Interiors*,
displayed in 2019 at the White Cube Mason's Yard, are two photographs side by
side depicting similar scenes of a man and a woman, sitting on the same sofa in
one room and in separate seating arrangements in the other. The juxtaposition
invites a narrative to work out or connect what has happened between them, but
Wall says that part of what he is doing in his work generally is "to bring things
together without submitting to the narrative because I think that pictures don't
narrate; they suspend impulses to narrate, they suspend our impulses to narrate
in order to be pictures."[41] Anti-narrative as they are anti-spontaneous, the prose
poetry of the image comes through in the way the image defies what we expect
from a photograph – captured spontaneity and a frozen extract from a bigger picture. The image is made as much from Wall's reconstructed thought process and
memory as it is his vision; that which was before his eye and mind's eye, akin to
Jarmusch's depiction of Paterson's movement between witnessing and reflection.
Likewise, prose poetry presents both and the story is made of us, artist, image, and
thought, whilst reconfiguring expectations around the form itself. In her essay,
"Why I Write," Joan Didion spoke of a similar interchange and mirroring between
pictures, the camera, and sentences:

> To shift the structure of a sentence alters the meaning of that sentence as
> definitely and inflexibly as the position of a camera alters the meaning of the
> object photographed. Many people know about camera angles now, but not
> so many know about sentences. The arrangement of the words matters, and
> the arrangement you want can be found in the picture in your mind. The
> picture dictates the arrangement ... and the arrangement of the words tells
> you, or tells me, what's going on in the picture.[42]

To create novels, Didion always started with pictures she saw that played on her
mind and the relationship between image and sentence was a devoted one; word
and picture alike tightly choreographed and composed so that the line between
them and their creation became invisible. Likewise, Wall's method progressed
from witnessing something, replaying it in his memory, understanding why it was
important, and then arranging and realising the photograph through to a highly
conceived and produced finish. As background to Didion's processing and interplay between pictures and sentences, in the early 1960s, she had a regular column
in Vogue and composed photo captions, which Walter Benjamin referred to as

"signposts," and which author and critic Brian Dillon recognised became "essential to the printed magazine page in the twentieth century."[43] Dillon calls her captions, "short, unattributed paragraphs" which "cannot be called essays, articles, or pieces."[44] His reading of her literary and visual practice through photo-captions and picture before the narrative is that not only did it give the writer her way of translating directly from image to text, then back again from what she saw and portrayed from life, but was a way of "getting used to putting one thing beside another."[45] This is the movement of the prose poem – sentence following sentence, image to image, horizontally propelled out of carefully composed and juxtaposed pieces of life seen or heard, thought about and processed and repurposed from memory. So too, with Wall's lightboxes, thought process and prose move around the pictures themselves. Given the parity between prose poetry and images exemplified in Didion's photo-captions and in Wall's photographs as prose poems, today is there a market for prose poetry away from the book and into the museum or gallery, via labels, captions, and catalogues? – what Julian Stallabrass calls "Museum Prose" in his essay on Wall?[46] Small, brief plaques on a wall balancing fact and fiction, information and interpretation, truth and possibility that would enable the viewer to move between picture and paragraph as if one piece, even as they are witnessed as self-contained units. Stallabrass calls Wall not only the most prominent museum photographer, instrumental during the late twentieth century in changing the former lowly status of photography in public spaces, but the most successful photographer to "generate a museum prose of the photograph."[47] Discussing the interdependence of Wall's prose and pictures, Stallabrass himself falls into a prose poem rendition of Wall's photo, "The Thinker" (1986). Strikethroughs are by me, to demonstrate where the balance between literal information, critical bias, and open, subtly guided interpretation would need very little tilting to render this a prose poem caption:

> The figure, a man in a suit and work boots, sits on a stump and pieces of concrete, overlooking a rail yard, the wheat silo of a long-established co-operative, and in the distance the towers of Vancouver. ~~The man is of an age that, had he lost his job, he would be unlikely to find work except of the most unskilled, casualized and low-paid kind. As in Dürer's print,~~ a sword protrudes from his back. Close above his head, the picture is divided by the heavy black of telephone lines, the data-carriers which spelt the end ~~of effective, nationally based working-class power. Wall was certainly concerned to describe this situation, but~~ nothing in these pictures points to resistance. The spilling of milk may indicate the pointlessness of shedding tears.[48]

As with so many examples, this is potentially a prose poem in the making. As a practitioner, once you start thinking along these lines, prose poetry appears everywhere as a possibility. As a theorist, this becomes less certain. Perhaps this is the same with the prose poem in its lesser spotted contexts, like art – that in practice it works, but in theory, there is more work to be done to draw these worlds together definitively. Akin to the question around whether the prose poem is poetry or prose, however, it is important to keep asking, or start asking: does it matter? Like the riddle, the prose poem thrives on paradox and uncertainty; hoping to move towards something, but never leaving the same spot, and by this alone is becoming increasingly relevant for the times we live in, irrespective of context. As Ruth Padel locates when opposites come together, they have everything in common:

> The deepest thing science and poetry share, perhaps, is the way they can tolerate uncertainty. They have a modesty in common: they do not have to say they're right. "A scientist should be the first to say he doesn't know," a tiger biologist told me when I asked some detail of tiger behaviour. "A scientist goes forward towards truth but never gets there."[49]

In summary, whether by chance or choice, the prose poem has and always will cross necessary borders both within and outside of itself. It is an eternally relevant form that questions assumptions around boundaries that are articulated around systems of duality and binary thinking. If visually and structurally the prose poem is sometimes too strange to reconcile in literature, however, then in practice, stand or sit in front of its equivalent – photograph, film, or window – and see how far you can travel, or at the very least find a way back in.

Notes

1 Charles Simic, "Essay on the Prose Poem," *Plume* 102 (February 2020), https://plumepoetry.com/essay-on-the-prose-poem-by-charles-simic/.

2 David Young, Introduction to *Models of the Universe: An Anthology of the Prose-Poem*, ed. Friebert, Stuart, and David Young (Oberlin, OH: Oberlin College Press, 1995), 17–20.

3 Claudia Rankine, "Interview with Claudia Rankine," interview by Kayo Chingonyi, *The White Review* (March 2018), www.thewhitereview.org/feature/interview-claudia-rankine/.

4 Rankine, "Interview."

5 Adrian Wanner, *Russian Minimalism: From the Prose Poem to the Anti-Story* (Evanston, IL: Northwestern University Press, 2003).

6 Cassandra Atherton and Paul Hetherington, eds. *Prose Poetry: An Introduction.* (Princeton, NJ: Princeton University Press, 2020).

7 Michel Delville and Mary Ann Caws, eds. *The Edinburgh Companion to the Prose Poem.* (Edinburgh: Edinburgh University Press, 2021).

8 Donna Stonecipher, *Prose Poetry and the City* (Anderson, SC: Parlor Press, 2018).

9 In publishing, poetry and prose distinctions are customary when collecting writers' works. See Simon Armitage, "Where is British Poetry Today?" panel discussion at British Academy Literature Week, May 2013, where he outlines the industry's rules on what is not accepted:

Illuminated initial letters in the shape of herons, poems in italics or capitals . . .
poems centrally justified . . . and those winning would be those clinging to the
left-hand margin like a non-swimmer at the side of the baths . . . using recognised
systems of punctuation and grammar.

10 Charles Baudelaire, "The Painter of Modern Life," *The Painter of Modern Life and Other Essays* (London: Phaidon Press, 1964), 3.
11 Sima Godfrey, "Baudelaire's Windows." *L'Esprit Créateur* 22, no. 4 (1982): 83–100.
12 Holly Iglesias, *Boxing Inside the Box: Women's Prose Poetry* (Niantic, CT: Quale Press, 2004), 98.
13 Atherton and Hetherington, *Prose Poetry: An Introduction*, 153.
14 Atherton and Hetherington, *Prose Poetry: An Introduction*, 175.
15 Tung-Hui Hu, "It's Not in Cleveland, But I'm Getting Closer," in McDowell, Gary L., and F. Daniel Rzicznek, eds. *The Rose Metal Press Field Guide to Prose Poetry: Contemporary Poets in Discussion and Practice.* (Brookline, MA: Rose Metal Press, 2010), 158.
16 *Paterson*, directed by Jim Jarmusch (Amazon Studios, 2016).
17 William Carlos Williams, *Paterson*, revised edition (New York, NY: New Directions, 1992), 9.
18 James Prestridge, "Cinematic Poetry: An In-Depth Reading of Jim Jarmusch's Film Paterson (2016)," *Close-Up Culture*, https://closeupculture.com/2017/05/04/cinematic-poetry-an-in-depth-reading-of-jim-jarmuschs-film-paterson-2016/.
19 Jim Jarmusch, "Creating a Cinematic Prose Poem: An Interview with Jim Jarmusch," interview by Leonard Quart, *Cinéaste* 42, no. 2 (2017): 28–30.
20 Jarmusch, "Interview," 29.
21 Wendy Haslem, "Maya Deren: The High Priestess of Experimental Cinema," *Senses of Cinema* 23 (December 2002), www.sensesofcinema.com/2002/great-directors/deren-2/.
22 See Maya Lin, *Boundaries* (New York: Simon & Schuster, 2000); Carol Vogel, "Maya Lin's World of Architecture, or Is It Art?," *The New York Times*, 9 May 1994, www.nytimes.com/1994/05/09/arts/maya-lin-s-world-of-architecture-or-is-it-art.html. Frequently referred to as an architect *or* artist, Lin uses the prose poem to describe her work. Sculpture to Lin is like poetry, architecture prose; Kriston, "Maya Lin, Prose Poet," *Eye Level*, Smithsonian American Art Museum, 16 February 2007, https://americanart.si.edu/blog/eye-level/2007/16/1193/maya-lin-prose-poet.
23 Young, "The Unbroken Line." In *Rose Metal Press Field Guide*, ed. McDowell and Rzicznek, 112–14.
24 Bechir Kenzari, "Windows," *Built Environment (1978–)* 31, no. 1 (2005): 38–48.
25 Nikki Santilli, "The Prose Poem and the City," *Prose Studies* 20, no. 1 (April 1997): 80.
26 Santilli, "Prose Poem and the City," 79–80.
27 Gaston Bachelard, *The Poetics of Space*, Translated by Maria Jolas. (Boston, MA: Beacon Press, 1994), 26–7.
28 Roger Robinson, "Woke," in *A Portable Paradise* (Leeds: Peepal Tree Press, 2019), 24.
29 Roger Robinson, "Ghosts," in *A Portable Paradise*, 16.
30 André Breton, *Manifeste du surréalisme* (Paris: Gallimard, 1963), 31–2 (my translation).
31 Iglesias, *Boxing Inside the Box.*
32 Gretchen E. Henderson, "Poetics/'Exhibits,'" in *Beauty is a Verb: The New Poetry of Disability*, ed. Jennifer Bartlett, Sheila Fiona Black, and Michael Northern (El Paso, TX: Cinco Puntos Press, 2011), 353.
33 David Lehman, "The Prose Poem: An Alternative to Verse," *The American Poetry Review* 32, no. 2 (March/April 2003): 48.

34 Roger Robinson, "Interview #4 Roger Robinson," interview by Gboyega Odubanjo, *bath magg* 4 (August 2020).

35 Jeff Wall, "Jeff Wall: 'I'm haunted by the idea that my photography was all a big mistake,'" interview by Sean O'Hagan, *The Guardian*, 3 November 2015, www.theguardian.com/artanddesign/2015/nov/03/jeff-wall-photography-marian-goodman-gallery-show.

36 Julian Stallabrass, "Museum Photography and Museum Prose," *New Left Review* 65 (September/October 2010). https://newleftreview.org/issues/ii65/articles/julian-stallabrass-museum-photography-and-museum-prose.

37 Stallabrass, "Museum Photography."

38 Jeff Wall, "Untitled Text, 1992," cited in Stallabrass, "Museum Photography."

39 "Jeff Wall," White Cube Gallery, https://whitecube.com/artists/artist/jeff_wall.

40 Jeff Wall, "Jeff Wall Interview: Pictures Like Poems," interview by Marc-Christoph Wagner, Louisiana Museum of Modern Art, 2015, www.youtube.com/watch?v=HkVSEVlqYUw.

41 Jeff Wall, "Jeff Wall on 'Pair of Interiors,'" White Cube Exhibition, 2019, www.youtube.com/watch?v=Nj0AqWHBwdY.

42 Joan Didion, "Why I Write," In *Let Me Tell You What I Mean* (London: 4th Estate, 2021), 50–1.

43 Brian Dillon, "The Perfect Prose of a Joan Didion Photo Caption," *The New Yorker*, 22 September 2020, www.newyorker.com/books/page-turner/the-perfect-prose-of-a-joan-didion-photo-caption.

44 Dillon, "Joan Didion."

45 Dillon, "Joan Didion."

46 Stallabrass, "Museum Photography."

47 Stallabrass, "Museum Photography."

48 Stallabrass, "Museum Photography."

49 Ruth Padel, "The Science of Poetry, the Poetry of Science," *The Guardian*, 9 December 2011, www.theguardian.com/books/2011/dec/09/ruth-padel-science-poetry.

BIBLIOGRAPHY

Admussen, Nick. "The Chinese Prose Poem: Generic Metaphor and the Multiple Origins of Chinese SANWENSHI." In *Edinburgh Companion*, edited by Mary Ann Caws and Michel Delville, 247–61. Edinburgh: Edinburgh University Press, 2021.

Agbabi, Patience. "The Wife of Bafa." In *Telling Tales*. Edinburgh: Canongate, 2015.

Agbabi, Patience. "The Wife of Bafa – Analysis." *Writers on Writing*, accessed 9 October 2021. www.transculturalwriting.com/radiophonics/contents/writersonwriting/patienceagbabi/thewifeofbafa-analysis/index.html.

Alexander, Lucy. "Reading in an Undiscovered Library: *Pulse – Prose Poems* as Collaboration." *Verity La*, 23 June 2017. https://verityla.com/2017/06/23/reading-in-an-undiscovered-library-pulse-prose-poems-as-collaboration/.

Allen, Grahame, Yago Zayed, and Rebecca Lees. *House of Commons Briefing Paper No. 8537: Hate Crime Statistics*. 2020.

Ambedkar, Bhimrao Ramji. *Annihilation of Caste: The Annotated Critical Edition*. London: Verso Books, 2014.

Arendt, Hannah. *The Human Condition*. Chicago: University of Chicago Press, 1998. Aristotle. *On the Art of Poetry, and the Categories*. Edited by Gilbert Murray. Translated by Ingram Bywater. Oxford: Clarendon Press, 1920.

Aristotle. *Nicomachean Ethics*. Edited and Translated by Roger Crisp. Cambridge: Cambridge University Press, 2002.

Armitage, Simon. "A Life in Writing: Simon Armitage." Interview by Sarah Crown. *The Guardian*, 9 December 2011. www.theguardian.com/culture/2011/dec/09/life-in-writing-simon-armitage.

Armitage, Simon. "Where is British Poetry Today?" Panel discussion at British Academy Literature Week, May 2013.

Armitage, Simon. "Interview with Simon Armitage." By Lisa Allardice. *The Guardian*, 7 June 2019. www.theguardian.com/books/2019/jun/07/simon-armitage-poet-laureate-ted-hughes-came-from-the-next-valley. Arshi, Mona. *Small Hands*. Liverpool: Liverpool University Press, 2015.

Ashbery, John. Preface to *Illuminations*, by Arthur Rimbaud, translated by John Ashbery, 13–16. Manchester: Carcanet, 2011.

Ashdown-Hill, John. *The Third Plantagenet: George, Duke of Clarence, Richard III's Brother.* Brimscombe Port: The History Press, 2014.

Atherton, Cassandra. *Exhumed.* Wollongong, AU: Grand Parade Poets, 2015.

Atherton, Cassandra. *Trace.* Braidwood, AU: Finlay Lloyd, 2015.

Atherton, Cassandra, and Paul Hetherington. "'Unconscionable Mystification'? Rooms, Spaces and the Prose Poem." *New Writing* 12, no. 3 (2015): 265–81.

Atherton, Cassandra, and Paul Hetherington. "Like a Porcupine or Hedgehog? The Prose Poem as Post-Romantic Fragment." *Creative Approaches to Research* 9, no. 1 (2016): 19–38.

Atherton, Cassandra, and Paul Hetherington. "The Ordinary and the Unreal: American and Australian Prose Poetry." *Axon: Creative Explorations* 7, no. 2 (December 2017). www.axonjournal.com.au/issue-13/ordinary-and-unreal.

Atherton, Cassandra, Jane Monson, and Ian Seed. "Insiders on and 'Outsider' Artform." Paper presented at Prose Poetry Symposium, Leeds Trinity University, 2019.

Athill, Diana. *Instead of a Letter.* London: Granta Books, 2001.

Atkins, Judi, and John Gaffney. "Narrative, Persona and Performance: The Case of Theresa May 2016–2017." *The British Journal of Politics and International Relations* 22, no. 2 (2020): 407–22.

Auden, W. H. *Selected Poems.* Edited by Edward Mendelson. New York: Random House, 2007.

Bachelard, Gaston. *The Poetics of Space.* Translated by Maria Jolas. Boston, MA: Beacon Press, 1994.

Bakhtin, M. M. *The Dialogic Imagination: Four Essays.* Translated by Caryl Emerson and Michael Holquist. Austin, TX: University of Texas Press, 1981.

Bakhtin, Mikhail. *Problems of Dostoevsky's Politics.* Minneapolis, MN: University of Minnesota Press, 1963.

Baral, Kailash C. "Articulating Marginality: Emerging Literatures from Northeast India." In *Emerging Literatures from Northeast India: The Dynamics of Culture, Society and Identity*, edited by Margaret Ch Zama, 3–13. New Delhi: Sage Publications India, 2013.

Barthes, Roland. *The Preparation of the Novel.* Translated by Kate Briggs. New York, NY: Columbia University Press, 2011.

Bartlett, Jennifer, Sheila Black, and Michael Northern, eds. *Beauty Is a Verb: The New Poetry of Disability.* El Paso, TX: Cinco Puntos Press, 2011.

Basho, Matsuo. *The Narrow Road to the Deep North and Other Travel Sketches.* Translated by Nobuyuki Yuasa. Harmondsworth: Penguin, 1966.

Baudelaire, Charles. *The Painter of Modern Life and Other Essays.* London: Phaidon Press, 1964.

Baudelaire, Charles. *Paris Spleen.* Translated by Louise Varèse. New York: New Directions, 1970.

Baudelaire, Charles. *Paris Spleen: Little Poems in Prose.* Translated by Keith Waldrop. Middletown, CT: Wesleyan University Press, 2009.

Baudelaire, Charles. *Paris Spleen.* Translated by Martin Sorrell. London: Alma Classics, 2010. BBC News. "Capitol Riots Timeline: The Evidence Presented Against Trump." *BBC News*, 12 February 2021. www.bbc.co.uk/news/world-us-canada-56004916.

Beach, Christopher. *Poetic Culture: Contemporary American Poetry between Community and Institution.* Evanston, IL: Northwestern University Press, 1999.

Beasley, Rebecca. *Ezra Pound and the Visual Culture of Modernism.* Cambridge: Cambridge University Press, 2007.

Bechir, Kenzari. "Windows." *Built Environment (1978–)* 31, no. 1 (2005): 38–48.

Beckel, Abigail. "Prose Poem Issue Introduction." *Beltway Poetry Quarterly* 14, no. 4 (Fall 2013). www.beltwaypoetry.com/prose-poem-issue-introduction/.

Benis White, Alison. *Small Porcelain Head*. New York: Four Way Books, 2013.

Berger, John. *Ways of Seeing*. London: Penguin, 1972.

Berger, John. *And Our Faces, My Heart, Brief as Photos*. London: Bloomsbury, 2005. Berman, Art. *Preface to Modernism*. Chicago: University of Illinois Press, 1994.

Berrigan, Anselm, ed. *What Is Poetry (Just Kidding, I Know You Know): Interviews from the Poetry Project Newsletter (1983–2009)*. Seattle, WA: Wave Books, 2017.

Berry, Emily. "Editorial." *Poetry Review* 109, no. 1 (Spring 2019): 5–6.

Berry, Liz. "Using Dialect in Poetry." *The Poetry School*, 2016. https://poetryschool.com/assets/uploads/2016/01/Liz-Berry-Using-Dialect-in-Poetry.pdf.

Bertrand, Aloysius. *Gaspard de la Nuit: Fantasies in the Manner of Rembrandt and Callot* by. Translated by Donald Sidney-Fryer. Encino, CA: Black Coat Press, 2004.

Black, Linda. "Begin with a Hook." *Magma* 54 (2014): 2.

Bök, Christian. *Eunoia*. Toronto, ON: Canongate Books, 2008.

Bolton, Gillie. *Write Yourself: Creative Writing and Personal Development*. London: Jessica Kingsley, 2011.

Bourdieu, Pierre. *The Field of Cultural Production: Essays on Art and Literature*. Cambridge: Polity, 1993.

Bowker, John, ed. *The Cambridge Illustrated History of Religions*. Cambridge: Cambridge University Press, 2002.

Bradley, John. Review of *Irradiated Cities*, by Mariko Nagai. *Rain Taxi* (Winter 2017–2018). www.raintaxi.com/winter-2017-2018/.

Brautigan, Richard. *A Confederate General from Big Sur*. New York: Grove Press, 1964.

Breton, André. *Manifeste du surréalisme*. Paris: Gallimard, 1963.

Breton, André, and Paul Éluard. "Notes on Poetry (excerpt)." In *Manifesto: A Century of Isms*, edited by Mary Ann Caws, 471–72. Lincoln, NE: University of Nebraska Press, 2001.

Breverton, Terry. *Richard III: The King in the Car Park*. Stroud: Amberley, 2015.

Brodskaya, Nathalia. *Symbolism: Art of Century*. New York: Parkstone Press, 2007.

Bronner, Yigal, David Dean Shulman, and Gary Alan Tubb. *Innovations and Turning Points: Toward a History of Kāvya Literature*. New Delhi: Oxford University Press, 2014.

Brooks-Motl, Hannah. "George Herbert: 'Love III': A 17th-Century Poet's Project Invites Its Reader to the Table." *Poetry Foundation*, 24 August 2012. www.poetryfoundation.org/articles/69843/george-herbert-love-iii.

Brophy, Kevin. "The Prose Poem: A Short History, a Brief Reflection and a Dose of the Real Thing." *TEXT: Journal of Writing and Writing Programs* 6, no. 1 (April 2002). www.textjournal.com.au/april02/brophy.htm.

Brophy, Kevin. *Portrait in Skin*. Wollongong, AU: Five Islands Press, 2002.

Broumas, Olga, and Jane Miller. *Black Holes, Black Stockings*. Middletown, CT: Wesleyan Poetry Series, 1985.

Brown, Andy. "'I Went Disguised in It': Re-evaluating Seamus Heaney's *Stations*." In *British Prose Poetry*, edited by Jane Monson, 177–91. Cham, CH: Palgrave Macmillan, 2018.

Bühler, Karl. *Theory of Language*. Translated by Donald Fraser Goodwin and Achim Eschbach. Amsterdam: John Benjamins, 1982.

Bullock, Owen. "Fresh Modes: Towards a Radical Ekphrasis." *Axon: Creative Explorations* 9, no. 1 (May 2019). www.axonjournal.com.au/issue-vol-9-no-1-may-2019/fresh-modes.

Bullock, Owen, "The Successful Prose Poem Leaves Behind Its Name." In *British Prose Poetry*, edited by Jane Monson, 227–46. Cham, CH: Palgrave Macmillan, 2018.

Byrd, Brigitte. "I Cannot Escape the Prose Poem." In *Rose Metal Press Field Guide*, edited by Gary L. McDowell and F. Daniel Rzicznek, 31–5. Brookline, MA: Rose Metal Press, 2010.

Caddy, David. "'Hidden' Form: The Prose Poem in English Poetry." In *British Prose Poetry*, edited by Jane Monson, 19–28. Cham, CH: Palgrave Macmillan, 2018.

Caldwell, Anne. *Slug Language*. Fife: Happenstance, 2008.

Caldwell, Anne. *Painting the Spiral Staircase*. Cardiff: Cinnamon Press, 2016.

Caldwell, Anne. "Reawakening Wonder: How Cartography can Act as Creative Research for Prose Poetry." *New Writing* 15, no. 4 (2018): 400–15.

Caldwell, Anne. *Alice and the North*. Scarborough: Valley Press, 2020.

Caldwell, Anne, and Oz Hardwick, eds. *The Valley Press Anthology of Prose Poetry*. Scarborough: Valley Press, 2019.

Carroll, Lewis. *The Complete Illustrated Works of Lewis Carroll*. Edited by Edward Giuliano. London: Chancellor Press, 1982.

Carroll, Monica, and Jen Webb. "'Defiant Formlessness': Prose Poem as Process." *TEXT Special Issue 46, Beyond the Line: Contemporary Prose Poetry* (October 2017): 1–15.

Carroll, Monica, and Paul Munden, eds. *Tract: Prose Poems*. Canberra, AU: Recent Work Press, 2017.

Carson, Anne. *Short Talks*. London: Brick Books, 2015.

Caws, Mary Ann. *Joseph Cornell's Theater of the Mind: Selected Diaries, Letters, and Files*. New York: Thames and Hudson, 1993.

Caws, Mary Ann, and Michel Delville, eds. *The Edinburgh Companion to the Prose Poem*. Edinburgh: Edinburgh University Press, 2021.

Chan, Mary Jean. *Flèche*. London: Faber and Faber, 2019.

Chandra, Amitabha. "The Naxalbari Movement." *The Indian Journal of Political Science* 51, no. 1 (1990): 22–45.

Chari, V. K. "The Genre Theory in Sanskrit Poetics." In *Literary India: Comparative Studies in Aesthetics, Colonialism, and Culture*, edited by Patrick Colm Hogan and Lalita Pandit, 63–80. Albany, NY: State University of New York Press, 1995.

Chuck, Elizabeth. "Donald Trump: 'Don't Worry, We'll Take Our Country Back.'" *NBC News*, 11 July 2015. www.nbcnews.com/politics/2016-election/donald-trump-freedomfest-you-cant-be-great-if-you-dont-n390546.

Clements, Brian, and Jamey Dunham. "Free-line Poems." In *An Introduction to the Prose Poem*, edited by Brian Clements and Jamey Dunham, 225. Newtown, CT: Firewheel Editions, 2009.

Clune, Michael W. "Theory of Prose." *NO: A Journal of the Arts* 6 (January 2008): 48–62.

Coles, Katharine. "The Poem in Time." *Axon: Creative Explorations* 7, no. 2 (December 2017). www.axonjournal.com.au/issue-13/poem-time.

Cook, Albert Spaulding. *Forces in Modern and Postmodern Poetry*. Edited by Peter Baker. New York: Peter Lang, 2008.

Corbett, Sarah. *A Perfect Mirror*. Liverpool: Liverpool University Press, 2018.

Creangă, Emil, Iuliana Ciotoiu, Gheorghiu Dragos, and George Nash. "Vernacular Architecture as a Model for Contemporary Design." In *Eco-Architecture III*, edited by Santiago Hernández, 157–71. Southampton: WIT Press, 2010.

Crystal, David. "Language and Time: RP and Its Successors." *BBC*, 29 October 2014. www.bbc.co.uk/voices/yourvoice/feature2_4.shtml.

Dabral, Manglesh. *This Number Does Not Exist: Selected Poems 1981–2013*. Translated by Nirupama Dutt, Sarabjeet Garcha, et al. Mumbai: Paperwall Poetrywala, 2014.

Davidson, Michael. "Ekphrasis and the Postmodern Painter Poem." *The Journal of Aesthetics and Art Criticism* 42, no. 1 (Autumn 1983): 69–79.

Dawson, Jill Eulalie. "A Brief Introduction to the Prose Poem." *Twelve Rivers* 8, no. 2 (Autumn/Winter 2017): 6.

Debney, Patricia. "Wrestling with Angels: The Pedagogy of the Prose Poem." In *British Prose Poetry*, edited by Jane Monson, 319–30. Cham, CH: Palgrave Macmillan, 2018.

DeKoven, Marianne. *A Different Language*. Madison, WI: University of Wisconsin Press, 1983.

Deleuze, Gilles, and Félix Guattari. *Anti-Oedipus: Capitalism and Schizophrenia*. London: The Athlone Press, 2000.

Delville, Michel. "The Prose Poem, Flash Fiction, Lyrical Essays and Other Micro-Genres." In *Edinburgh Companion to the Prose Poem*, edited by Caws and Delville, 137–49. Edinburgh: Edinburgh University Press, 2021.

Delville, Michel. *The American Prose Poem: Poetic Form and the Boundaries of Genre*. Gainesville, FL: University of Florida Press, 1998.

deNiord, Chard. "Blurred Lines, Some Thoughts on Hybrid, Liminal, and Prose Poetry." *Plume* 100 (December 2019). https://plumepoetry.com/blurred-lines-some-thoughts-on-hybrid-liminal-and-prose-poetry/.

Dewey, Anne. "Gender and the 1980s Prose Poem: Rosmarie Waldrop's *Curves to the Apple*." *Revue française d'études américaines* 147, no. 2 (2016): 66–77.

Dewey, John. *Art as Experience*. New York, NY: Penguin, 2005.

Dhar, Nandini. *Historians of Redundant Moments: A Novel in Poems*. Los Angeles: Agape Editions, 2016.

Dhar, Nandini. "Interview with Nandini Dhar on Historians of Redundant Moments." By Julianna DeMicco. *Agape Editions*, 20 March 2017. https://bloggingthenuminous.com/2017/03/20/interview-with-nandini-dhar-on-historians-of-redundant-moments/.

Didion, Joan. "Why I Write." In *Let Me Tell You What I Mean*. 45–57. London: 4th Estate, 2021.

Dillon, Brian. "The Perfect Prose of a Joan Didion Photo Caption." *The New Yorker*, 22 September 2020. www.newyorker.com/books/page-turner/the-perfect-prose-of-a-joan-didion-photo-caption.

Doolittle, Hilda. "The Borderline Pamphlet." In *The Gender of Modernism*, edited by Bonnie Kime Scott, 110–24. Bloomington, IN: Indiana University Press, 1990.

Duhamel, Denise. "Happy (or How It Took Me Twenty Years to Almost 'Get' The Prose Poem)." In *Rose Metal Press Field Guide*, edited by Gary L. McDowell and F. Daniel Rzicznek, 25–30. Brookline, MA: Rose Metal Press, 2010.

Duhamel, Denise, and Maureen Seaton. "Featured Selection: A Poem Cycle." *Plume* 26 (August 2013). https://plumepoetry.com/featured-selection-a-poem-cycleby-denise-duhamel-and-maureen-seaton/.

Duhamel, Denise, Maureen Seaton, and David Trinidad, eds. *Saints of Hysteria: A Half-Century of Collaborative American Poetry*. Brooklyn: Soft Shell Press, 2007.

East, Ben. "Grief Is the Thing with Feathers Review – A Fable of Magic and Mourning." Review of *Grief Is the Thing with Feathers*, by Max Porter. *The Guardian*, 11 September 2016. www.theguardian.com/books/2016/sep/11/grief-is-the-thing-with-feathers-max-porter-paperback-of-the-week.

Eco, Umberto. *The Open Work*. Translated by Anna Cancogni. Cambridge, MA: Harvard University Press, 1989. Edson, Russell. "The Prose Poem in America." *Parnassus* 5, no. 1 (1976): 321–5.

Edson, Russell. *The Reason Why the Closet-man Is Never Sad*. Middletown, CT: Wesleyan University Press, 1977.

Edson, Russell. "Portrait of the Writer as a Fat Man: Some Subjective Ideas or Notions on the Care and Feeding of Prose Poems, 1975." In *Claims for Poetry*, edited by Donald Hall, 95–103. Ann Arbor, MI: University of Michigan Press, 1983.

Edson, Russell. *The Tunnel: Selected Poems*. Oberlin, OH: Oberlin College Press, 1994.

Edson, Russell. "An Interview with Russell Edson." By Mark Tursi. *Double Room* 4 (Spring/Summer 2004). www.doubleroomjournal.com/issue_four/ Russell_Edson.html.

Edson, Russell. "Interview: The Art of the Prose Poem. Russell Edson." By Peter Johnson. In *Truths, Falsehoods, and a Wee Bit of Honesty: A Short Primer on the Prose Poem with Selected Letters from Russell Edson*, edited by Peter Johnson, 37–52. Cheshire, MA: MadHat Press, 2020.

Eliot, T. S. "The Three Voices of Poetry." In *The Lyric Theory Reader: A Critical Anthology*, edited by Virginia Jackson and Yopie Prins, 192–200. Baltimore, MD: John Hopkins University Press, 2014.

Etter, Carrie. "The Prose Poem." In *The Portable Poetry Workshop*, edited by Nigel McLoughlin, 71–5. London: Palgrave, 2017.

Evans-Bush, Katy. "The Line." In *Stress Fractures: Essays on Poetry*, edited by Tom Chivers, 191–212. London: Penned in the Margins, 2010.

Farley, Paul, and Michael Symmons Roberts. *Edgelands, Journeys into England's True Wilderness*. London: Jonathan Cape, 2011.

Finlay, Alec, and Ken Cockburn. *The Road North*. Swindon: Shearsman, 2014.

Fitterman, Robert. "Does American Political Poetry Have a Future?" *Vice*, 8 July 2014. www.vice.com/en_us/article/9bznvp/does-american-political-poetry-have-a-future-707.

Foucault, Michel. "What Is an Author?" Translated by Josué Harari. In *The Foucault Reader*, edited by Paul Rabinow, 101–20. New York, NY: Pantheon Books, 1984.

Francis, James. "Metal Maidens, Achilles's Shield, and Pandora: The Beginnings of Ekphrasis." *American Journal of Philology* 130, no. 1 (Spring 2009): 1–23.

Frank, Arthur W. *The Wounded Storyteller*. Chicago: University of Chicago Press, 1995.

Franklin, Ralph W., ed. *The Poems of Emily Dickinson: Reading Edition*. Cambridge, MA: Harvard University Press, 1988.

Fredman, Steven. *Poet's Prose: The Crisis in American Verse*. Cambridge: Cambridge University Press, 1990.

Friebert, Stuart, and David Young, eds. *Models of the Universe: An Anthology of the Prose-Poem*. Oberlin, OH: Oberlin College Press, 1995.

Garnham, Trevor, and Randall Thomas. *The Environments of Architecture: Environmental Design in Context*. London: Taylor and Francis, 2007.

Gemmell, Rosi, Jasmin Williams, and Oz Hardwick, eds. *Mystery*. Beaworthy: Wordspace/Indigo Dreams Publishing, 2019.

Gilbert, Margaret. "Walking Together: A Paradigmatic Social Phenomenon." *Midwest Studies in Philosophy* 15 (1990): 1–14.

Glück, Louise. "The Archipelago." *Poetry* (May 1971): 65.

Glück, Louise. *The Wild Iris*. Hopewell, NJ: Ecco, 1992.

Godfrey, Sima. "Baudelaire's Windows." *L'Esprit Créateur* 22, no. 4 (1982): 83–100.

Goldfarb, Lisa. *Unexpected Affinities: Modern American Poetry and Symbolist Poetics*. Brighton: Sussex Academic Press, 2018.

Goldsmith, Kenneth. "Flarf Is Dionysus. Conceptual Writing Is Apollo." *Poetry* (July/August 2009). www.poetryfoundation.org/poetrymagazine/articles/69328/flarf-is-dionysus-conceptual-writing-is-apollo.

Goswami, Joy. *After Death Comes Water: Selected Prose Poems*. Translated by Sampurna Chattarji. New Delhi: Harper Perennial, 2021.

Gottschall, Jonathan. *The Storytelling Animal: How Stories Make Us Human*. Boston, MA: Mariner Books, 2013.

Gould, Evlyn. "Penciling and Erasing Mallarmé's 'Ballets.'" *Performing Arts Journal* 15, no. 1 (1993): 97–105.

Graham, John, ed. *The Shetland Dictionary*. 3rd Edition. Lerwick: Shetland Times, 1993.

Gumpert, Matthew. *The End of Meaning: Studies in Catastrophe*. Newcastle-upon-Tyne: Cambridge Scholars Publishing, 2012.

Guthrie, Camille. "Writing Poetry about Art." *Poetry Foundation*, 12 April 2013. www.poetryfoundation.org/harriet/2013/04/writing-poetry-about-art.

Hadfield, Jen. *Nigh-No-Place*. Tarset: Bloodaxe Books, 2008.

Haidt, Jonathan. *The Righteous Mind: Why Good People are Divided by Politics and Religion*. London: Penguin, 2013.

Harding, Cory. *Blue, Yellow & Green*. Croydon: The X Press, 1980.

Hardwick, Oz. "Shaping Loss: Prose Poetry and the Elegiac Mode." *Axon: Creative Explorations* 9, no. 1 (May 2019). www.axonjournal.com.au/issue-vol-9-no-1-may-2019/shaping-loss.

Hardwick, Oz. *Wolf Planet*. Clevedon: Hedgehog Poetry Press, 2020.

Harris, James "'Goodtime Jesus' and Other Sort-of Prose Poems." In *Rose Metal Press Field Guide*, edited by Gary L. McDowell and F. Daniel Rzicznek, 7–13. Brookline, MA: Rose Metal Press, 2010.

Harrison, Tony. "Them and [uz]." In *Selected Poems*. London: Penguin, 1979.

Haslem, Wendy. "Maya Deren: The High Priestess of Experimental Cinema." *Senses of Cinema* 23 (December 2002). www.sensesofcinema.com/2002/great-directors/deren-2/.

Hass, Robert. *A Little Book on Form: An Exploration into the Formal Imagination of Poetry*. New York: HarperCollins, 2017.

Heffernan, James. *Museum of Words: The Poetics of Ekphrasis from Homer to Ashbery*. Chicago: University of Chicago Press, 2004.

Hejinian, Lyn. *The Language of Inquiry*. Berkeley, CA: University of California Press, 2000.

Hejinian, Lyn. "The Rejection of Closure." *Poetry Foundation*, 13 October 2009. www.poetryfoundation.org/articles/69401/the-rejection-of-closure.

Henderson, Gretchen E. "Poetics/'Exhibits.'" In *Beauty Is a Verb: The New Poetry of Disability*, edited by Jennifer Bartlett, Sheila Fiona Black, and Michael Northern, 353–5. El Paso, TX: Cinco Puntos Press, 2011.

Herbert, George. "Love III." In *George Herbert and the Seventeenth-Century Religious Poets*, edited by Mario A. Di Cesare, 69. New York: W. W. Norton, 1978.

Hetherington, Paul. *Gallery of Antique Art*. Canberra, AU: Recent Work Press, 2016.

Hetherington, Paul. *Palace of Memory: An Elegy*. Canberra, AU: Recent Work Press, 2019.

Hetherington, Paul, and Cassandra Atherton. "'Unconscionable Mystification'? Rooms, Spaces and the Prose Poem." *New Writing* 12, no. 3 (2015): 265–81.

Hetherington, Paul, and Cassandra Atherton. "Breaking Boundaries and Crossing Lines: English-Language Prose Poetry Today." Keynote address at the Prose Poetry Symposium, Leeds Trinity University, 2019.

Hetherington, Paul, and Cassandra Atherton. "Double Vision: Ekphrasis as a Way of Looking Twice." Paper presented at Art and Soul Symposium, University of Winchester, 2019.

Hetherington, Paul, and Cassandra Atherton. "An Intertextual Poiesis: The Luminous Image and a 'Round Loaf of Indian and Rye,'" *New Writing* 17, no. 3 (2020): 259–71.

Hetherington, Paul, and Cassandra Atherton, eds. *Prose Poetry: An Introduction*. Princeton, NJ: Princeton University Press, 2020.

Hetherington, Paul, and Cassandra Atherton. "The Prose Poem's Post-Romantic Inheritance." In *Prose Poetry: An Introduction*, edited by Hetherington and Atherton, 28–50. Princeton, NJ: Princeton University Press, 2020.

Hetherington, Paul, and Cassandra Atherton. "Prose Poetry and TimeSpace." In *Prose Poetry: An Introduction*, edited by Hetherington and Atherton, 128–50. Princeton, NJ: Princeton University Press, 2020.

Hetherington, Paul, and Cassandra Atherton. "Singing the Quotidian: The Lyric Voice and Contemporary American Prose Poetry by Women." *New Writing* 1, no 4 (2021): 386–99. https://doi.org/10.1080/14790726.2021.1876097..

Hipshon, David. *Richard III.* Abingdon: Routledge, 2010.

Hollander, John. "The Poetics of Ekphrasis." *Word & Image* 4, no. 1 (1988): 209–19.

Homer. *The Odyssey.* Revised Edition. Translated by E. V. Rieu. London: Penguin, 1991.

Horspool, David. *Richard III: A Ruler and His Reputation.* London: Bloomsbury Continuum, 2017.

Howell, Anthony. "The Prose Poem." *Fortnightly Review* 1 (April 2016). http://fortnightlyreview.co.uk/2016/04/prose-poetry.

Hu, Tung-Hui. "It's Not in Cleveland, But I'm Getting Closer." In *Rose Metal Field Guide*, edited by Gary L. McDowell and F. Daniel Rzicznek, 157–9. Brookline, MA: Rose Metal Press, 2010.

Iglesias, Holly. *Boxing Inside the Box: Women's Prose Poetry.* Niantic, CT: Quale Press, 2004.

Irwin, Mark. "Distortion and Disjunction in Contemporary American Poetry." *The American Poetry Review* 40, no. 6 (November/December 2011): 39–42.

Iser, Wolfgang, "The Reading Process: A Phenomenological Approach." *New Literary History* 3, no. 2 (Winter 1972): 279–99.

Ivory, Helen. *Maps of the Abandoned City.* Dublin: SurVision, 2019.

Jacob, Max. *The Dice Cup.* Translated by Ian Seed. Cambridge, MA: Wakefield Press, forthcoming 2023.

Jarmusch, Jim, dir. *Paterson.* Amazon Studios, 2016.

Jarmusch, Jim. "Creating a Cinematic Prose Poem: An Interview with Jim Jarmusch." By Leonard Quart. *Cinéaste* 42, no. 2 (2017): 28–30.

Jin'Ichi, Konishi. "The Art of Renga." Translated by Karen Brazell and Lewis Cook. *The Journal of Japanese Studies* 2, no. 1 (Autumn 1975): 29–61.

Johnson, Javon. *Killing Poetry: Blackness and the Making of Slam and Spoken Word Communities.* New Brunswick, NJ: Rutgers University Press, 2017. Johnson, Peter. Introduction. In *The Best of the Prose Poem: An International Journal*, edited by Peter Johnson, 10–18. Buffalo, NY: White Pine Press, 2000.

Johnson, Peter, ed. *A Cast-Iron Aeroplane that Can Actually Fly: Commentaries from 80 American Poets on their Prose Poetry.* Cheshire, MA: MadHat Press, 2019.

Johnson, Peter. "Vaccination, in the Broadest Sense of the Term." In *Old Man Still Howling at the Moon: Collected and New Prose Poems.* Cheshire, MA: MadHat Press, forthcoming.

Keller, Lyn. *Thinking Poetry: Readings in Contemporary Women's Exploratory Poetics.* Iowa City, IA: Iowa University Press, 2010.

Kennard, Luke. "'Man and Nature in and Out of Order': The Surrealist Prose Poetry of David Gascoyne." In *British Prose Poetry*, edited by Jane Monson, 249–64. Cham, CH: Palgrave Macmillan, 2018.

Khair, Tabish. "Artist in Action: On the Lack of an Adequate Critical Vocabulary." In *The Routledge Companion to World Literature and World History*, edited by May Hawas, 31–41. London: Routledge, 2018.

King, Bruce. *Modern Indian Poetry in English*. New Delhi: Oxford University Press, 2001.

Kinsella, John. "Film Shoot." In *Anthology of Australian Prose Poetry*, edited by Cassandra Atherton and Paul Hetherington, 112. Carlton, AU: Melbourne University Press, 2020.

Kittay, Jeffrey, and Wlad Godzich. *The Emergence of Prose: An Essay in Prosaics*. Minneapolis, MN: University of Minnesota Press, 1987.

Koch, Kenneth. "A Note on this Issue," and "Individual Notes on Works and Authors." *Locus Solus II: A Special Issue of Collaborations* (Summer 1961): 193–204.

Kovalik, Kate, and Jen Scott Curwood. "#poetryisnotdead: Understanding Instagram Poetry Within a Transliteracies Framework." *Literacy* 53, no. 4 (November 2019): 185–95.

Kriston. "Maya Lin, Prose Poet." *Smithsonian American Art Museum*, 16 February 2007. https://americanart.si.edu/blog/eye-level/2007/16/1193/maya-lin-prose-poet.

Ladsaria, Seema K., and Rajni Singh. "The 'Semiotic Animal' in Roland Barthes: A Reflection on Calculating the Self as 'Difference in Man.'" *Rupkatha Journal on Interdisciplinary Studies in Humanities* 8, no. 3 (August 2016): 24–34. DOI:10.21659/rupkatha.v8n3.04.

Laird, Holly. "Contradictory Legacies: Michael Field and Feminist Restoration." *Victorian Poetry* 33, no. 1 (Spring 1995): 111–28.

Lea, Bronwyn. "Poetics and Poetry." In *The Cambridge Companion to Creative Writing*, edited by David Morley and Philip Neilsen, 67–86. Cambridge: Cambridge University Press, 2012.

Lehman, David. "The Prose Poem: An Alternative to Verse." *The American Poetry Review* 32, no. 2 (March/April 2003): 45–9.

Lehman, David, ed. *Great American Prose Poems: From Poe to the Present*. New York: Scribner, 2003.

Leitch, Thomas. "Collaborating with the Dead: Adapters as Secret Agents." In *Adaptation Considered as a Collaborative Art,* edited by Bernadette Cronin, Rachel MacShamhráin, and Nikolai Preuschoff, 19–35. Cham, CH: Springer, 2020.

Lepine, Ayla, and Caroline Levitt. "Intersections: Architecture and Poetry (London, 3–4 June 2011)." *ArtHist.net*, 5 May 2011. https://arthist.net/archive/1337/.

Léveillé, Laurence. "Collins Shares Thoughts on Shift in Methods of Writing Poetry." *The Chautauquan Daily*, 28 June 2012. https://chqdaily.wordpress.com/2012/06/28/coll ins-shares-thoughts-on-shift-in-methods-of-writing-poetry/.

Levine, Caroline. *Forms: Whole, Rhythm, Hierarchy, Network*. Princeton, NJ: Princeton University Press, 2015.

Levine, Caroline. "Forms: Literary and Social." *Dibur Literary Journal* 2 (Spring 2016): 75–9.

Lewis, Matthew. *Richard III: Loyalty Binds Me*. Stroud: Amberley, 2018.

Lienhard, Siegfried. *A History of Indian Literature: A History of Classical Poetry Sanskrit – Pali – Prakrit*. Wiesbaden, Germany: Otto Harrassowitz, 1984.

Lin, Maya. *Boundaries*. New York: Simon and Schuster, 2006.

Loidolt, Sophie. "Hannah Arendt on Plurality, Action, and Forms of the 'We.'" Paper presented at Shared Commitment in Crisis: Social Ontology, Engagement, and Politics, Institute for Philosophy and Social Theory, University of Belgrade, September 2018.

Loizeaux, Elizabeth. *Twentieth-Century Poetry and the Visual Arts*. Cambridge: Cambridge University Press, 2008.

Long, Alexander. "Something Like a Meditation." In *Rose Metal Press Field Guide*, edited by Gary L. McDowell and F. Daniel Rzicznek, 41–7. Brookline, MA: Rose Metal Press, 2010.

Longley, Michael. *Selected Poems*. London: Cape Poetry, 1999.

Loydell, Rupert and David Miller, ed. *A Curious Architecture: A Selection of Contemporary Prose Poems*, 115. Exeter: Stride Books, 1996.

Loydell, Rupert. "The Untaught Module." *TEXT Special Issue 46, Beyond the Line: Contemporary Prose Poetry* (October 2017): 8–10.

Lyons, John. *Semantics*. Vol. 2. Cambridge: Cambridge University Press, 1977.

Magritte, René. *Poetry is a Pipe: Selected Writings of René Magritte.* Edited by Kathleen Rooney and Eric Plattner. Translated by Jo Levy. *Literary Hub* (29 September 2016). https://lithub.com/poetry-is-a-pipe-selected-writings-of-rene-magritte/.

Maitreya, Yogesh. "Call for Submissions." *nether Quarterly*, accessed 18 August 2021. https://netherquarterly.com/about/.

Mallarmé, Stéphane. "Interview with Stéphane Mallarmé. By Jules Huret." In *Enquete sur l'evolution litteraire*, edited by Jules Huret 55–65. Paris: Bibliothèque Charpentier, 1891. Translated by Aaron Robertson. www.aaronrobertson.co/translations/mallarme-interview/.

Mallarmé, Stéphane. *Un Coup de Dés & Other Poems.* Translated by A. S. Kline. *Poetry in Translation*, 2004. www.poetryintranslation.com/klineasmallarme.php.

Manguso, Sarah. "Why the Reader of Good Prose Poems Is Never Sad." *The Believer* 11 (March 2004). https://believermag.com/why-the-reader-of-good-prose-poems-is-never-sad/.

Maxwell, Glyn. *On Poetry.* London: Oberon, 2012.

McCullough, John. *Reckless Paper Birds.* London: Penned in the Margins, 2019.

McDowell, Gary L., and F. Daniel Rzicznek, eds. *The Rose Metal Press Field Guide to Prose Poetry: Contemporary Poets in Discussion and Practice.* Brookline, MA: Rose Metal Press, 2010.

McGrath, Campbell. "Rifle, Colorado." In *A Cast-Iron Aeroplane that Can Actually Fly: Commentaries from 80 American Poets on their Prose Poetry*, edited by Peter Johnson, 154. Cheshire, MA: MadHat Press, 2019.

McGookey, Kathleen. "Why I Write Prose Poems." In *Rose Metal Press Field Guide*, edited by Gary L. McDowell and F. Daniel Rzicznek, 48–51. Brookline, MA: Rose Metal Press, 2010.

McHale, Brian. "Beginning to Think about Narrative in Poetry." *Narrative* 17, no. 1 (2009): 11–30.

McMillan, Andrew. "Recommendation of *Grief Is the Thing with Feathers*, by Max Porter." *The Guardian*, 28 November 2015. www.theguardian.com/books/ng-interactive/2015/nov/28/best-books-of-2015-part-one.

Mehrotra, Arvind Krishna. *Partial Recall: Essays on Literature and Literary History.* Ranikhet, India: Permanent Black, 2012.

Milkova, Stiliana. "Ekphrasis and the Frame: On Paintings in Gogol, Tolstoy, and Dostoevsky." *Word & Image* 32, no, 2 (2016): 153–62.

Miller, Brenda. "A Braided Heart: Shaping the Lyric Essay." In *Writing Creative Nonfiction*, edited by Philip Gerard and Carolyn Forché, 41–50. Cincinnati, OH: Story Press, 2001.

Misra, Tillotama. "Speaking, Writing and Coming of the Print Culture in Northeast India." In *Emerging Literatures from Northeast India: The Dynamics of Culture, Society and Identity*, edited by Margaret Ch Zama, 14–27. New Delhi: Sage Publications India, 2013.

Mix, Deborah. "Tender Revisions: Harryette Mullen's Trimmings and S*PeRM**K*T." *American Literature* 77, no. 1 (2005): 65–92.

Mix, Deborah. *Vocabulary of Thinking: Gertrude Stein and Contemporary North American Women's Innovative Writing.* Iowa City, IA: University of Iowa Press, 2007.

Monk, Geraldine. "Collaborations with the Dead." In *The Salt Companion to Geraldine Monk*, edited by Scott Thurston, 178–87. Cambridge: Salt Publishing, 2007.

Monroe, Jonathan. *A Poverty of Objects.* Ithaca, NY: Cornell University Press, 1987.

Monson, Jane, ed. *British Prose Poetry: The Poems Without Lines.* Cham, CH: Palgrave Macmillan, 2018.

Monson, Jane. Introduction. In *British Prose Poetry*, 1–16. Cham, CH: Palgrave Macmillan, 2018.

Moore, Fabienne. *Prose Poems of the French Enlightenment: Delimiting Genre*. Farnham: Ashgate Publishing, 2009.

Moréas, Jean. "The Manifesto of Symbolism." In *Symbolism: Art of Century*, edited by Nathalia Brodskaya, 8–23. New York, NY: Parkstone Press, 2007.

Mullen, Harryette. "Optic White: Blackness and the Production of Whiteness." *Diacritics* 24, no. 2/3 (Summer-Autumn 1994): 71–89.

Mullen, Harryette. "Interview with Harryette Mullen." By Cynthia Hogue. *Postmodern Culture* 9, no. 2 (January 1999). Mullen, Harryette. *Recyclopedia: Trimmings, S*PeRM**K*T, and Muse & Drudge*. Minneapolis, MN: Graywolf Press, 2006.

Munden, Paul. "Playing with Time: Prose Poetry and the Elastic Moment." *TEXT Special Issue 46, Beyond the Line: Contemporary Prose Poetry* (October 2017): 1–13.

Murphy, Margueritte S. "The British Prose Poem and 'Poetry' in Early Modernism." In *British Prose Poetry*, edited by Jane Monson, 29–45. Cham, CH: Palgrave Macmillan, 2018.

Murphy, Margueritte S. *A Tradition of Subversion: The Prose Poem in English from Wilde to Ashbery*. Amherst, MA: University of Massachusetts Press, 1992.

Murphy, Sheila. *Proof of Silhouettes*. Exeter: Stride Books, 1996.

Nagai, Mariko. *Irradiated Cities*. Los Angeles: Les Figues Press, 2015.

Narayanan, Vivek. *Life and Times of Mr. S.* New Delhi: HarperCollins India, 2012.

Nash, Clare. *Contemporary Vernacular Design: How British Housing Can Rediscover Its Soul*. Newcastle-upon-Tyne: RIBA Publishing, 2016.

Naskar, Goutam, and Ranjit Mandal. "Casteist Language/s: Situating English and Vernacular Languages in Indian Educational Context." In *Caste, Gender and Media: Significant Sociological Trends in India*, edited by Srabanti Chodhuri and Chandan Basu, 431–42. Kolkata: Netaji Subhas Open University, 2017.

Neginsky, Rosina, ed. *Symbolism, Its Origins and Its Consequences*. Cambridge: Cambridge Scholars, 2011.

Noel-Tod, Jeremy, ed. *The Penguin Book of the Prose Poem: From Baudelaire to Anne Carson*. London: Penguin, 2018.

Noel-Tod, Jeremy. "Introduction: The Expansion of the Prose Poem." In *Penguin Book of the Prose Poem: From Baudelaire to Anne Carson*, edited by Jeremy Noel-Tod, xix–xliv. London: Penguin, 2018.

Northumberland County Council. *Northumberland Coast AONB Management Plan*. 2014. www.northumberlandcoastaonb.org/management-plan/.

Novalis. *Novalis: Philosophical Writings*. Edited and Translated by Margaret Mahony Stoljar. Albany, NY: State University of New York Press, 1997.

O'Brien, Sean. "Introduction to Poetry." In *The Handbook of Creative Writing*, edited by Stephen Earnshaw, 183–98. Edinburgh: Edinburgh University Press, 2007.

Ogawa, Tadashi. "The Trans-subjective Creation of Poetry and Mood: A Short Study of Japanese Renga." *Comparative and Continental Philosophy* 1, no. 2 (2009): 193–209.

Oliver, Mary. *Long Life: Essays and Other Writings*. Boston, MA: Da Capo Press, 2004.

Olson, Charles, "Projective Verse." In *Collected Prose*, edited by Donald Allen and Benjamin Friedlander, 239–49. Berkeley, CA: University of California Press, 1997.

Olson, Ray. Review of *The Tormented Mirror*, by Russell Edson. *Booklist*, April 2001. www.booklistonline.com/The-Tormented-Mirror-/pid=416619.

O'Neill, Michael. "The Marvellous Clouds: Reflections on the Prose Poetry of Woolf, Baudelaire and Williams." In *British Prose Poetry*, edited by Jane Monson, 73–89. Cham, CH: Palgrave Macmillan, 2018.

Orozco, Gaspar. *Autocinema*. Translated by Mark Weiss. Victoria, TX: Chax Press, 2016.

Orozco, Gaspar. *Book of the Peony*. Translated by Mark Weiss. Bristol: Shearsman, 2017.

Over, Jeremy. "Fishing for the Moon: Some Recent Prose Poetry in the UK." *Hard Times: Contemporary British Poetry* 80 (2006): 39–44.

Padel, Ruth. "The Science of Poetry, the Poetry of Science." *The Guardian*, 9 December 2011. www.theguardian.com/books/2011/dec/09/ruth-padel-science-poetry.

Patchen, Kenneth. *Collected Poems*. New York: New Directions, 1952.

Patchen, Kenneth. *Love and War Poems*. Derby: Whisper & Shout, 1968. Paterson, Don. *101 Sonnets from Shakespeare to Heaney*. London: Faber and Faber, 1999.

Patke, Rajeev S. *Postcolonial Poetry in English*. Oxford: Oxford University Press, 2006.

Paz, Octavio. "Introduction." In *Renga: A Chain of Poems*, edited by Octavio Paz, Jacques Roubaud, Edoardo Sanguineti, and Charles Tomlinson. New York, NY: George Braziller, 19–30. 1972.

Perloff, Marjorie. "Book Review: Michel Delville's *The American Prose Poem: Poetic Form and the Boundaries of Genre*." *The Prose Poem: An International Journal* 8 (1999): 134–8.

Perloff, Marjorie, *Differentials: Poetry, Poetics, Pedagogy*. Tuscaloosa, AL: University of Alabama Press, 2004.

Peyre, Henri. *What is Symbolism?* Translated by Emmett Parker. Tuscaloosa, AL: University of Alabama Press, 2010.

Philokyprou, Maria, Michael Aimillios, Eleni Malaktou, and Andreas Savvides. "Environmentally Responsive Design in Eastern Mediterranean. The Case of Vernacular Architecture in the Coastal, Lowland and Mountainous Regions of Cyprus." *Building and Environment* 111 (January 2017): 91–109.

Pollard, A. J. *The Worlds of Richard III*. Brimscombe Port: Tempus, 2001.

Pont, Antonia, and Cassandra Atherton. "Poetics of Collaboration: Introduction." *Axon: Creative Explorations* 6, no. 1 (March 2016). www.axonjournal.com.au/issue-10/introduction.

Porter, Max. *Grief Is the Thing with Feathers*. London: Faber & Faber, 2015.

Preminger, Alex, Frank J. Warnke, and O. B. Hardison, Jr., eds. *Princeton Encyclopedia of Poetry and Poetics*. Princeton, NJ: Princeton University Press, 1965.

Prestridge, James. "Cinematic Poetry: An In-Depth Reading of Jim Jarmusch's Film *Paterson* (2016)." *Close-Up Culture*. https://closeupculture.com/2017/05/04/cinematic-poetry-an-in-depth-reading-of-jim-jarmuschs-film-paterson-2016/.

Purushotham, K. *Dalit Literature: Emerging Trends*. Warangal, India: DRS I Kakatiya University, 2018.

Rainey, David. *The Hoax and Beyond*. Melbourne: Heide Museum of Modern Art, 2009.

Rajendran, C. "The Actual and the Imagined: Perspectives and Approaches in Indian Classical Poetics." In *Approaches to World Literature*, edited by Joachim Küpper, 121–32. Berlin: Akademie Verlag, 2013.

Ramakrishnan, E. V. "Language, Power and Ideology: The Changing Contexts of Bhasha in India." In *Language Policy and Education in India*, edited by M. Sridhar and Sunita Mishra, 57–69. London: Routledge India, 2016.

Ramanujan, A. K. *Speaking of Śiva*. Harmondsworth: Penguin Books, 1973.

Rankine, Claudia. "Interview with Claudia Rankine." By Kayo Chingyoni. *The White Review* (March 2018). www.thewhitereview.org/feature/interview-claudia-rankine/.

Rankine, Claudia, and Beth Loffreda. "On Whiteness and the Racial Imaginary." *Literary Hub* (9 April 2015). https://lithub.com/on-whiteness-and-the-racial-imaginary/.

Rapatahana, Vaughan. "Bending Genres: Flash Fiction/Prose Poetry in Aotearoa New Zealand." *Jacket2* (26 March 2018). https://jacket2.org/commentary/flash-fictionprose-poetry-aotearoa-new-zealand.

Reverdy, Pierre. *Pierre Reverdy.* Translated by Vivienne Finch. Croydon: X-Press, 1980.

Reverdy, Pierre. *The Thief of Talant.* Translated by Ian Seed. Cambridge, MA: Wakefield Press, 2016.

Riffaterre, Michael, *Semiotics of Poetry.* Bloomington, IN: Indiana University Press, 1978.

Riley, Denise. *Words of Selves: Identification, Solidarity, Irony.* Stanford, CA: Stanford University Press, 2000.

Robbins, Amy Moorman. *American Hybrid Poetics: Gender, Mass Culture, and Form.* New Brunswick, NJ: Rutgers University Press, 2014.

Robinson, Roger. *A Portable Paradise.* Leeds: Peepal Tree Press, 2019.

Robinson, Roger. "Interview #4 Roger Robinson." By Gboyega Odubanjo. *bath magg* 4 (August 2020). www.bathmagg.com/interview4/.

Rodia, Becky. "Comments – Editorial and Otherwise." In *Always the Beautiful Answer: A Prose Poem Primer*, edited by Ruth Moon Kempher. 237–50. St Augustine, FL: Kings Estate Press, 1999.

Rosenblatt, Louise M. "Towards a Transactional Theory of Reading." *Journal of Reading Behavior* 1, no. 1 (1969): 31–49.

Ross, Charles. *Richard III.* New Haven, CT: Yale University Press, 1999.

Russell, Lauren. "Requiem for Elementary Language Acquisition." *The Brooklyn Rail* (June 2021). https://brooklynrail.org/2021/06/poetry/Requiem-for-Elementary-Language-Acquisition.

S. Chandramohan. "Claiming the English Language as a Dalit Poet." *The Indian Express*, 17 April 2021. https://indianexpress.com/article/opinion/columns/claiming-the-english-language-as-a-dalit-poet-7277032/.

Saikia, Rosy. "Image and Beyond: A Re-reading of Basho's Haiku." In *Consciousness, Theatre, Literature and the Arts 2015*, edited by Daniel Meyer-Dinkgräf, 128–35. Newcastle-upon-Tyne: Cambridge Scholars Publishing, 2016.

Santilli, Nikki. "The Prose Poem and the City." *Prose Studies* 20, no. 1 (April 1997): 77–89.

Santilli, Nikki. "Prose Poetry and the Spirit of Jazz." In *British Prose Poetry*, edited by Jane Monson, 279–98. Cham, CH: Palgrave Macmillan, 2018.

Santilli, Nikki. "Foreword." In *This Line Is Not for Turning: An Anthology of Contemporary British Prose Poetry*, edited by Jane Monson, 9–11. Blaenau Ffestiniog, Wales: Cinnamon Press, 2011.

Schopenhauer, Arthur. *The World as Will and Representation.* New York: Dover, 1969.

Shirane, Haruo. *Traces of Dreams: Landscape, Cultural Memory, and the Poetry of Basho.* Palo Alto, CA: Stanford University Press, 1998. Seed, Ian. *Anonymous Intruder.* Exeter: Shearsman, 2009.

Seed, Ian. *Amore Mio.* Lancaster: Flax Books, 2010.

Seed, Ian. *Shifting Registers.* Exeter: Shearsman, 2011.

Seed, Ian. *Makers of Empty Dreams.* Bristol: Shearsman, 2014.

Seed, Ian. *Identity Papers.* Bristol: Shearsman, 2016.

Seed, Ian. Interview by Ian McMillan. "New Towns." *The Verb*, BBC Radio 3, March 2016. Seed, Ian. *New York Hotel.* Bristol: Shearsman, 2018. Seward, Desmond. *Richard III: The Black Legend.* London: Penguin, 1997.

Shepherd, Reginald. "The Other's Other: Against Identity Poetry." *Michigan Quarterly Review* XLII, no. 4 (Fall 2003). http://hdl.handle.net/2027/spo.act2080.0042.407.

Silliman, Ron. *The New Sentence.* Berkeley, CA: Roof Press, 1987.

Silliman, Ron. Comments on *Rain Taxi. Silliman's Blog: A Weblog Focused on Contemporary Poetry and Poetics*, June 2003. https://ronsilliman.blogspot.com/2003_06_15_archive.html

Silverberg, Mark, ed. *The New York School Collaborations: The Colour of Vowels.* New York: Palgrave, 2010.

Simic, Charles. *Dime-Store Alchemy: The Art of Joseph Cornell.* New York: New York Review Books, 1992.

Simic, Charles. "Essay on the Prose Poem." *Plume* 102 (February 2020). https://plumepoe try.com/essay-on-the-prose-poem-by-charles-simic/.

Skidmore, Chris. *Richard III: Brother, Protector, King.* London: Weidenfeld & Nicolson, 2017.

Smiles, Sam, "Unfinished? Repulsive? Or the Work of a Prophet? Late Turner." *Tate*, 1 January 2009. www.tate.org.uk/tate-etc/issue-15-spring-2009/unfinished-repulsive-or-work-prophet.

Smith, Hazel. *The Writing Experiment: Strategies for Innovative Creative Writing.* Crows Nest, AU: Allen & Unwin, 2005.

Solnit, Rebecca. *A Field Guide to Getting Lost.* Edinburgh: Canongate, 2017.

Soto, Christopher. "What Constitutes Political Poetry?" *Poetry Foundation*, 5 September 2017. www.poetryfoundation.org/harriet/2017/09/what-constitues-as-political-poetry.

Spahr, Juliana. *Everybody's Autonomy: Connective Reading and Collective Identity.* Tuscaloosa, AL: University of Alabama Press, 2001.

Stallabrass, Julian. "Museum Photography and Museum Prose." *New Left Review* 65 (September/October 2010). https://newleftreview.org/issues/ii65/articles/julian-stal labrass-museum-photography-and-museum-prose.Stein, Gertrude. *Tender Buttons.* Mineola, NY: Dover Publications, 1997.

Stein, Gertrude. *The Autobiography of Alice Toklas.* London: Penguin, 2001.

Stewart, Heather, and Rowena Mason. "Nigel Farage's Anti-migrant Poster Reported to Police." *The Guardian*, 16 June 2016. www.theguardian.com/politics/2016/jun/16/nigel-farage-defends-ukip-breaking-point-poster-queue-of-migrants.

Stonecipher, Donna. *Prose Poetry and the City.* Anderson, SC: Parlor Press, 2018.

Strange, Shane, ed. *Seam: Prose Poems.* Canberra: Recent Work Press, 2015.

Strange, Shane, and Monica Carroll, eds. *Pulse: Prose Poems.* Canberra: Recent Work Press, 2016.

Stockdale, Edwin. "Old Year's Night." *Dream Catcher* 42 (2020): 48.

Sweeney, Dennis James. "'there is only one narrative & nothing else': Building the One-Legged Shrine." Review of *Irradiated Cities*, by Mariko Nagai. *Newfound* 9, no. 1. https://newfound.org/archives/volume-9/issue-1/reviews-irradiated-cities/.

Symons, Arthur. *The Symbolist Movement in Literature.* London: Lightening Source, 1899.

Symmons Roberts, Michael, *Mancunia.* London: Cape Poetry, 2017.

Tahir, Abu. "Indian English Literature and Its Caste Discrimination; A Great Blow on Cultural Diversity, with a Special Reference to Mulk Raj Anand's 'Untouchable.'" *The Literary Herald* 1, no. 4 (2016): 59–64.

Talbot, Bryan. *Alice in Sunderland.* Milwaukie, OR: Dark Hores Books, 2007.

Taylor, John. "Two Cultures of the Prose Poem." *Michigan Quarterly Review* 44, no. 2 (Spring 2005). http://hdl.handle.net/2027/spo.act2080.0044.223.

Tóibín, Colm. *The Master.* London: Picador, 2004.

Tookey, Helen. "Halb Null." In *Valley Press Anthology*, edited by Anne Caldwell and Oz Hardwick, 70.

Tremblay-McGaw, Robin. "Enclosure and Run: The Fugitive Recyclopedia of Harryette Mullen's Writing." *Multi-Ethnic Poetics* 35, no. 2 (2010): 71–94.

Upton, Lee. "Structural Politics: The Prose Poetry of Russell Edson." *South Atlantic Review* 58, no. 4 (November 1993): 101–15.

Upton, Lee. "Counting Russell Edson." *Field* 93 (Fall 2015): 20–2.

Valéry, Paul. *Collected Works of Paul Valéry. Volume 14: Analects.* Translated by Stuart Gilbert. Bollingen Series XLV, 14. Princeton, NJ: Princeton University Press, 1970.

Vincent, Bridget. "Object Lessons: Derek Mahon's Material Ekphrasis." *Interdisciplinary Literary Studies* 20, no. 3 (2018): 371–84.Vincenz, Marc. *Here Comes the Nightdust.* County Clare, Ireland: Salmon Poetry, 2019.

Vincenz, Marc. "Switzerland 911." *Westerly Magazine* 66, no. 2 (2021), 35.

Virdee, Satnam, and Brendan McGeever. "Racism, Crisis, Brexit." *Ethnic and Racial Studies* 41 (2018): 1802–19.

Vogel, Carol. "Maya Lin's World of Architecture, Or Is It Art?" *The New York Times*, 9 May 1994. www.nytimes.com/1994/05/09/arts/maya-lin-s-world-of-architecture-or-is-it-art.html.

Waldman, Diane. *Joseph Cornell: Master of Dreams.* New York: Harry N. Abrams, 2002.

Wall, Alan. "Questioning the Prose Poem: Thoughts on Geoffrey Hill's *Mercian Hymns.*" In *British Prose Poetry*, edited by Jane Monson, 167–76. Cham, CH: Palgrave Macmillan, 2018.

Wall, Jeff. "Jeff Wall: 'I'm Haunted by the Idea that My Photography Was All a Big Mistake.'" Interview by Sean O'Hagan. *The Guardian*, 3 November 2015. www.theguardian.com/artanddesign/2015/nov/03/jeff-wall-photography-marian-goodman-gallery-show.

Wall, Jeff. "Jeff Wall Interview: Pictures Like Poems." By Marc-Christoph Wagner. Louisiana Museum of Modern Art, 2015. www.youtube.com/watch?v=HkVSEVlqYUw.

Wall, Jeff. "Jeff Wall on 'Pair of Interiors,'" White Cube Exhibition, 2019. www.youtube.com/watch?v=Nj0AqWHBwdY.

Wall, Jeff. "Jeff Wall." White Cube Gallery. https://whitecube.com/artists/artist/jeff_wall.

Wallace, Mark. "Split: Seam and Abyss in the Prose Poem." In *Rose Metal Press Field Guide*, edited by Gary L. McDowell and F. Daniel Rzicznek, 74–8. Brookline, MA: Rose Metal Press, 2010.

Wanner, Adrian. *Russian Minimalism: From the Prose Poem to the Anti-Story.* Evanston, IL: Northwestern University Press, 2003.

Webb, Jen, and Monica Carroll. "A Seethe of Poets: Creativity and Community." *TEXT Special Issue 40, Making It New: Finding Contemporary Meanings for Creativity* (April 2017): 1–15.

Webb, Ruth. "*Ekphrasis* ancient and modern: the invention of a genre." *Word & Image* 15, no. 1 (1999): 7–18.

Webb, Ruth. *Ekphrasis, Imagination and Persuasion in Ancient Rhetorical Theory and Practice.* Aldershot: Taylor & Francis Group, 2009.

Weir, Alison. *The Princes in the Tower.* London: Pimlico, 1997.

Weir, Alison. *Richard III and the Princes in the Tower.* London: Vintage, 2014.

Wheatley, David. "By Soft Return." Review of *The Penguin Book of the Prose Poem: From Baudelaire to Anne Carson*, edited by Jeremy Noel-Tod. *The Poetry Review* 109, no. 1 (Spring 2019). https://poetrysociety.org.uk/review-by-soft-return/.

Wilkinson, Josephine. *Richard, The Young King to Be.* Chalford: Amberley, 2008.

Will, Barbara. *Gertrude Stein, Modernism and the Problem of "Genius."* Edinburgh: Edinburgh University Press, 2000.

Williams, James. "Deleuze on J.M.W. Turner: Catastrophism in Philosophy?" In *Deleuze and Philosophy: The Difference Engineer*, edited by Keith Ansell-Pearson, 233–46. London: Routledge, 1997.

Williams, Raymond. "Metropolitan Perceptions and the Emergence of Modernism." In *The Politics of Modernism: Against the New Conformists*, edited by Tony Pinkney, 37–48. London: Verso, 1989.

Williams, William Carlos. Paterson. Revised edition. New York, NY: New Directions, 1992.

Wilson, Chloe. "A Shrine to the Fragment. Review of *Pulse: Prose Poems.*" *TEXT: Journal of Writing and Writing Courses* 20, no. 2 (October 2016).

Wolfe, Jan. "Four Officers Who Responded to U.S. Capitol Attack Have Died by Suicide." *Reuters*, 2 August 2021. www.reuters.com/world/us/officer-who-responded-us-capitol-attack-is-third-die-by-suicide-2021-08-02/.

Wong, Nicholas. Testimonial about *Irradiated Cities*. Accessed 2 February 2021. www.mariko-nagai.com/irradiated-cities.

Woolf, Virginia. "The Cinema." In *The Crowded Dance of Modern Life*, edited by Rachel Bowlby, 54–8. Harmondsworth: Penguin, 1993.

Wordsworth, William. *Poetical Works*. London: Oxford University Press, 1904.

Yeung, H. H. *Spatial Engagement with Poetry*. New York: Palgrave Macmillan, 2015.

Yoko's Dogs. *Whisk*. Toronto: Pedlar Press, 2013.

You, Mia. "Sublime Deformations of Nature." *Poetry Foundation*, 4 April 2017. www.poetryfoundation.org/harriet-books/2017/04/sublime-deformations-of-nature.

Young, David. Introduction. In *Models of the Universe*, edited by Stuart Friebert and David Young, 17–20. Oberlin, OH: Oberlin College Press, 1995.

Young, Gary. "The Unbroken Line." In *Rose Metal Press Field Guide*, edited by Gary L. McDowell and F. Daniel Rzicznek, 112–14. Brookline, MA: Rose Metal Press, 2010.

Yule, George. *The Study of Language*. 6th Edition. Cambridge: Cambridge University Press, 2016.

Zaidi, Nishat. "Center/Margin Dialectics and the Poetic Form: The Ghazals of Agha Shahid Ali." *Annual of Urdu Studies* 23 (2008): 55–66.

INDEX

vernacular 14, 77–92, 125, 129, 132, 134, 147–8
Vincenz, Marc 11–4, 20
violence 48, 53–4, 58, 61, 64, 72, 98–9, 178, 206

Waldrop, Rosmarie 20, 118, 146
Wall, Alan 172, 180
Wall, Jeff 208–11
Wallace, Mark 165
Waterhouse, John William 191
Webb, Jen 159, 171
Weir, Alison 177

Wheatley, David 35, 158
white space 11, 14, 103–4, 163, 172–3, 176, 193–4, 202
Wilkinson, Josephine 179–80
Wong, Nicholas 9
word problem 52–4
Wordsworth, Dorothy 80
Wordsworth, William 40, 80, 145

Yeats, William Butler 189
Young, Gary 39, 205
Yuasa, Nobuyuki 144–5
Yule, George 78

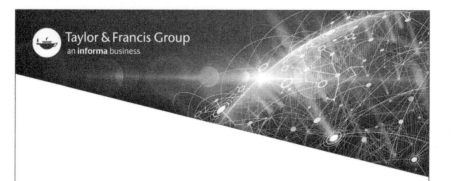